CW01667103

CITY MERCHANT AND THE ARTS 1670–1720

THE CORPORATION OF LONDON

THE CORPORATION OF LONDON is the provider of local government services for the Square Mile – the financial and commercial heart of the City. It is a unique organisation, older than Parliament itself, and which offers an enormous array of services to London and the nation. It is the third largest sponsor of the arts in this country. It owns and manages the internationally renowned Barbican Centre, Europe's largest multi-arts and conference venue, and a prestigious conservatoire, the Guildhall School of Music and Drama. The Guildhall Art Gallery and Roman London's Amphitheatre welcome visitors on the Guildhall site. The Corporation part-funds the popular Museum of London, and owns and manages several well-known landmarks including Tower Bridge, Hampstead Heath, Epping Forest and other open spaces.

THE EDUCATION COMMITTEE works to provide a high quality, informed and responsive service to City residents and businesses. It has the duty to secure nursery education and school places for children; it provides services for young people, including play and youth provision, and the Duke of Edinburgh's Award. It maintains the Sir John Cass's Foundation Primary School. It offers an adult education initiatives programme of courses, lectures and cultural events; study vouchers for City residents and workers; the administration of student scholarships; and careers and education advice for adults. The Corporation uses its private funds to maintain three independent secondary schools. It has sponsored a new City Academy, and gives substantial financial support to London schools and higher education institutions.

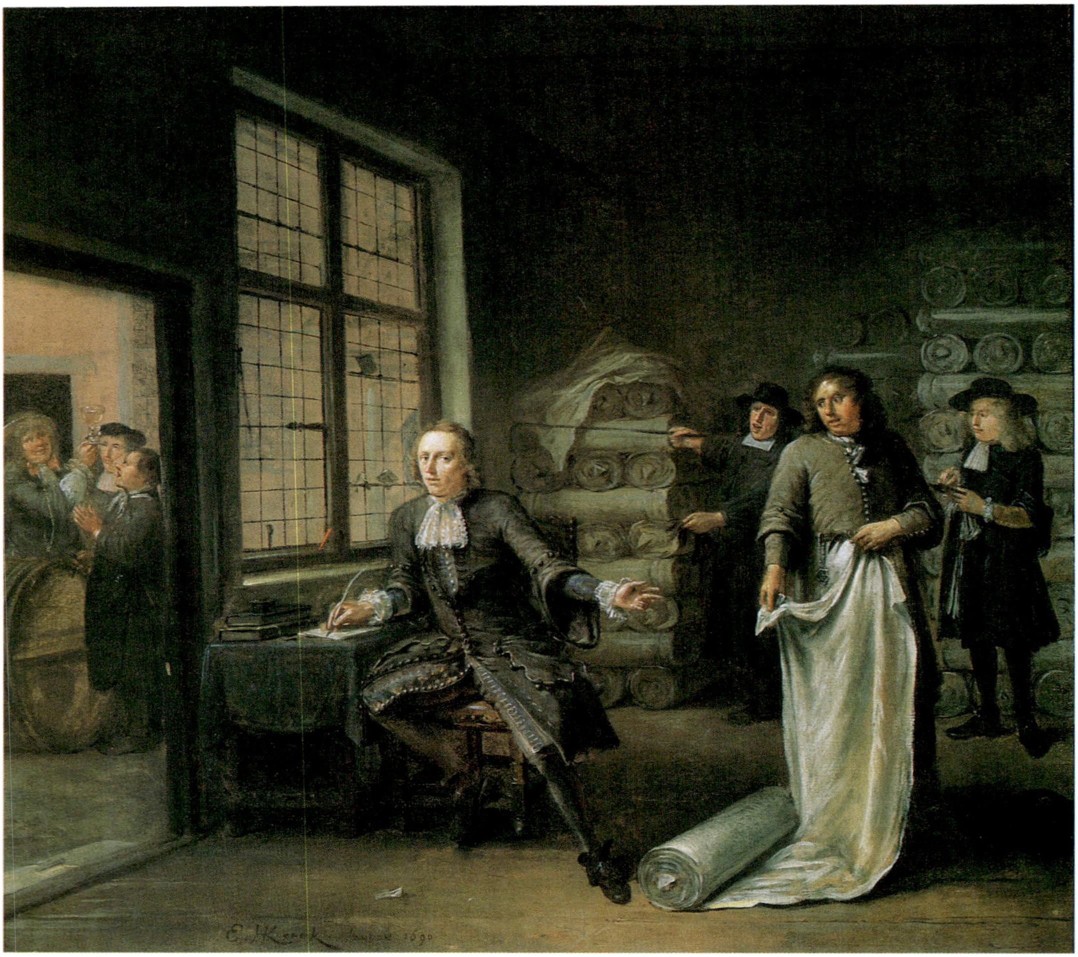

Frontispiece *The Interior of a Cloth Merchant's, with a buyer inspecting bales of cloth, 1690, oil on canvas by Egbert van Heemskerk the Younger. This is a unique depiction of a London merchant at work (the painting is inscribed 'London'). The interior has not been identified but could conceivably depict Blackwell Hall, or an area of the Royal Exchange or the premises of a London merchant.* © *The Museum of London*

CITY MERCHANTS AND THE ARTS 1670–1720

Edited by Mireille Galinou

Published by

OBLONG

for the

Corporation of London

2004

CORPORATION OF LONDON

First published in 2004 by Oblong Creative Ltd
for the Corporation of London

Distributed in the UK by: Oblong Creative Ltd
416B Thorp Arch Estate
Wetherby LS23 7BJ

ISBN 0 9536574 4 2

This book is dedicated to the painter Robert Robinson (1651–1706), author of the Painted Room in the City of London.

Sub-editors: Jackie Maidment and Stephen Denny
Designer: Derek Brown
Index: Elizabeth Wiggans
Printed by: A1 Press, Wetherby
Bound by: Woods of Bradford

This book was inspired by the Conference 'City Merchants and the Arts' held at Guildhall Art Gallery on 1 November 2002. Not all chapters included in this book relate to the Conference.

FRONT COVER: *Fishing and cooking scene by a stream: a group of three dark Indians are attempting to capture a narwhal from a moored boat while another group behind them have started a huge fire against the rock to cook their catch. They are being watched by a party of three sheltering in a hut-like structure at the top of a huge rock. The central figure in this group is a white woman who is barely clothed.*

BACK COVER: *Catching flying fish on stormy seas. The scene echoes the words of Monsieur de Monts in the seventeenth-century voyage account found in the publication,* Nova Francia: or the Description of that part of New France which is one Continent with Virginia*: 'Tempest, porpoises … some men waited for them at the beak head which is the forepart of the ship with harping irons in their hands'.*

Details from the Painted Room by Robert Robinson, 1696, at 32 Botolph Lane. *(See p. 113)*

Contents

Acknowledgements

This book has been a labour of love, quite literally. It would not have seen the light of day had it not been for the many people who most generously gave of their time and their expertise, who granted free reproduction rights or helped the project in financial terms.

They say charity begins at home and this is exactly what happened with the Corporation of London. Stephen Denny, the Assistant Education Officer and Barry Cropper, the Assistant Director in Libraries and Guildhall Art Gallery, have been generous and supportive to this project far beyond the call of duty. The staff of the Guildhall Library Print Room (and in particular Jeremy Smith), of the Guildhall Art Gallery (in particular Vivien Knight and Naomi Allen) and of London Metropolitan Archives (in particular Rhys Griffith) have provided outstanding service at all times.

The book also owes a substantial debt to the Paul Mellon Centre for Studies in British Art. This institution had backed the publication of the 2002 Corporation pamphlet on The Painted Room, and the present volume, an offshoot of this earlier publication (see the Introduction), has also benefited from a publication grant.

The editor and the Corporation of London are also immensely grateful to all the contributors to this book. They have met, discussed, written, corrected, checked and double checked with good humour and with enormous professionalism. They have also given their time, without financial reward.

We are enormously grateful too, to all the institutions, private owners, or photographers who have kindly granted permission to use their photographic material. It would perhaps not be realistic to thank everyone individually (there are 130 images in this volume and a complete list of acknowledgements is found at the end of the book) but we particularly wish to thank for their generosity the Corporation of London's image collections; the Schroder Collection; the Worshipful Company of Goldsmiths; the Governor and Company of the Bank of England; the London Topographical Society; the Sutton Local Studies Library; the owners of Norton Court; Mrs Sam Dunkerley; Scarthin Books; Squerryes Court; Harris Lindsay; S. Marchant & Son; Tate London; Nottingham Castle Museum; the River and Rowing Museum at Henley-on-Thames; the Hon. Michael Willoughby; the Hon. Christopher Lennox-Boyd; Ruth Bubb; the Yale Center for British Art; Alastair Laing at the National Trust; the Sir John Cass's Foundation; the Paul Mellon Centre for British Art; the Conway Library and the Photographic Survey at the Courtauld Institute of Art.

Finally, the book would not look as good as it does were it not for the very high standards of the publishers, Oblong Creative Limited. We thank Derek Brown for the elegant design and for providing, tirelessly, advice on all aspects of the publication. Jackie Maidment had the delicate but crucial task of ensuring the commercial viability of the book and everyone knows what a vital job this has become in our times.

Introduction

You may be surprised to read that this book is dedicated to the little known painter Robert Robinson. Who was he? A talent that has been overlooked? Almost certainly. A potential source of inspiration for art lovers? Definitely. The possibility of attracting the attention of a wider public to Robinson's series of pictures for the Painted Room first caught the imagination of Stephen Denny, the Corporation of London's Assistant Education Officer, in spring 2000. This late-seventeenth-century Painted Room has been housed in the Primary School of the Sir John Cass's Foundation since 1906. The Corporation commissioned a guide as they were keen to see the Room included in the Open House weekend in September 2000 and thereafter. I was the lucky art historian who landed the job. The Painted Room then caught my own imagination and fuelled the development of several new proposals. One was an annual series of one day conferences on the theme of City Merchants and the Arts; another was turning the proceedings of the first Conference, on Friday 1 November 2002, into a book entirely devoted to the period of Robert Robinson and the Painted Room. This is the result.

SETBACKS AND BREAKTHROUGHS

The project was not without its setbacks. The most disastrous event took place in July 2000, when enormous damage was sustained by the Painted Room, weeks before the expected Open House viewing. For a number of hours one weekend, the air conditioning blew out steam and the excessive moisture completely blanched the varnish and in some cases, too, the layer of paint underneath. It was literally impossible to see the paintings. In the end, restoring the panels to their former glory took close to three years and for the first year or so the project was paralysed. Negotiations with the insurers and other official bodies were delaying the restoration of the paintings, preventing access to the works and postponing publication of the guide book. Eventually, a grant from the Paul Mellon Centre for British Art to help publish the Painted Room guide heralded a more active and creative phase. The next project was an attempt to capture in a one-day conference the varied array of artistic endeavours in the City of London at the end of the seventeenth century — ranging from those which burnished the self-esteem of merchants to those which transformed the buildings or streets of London after the devastation of the Great Fire.

A LITTLE-KNOWN SUBJECT

The conference was a great success. Most people there, speakers and members of the public, found a subject that was little recorded but fascinating. Historians of architecture, furniture and sculpture realised, sometimes to their surprise, that their papers cross-referenced a number of the same merchants. Amongst the most quoted was Sir Robert Clayton. His London house is illustrated in Chapter 3, his property dealings and art commissions are discussed by Laura Wortley in Chapter 8 and his tomb is analysed by Anthony Hotson in Chapter 11.

Everyone involved with this publication has worked towards a 'Book of the Conference' rather than the more usual 'publication of conference papers'. Most papers were re-written to fit the more structured format of a book, adding notes, bibliography, merchants' biographies, illustrations and additional information. The content was revised and a couple of chapters were added to ensure more complete coverage of the subject. One additional chapter examines the life and work of Robert Robinson; its author, James Ganz, could not attend the conference but his doctoral thesis provides the most recent work on this artist. The other addition is David Mitchell's scene setting chapter which complements the rich and lively essay by Gordon and Philippa Glanville.

NEW INSIGHTS

Although we set out to document relatively uncharted territory, namely the relationship between the City and the Arts, the range and content of the contributions, suggested the almost endless ramifications of this theme. We were all familiar with the idea of the City being the engine of Britain's wealth; but reading this book conjures up this community of merchants as they make money and then spend it. Many of their habits and motives have been unmasked: where they chose to live, where they went to see art, the way they dined, slept, sat, or bought their houses. Adriana Turpin successfully describes the vanished interiors of their houses in Chapter 5 — despite the scarcity of documentation on mercantile taste. In this respect, Ann Saunders' unusual and original essay (Chapter 13), by adopting a fictional voice in an otherwise well documented case history, allows the reader to feel at home in this post-Fire London.

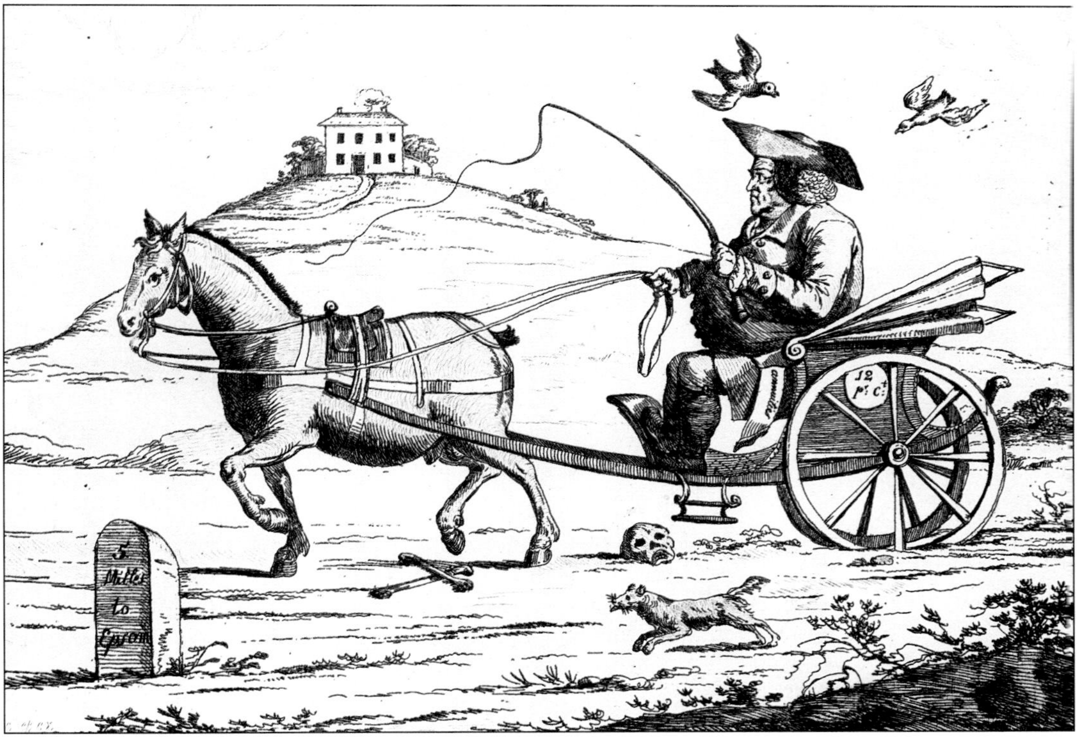

Another theme which emerged from this project was the impact made by City merchants outside the capital. This worked in two ways; either London merchants came from the province (for example Yorkshire for William Turner) or they created roots in the Home Counties through the purchase of estates (for instance Carshalton House in the case of Edward Carleton and Sir John Fellowes). In both cases, merchants lavished time, energy and money on their property or on local charitable works. This trend, which started in the late sixteenth century, grew during the period under review and did not escape the sharp eye of London's satirical artists later in the eighteenth century.

1 *'The Sally from Mincing Lane to Little Hell', engraving published by W. Humphrey on 13 February 1777. The anonymous artist has captured with great verve the potentially exhausting hazards of eighteenth-century 'commuting' between the City and the Home Counties.*

Illus. 1

WHAT IS A MERCHANT?

The concept and shape of the book evolved gradually through a series of conversations and meetings, one of which was held in the fine historic house described in Chapter 4 of this book. Our host and contributor, Katharine Goodison, has succeeded in providing evidence of the house's origins and owners in her chapter. Yet although the first owner's name has come down to us, his precise activities as a merchant have remained obscure. More frustrating still is the unknown name of the merchant who commissioned the

Painted Room; luckily in this case, the subject of the paintings have helped establish his activities as a tobacco merchant. There have been hundreds of books on London which refer to London's community of merchants or to such and such merchant, without their authors defining who a merchant is and what he actually does. 'Buying and selling' is the widest possible definition of mercantile activities, though the phrase does not differentiate between a merchant and a tradesman. Both these professions will at times be mentioned and indeed illustrated in this volume (See *Frontispiece* and *Illus. 67*).

Yet definitions can be very useful: they provide a yardstick by which to measure commercial activity. Perhaps one of the most useful definitions is that given by David Hancock in his book *Citizens of the World*:

> *'Merchant' originally meant any trader in goods, but by the middle of the eighteenth century, its original meaning had been considerably narrowed. General dictionaries, like those written by Samuel Johnson or Thomas Sheridan, defined a merchant as one 'who trafficks to remote countries.' Trade experts like Timothy Cunningham, the author of a popular treatise on the law of bills of exchange [1761], described a merchant as not 'every one who buys or sells' but rather one who moves in the 'Way of Commerce' by 'Importation or Exportation,' who 'makes it his Living to buy and sell, and that by a continued Assiduity, or frequent Negotiation in the Mystery of Merchandizing.' Most contemporaries agreed that a merchant was a wholesale trader who had dealings with foreign countries. Many groups of critical importance to the domestic economy, such as 'artificers' (manufacturers), skilled tradesmen, retailers, and shopkeepers, were not labelled 'merchants'.*[1]

This definition is also valid in the second half of the seventeenth century, even if, as stated here, documents confirming its veracity only turn up later in the eighteenth century. The significant place which exotic lands occupied in the life of merchants found a visual echo in the 1661 Lord Mayor's Show scene described by William Schellinks: 'in the afternoon he [the Lord Mayor] was met at Foster Lane by a display of Americans trading with the Christians. First appeared some Europeans, in the dress and fashions of various nations. Their leader was sitting on a camel and addressed the Lord Mayor with a speech about the increase and growth of the trade'.[2] Both Hancock's definition and the pageant scene conjure up a world of distant lands and risky business transactions. In the social hierarchy of the City, merchants were indeed at the top, just as the 'houses of the greatest bigness' inhabited by so many of them were at the apex of the housing hierarchy in London's streets.

At the end of the seventeenth century, however, things changed again with the emergence of the banking system and of a new class of merchants — the goldsmith-banker. At times they combined lending activities with trading activities, at other times they concentrated on money lending only, thus modifying the definition above, by placing the 'exotic' activities in second place. Sir Robert Vyner, discussed in Chapter 10, was an obvious example but the more obscure figure of John Coggs has also been brought into focus in Karen Hearn's Chapter 7. This book covers many social categories, very occasionally venturing into a non-mercantile arena though one which is always firmly associated with the City.

DO MERCHANTS FOLLOW THEIR OWN SEPARATE SET OF RULES IN ARTISTIC PURSUITS?

There are various views on this particular theme and the issue may therefore not be as clear cut as was originally assumed. Previous thinking has tended to regard merchants' artistic taste being driven by the emulation of the aristocratic classes. Susan Wyman's book on the Verneys (see Bibliography) challenged these assumptions by showing that the merchant elite was so powerful and influential that it had its own momentum and independence. However, the evidence provided by some of the contributors here still rightfully describes the impact of aristocratic taste, for instance in terms of costume (see Valerie Cumming in Chapter 10) or in terms of large scale commissions such as the judges portraits for Guildhall (see Vivien Knight in Chapter 12).

Yet two factors are shown here to undermine the idea that 'merchant taste follows aristocratic taste'. Valerie Cumming argues the case for 'social fluidity' and Laura Wortley points out that 'bankers and artists have cultivated overlapping networks of clients among merchants and landowners'. In this instance the artist may be seen as a catalyst, at the service of his patrons but also setting the pace for many commissions, whatever their origins.

I should also like to offer another interpretation of the information that is available to us. What drove me to investigate the theme of City Merchants and the Arts was the intimation of a type of patronage unrelated to aristocratic patronage, with the courage of its own distinct convictions. In a country which at times seems burdened by the weight of its royal connections, it is refreshing to encounter alternatives. The taste for the exotic which so appealed to the aristocracy in the eighteenth century owed much of its existence to the mercantile class, their trading links with the East and the Americas, and their imports of luxury goods. The introduction of solid reality into the fantastic world of the exotic can also be regarded as influenced by mercantile taste. The Painted Room scheme, for example, probably shows the earliest representations of tobacco manufacture and the detail in several panels is remarkably precise. The same sharp reality is encountered in the rare portrait of a cloth merchant in his warehouse: an example of mercantile patronage creating a new type of painting, a hybrid of Dutch genre scenes and portraiture.

In conclusion it should be stressed that differences in the interpretation of the artistic evidence have not been ironed out to fit a single vision. We leave it up to you, gentle reader, to make up your own mind ...

Mireille Galinou
January 2004

LONDON AFTER THE GREAT FIRE

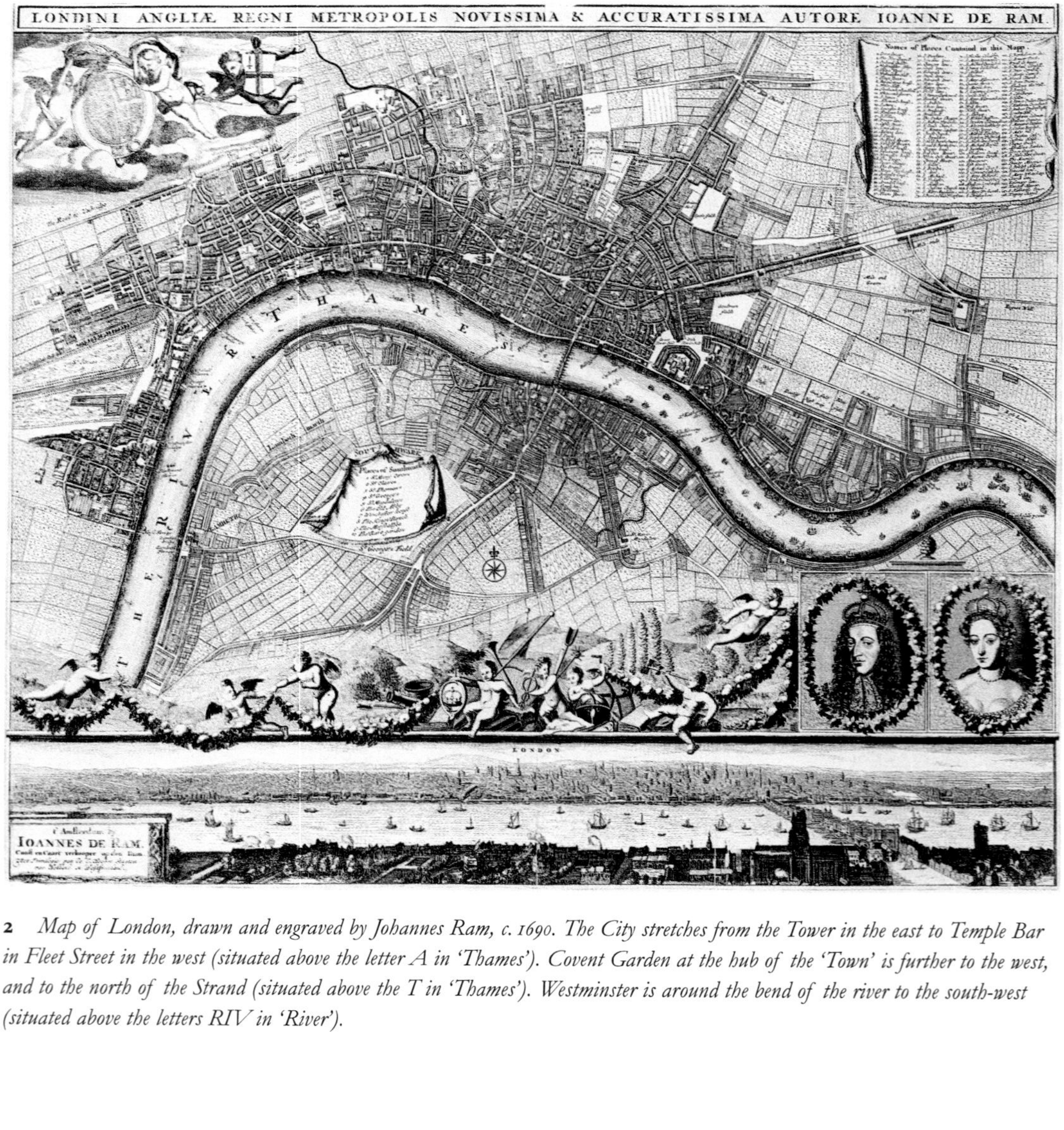

2 *Map of London, drawn and engraved by Johannes Ram, c. 1690. The City stretches from the Tower in the east to Temple Bar in Fleet Street in the west (situated above the letter A in 'Thames'). Covent Garden at the hub of the 'Town' is further to the west, and to the north of the Strand (situated above the T in 'Thames'). Westminster is around the bend of the river to the south-west (situated above the letters RIV in 'River').*

'The Three Londons'

Chapter One

DAVID MITCHELL

In 1652 John Evelyn compared the virtues of Paris and London:

This I will boldly affirm, that for the streets, suburbs, and common buildings, it [Paris] infinitely excels any City else in Europe.

But what our City of London hath not in houses and Palaces, she hath in Shops and Taverns; which render it so open by day, and cheerful in the night, that it appears to be a perpetual Wake, or Wedding to the beholder; for so mad and lowd a Town, is no where to be found in the whole World.[1]

Evelyn complained of the tiresome bustle of Paris, to which the anonymous French author of *A Character of England* of 1659, responded that London was, 'a large, yet very ugly Town, pestred with Hackney-Coaches, ... Shops and Taverns, Noyse, and ... a cloud of Sea-Coal'.[2] This 'Slanderous Pamphlet' elicited an immediate reply with the retort that Paris was 'a world of confusion, a world of dust, ... and indeed a world of fooleries and vanities'.[3] It continued with an angry response to the Frenchman's disdain that 'our City is a wooden, Northern, and an artificial congestion of houses'; 'this Monsieur, I perceive is no curious Architect, for finding fault with our wooden Buildings, which consider London, as a Mercantile City, strong and beautiful'.[4]

Two foreign visitors, the French savant Samuel Sorbière in 1663 and the Tuscan Count Lorenzo Magalotti in 1669, both commented upon the commerce and overseas trade of London. They admired the New Exchange and its 'Fine Shop-Women', with Sorbière concluding that 'perhaps there is no City in the World that has so many, and such Fine Shopps'.[5] He was also struck by the 'Multitudes ... Imploy'd in Building and Fitting out Vessells for Sea, on each side of the river', with Magalotti stating that, 'it is said, that there are more than one thousand four hundred [large ships] betwixt Gravesend and London Bridge'.[6]

The Great Fire of 1666 destroyed much of the 'wooden' city which had been so derided and stoutly defended by the opposing

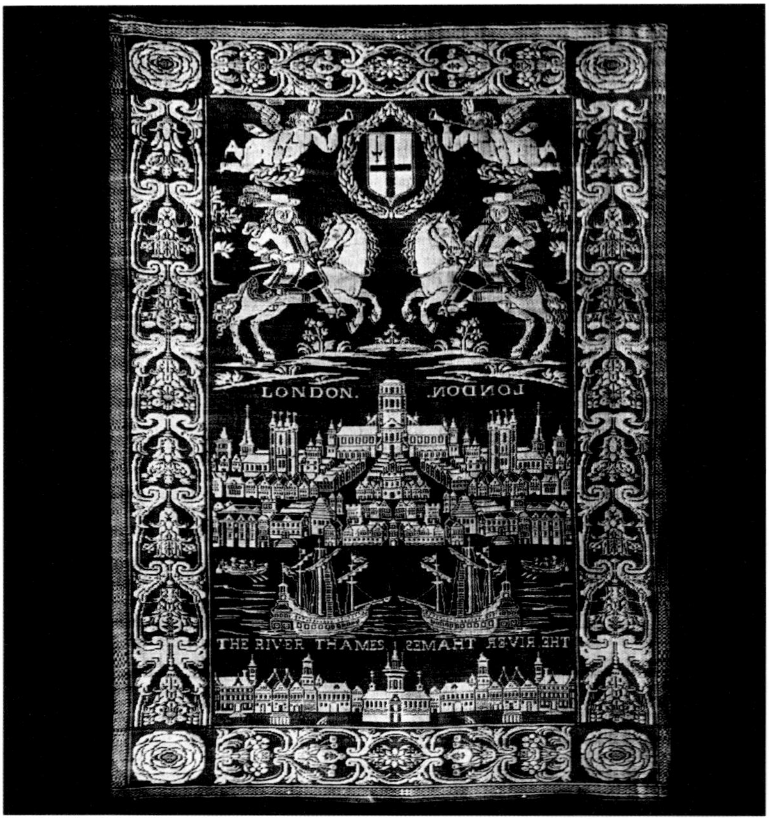

3 *View of the City of London on a linen damask napkin, probably woven at Kortrijk in the Spanish Netherlands, c. 1665. The design is possibly derived from Wenceslaus Hollar's frontispiece to James Howell's book 'Londinopolis', published in London in 1657. The napkin is woven in point repeat, being symmetrical about its centre line, and depicts the City to the west of the tower of St Paul's Cathedral. On the northern waterfront, Baynard's Castle and the Waterhouse are clearly recognisable and across the river in Southwark, St Mary Overy and Winchester House. The large ocean-going ships in the river are presumably to emphasize London's overseas trade, for it was impossible to get such ships upstream of London Bridge after its drawbridge ceased to be operational during the sixteenth century.*

pamphleteers of 1659. The City was rebuilt in brick and stone, and the areas of gentry housing to the west were greatly extended, so that by 1689, the developer Nicholas Barbon could boast,

The artists of this age have already made the City of London the metropolis of Europe, and if it be compared for the number of good houses, for its many and large piazzas, for the richness of inhabitants it must be allowed the largest, best built, and richest city in the world.[7]

Thus London seems to have been characterized by its size and shops and ships! It was certainly large, with a population of 575,000 in 1700, when it had overtaken Paris with 510,000 as the largest city in Europe. It was the centre of government, the court, commerce, manufacturing and the principal port accounting for some three quarters of foreign trade. England was dominated by the metropolis which represented about 10 per cent of the population of 5.5 to 6 millions, with the other major towns such as Norwich, Bristol and Newcastle being tiny in comparison, with populations in 1700 of about 29,000, 25,000 and 14,000 respectively.

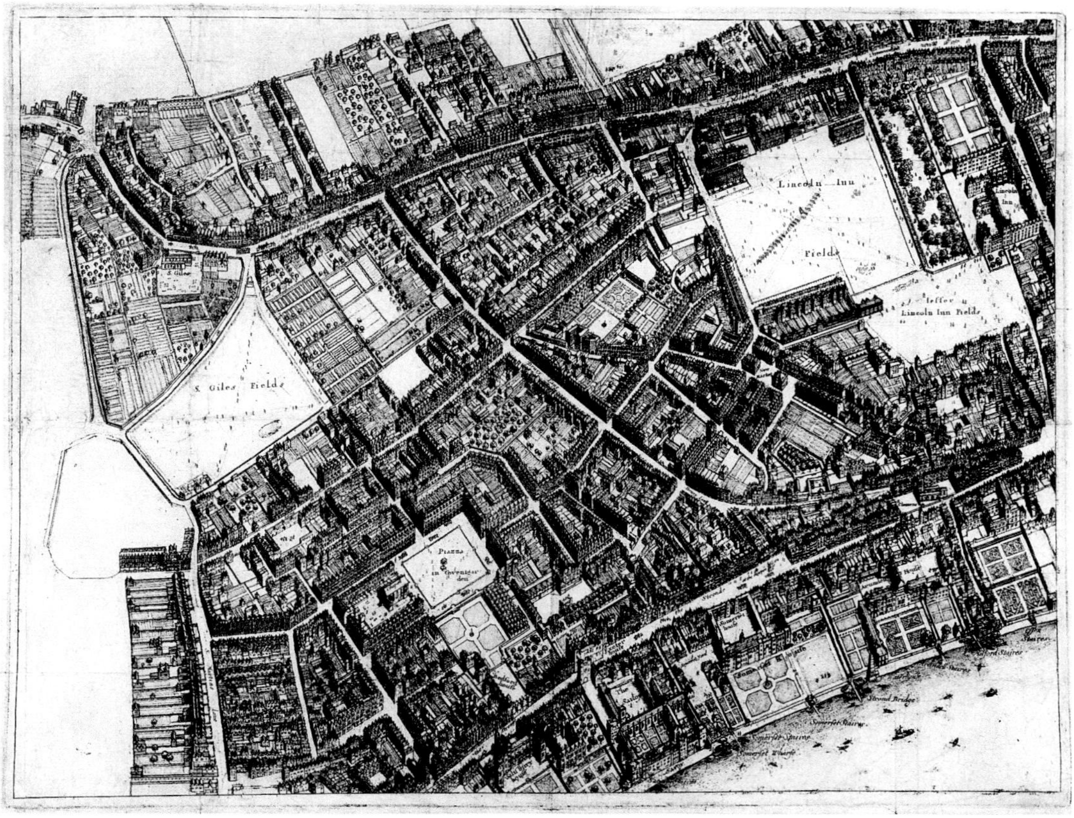

4 *Bird's-eye view of the 'Town', etching by Wenceslaus Hollar, undated, c. 1658. This is the only section Hollar published of his projected 'Great Map of London'. The growth of the Town was largely articulated around the square, ushered in at Lincoln's Inn Fields (top right) but fully developed at Covent Garden for the first time, as shown in this view.*

This was in marked contrast to France where the total population of nineteen millions was more than three times that of England, with Paris representing less than three per cent. Further, provincial cities such as Bordeaux, Rouen, Marseilles and Lyon had large populations compared with their English counterparts, ranging between 50,000 and 100,000. The other major European cities had considerably smaller populations than London and Paris: for example, Naples had 216,000, Amsterdam 200,000 and Lisbon 165,000.

Accordingly, before the dispersal of much of London's manufacturing capacity and the growth of cities such as Manchester, Birmingham and Glasgow following the 'Industrial Revolution', the metropolis arguably held a greater sway over national, cultural, social, political and economic attitudes than other major capitals.

At the Restoration in 1660, the Royal Family and other exiles returned from France and the Low Countries where they had observed, and in some cases adopted, the current fashions in dress, manners and cuisine. Both at court and in the 'Town', all things

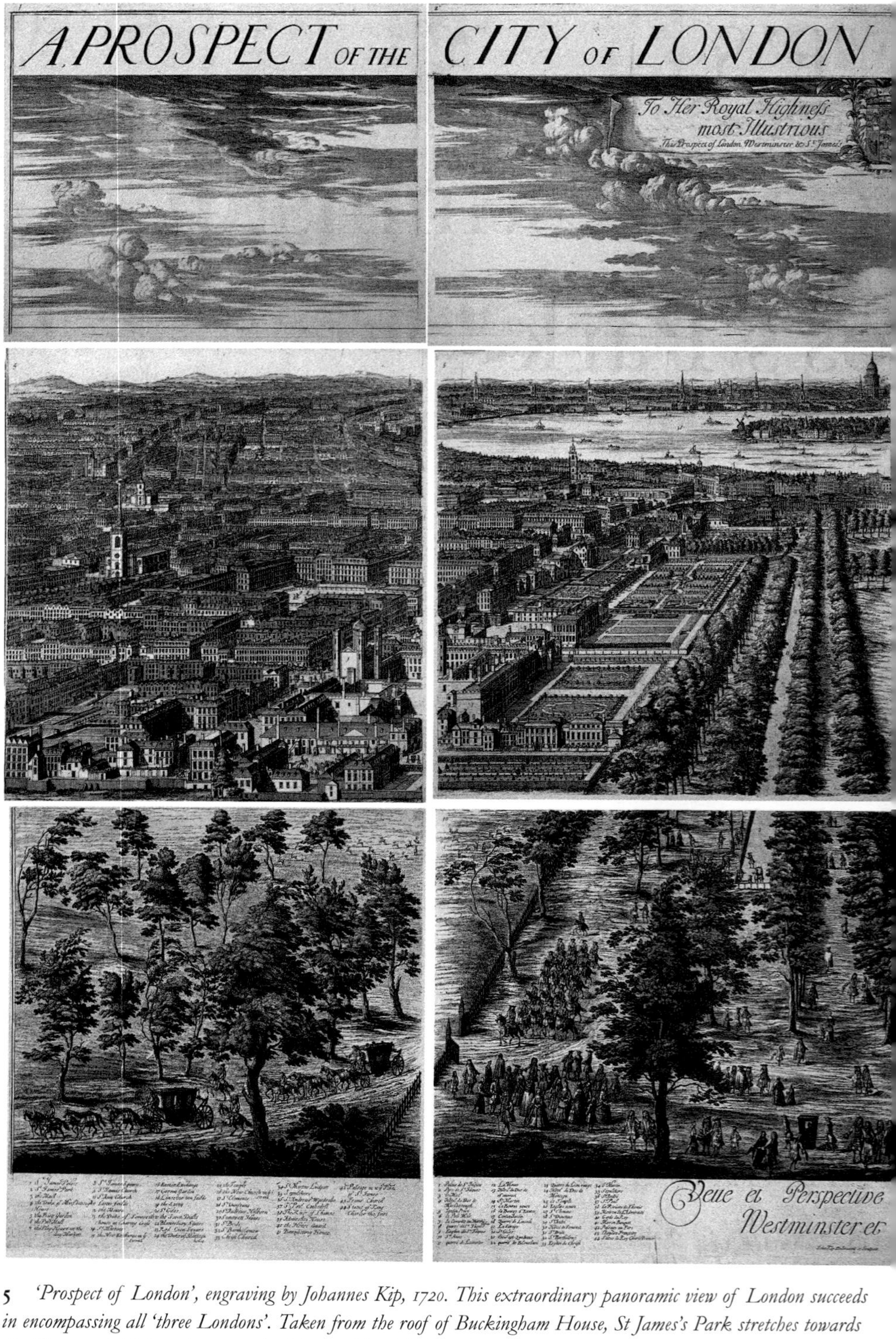

5 *'Prospect of London', engraving by Johannes Kip, 1720. This extraordinary panoramic view of London succeeds in encompassing all 'three Londons'. Taken from the roof of Buckingham House, St James's Park stretches towards the Thames with Westminster on the right, the West End on the left and the City in the far distance.*

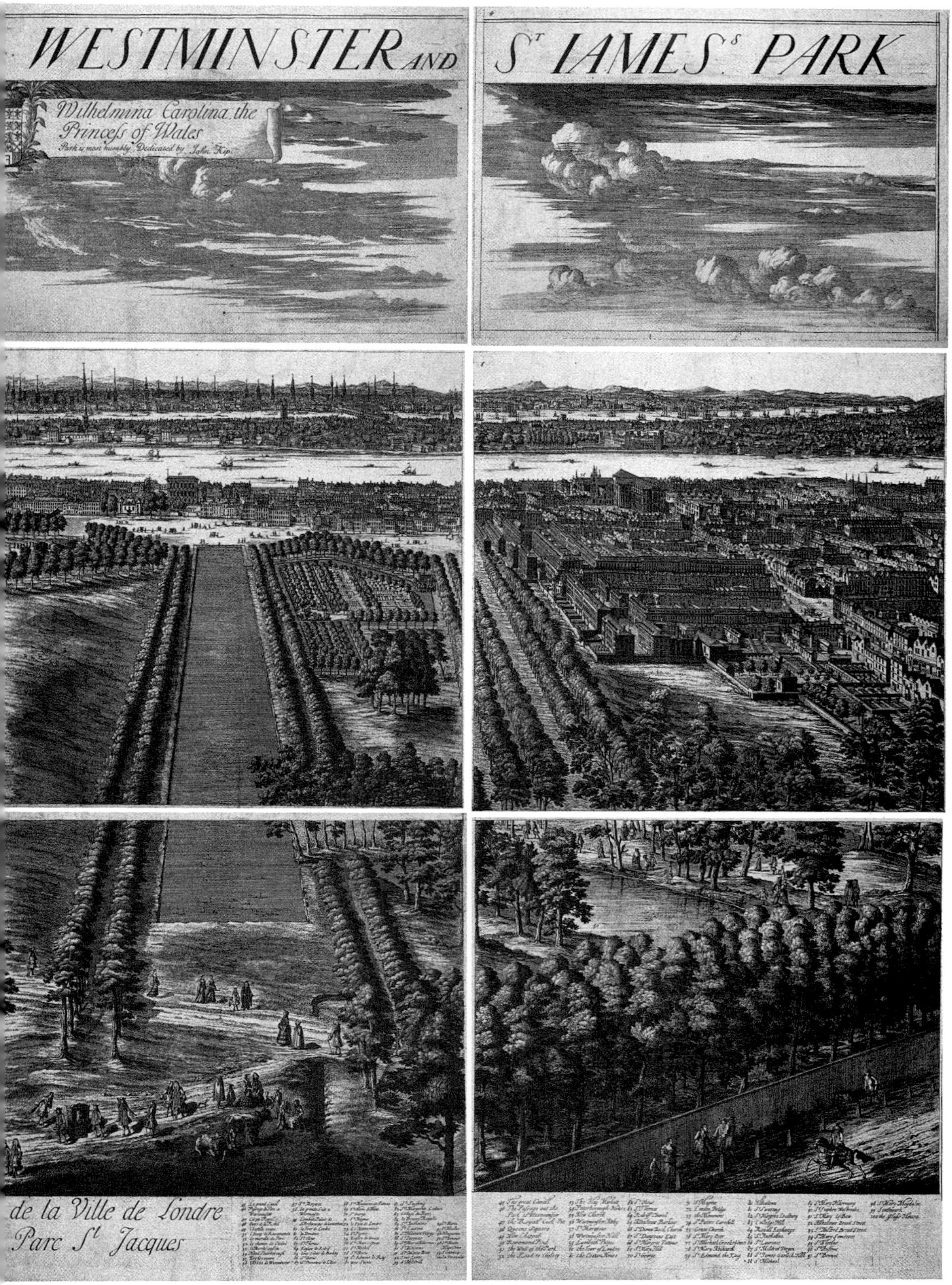
WESTMINSTER AND St IAMES's PARK
Wilhelmina Carolina, the Princess of Wales
Park is most humbly Dedicated by John Kip
de la Ville de Londre
Parc St Jacques

French seemed à la mode.[8] In this period, the 'Town' centred on Covent Garden was becoming the fashionable heart of London in contrast to the centre of commerce and trade in the City, and to the Court and Government at Westminster. Larry Klein has argued that the 'Town' was a concept as well as a physical place, citing Richard Steele in Town Talk of 1715:[9]

Illus. 2, 3, 4, 5

> *The Town is the upper part of the World, or rather the fashionable People, those who are distinguished from the rest by some Eminence. These compose what we call the Town, and the Intelligent very well know, that many have got Estates both in London [i.e. the City] and Westminster . . . that could never get into Town.*[10]

However, these three separate physical and conceptual geographies — the City, the Town and the Court — were not isolated, for both the Court and the City had close links with the Town, with merchants serving together with courtiers and landed gentry on various councils of state, such as that for Trade, or for the Plantations. They also formed consortia for overseas adventures, for example in diamonds from India.[11]

Susan Whyman in her study of John Verney, a Levant merchant who in middle age inherited his father's baronetcy, argued that the social behaviour and attitudes of younger gentry sons apprenticed to elite trades in the City were little different from their elder

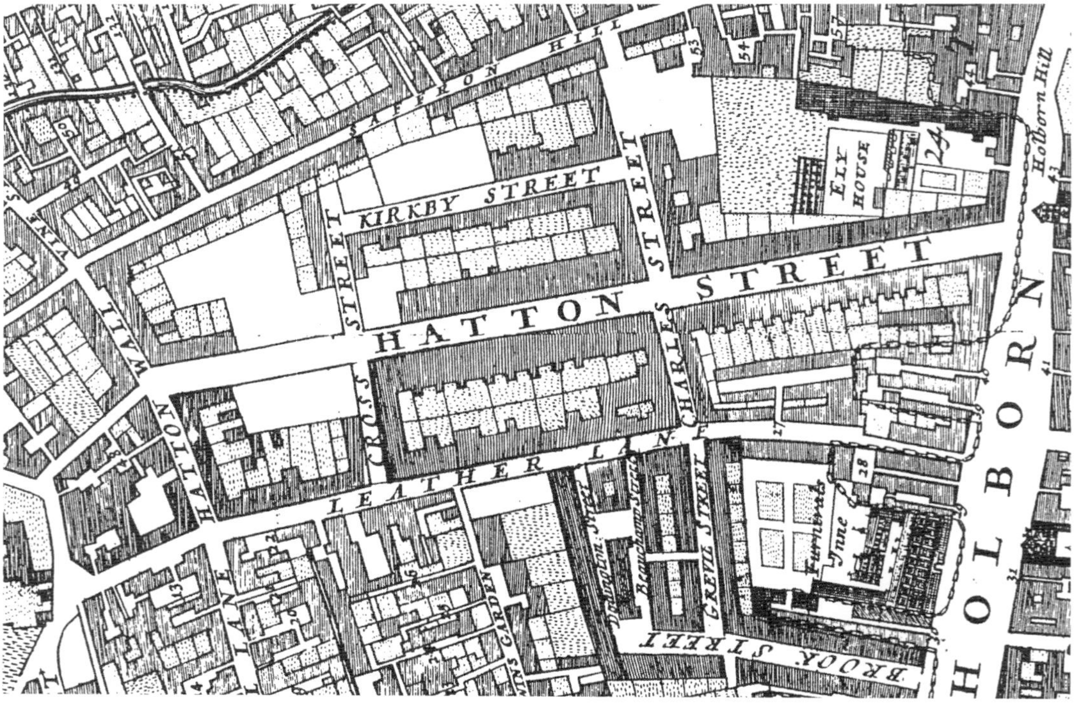

6 *Hatton Garden, detail of William Morgan's Map of London, 1682. By 1681 John Verney was living 'at the first wooden balcony on the left hand near Holborn in Hatton Garden [Hatton Street]'.*

brothers. An observer wrote in 1695, 'the interests of trade and land are the same, for the mutation frequently happens; the moneyed man today is the landed man tomorrow'.[12] Whilst still a 'moneyed man', John Verney lived between the City and the Town in Hatton Garden,[13] whence he walked into the City and his business on the Exchange and at the Customs House, or alternatively visited his family and Buckinghamshire neighbours at their town houses in Covent Garden.[14] Like Verney, another younger son who plied a very successful trade as a 'Turkey merchant', Sir Dudley North, also dined in 'exquisite . . . harmony' with 'courtiers, bankers, and divers of the nobility'.[15] Apart from elite overseas merchants, a number of goldsmith-bankers as well as brewers, sugar-refiners and others led lives in the City, but were also members of the 'Town'.

Illus. 6

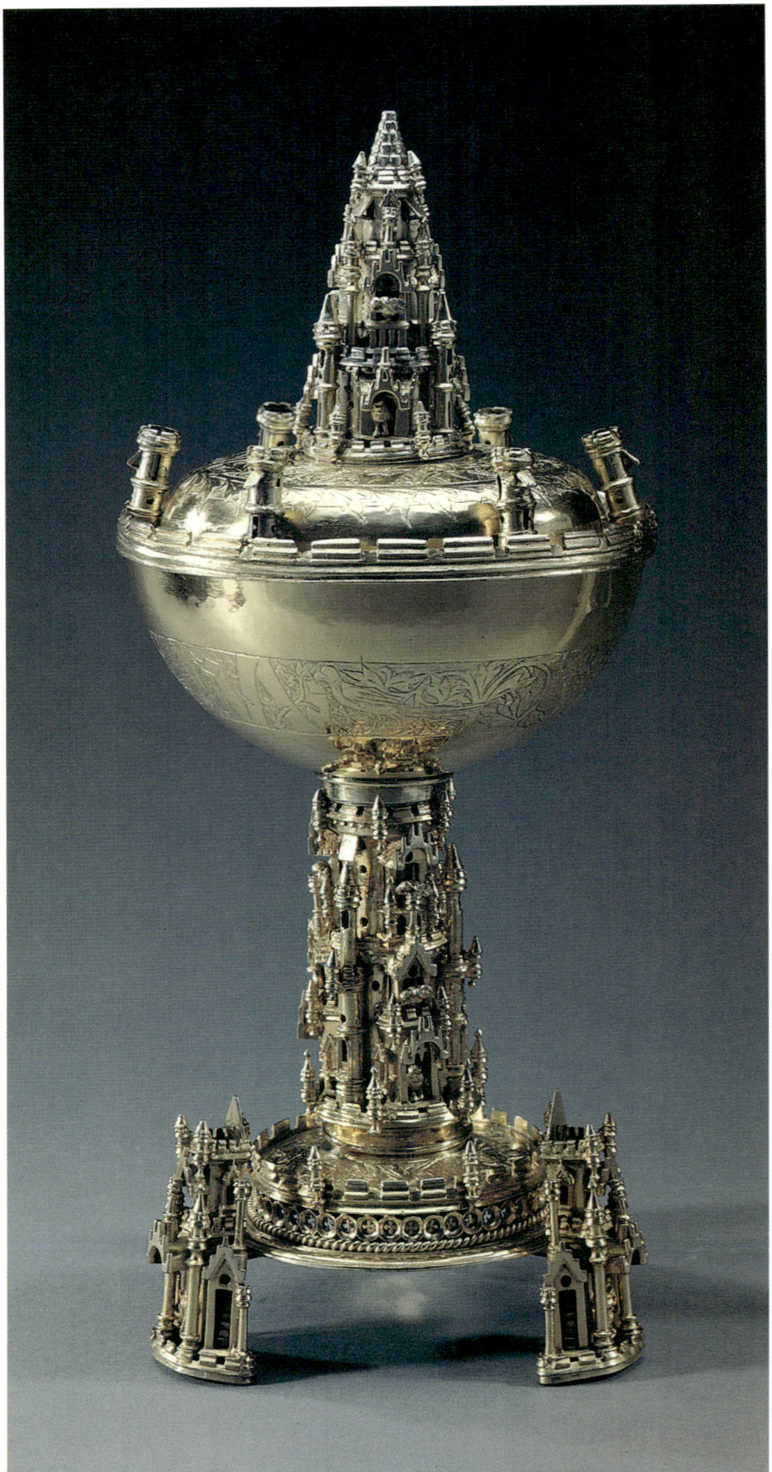

7 *Late fifteenth-century silver gilt Cup owned by goldsmith-banker Robert Clayton.*

The Art Market and Merchant Patronage in London 1680 to 1720

Chapter Two

GORDON AND PHILIPPA GLANVILLE

Historians have beavered away with considerable success in identifying the possessions of the 'middling sort' and of the aristocracy, but have neglected the lifetime accumulations of those described loosely as London merchants. This category includes financiers, tax farmers, brokers, government agents and contractors, those described as 'eminent merchants' by Gregory King.[1]

For this distinctive group, 'new men' perceived as a phenomenon at the time, their position in society was not necessarily judged by their baronetcy or their knighthood, their roles as Members of Parliament or participants in City government, but by their reputed wealth. Still mostly living within the boundary of the City, they also owned houses in the leafy parishes around London or further afield. Their City houses have long disappeared, the leafy parishes have become overbuilt commuterland, and their country estates passed by marriage or default of heir to others or obscured behind the acquisition of a title. An intensive search among family papers might uncover the chronology and nature of their once fashionable acquisitions and the commissions, public and private, which they chose and funded.

THE SOUTH SEA INVENTORIES

Happily, a snapshot appears in the submission of accounts forced upon the thirty-three directors and officials of the South Sea

Company by the terms of the South Sea Sufferers Bill (Appendix I). They had to provide not only an inventory of their wealth but also the details of their expenditure between 1 June 1720 and 31 March 1721, to indicate the extent of their gain from the Bubble. This is not the forum for a detailed analysis, but simply to highlight that of the twenty-four serviceable individual inventories, one listed more than 200 pictures, one more than 100, eight between 50 and 100, and five between 20 and 50.* Very rarely are prices given except for purchases between 1 June and 31 March. Family portraits or pictures are common; there are vague references to landscapes, battle scenes and horses but the single identification is a portrait of Jane Shore, a London character and mistress of Edward IV, valued at 75 pence in the Manchester house of Thomas Reynolds. Overall, pictures are perfunctorily listed compared with the attention given to plate and jewels.

*The goldsmith-banker John Hinde had 45 pictures on the great staircase and 19 in the matted gallery of his Highgate house in 1685. Roger North had 219 in 1701, comparable with noble family holdings. The three Northumberland houses held 161 in 1670, Ham House 182 in 1680 and Kimbolton 167 in 1687.

A useful example is the inventory of the Customs farmer Francis Hawes, owner of 132 pictures in his house at Purley Hall near Reading, and another 133 at his house in Winchester Street, the stairs of 'the first story painted with landscapes.' Hawes was a collector on a grand scale. His London house was a veritable cabinet of curiosities and he was still buying up to and beyond the collapse of the Bubble, although paintings were a minor expense. His expenditure reveals his priorities; 'August 2nd 1720 paid Mr Lockyer for pictures £120; Dec 1st North the upholster in part £2000; January 4th Mr Hutt the Upholster in part £400: the Jewelers Bill £1190'. Although perhaps manipulated, the overall figures reveal where true value was to be sought: 'My Household goods at Purley in Berkshire £630-12; My Household goods at home in Town £1041-19-6; My Wifes Jewels, Watches £1,960-0; My plate £693-4'.[2]

BUYING PAINTINGS

Historians have analysed the late Stuart art market in terms of auctions, the nature of the pictures sold and prices paid, in line with the modern perception of these as the principal form of art. But few paintings sold at auction cost more than £4 to £10 (apart from the occasional spectacular sales such as Peter Lely's in 1682, Lord Melfort's in 1693 or Mr Graham's in 1712, when connoisseurs competed for exceptional treasures by Rubens, Poussin or Van Dyck) whereas expenditure on tapestry, furnishings, plate or decorated furniture was far higher. Value was attached to rich effects, figurative ornament and fine workmanship, and these costly artefacts were appreciated rather more than works on canvas (many of which were copies), the attitude deplored by Shaftesbury in his *Characteristics*. Designs had to be created 'in the latest fashion' for these luxurious and essential items, but Court patronage alone has attracted analysis to date.[3]

Expenditure on art encompassed a far wider variety of products in many media, often ephemeral, including interior painting, goldsmiths' work and textiles, plus art forms such as the Lord Mayors' pageants, than modern orthodoxy, with its emphasis on the individual canvas, acknowledges. Post-Fire London was rich in decorative effects — painted interiors, carving in wood and stone, gilded ironwork, stained glass and colourful monuments.

Illus. 97

Commissioned by City merchants, these were prestigious creations, devised by sculptors, metalworkers and artists better known today for work outside the City, such as Edward Pearce, Grinling Gibbons, Jean Tijou, Antonio Verrio or James Thornhill.* Many parish churches and livery halls were embellished.† But these examples of aesthetic decisions originating within a City elite have vanished or been dramatically modified and the art works dispersed, destroyed or at the least, now without their original setting.

*In the City these artists are best remembered for statues of Gresham and Edward III at the Royal Exchange and for the dragons on the Monument (Pearce; Bushnell's magnificent Charles I and Charles II now greet visitors to the Old Bailey); another Royal Exchange statue, James I (Gibbons); screens at St Paul's (Tijou); the commemorative group portrait at Christ's Hospital (Verrio); and scenes from the life of St Paul, formerly in the cupola of the Cathedral (Thornhill).

†In 1679 the Clothworkers Company spent £54 on gilded statues of Charles I and James I to ornament their Hall, and ten years later they commissioned stained glass to honour their members and benefactors Samuel Pepys and Sir Joseph Williamson. A less wealthy company, the Weavers, was given a set of tapestries from a Dutch merchant for their Hall.

Picture imports are one aspect of the burgeoning London art market to have been analysed exhaustively, although the buyers are not necessarily identifiable. The Calendar of Treasury Books for the period 1660–94 reveals the Crown's changing attitude towards the importation of paintings. Although prohibited by earlier legislation and subject to the provision 'for private use', the government appears to have made no effort to monitor imports in the 1660s. Following reforms in the early 1670s, Treasury warrants were issued to the Customs Commissioners to release or charge duty on pictures held in the Customs House. Eighty-five warrants were issued in that decade but from 1680 to 1689, only thirty-five. From 1689 no more warrants appear in the Calendar although the 'ad valorem' tax of 5% is doubled in 1693. In 1695 the ambiguity of the system is removed: pictures can be imported for sale on payment of a duty of 20%, raised to 60% in 1704. The survival of customs records for London and the Outports has enabled one historian to calculate the total valuation of the importation of pictures country by country for the period 1696–1720. The modest total for painting and prints of £12,575-17-0, a yearly average of a fraction under £524, presumably reflects market dislocation from the War of the Spanish Succession. Imports from France were banned for much of these years.[4]

If the number, value and quality of the paintings imported before 1695 is unrecoverable, how they were sold before the advent of the auction is also obscure. William Cartwright, the actor and bookseller bequeathed a collection of 215 paintings to Dulwich College in 1687.[5] His role as a bookseller would have placed him among the print sellers and shops selling pictures. That they existed is borne out by Pepys' visits to John Cade the stationer in Cornhill 'to chose some pictures for our house'.* Pictures also found their way into the hands of painters who dealt in the works of others.[6]

*Thomas Taylor of the Golden Lion, Fleet Street, offered 'all sorts of fine French Italian and Dutch prints and map ... Indian picters, oil paintings and glass paintings ... all sorts of gilt frames ... likewise fitteth up staircases and rooms at reasonable rates.'

The most striking development of the London market in the late 1680s and the early 1690s was the refinement of an auction system, hitherto a somewhat ill-managed monopoly activity of the City's Outroper, selling all manner of property of deceased citizens for the benefit of the Orphans' Fund (Appendix II). After the first private auction of 1674, another is advertised in the *London Gazette* 3 May 1677 for the sale 'of the late deceased Mr Remy picture drawer'. Another auction in 1679 was followed by the very successful sale of Sir Peter Lely's paintings and collection of paintings. No picture auctions are recorded in 1683, one in 1684, two in 1685, twelve in 1686, seven in 1687, fourteen in 1688, thirty in 1689 and climaxing in 1691 at 92.[7] On the basis of 132 surviving catalogues of auctions between 1689 and 1694, it has been calculated that 24,000 pictures changed hands in 1691 alone.

Several explanations have been offered for the sudden surge in auction sales in 1689: a relaxation of the import restrictions on Dutch paintings, courtesy of William III; the Glorious Revolution of 1689 producing 'a volatile period of speculative activity as the public clambered to support Parliament's plea for public funds'; the belief that auction sales 'developed in response to an imbalance between an inelastic supply and a high demand for commodities such as art work, books'. However, those Dutch, Flemish and French migrants encouraged by Charles II in 1671 and 1674 may have played a role. Auctions were a familiar feature of Dutch society in the early seventeenth century, painters brought with them a wider range of subject matter, the product of the 'Golden Age' of Dutch painting. Not only artists but also merchants already established in their occupations brought with them family portraits and collections. Without the immigrants, would there have been sufficient paintings in the country to spark the auction boom of 1689–91?[8]

The breaking of the Outroper's monopoly brought forward a number of promoters of auctions. At least fourteen individuals were running auctions in the boom at coffee houses and taverns in the West End. Auctions and viewings were advertised in news sheets; two thirds of the 1694 issues of the *Athenian Mercury* contained auction sales for luxury items. This was a new kind of town pleasure, and one which women could enjoy too, unlike most public gatherings.[9]

The art historians H. V. S. and M. S. Ogden identified three levels of auctions: those of high class works by named authors whose works fetched high prices such as Paolo Veronese's '*The Blessed Virgin, The Child Jesus, Joseph and St Catherine* as big as the life' bought by the Earl of Peterborough at the Lely sale in 1682; sales such as Prosper Henry Lankrinck's collection of competent works and good copies; and the bottom end of the market containing 'the highest proportion of anonymous paintings' where catalogues 'often advertise the pictures as fit for ladies' closets, staircases overdoors and the like'.[10]

Why did the auction boom of 1689 to 1694, that had peaked at 92 recorded auctions in 1691, collapse so dramatically, falling to only sixteen recorded auctions in 1695, seven in 1696, and one each in the following two years? Had the market become sated? More to the point was Sir John Banks's rather sombre calculation of his tax payments: in the 1660s (when he lived in the City) 2% of this successful merchant's income went in tax, increasing to between 15 and 20% on a larger income in the 1690s, by which time he lived in some splendour in Lincoln's Inn Fields.* Any spare cash was better invested in funds to sustain the government than in the purchase of pictures. Although auction sales recovered to 46 in 1710 and may have further increased after the War of Spanish Succession in 1713 they did not reach the levels of 1691 and 1692.[11]

*Funding the Nine Years War with Louis XIV required a quarterly poll tax, a land tax of 20 p in the pound, increases in the beer and liquor excise, higher customs duties on luxury imports, still leaving the government with an overall deficit for 1688–1702 of £13.5 m.

MOTIVATIONS

Competition and nationalism drove decisions in the arts, a defensive frame of mind caught in the 1714 project to create a monument to the Stuarts in the Strand: 'Something be done in England that Strangers may not say that we think only of eating and drinking (but) admire us for Polite people in Arts'.[12]

These motives and values are made explicit in City commissions such as the statues at the Royal Exchange 'for the reputation . . .', the Monument and the royal portraits at Christ's Hospital. Popular festivities at Bartholomew Fair included painterly exhibits, such as Peter Tillemans's patriotic 'Fine Musical Picture of the Royal Family' in 1717.[13] The Mercers' Chariot of the Virgin Queen, centrepiece of the 1686 Lord Mayor's show, was praised for 'the Magnificence of the Structure, the Elegance of the Contrivance and the Costliness of the Work', a summary of the prevailing

Illus. 97

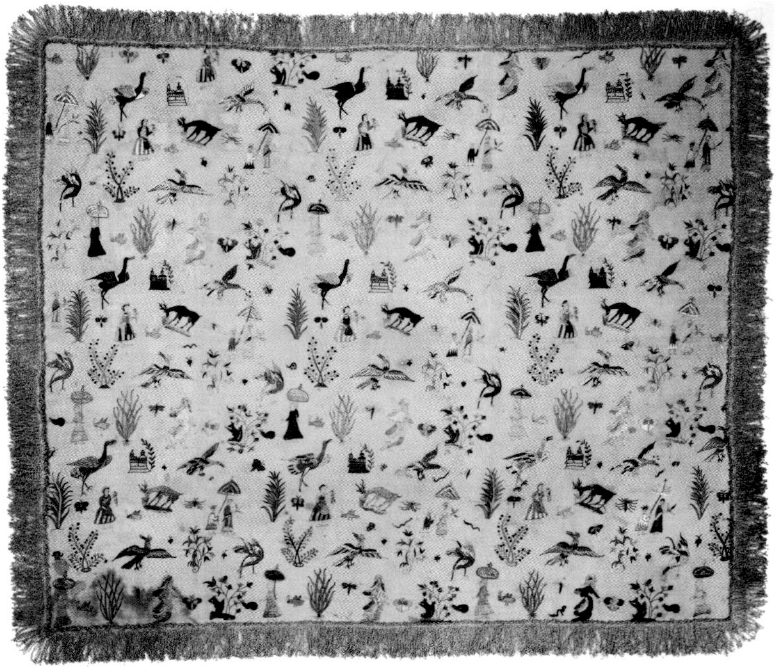

8 *This embroidered bed cover with chinoiseries, c. 1700, was made in London. The label shows the name and address of the pattern drawer: John Stilwell, of the Flaming Sword Russell Street. Nine pattern-drawers are listed in the 1692 poll tax.*

criteria which finds echoes in many contemporary commissions.[14] Sir Samuel Dashwood's lavish Lord Mayor's show devised for the Vintners' Company in 1702 was an eclectic mix of classical and trade themes, St Martin on horseback flanked by twenty satyrs, ten halberdiers and ten Roman lictors. Set pieces included an Indian galleon, Ariadne's chariot and the Arbour of Delights with Bacchus.[15]

Exotic images, drawn from a theatrical melange of Indian, Persian and Japanese sources, adorned plate, ceramics, lacquer, tapestries, wallpaper and painted cloths, as well as screens, wall panels and cabinets. Although there were few drawing academies before the 1690s and, unlike Paris, few English apprentices were taught to design and model, pattern drawers designed images for copying in many media.[16]

Upholders, forerunners of interior decorators, brought together all these costly ingredients, including decorative painting, into fashionable ensembles. So any discussion of art patronage needs to take account of these less familiar vanished media too, whose subject matter is documented only in bills. Both decorative painting, schemes like Isaac Fuller's at the Mitre public house in Fenchurch Street depicting classical deities life size, and individual canvases,[17] were inexpensive and ubiquitous, even in coffee houses and taverns. In 1714 Joseph Highmore encountered a Dutch artist in

Drury Lane who specialized in painting long strips of landscape, which he then cut and sold in sections. 'Those who dealt in this way would go to his house and buy . . . any number of feet of landscape'.[18]

STRATEGIC PATRONAGE

For City institutions a display of royal portraits in a time of political turbulence was expedient.* A well-documented commission, recently reassessed, is Gaspars's portrait of Charles II with mathematical instruments, painted for the Great Hall at Christ's Hospital. He was paid £50. This faced Verrio's massive 'fair Table', the commemorative group portrait which took so long to complete from its initial commission by Pepys in 1678 that James II replaced Charles as the central figure. These were institutional obligations, not calculated to appeal to the connoisseurs, for whom 'History Painting' was pre-eminent.[19]

Sculpture was another vehicle for patronage, driven by family and civic pride and widely visible across the City.† Statues of monarchs were quickly reinstated in Edward Jarman's new Royal Exchange, essential to beautify the heart of the City's commerce, although there is a marked discrepancy in style between Bushnell's baroque figures of the two Charles and others by Quellin, Cibber and Pearce. More challenging and intended to stimulate both pity and charity are Cibber's painfully expressive figures of Madness and Melancholy, commissioned for the gateway at Bethlem Hospital.[20] *Illus. 9*

Status was reinforced through the display and exchange of portraits which reinforced the sense of belonging to social or business circles. As Steele wrote in 1712, 'No Nation in the World delights

*In 1676 the Court of the Painter-Stainers commissioned portraits of the King and Catherine from John Baptist Gaspars and Jacob Huysman, of Anne Hyde from John Greenhill and later Michael Dahl (Queen Anne) and of William III from Godfrey Kneller. Closterman painted Queen Mary for the Vintners in the 1690s and won the 1702 competition for the Guildhall portrait of Queen Anne, which cost £100, frame and all.

†The splendid reclining monuments of Thomas and Robert Vyner, now in a remote Lincolnshire church, were commissioned for St Mary Woolnoth, Lombard Street. At St Olave Hart Street, Pepys's pew faced John Bushnell's vivid image of his dead wife. Edward Pearce the younger created carvings and busts for his City circle, such as that of Thomas Evans, Master and benefactor of the Painter-Stainers.

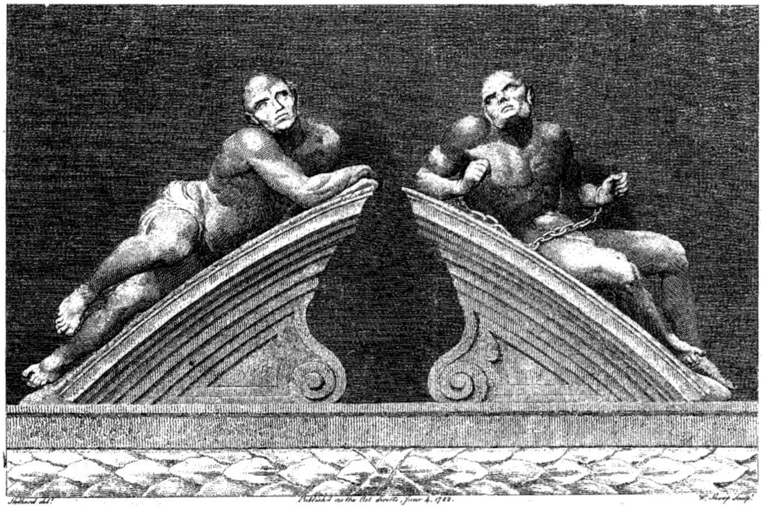

9 *The figures of 'Madness' and 'Melancholy' by Caius Gabriel Cibber on the pedimented entrance gate to the Hospital of St Mary of Bethlehem in Moorfields, better known as Bedlam. From a 1783 engraving by William Sharp after Thomas Stothard.*

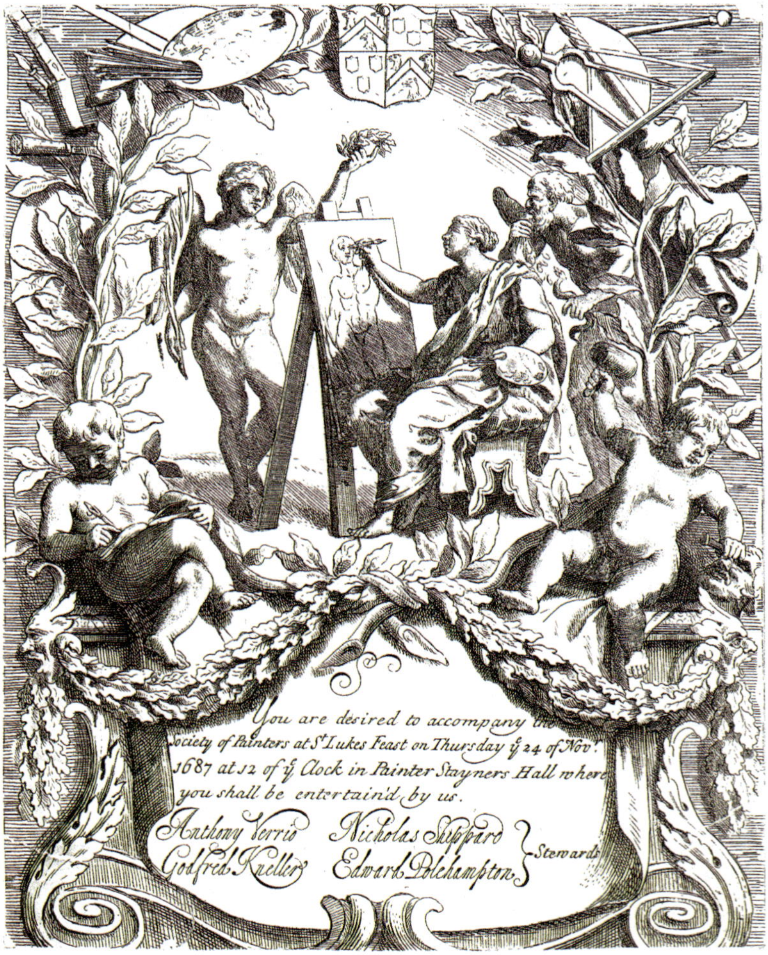

10 *Invitation to St Luke's Feast held at Painter-Stainers' Company on 24 November 1687, etching.*

so much in having their own or Friends or Relations Pictures,' a list to which benefactors might be added. In July 1689 John Evelyn sat to Kneller, 'holding my Sylva in my right hand' at Pepys's 'long and earnest request'. Pepys's Buckingham Street library had a total of fourteen portraits hanging above the bookcases by 1690 and he exchanged images with the Houblon family too. *Illus. 23*

In 1680, unlike Paris or Brussels, London had no official academy of art, few drawing classes, and no public display to inform the eye; and inexpensive and poor quality paintings flooded the market. At this time the canvases and wall paintings at Painter-Stainers' Hall helped to inform merchant taste. Although there was no formal society of St Luke on the longstanding Flemish, Italian and German models nor an official academy of painting as in Paris (founded in the 1660s), the origins of Kneller's and Thornhill's academies lie in

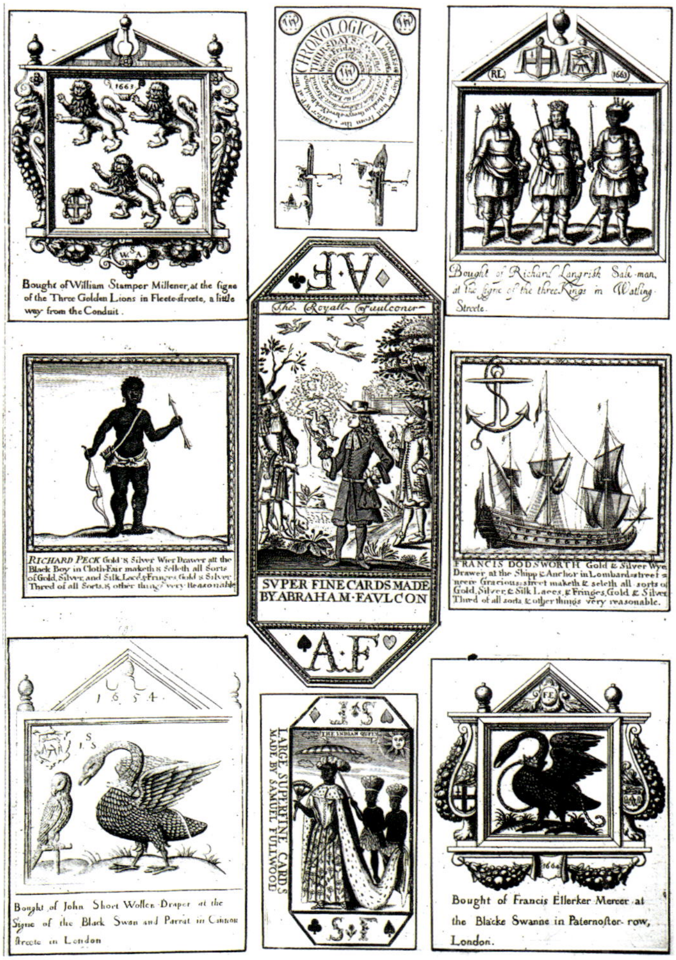

11 *A sheet of London trade cards from the famous collection formed by the diarist Samuel Pepys (1633–1703).*

the 1680s informal club of artists and designers called the Society of Painters, sharing members but not coterminous with the Painter-Stainers. These Virtuosi held an annual St Luke's feast and in effect stimulated art education. The City merchants Col. James Seymour and Sir Robert Child were both members.[21] *Illus. 10*

A TASTE FOR COLLECTING

A cabinet of curiosities, with assemblages of medals, old coins, engravings and antiquities, belonged to one South Sea Director but the taste had deep roots. Such items were available from Cheapside goldsmiths in the 1590s and 'antiquaries' had been mocked by Jacobean dramatists. By 1700 rarities were taken more seriously as an aspect of art and admired in the circle of John Talman, which included merchants and from which the Society of Antiquaries,

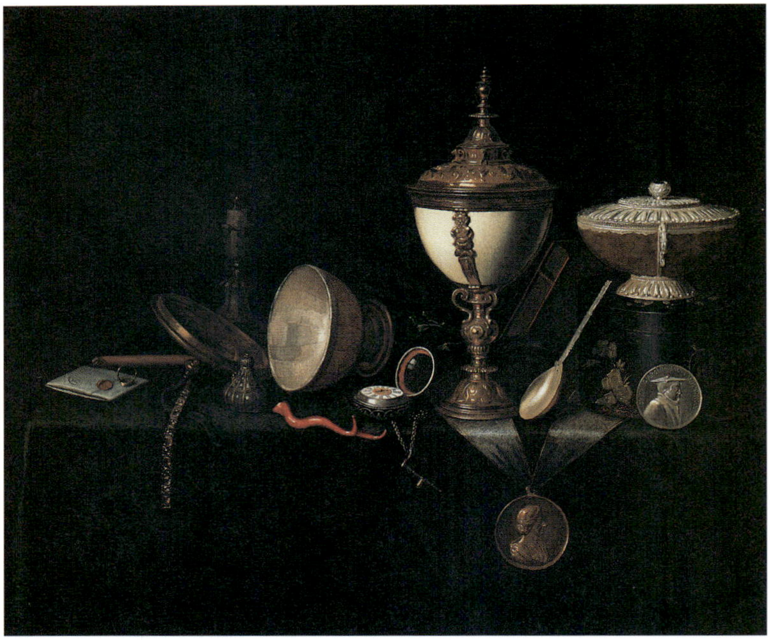

12 *Still life painting with Elizabethan Cup by Pieter Gerritsz van Roestraten (1630–1700).*

with Talman and Vertue as contributors, was to emerge in 1717. Evelyn's *Numismata* (1697) praised the study of coins and medals as expressing history and the character of famous men.[22]

Illus. 80–82, 84, 126

The taste for collecting mezzotints and engravings stimulated magnificent printed images,* some commemorating City events and achievements, such as the re-opening of the Royal Exchange or the building of Bedlam. Large maps of London were also a feature of late Stuart decorative printing, sold by William Morgan. Although relatively expensive, these sheets of paper have proved ephemeral, many editions surviving as single copies. In the unique collection of London views, ephemera and other works on paper at Magdalene College, Cambridge left by Pepys, some came via the book agent Bagford, and the Continental topographical prints were assembled on a kind of art lover's Grand Tour orchestrated by Pepys for his nephew in 1699.[23]

Illus. 11

*The *London Gazette* advertised in May 1697 an imported 'parcel of extraordinary fine large prints, fit for rooms and staircases, as is now in use by most people of quality'.

SILVER

Illus. 12

Something peculiarly English happens to the Vanitas paintings of Pieter Gerritz van Roestraten during his long London career (*c.* 1666–1700), presumably driven by his London patrons such as the goldsmith-banker Robert Vyner discussed in Valerie Cumming's essay. Ornamental gilt cups, the standard northern European motif of luxury, are metamorphosed into hallmarked silver, recognisably the work of London goldsmiths (this may also be observed in the mezzotints as well as the paintings of Robinson). The objects depicted, fashionable tea and wine vessels, fancy candelabra or unusual antique pieces such as the Elizabethan ostrich egg cup which survives and was on loan to the Victoria and Albert Museum until 1993, are clearly specific 'portraits'. As royal goldsmith, Vyner probably commissioned Roestraten's painting of the regalia at the Tower of London.[24]

This preference says a great deal about late Stuart taste. Glitter, colour and lustre characterized interiors, in which silver fire furniture, lighting and tea wares, alongside the gleam of lacquer screens, the brilliance of porcelain and the shimmer of silk, created dazzling effects.* The gilded or silvered frames of paintings played their part in this interplay of reflections and illusions.

*Consumers wanted splendour, or as Celia Fiennes put it, when describing lavish upholstery for a state bed, 'these fooleries are requisite sometimes to create admiration and regard.'

Plate, a costly status symbol, was a feature of all interiors, whether churches, livery halls† or private houses. Altars were embellished with gilded alms basins and in dining halls buffets displaying elaborate pieces expressed standing, history and wealth alongside the fashionable dinner plates, cruets, casters and flatware on the table. Older pieces, valued for their associations and 'curious' workmanship, were increasingly treasured, like the striking German covered cup of around 1500, by tradition presented to Clayton to mark his mayoralty, and repaired, as the Barber-Surgeons did with their bell-hung Redman cup, supposed to be a gift from Henry VIII. *Illus. 7*

†After the Fire, many livery companies disposed of plate to help with the cost of rebuilding, but a growing antiquarian spirit appears at the Fishmongers Company, which retains Richard Rushout's striking Dutch shell centrepiece, a bequest of 1654.

A watercolour of the 1690s shows a prominent buffet niche for the Goldsmiths' state plate, facing the Court dining table. The Fishmongers Company retains a 1706 gilt ewer and basin, presented by Sir James Bateman from his household plate in 1717, expressing the obligations of a wealthy liveryman. The goldsmith-banker and property developer John Hinde (1639–87) at Lauderdale House Highgate in 1685 had a similar carved buffet, a reminder of the enormous late Stuart demand for plate.[25] By June 1694 the assay office was assaying more than half a million ounces of plate a year. In 1697 Isaac Newton as Master of the Mint was forced to introduce the higher Britannia standard for wrought plate, to reduce the demand from the goldsmiths and protect the coinage.[26] *Illus. 13*

NETWORKS

Robert Hooke's daily encounters with engravers, draughtsmen and map makers in City coffee houses show that those interested in architecture, art, science and collecting had easy access to such overlapping circles in the 1680s.[27] Artists' studios operated as clubs for buying and discussing art.[28] *Illus. 14* *Illus. 15*

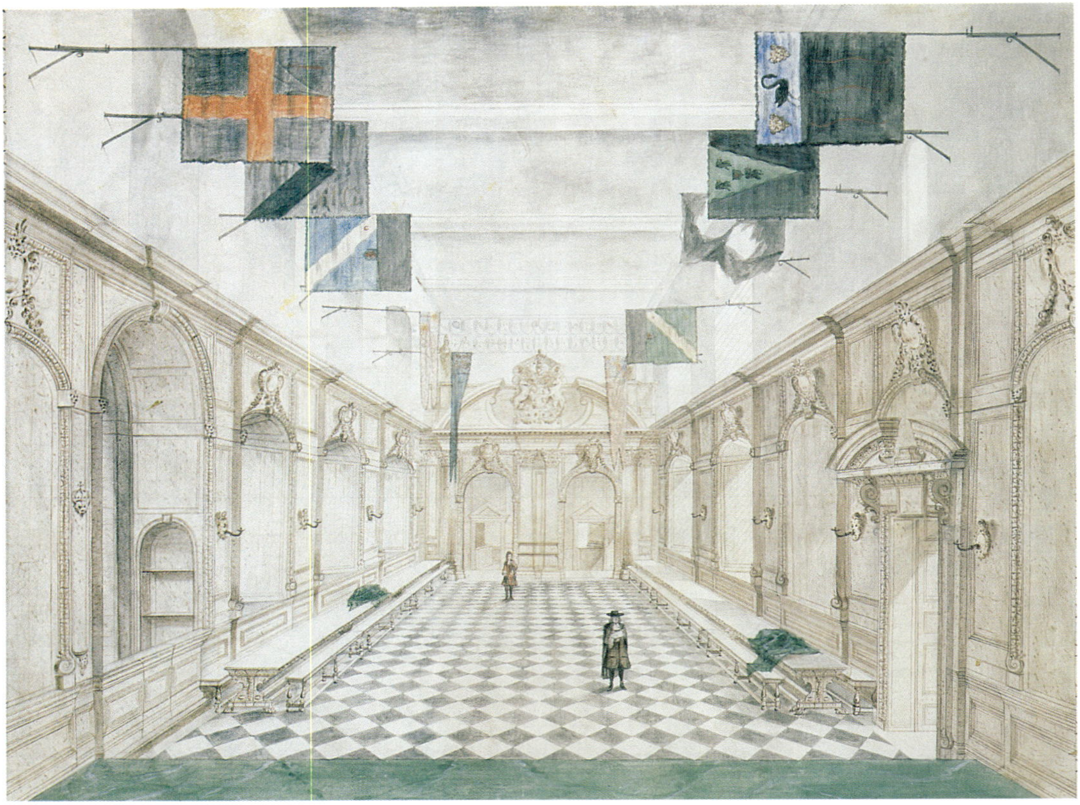

13 *Interior view of Goldsmiths' Hall, 1692. Watercolour by John Ward. A 'grand niech . . . to be set out with plate on solemn days' was a standard institutional feature, included by John Talman in designs for All Souls in 1708.*

City and country elites were closely linked, through marriage, inheritance and a myriad of political and personal circumstances, as in the careers of John Verney, Levant Company merchant and baronet or Robert Child, banker, described by 1706 as 'one of the foremost art collectors in England'. Their attitudes to luxury and aesthetic preferences were shared although their conspicuous consumption might not be approved by an older generation, nervous about the morality and excessive profits of these great merchants. Sir Josiah Child, who bought Wanstead House in 1673, was criticized by John Evelyn for alterations and interior decoration that were 'vast and tasteless'. And Sir Gilbert Heathcote, the East India clerk who became 'the richest commoner', shared the prevailing taste for rich effects. In three generations the Batemans* rose through the City and the mayoralty to marry into the aristocratic Spencer family in 1720.[29]

*William Bateman was a recognized connoisseur. 'He made a better figure than some of the foreign princes through whose domains he passed', buying art and commissioning the latest costly French silver, although George I was sceptical of his claim to gentility: 'I can make him a lord but cannot make him a gentleman'.

TASTE AND TRAVEL

How did these merchants select their possessions? Where could they see art? Who advised them? What aesthetic authorities shaped

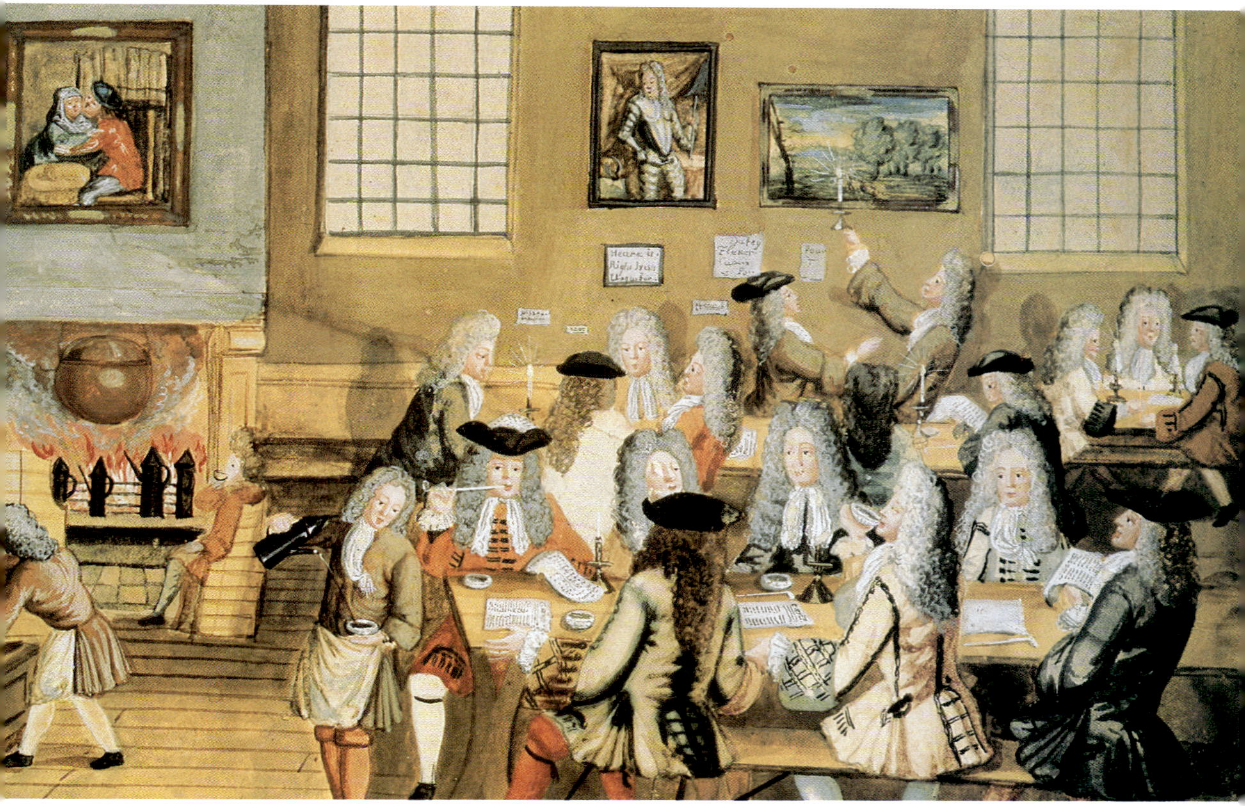

14 *A London Coffee House, c. 1705, anonymous gouache drawing (detail). Political and literary coffee houses tended to be found in the 'Town' while financiers and shipping merchants would congregate at Jonathan's and Edward Lloyd's in The City. The interest shown by two customers, armed with a candle, in the paintings which decorate the walls confirms the role of inns and coffee houses in offering access to art.*

their choices? A school curriculum introduced classical history and Ovid's *Metamorphoses*, supplemented by the stimulus of travel, languages and cultural exchange. The Grand Tour was by no means an aristocratic monopoly; Robert Clayton's son (who died during his travels) and Caleb Banks are two examples.

How far this mercantile equivalent of the Grand Tour sharpened their eyes for art has not been assessed, although it was clearly expected to do so. Sir Stephen Fox (1627–1717), now seen as of great significance in the City as well as Whitehall, commissioned Verrio and Gibbons for his Chiswick house and sent his son Charles (d. 1713) on a European tour in 1676/77. In Rome Charles sat to Carlo Maratti and the tutor Mr Younger described the result; 'Tis made to be hang'd in a high Roome: ye Italian paintings being drawn in proportion to their Way of building'. The youth was expected to study Italian baroque architecture, so as to be able to compare it with the scheme initiated by Charles II at Windsor.[30]

Ingamells's and Ford's wideranging and comprehensive listing of English travellers to Italy in the eighteenth century has revealed

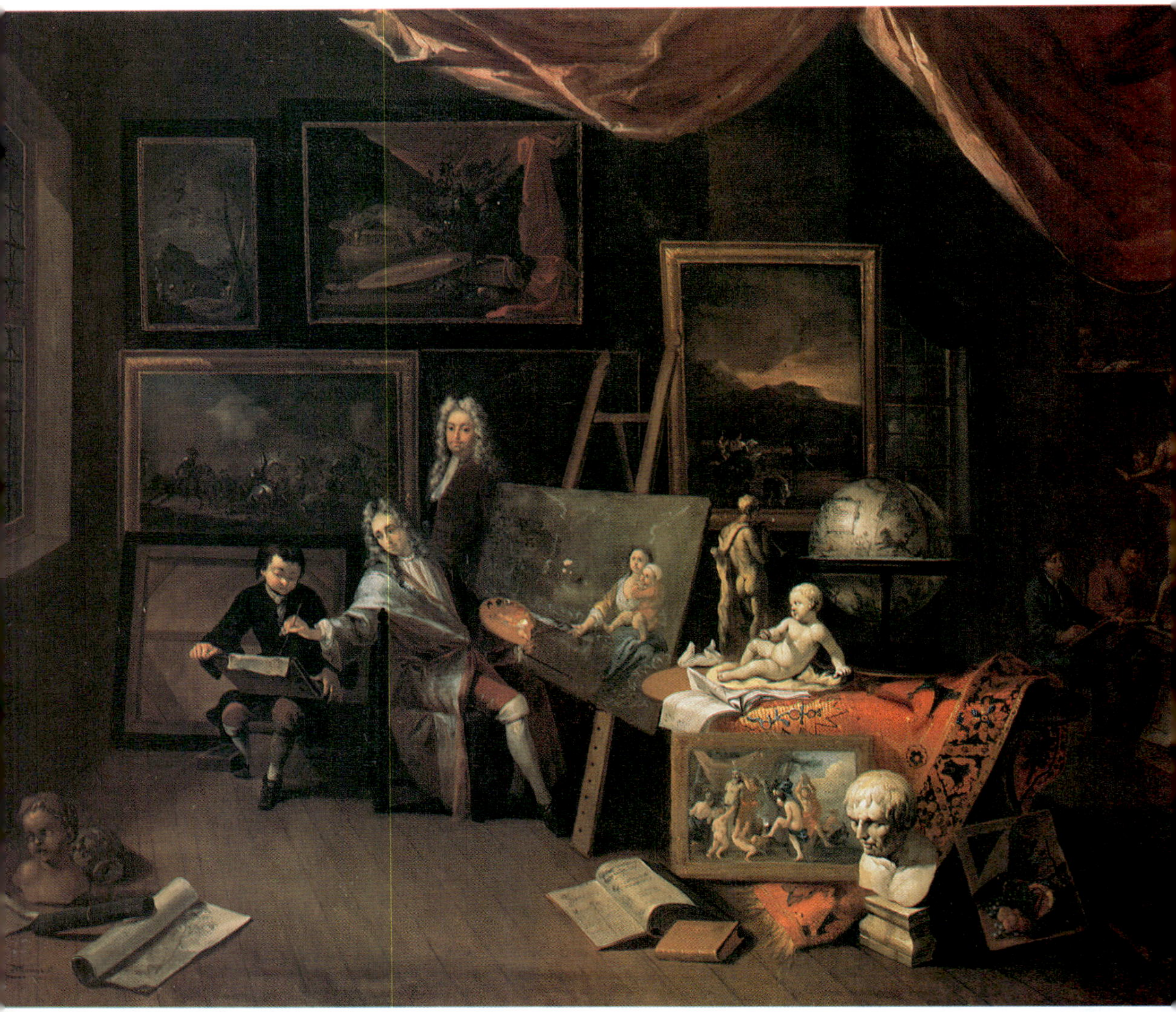

15 *The artist in his studio, c. 1716, oil painting on canvas by Peter Tillemans (1684–1734). A vivid expression of the role played by art and artists is Tillemans's Covent Garden studio, depicted for his Norfolk patron Cox Macro, in which the artist is simultaneously conducting a drawing class, showing sculpture and Old Masters to his patron and not so subtly, advertising his work in progress on an easel.*

how highly some of the merchant class valued this educational experience for their sons.[31] This aspect of the cultural environment of London merchants merits further research. No doubt commercial as well as social imperatives were at work. Around 1700, in Leghorn alone, there were almost twenty London agencies, which handled payments, shipped goods and exposed City youths to linguistic, architectural and cultural diversity.

Merchants' Houses

Chapter Three

MIREILLE GALINOU

The Victorian novelist Charlotte Eliza Lawson Riddell, better known as Mrs Riddell, is barely remembered today, and this is a shame. She wrote most passionately about the City of London, blending historical fact and fiction, a formula which was very successful while she was alive but which does not appear to have stood the test of time.[1]

In 1885, in a novel called *Mitre Court*, she pledged her commitment to saving the City:

Were I, the writer of this book, ... in any capacity free of the City of London — say liveryman, common councillor, deputy-sheriff, sheriff, alderman, Lord Mayor — I would make the City — which after all cannot be accounted so very big, though undoubtedly it is very great — my study: I would know every court, lane, alley, house exhaustively: and were there still left an old mansion, hallowed by fact and tradition, I should try to save it.[2]

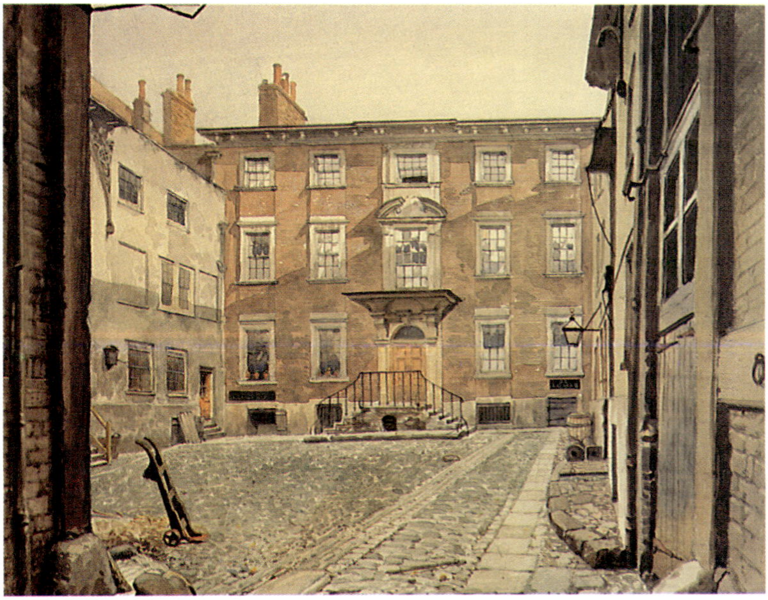

16 *View of a merchant's house, 1886, watercolour by John Crowther. The artist positioned himself at the street entrance of 32 Botolph Lane; on the other side the house backed on to Love Lane. Both streets ran parallel (they still do) leading to Billingsgate Market. We know from another Guildhall Library watercolour that the entrance gate was similar to that of Robert Clayton's house (Illus. 26) albeit on a considerably more modest scale.*

The old mansion about which Mrs Riddell felt so strongly stood
Illus. 16 at 32 Botolph Lane in the ward of Billingsgate. It belonged to the last (and grandest) category of domestic buildings described in the Rebuilding Act of 1667: 'the Fourth Sort of Building, being Mansions Houses and of the Greatest Bigness'.[3] This essay will concentrate on houses of 'The Greatest Bigness'. This is not just to provide a clear focus within the scope of this vast subject but also because art patronage in the City — or anywhere else in the world — is connected to wealth. These grand mansions spoke of wealth and status and indicated that their owners were ready to spend money on fine or decorative arts.

BACKGROUND

Before we penetrate the world of these hidden, now mostly lost, historic treasures, it would be useful to remind ourselves of the extraordinary changes that befell the City of London after the Great Fire of London. Monsieur (Francis Maximilien) Misson recorded in great detail many of his impressions of London in a book called *Mémoires d'Angleterre*. This is my own modern translation of the passage where he describes the appearance of the City before and after the Great Fire.[4] It illustrates perfectly the astonishing contrast between the two eras:

> *Before* [the Great Fire]*, their houses were the nastiest thing in the world, as may still be seen in whole areas. They were all wood and plaster with horrid little windows of which only one could be open. The storeys were low and became wider and wider as they went up. Everything was askew and looked as if it was about*
> *Illus. 17* *to collapse.*
>
> *Nowadays,* [Mr Misson goes on] *they build houses in brick and they go up with an even facade, without any magnificence or anything remotely like it, but with symmetry and neatness. Everything is well fenestrated and well lit, the windows tall and with window sashes. Wooden floors are universally fitted with a ceiling; and ground floor rooms and first floor rooms are wainscoted. Sometimes even the second floor is wainscoted as well.*

The result was surprisingly dynamic: neat harmonious streetscapes of red and white brick and stone gave the City a warm red glow which was well captured by the anonymous painter who depicted
Illus. 18 the mouth of the Fleet River and the North Bank of the Thames.[5]

REBUILDING LONDON

This new look for the City was the outcome of the Rebuilding Act which Parliament passed on 8 February 1667, barely five months after the conflagration. In the building hierarchy that was spelt out
Illus. 16 (see INSET, p.29), the Botolph Lane property was placed at the top.

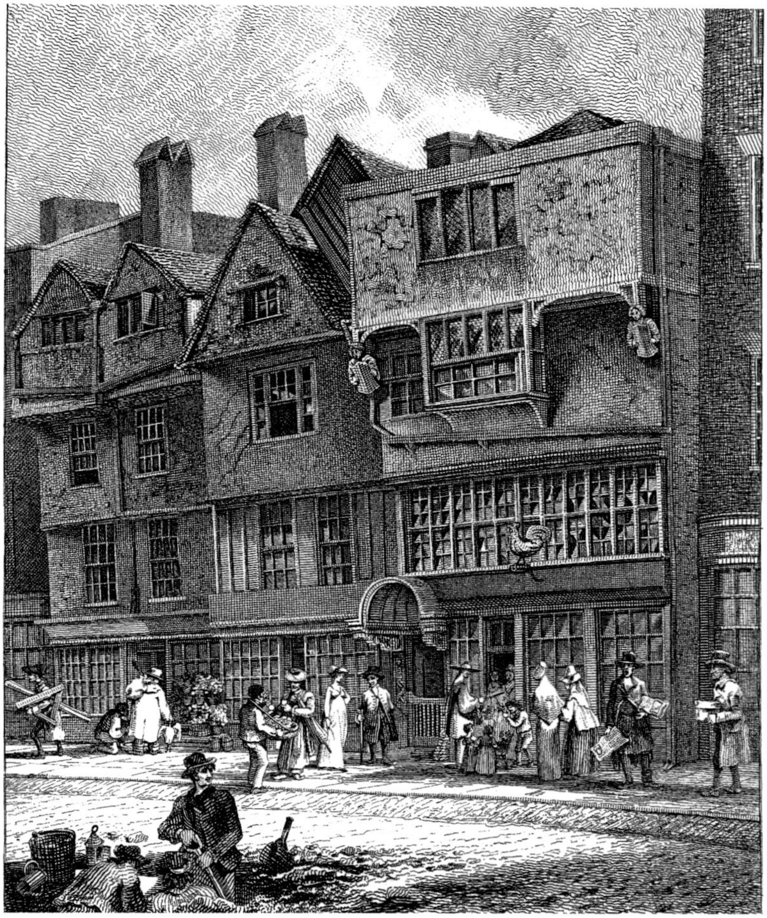

17 *Houses on the South Side of Leadenhall Street, drawn in 1796 by J. T. Smith and published by him in 1814. These pre-Fire houses echoed Mr Misson's comment that 'everything was askew and looked as if it was about to collapse'.*

The guidelines for rebuilding made sense and were simple. People had to use brick or stone only on the outside: 'Brick is not only more comely and durable, but also more safe against future Perils of Fire'.[6] Timber would now be restricted to such essential accessories as doors, windows, flooring or roofing.

The team who dealt with the reconstruction of London was made up of two groups: 'The King's Commissioners' who consisted of Christopher Wren, Hugh May and Roger Pratt; and the 'Surveyors of New Buildings', i.e. the City representatives who from 13 March 1667 consisted of Peter Mills, Edward Jarman, Robert Hooke and John Oliver.[7] As Jarman chose to concentrate exclusively on the task of rebuilding the Royal Exchange, and Hooke was juggling with a large number of other projects, the traditional assumption was that Mills and Oliver led the process of staking out the foundations. This view has recently been challenged in favour of Hooke, who is now seen as taking a more

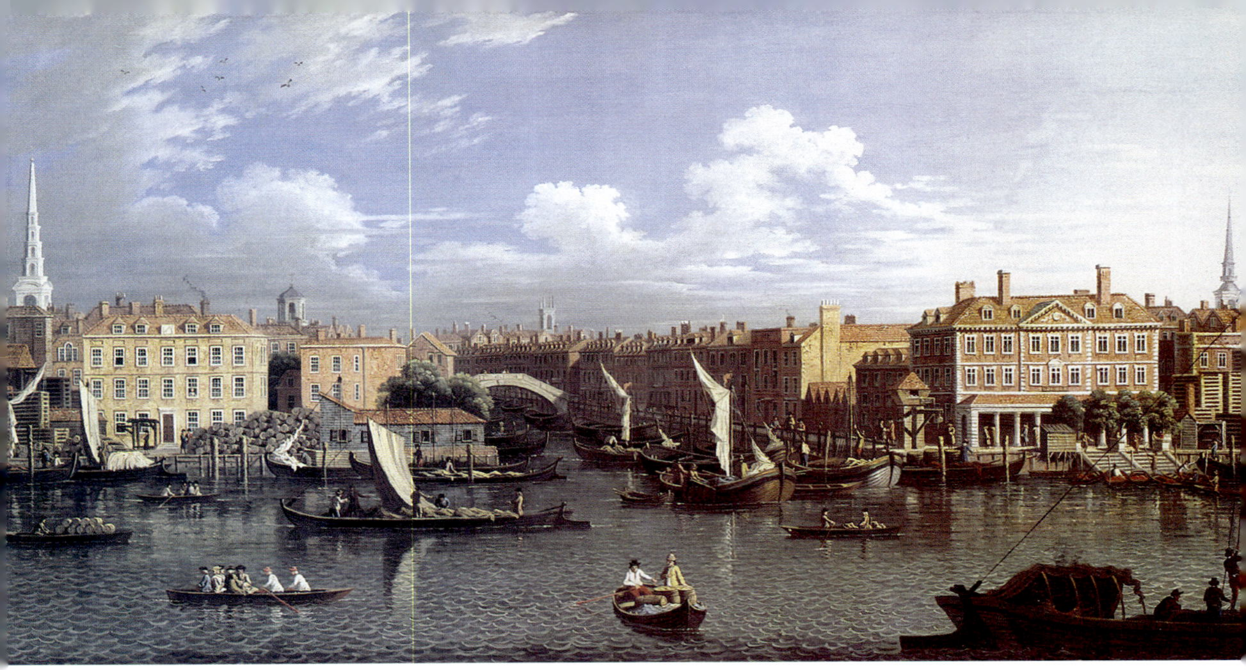

18 *Entrance to the Fleet River, c. 1750, anonymous oil on canvas, school of Samuel Scott. This work is slightly later than the period under review but it is particularly successful in giving us an idea of London's warm and bright colours after the rebuilding.*

active role.[8] Unfortunately the original surveys carried out by all three men have not survived. Mills and Oliver duly returned their surveys to the Corporation while Hooke chose to keep his documents. A facsimile of Mills and Oliver surveys was produced for the Corporation in the eighteenth century — a precious record of many properties (see for instance *Illus. 30*), their size, the names of the owners and adjoining neighbours.[9] Sadly, the Botolph Lane property was situated in the area east of Walbrook, Hooke's patch, for which no records at all survive.

MERCHANTS' HOUSES – SINGLE OR DOUBLE

As a general rule, merchants' houses were three or four stories high to be able to accommodate business premises and living accommodation, both for the merchants and their employees. However, the final size of these houses also depended on the wealth of individual merchants. In his thoroughly researched book *Citizens of the World*, David Hancock follows a handful of eighteenth-century merchant dynasties whose roots are traced back to the seventeenth century.[10] Hancock usefully points out that architectural designs for merchants' houses boil down to just two plans: the rectangular single house or the square double house. The single house was by far the most common of the two forms though the double format was a favourite for wholesale merchants with large-scale operations.

Illus. 24 & 25

To modern minds, the most unexpected feature of the merchants' double house type is its location.[11] The Rebuilding Act clearly described them as 'not fronting upon any of the Streets or

The 1667 Rebuilding Act offered guide lines for builders and landowners involved in the great task of rebuilding London. Domestic architecture fitted into four categories:[43]

The First and least Sort of Building fronting Bye Streets or Lanes as aforesaid shall be of Two Stories high, besides Cellars and Garrets.

This type of building has all but disappeared except for one example: a little building on the corner of Cheapside and Wood Street. The façade has long been stuccoed and painted but if you have your lunch amid the unexpected palm trees of the small courtyard at the back of the building you will see the original brick finish and a small plaque, at the top which reads: 'Erected on Ye sole Cofts & charges of the Parish of St Peters Cheape Ao: Dni 1687', (followed by the names of the Church Wardens).

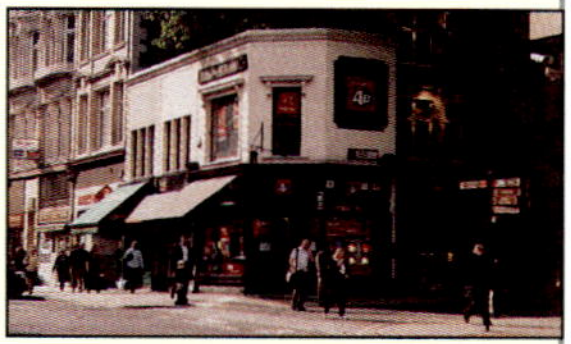

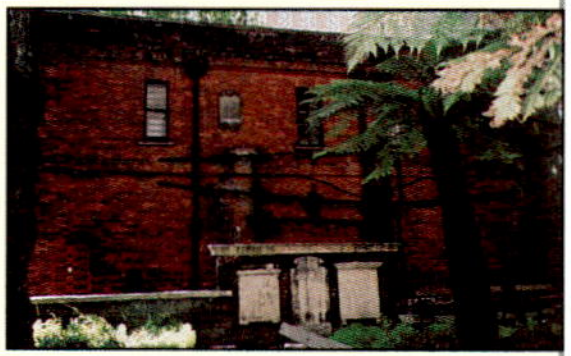

19–20

The Second Sort of Building fronting Streets and Lanes of Note and the River Thames shall consist of Three Stories high, besides Cellars and Garrets, as aforesaid.

Here is a familiar example, a favourite pub haunt, Ye Olde Watling, in Watling Street which runs parallel with Cheapside. It dates from 1672–74.

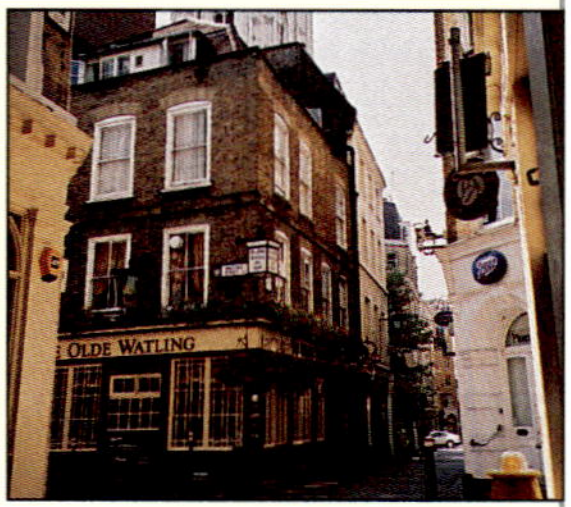

21

The Third Sort of Buildings fronting the high and principal Streets shall consist of Four Stories high, besides Cellars and Garrets, as aforesaid.

When Walter George Bell was writing in 1922 the list of surviving buildings was quite long. However, a number of these, notably in the Cheapside area, have sadly been destroyed during the last war. This prototype may be viewed in one of the most delightfully hidden corners of the City: Wardrobe Place, off Carter Lane (right-hand block). Another example which was recently given a new lease of life is the house at 7a Laurence Pountney Hill. (See Illus. 24)

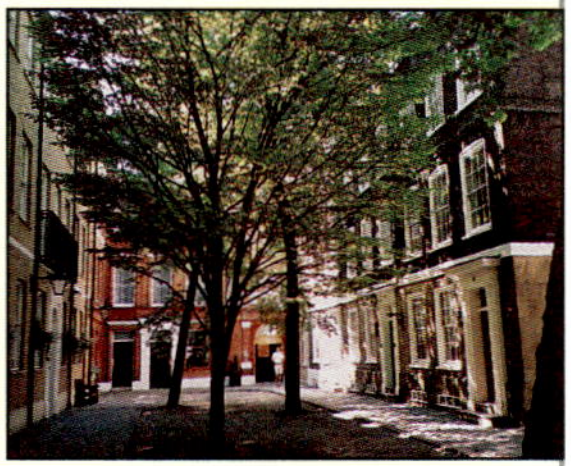

22

All Houses of the Fourth Sort of Building, being Mansion Houses and of the greatest Bigness, not fronting upon any of the streets or Lanes as aforesaid etc. etc. the Number of Stories and the Height thereof be left to the Discretion of the Builder so as he exceed not Four Stories.

There we have our Botolph Lane property (see Illus. 16), its entrance removed from Botolph Lane, although its back facade opened directly on to the street (Love Lane) thus affording the house a great amount of flexibility. Another notable house of the greatest Bigness was that of Sir John Houblon in Threadneedle Street (reproduced here).

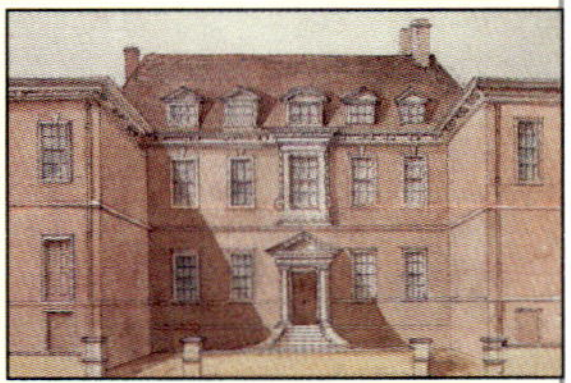

23

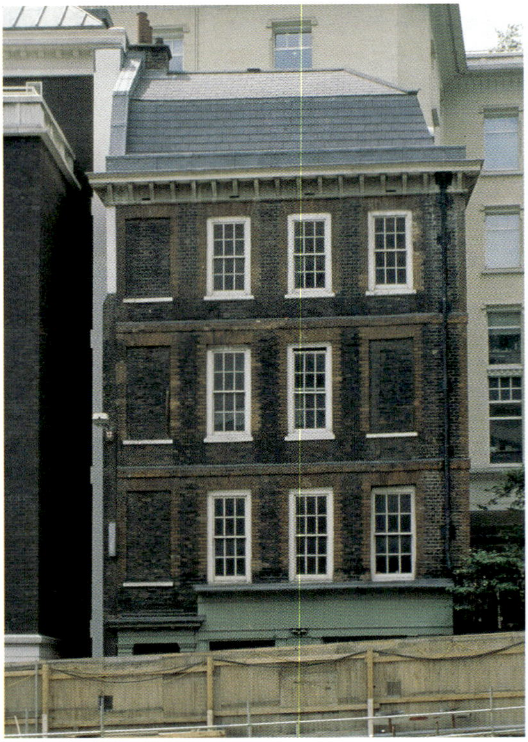

24 *This large single house at 7a Laurence Pountney Hill has recently been restored (2003) and was the object of a brief archaeological investigation by Nick Holder from the Museum of London Archaeology Service (see Bibliography). It is no longer possible to view the house from this angle. A large office block now stands opposite the house.*

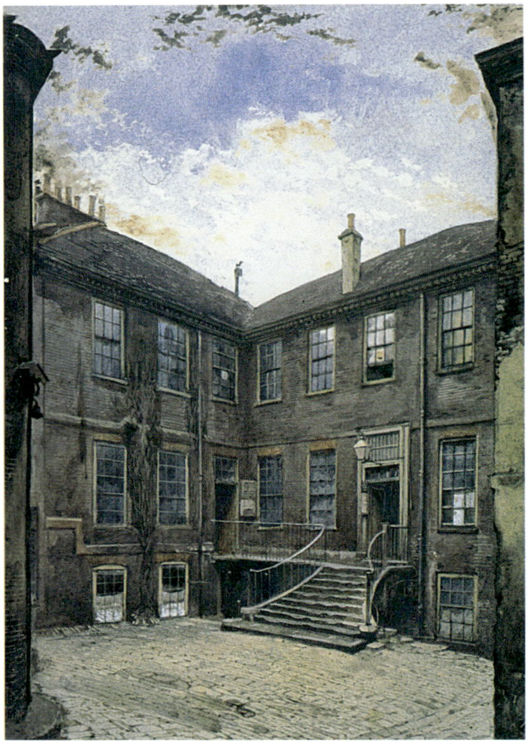

25 *No. 23 Great Winchester Street, 1880, watercolour by John Crowther. Several illustrations exist for this striking property, the captions sometimes confusing it with its more famous neighbour 'Winchester House'. This property is as mysterious as the Botolph Lane property and would deserve to be further researched.*

Lanes as afore said'. Most of them were indeed completely hidden from view and our determined nineteenthth-century guide, Mrs Riddell, has captured perfectly the somewhat contradictory character of these grand houses — hidden from view but of magnificent size and ostentatious appearance. *Illus. 26*

HIDDEN OSTENTATION

In a courtyard that might well escape the observation of passers-by, entered as it is through an archway of the most unassuming appearance, there stands ... an old and most beautiful house ... To pass out of the City streets — into that spacious hall paved with black and white marble, is like stepping back a couple of centuries in England's history.[12] *Illus. 16*

The author James Ogilvy confirms this description and adds further details about one of the property's most special features — its Painted Room:

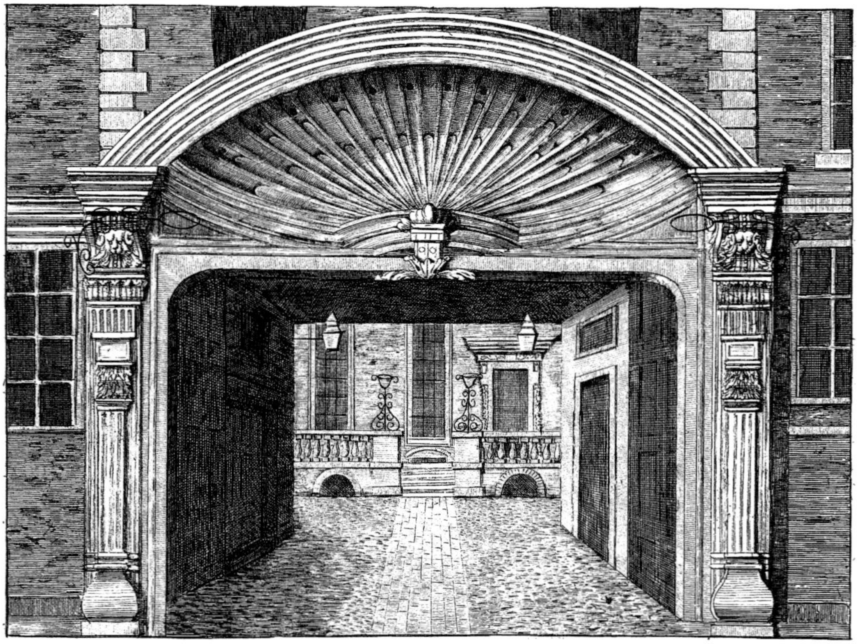

26 *The house built by Robert Clayton off Old Jewry near the Guildhall is remarkable for the way in which it reconciles private location and public ostentation. It follows the mercantile pattern of an entrance removed from the street, with courtyard, but Clayton clearly could not resist signalling at street level the importance of this particular residence: the use of a shell hood on a gigantic scale could not fail to attract attention.*

From Botolph Lane it was reached by a large courtyard with fruit warehouses on three sides, the house occupying the fourth. A curious dog-kennel occupied the space under the double stair outside — the entrance hall was laid with squares of black and white marble; on the left a fine panelled room, the panels having pictures painted on them, much obscured by dirt and smoke.[13] *Illus. 28*

There are further examples of these hidden vistas in the heart of the City: the cluster of houses near Guildhall and the house at 23 Winchester Street. While many of the houses' occupants could be described as merchants, we should be cautious about generalisations. The house known as The Deanery follows very closely the type we have been reviewing here though it has no mercantile associations.

Illus. 27
Illus. 25
Illus. 29

However, it is possible to generalise where in the City you could find a high concentration of 'Houses of the Greatest Bigness'. John Ogilby and William Morgan's *1676 Map of London*[14] indexes all the important houses and plotting them on the map clearly reveals that most of these houses were found in three principal areas. By far the most popular was Farringdon Without, close to the City but just outside the walls in the north west corner, around the Smithfield area. The next most popular areas were the adjoining Farringdon Within, followed by Castle Baynard.[15] There are also of course some notable exceptions, principally the area around Old Jewry which has already been discussed. *Illus. 27*

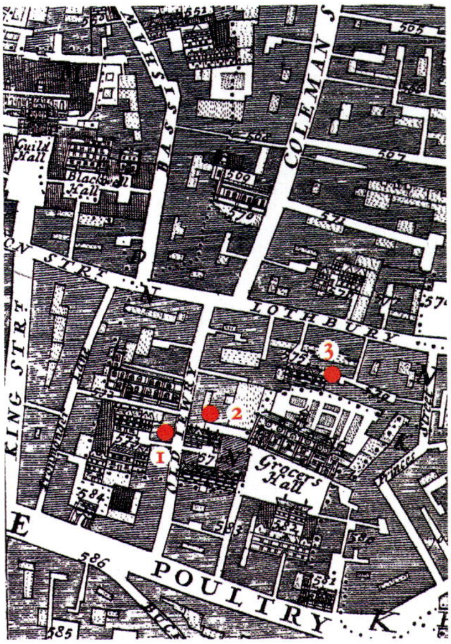

27 *This detail from Morgan's 1682 Map of London shows well the substantial number of grand houses clustered on the south west side of the Guildhall. From left to right, the 'hidden' houses of the following may be picked out:*

1. Sir John Frederick, an East India Merchant who was Lord Mayor in 1661. The site of the house was developed by the Adam Brothers in 1776 as Frederick's Place and has survived to this day.

2. The House of Sir Robert Clayton, exactly opposite Frederick's House.

3. The House of Nathaniel Herne.

THE BOTOLPH LANE PROPERTY

Illus. 28 & 86–88

Both in terms of layout and appearance, the Botolph Lane property typifies the genre of the Post-Fire merchant's house. The splendid size of the property, its survival for over 200 years and most of all the extraordinary legacy of its Painted Room are factors that lead one to assume that it had been well recorded over time. Alas, this is not the case; the property has remained tantalisingly mysterious. No amount of searching has yielded the definite name of its owner or occupier. The legend that it was built and inhabited by Christopher Wren echoes the similar belief surrounding another merchant's house: the Manor House at Greenwich.* Both attributions are Victorian fabrications which cannot be substantiated.

*The Manor House on Croom's Hill, Greenwich, bears similarities with the Botolph Lane property and was also ascribed to Christopher Wren in the same unfounded way. Interestingly, the Manor House was built for a London merchant, Sir Robert Robinson, in 1695.

So who was the owner? The first port of call for the historian is of course the rate books, always exceedingly difficult to interpret and in this case yielding no clues (see Chapter 9, p. 116). An alternative source is the list of the Botolph Lane proprietors who applied to the City surveyors prior to rebuilding. Is the name of the Botolph Lane house owner amongst these?[16] Or does it feature instead on the list of Botolph Lane Merchants which can be pieced together using the 1677 trade directory?[17] Both lists of course have been cross-referenced but they offered no obvious candidate.

Further potential clues exist. As Jim Ganz explains in his Robinson essay (Chapter 9, p. 113) it is likely that the owner was a tobacconist, and we have a list of tobacco merchants for the

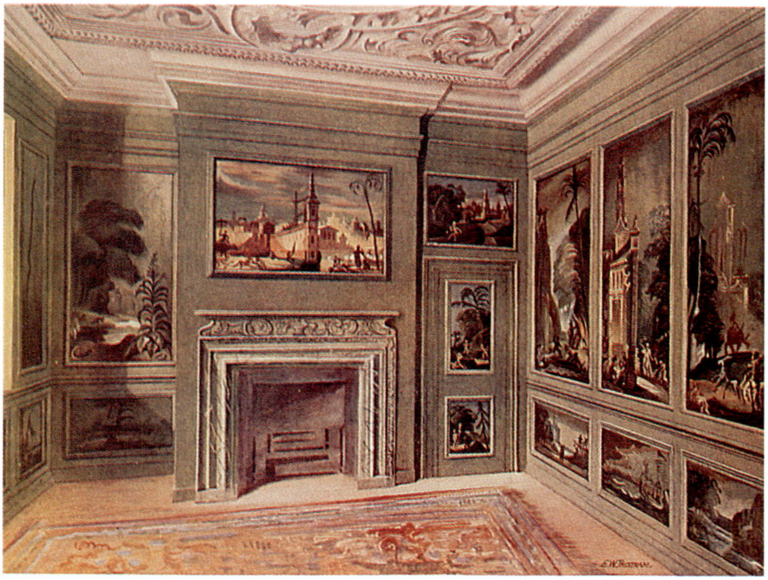

28 *A view of the Painted Room at 32 Botolph Lane, watercolour by E. W. Tristram. Tristram restored the paintings after they were saved from destruction when the house was pulled down in 1905–06. He also re-installed them in the Sir John Cass's Primary School at Aldgate.*

Restoration period.[18] Alas, no tobacco merchants match any of the names in the 1677 directory or the surveyors' records.

When the building became used as a school in 1852, a Phoenix Fire Insurance policy was taken out for the period May 1852 until December 1853. Its number, 1033587 has been recorded in the School's Treasurer's Journal.[19] Alas this, too, cannot be traced.[20] Would the insurance entry have contained some lost piece of information? The key to the puzzle, or at least a piece of it?

Or could the owner of the Botolph Lane property be the man who commissioned, no doubt at vast expense, the funeral monument which once stood in the church of St George Botolph Lane in whose parish the house stood? The church was demolished in 1904 but we have a description of that monument, the only one apparently of any note in the church:

At end of Church in Chancel, neat white Marble Monument, enrich'd with Mantling, Cherubins, Urn & these Arms Ermin 2 Bars Sable, each charged with 5 leaves Or. And in another place these Arms

> *Ermin 2 Bars Sable, each charged with 5 — Leaves Or*

And in another place these Arms

> *Sable a Sword in pale Argent, hilted Or; on a chief Indented Gules, a Ducal Coronet of the third.*

This monument is in memory of Daniel Wigfall, Merchant, who died March the 18th 1698.[21]

Unfortunately, once again, the name Daniel Wigfall cannot be reconciled with any of those already discussed although there is an

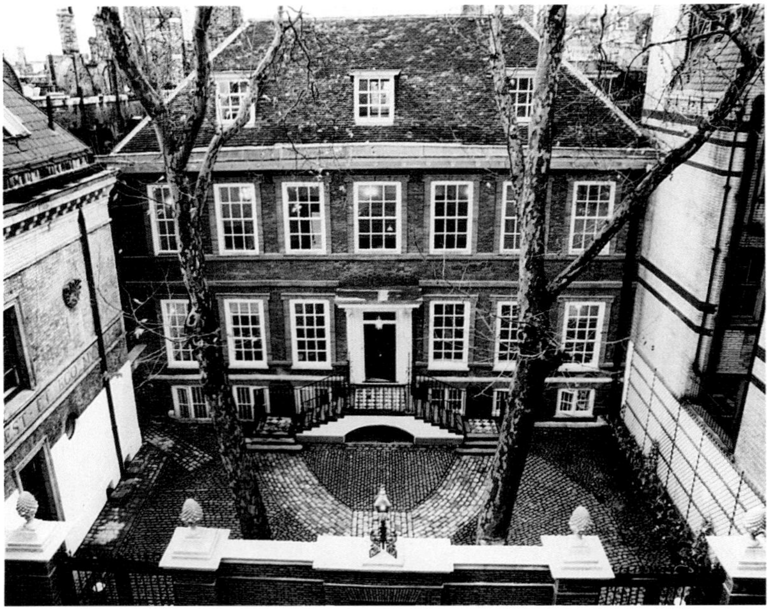

29 *Dean's Court, south of St Paul's Cathedral, now the residence of the Bishop of London, was built on the site of Doctors' Common in 1670, the same year as the Botolph Lane property. Both buildings clearly belong to the same type of courtyard house. This was never a merchant's house, however, since the residence of the Dean of London was established on this site as early as 1145. This is the only house of this type to have survived in the City.*

outside chance that Daniel Wigfall may in fact be the Daniel Wagfield listed in the 1677 trade directory (see note 17). All one can say is that this catalogue of failed attempts to identify the owner of the Botolph Lane house has been a useful exercise as it has encouraged the exploration of facts and records which at other times can genuinely solve such riddles.

BRIEF SURVEY OF 'HOUSES OF THE GREATEST BIGNESS'

By contrast with the Botolph Lane property, the Maiden Lane house of poor Tom Bludworth, the Lord Mayor who became infamously known for his totally inappropriate handling of the Great Fire[22]* offers the type of documentation one hoped to find for Botolph Lane. Part of the property is recorded in the Mills and Oliver survey,† and also appears, primitively drawn and identified, on the William Morgan 1682 map which has been used throughout this publication (it is visible on p. 164). Its final appearance has also tentatively been reconstructed.[23]

*The Lord Mayor was recorded to have cried 'like a fainting woman "Lord! What can I do? I am spent: people will not obey me. I have been pulling down houses; but the fire overtakes us faster than we can do it."'

Illus. 30

†This survey (full details in Bibliography) is a key document for the post-Fire City.

Historian Bridget Cherry hit the jackpot with Pollexfen's House which was built in Walbrook.[24] A series of leases survive as do the original building accounts, providing a wealth of documentation on the mercantile house and its layout: 'an account of ye cost and charges of ye ground and building of my house in Walbrook begun ye 13 March 1668'. Both sets of documents more than compensate for the fact that Hooke's records relating to this building do not

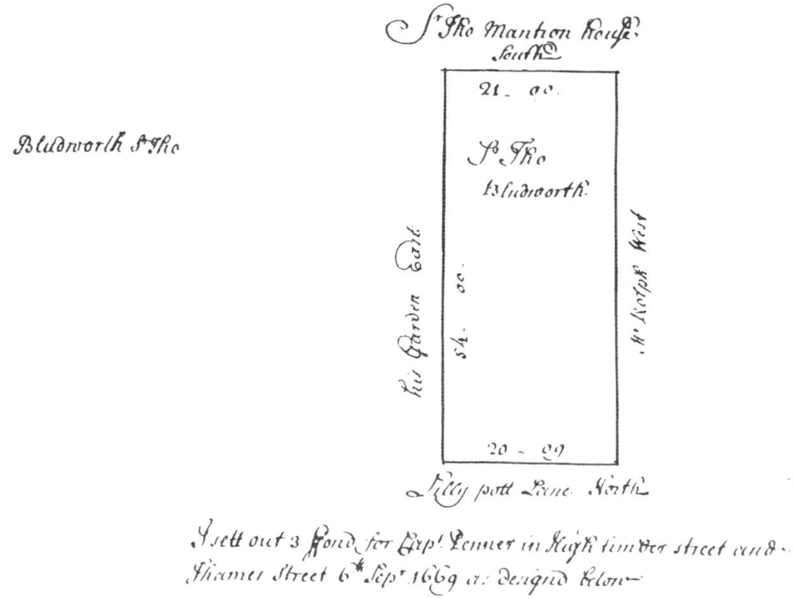

30 *This plan from Mills & Oliver's Survey shows the size and shape of the land surveyed for Lord Mayor Tom Bludworth in 1669 in Lillypott Lane, the back entrance to his Maiden Lane property, west of Guildhall.*

survive. The house was built for John Pollexfen (*c.* 1638–1715) in 1668 and was leased to William Scawen in 1684, a merchant we will encounter later in this essay at Carshalton House. The leases are helpful because they itemise all the rooms and also the outbuildings, an essential but little documented requisite for many if not all of those mercantile courtyard houses. They record two sets of street gates — 'wainscot' on the street side, and 'perspective' metalwork gates on the inner side.* They describe a counting house (as distinct from the house), a washhouse and house of office over which was a large warehouse and another counting house.[25] When Scawen took over the house he added an extra floor to the warehouse. The leases also throw light on another little documented feature: the cellar, visible in a number of the illustrations for this essay — 'a vault of the length of the front of the house and Backwards a beer cellar and cellar for coale' as well as 'two partitions, one to make a wett larder and the other a wine cellar'.[26]

Before leaving Pollexfen's House, it is worth observing the paving with black and white marble applied to the second, grander, parlour on the ground floor as well as the adjoining entry. This choice of flooring is also found at Botolph Lane and at Goldsmiths' Hall.[27] It delightfully echoes the floors depicted in so many Netherlandish paintings of that period.

Illus 13 & 31

The other extremely well documented merchant's house of the 'Greatest Bigness' is 34 Great Tower Street.[28†] The idea of the individual house bearing marks of the taste of various significant

*The Botolph Lane property also had elaborate metal gates which may be admired in the permanent galleries of the Museum of London. They are recorded as adorning the house's back entrance, in Love Lane, in James Ogilby's *Relics and Memorials of London City* (1910) and were purchased by the Museum in 1937.

†It is a tragedy that this house, which was built in 1668 for Richard Beckford (no connection with Alderman Beckford, Lord Mayor in 1762 and 1769) — the only City merchant's house to have survived well into the 20th century — should have been destroyed during the Second World War.

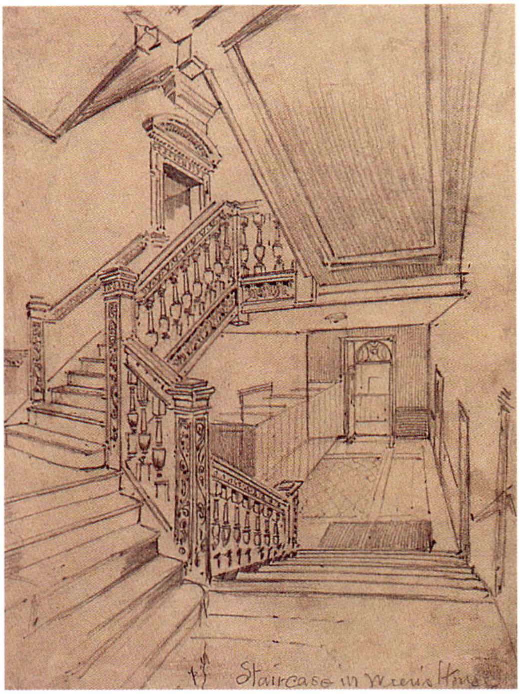

31 *The staircase of the Botolph Lane property, by Robert Randoll, around 1900. In this pencil drawing, the artist has positioned himself on the staircase entrance landing, where he looks across the hall, paved with black and white marble, to the main entrance door. There are two doors visible on the right hand side. The one nearest to the entrance led to the Painted Room.*

owners is somewhat challenged by the longish list of names of its successive inhabitants between 1683 and the early years of the 19th century, many of whom appear to have come and gone in fairly rapid succession.[29]

PLAN/USE OF ROOMS

Alongside the evidence provided by Pollexfen's House and Great Tower Street, David Hancock reconstructed the interior of another well documented double house in Mincing Lane.[30] It offers close similarities to the properties we have discussed so far, and will enable us to make a few general points.

Illus. 32

The layout of these large houses is usually four rooms to a floor, an arrangement which architectural historians describe as 'double pile'[31] as opposed to the rambling and costly houses with a one room deep arrangement.* In the City, much of the recorded evidence dates from the period after the Great Fire though there is a well documented group of sixteenth-century houses in Leadenhall Street at the back of which was a 'Great House', described in 1699 as the 'new brick house' but which was built for Henry Boone, a prominent member of the Barber-Surgeons Company, around 1660. This house was three storeys high, with garret and cellar though not yet symmetrical.[32] It was recorded in plan by William

*The double pile layout is credited to the architect Roger Pratt (1620–84), who designed Coleshill House in Oxfordshire, a very influential building finished in 1662 and pulled down after a fire in 1952. As this seminal building post dates some of the examples quoted here, perhaps Roger Pratt drew inspiration from some of London's building practices?

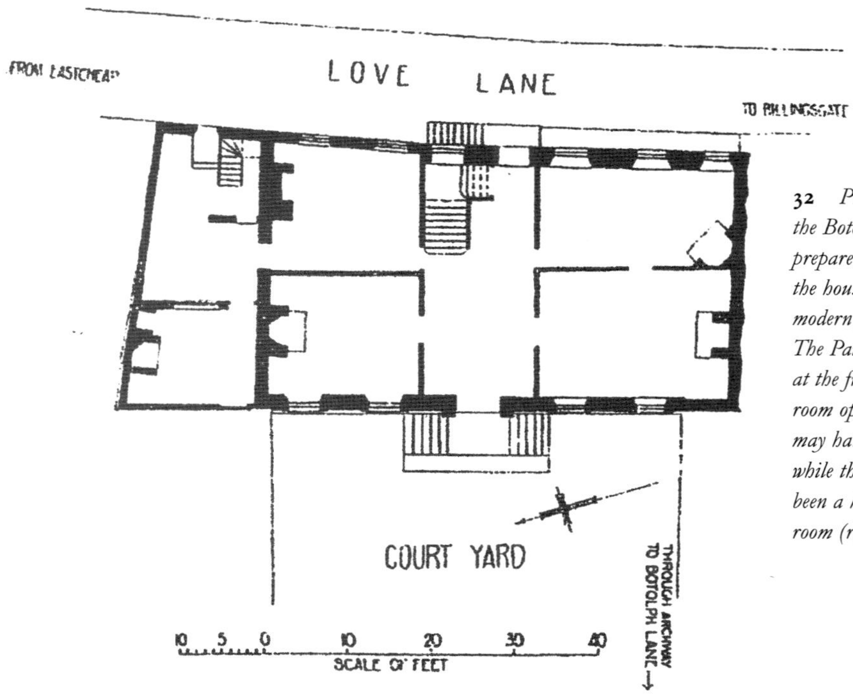

32 *Plan of the ground floor of the Botolph Lane property, prepared in 1906, shortly before the house was demolished. The modern partitions are not shown. The Painted Room is on the left at the front of the house. The room opposite across the corridor may have been a clerks room, while the back rooms may have been a kitchen (left) and dining room (right).*

Leybourne around 1680 alongside the three houses spared by the Great Fire — 'a frame of three fayre houses, set up in the year 1590 on the high streete'.[33] It provided a touching example of the old and the new existing side by side on the streets of London. There are further instances of double pile layout being used prior to the Great Fire in mercantile buildings, notably at Kew Palace, best known as a royal residence though it was in fact built, in brick, by a City merchant called Samuel Fortrey in 1630. Although the insertion, in the Georgian period, of an entrance corridor and stairs have interfered with the original layout, it is clear that Kew was an early example of this compact arrangement.[34]

To return to the Mincing Lane property, the 'Partners Room' at the front of the house would have corresponded to the 'Painted Room' of the Botolph Lane property. Opposite was the Clerks' Room and at the back, the kitchen and dining room. The first floor was the proprietors' floor with drawing rooms and bedrooms. The last floor was reserved for employees and utility rooms. *Illus. 28*

We gain further insight into the significance of rooms and layout from a rare document 'Explanation of the Draughts of a House Proposed for a Merchant' dated 1724.[35] Although the manuscript relates to Bristol, another mercantile city, the overall plan of the house fits the standard arrangement of four rooms to a floor.

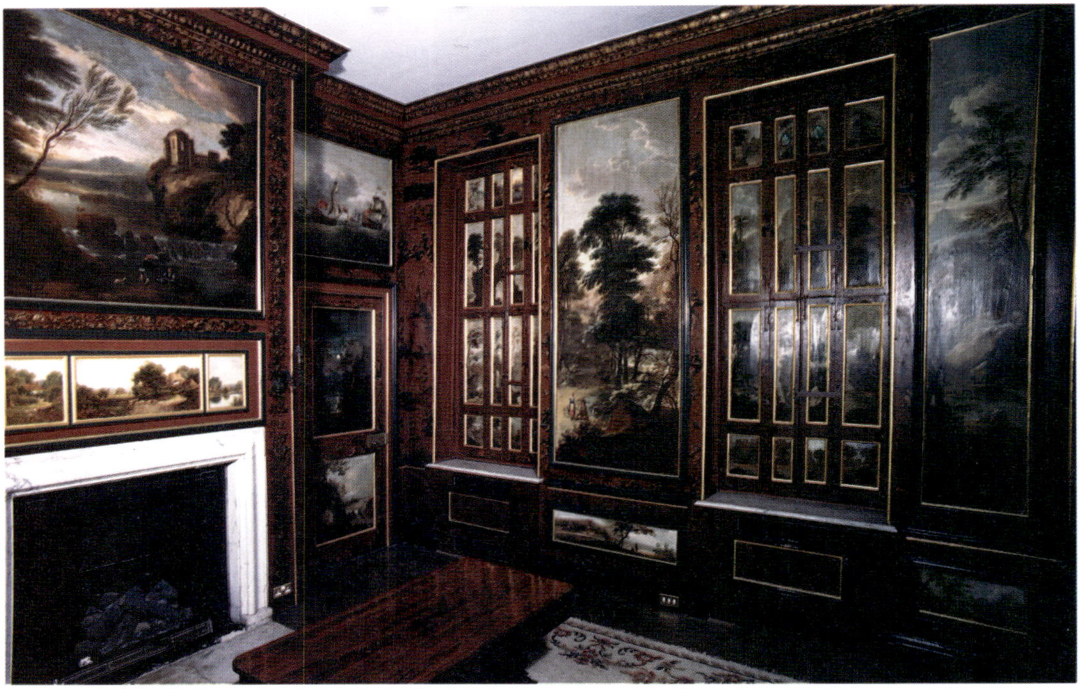

33 *View of the Painted Room at Carshalton House. Unlike the Painted Room in Botolph Lane, this survives in situ and we know it was commissioned by Edward Carleton, a tobacco merchant who went bankrupt in the early years of the eighteenthth century, having lavished substantial sums of money on this property.*

34 (opposite margin) *This panel comes from the Painted Room at Norton Court in Kent, probably commissioned by London merchant Benjamin Godfrey shortly after 1700. The main scheme appears to consist of 15(?) large monochrome paintings, all inviting the onlooker to travel to far away places. One panel, traditionally described as a 'portrait' of Norton Court echoes that found in the Painted Room at Carshalton House also purporting to depict this residence.*

Here the room which corresponds to the Painted Room is described as a 'handsome withdrawing room for the Mistress of the House to entertain company in'. We learn about the Dining Room 'which for many good reasons is generally avoided to be in the Front of the House where every Passenger looks in'.[36]

CITY VERSUS COUNTRY

This brief survey started with a City Painted Room and will close with a couple of country Painted Rooms. Both are the outcome of mercantile commissions and both are so integral to the fabric of the house that they have survived when individual paintings might have been dispersed.

The trend for acquiring houses in the countryside around London was firmly established by the seventeenth century (see Introduction, p. ix) and ought to be further researched.[37] Other essays in this book describe examples of this 'double life' — for instance Robert Clayton at Marden, the Warde family at Squerryes Court, Robert Vyner at Swakeleys, Edward Carleton at Carshalton House. I should like to evoke two further examples, those of John Fellowes and Benjamin Godfrey.

Sir John Fellowes and Edward Carleton (also see Chapter 9, p. 113) had several things in common: they both lived at Carshalton

House — and each would have spent time in its Painted Parlour. *Illus. 33* They also both suffered heavy financial losses, Carleton going bankrupt in 1713, a fate that was not uncommon in this line of business while Fellowes fell victim to the famous South Sea Bubble in 1720. So far it has not been possible to discover Carleton's London address, but we know that Fellowes lived in Old Jewry and we reproduce his London inventory in Appendix I. There he leased a house whose description seems to fit the building erected by City magnate Sir Robert Clayton a few years previously. The *Illus. 26* contents of both of Fellowes's homes were valued: £604 for London and £753 for Carshalton. He retired and died at Carshalton in 1728 after his fall from grace in the City. His austere tomb at Carshalton Church is in stark contrast with the tomb opposite in the south aisle — the large and elaborate monument of Sir William Scawen, who became Governor of the Bank of England in 1697 and a Director of the South Sea Company in 1710. He owned the Manor of Carshalton.[38]

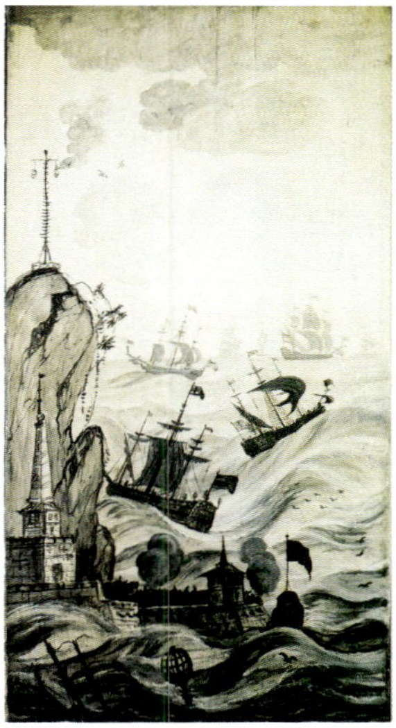

The other merchant who was active both in London and his native Kent was Benjamin Godfrey (1632–1727), seventeenth child of Thomas Godfrey.[39] His brother, Edmund-Berry Godfrey (1621–1678), justice of the peace for Westminster, has been the object of many books as he died in circumstances which remain mysterious to this day.[40] Little is known about Benjamin himself, but his marriage certificate records both his London address and that of his father in law: 'Benjamin Godfrey of Bury Street, in

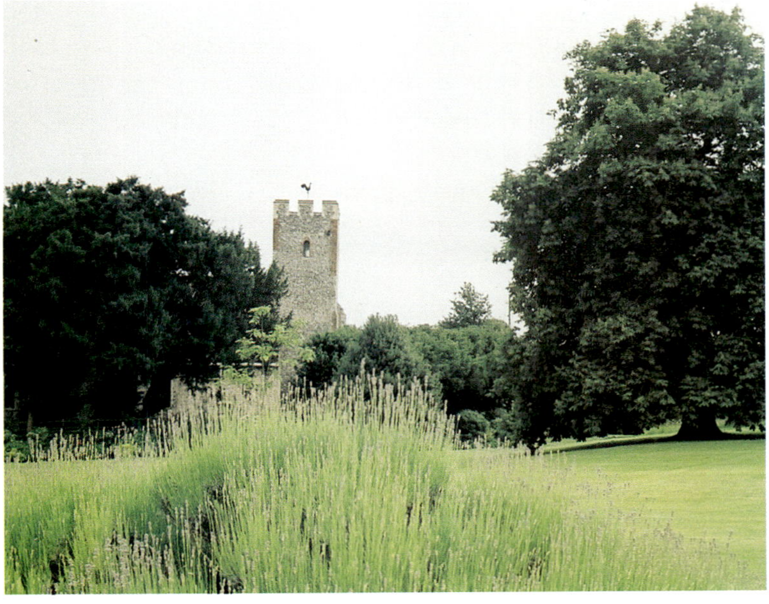

35 (left) *As with many of the churches in London's suburban belt, the picturesque and modest church at Norton Court holds the key to a number of London's merchant families who would have wanted to be buried close to their roots, old or new.*

London, merchant, bachelor about 30, and Mary Piggott, spinster, 20, daughter of Baptist Piggott, of Cannon Street, London, grocer.'[41] Godfrey also clearly spent time in his Kent residence at Norton Court near Sittingbourne where he is credited as the commissioner of the Painted Room. The House suffered a fire in 1961 but the Painted Room escaped the tragedy although it is likely to have been relocated as each panel is now movable and detachable rather than fixed in place in the wainscoting.[42] Its artist was *Illus. 34* probably a provincial painter with a good eye for composition. However naive the execution may seem, it shares with the Painted Rooms of Carshalton and Botolph Lane the same interest in the exotic and the same allusions to shipping and far away lands.

In the nearby church at Norton Court, the tomb of Baptist *Illus. 35* Piggot is packed with references to London merchants: 'Here are placed the remains of Baptist Piggott of Norton Court Gent whose first wife was Margaret the daughter of John Minn of London Grocer by whom he had 5 children of which Mary his sole Heire (married to Benjamin Godfrey Merchant) survived only at his death. His second wife was Katharine ye daughter of Will. Robinson of London, merchant . . .'.

CONCLUSION

The Great Fire of London and its aftermath produced a solid, practical and often austere form of 'houses of the greatest Bigness'. Compare for instance the Jacobean, florid style of Scawen's *Illus. 16 & 129* House with the Botolph Lane property. However, the painted rooms, which in most cases formed such an integral part of the fabric of the house, tell another story: with their mix of realistic and imaginary detail they evoke the fantastically exotic world of merchants, many of whom, refreshingly, never commissioned the complicated allegorical and mythological paintings so favoured by the aristocracy. In their 'houses of the greatest Bigness' merchants created instead their own vision of a world fuelled by solid reality but also magical encounters.

ART IN PRIVATE LIVES

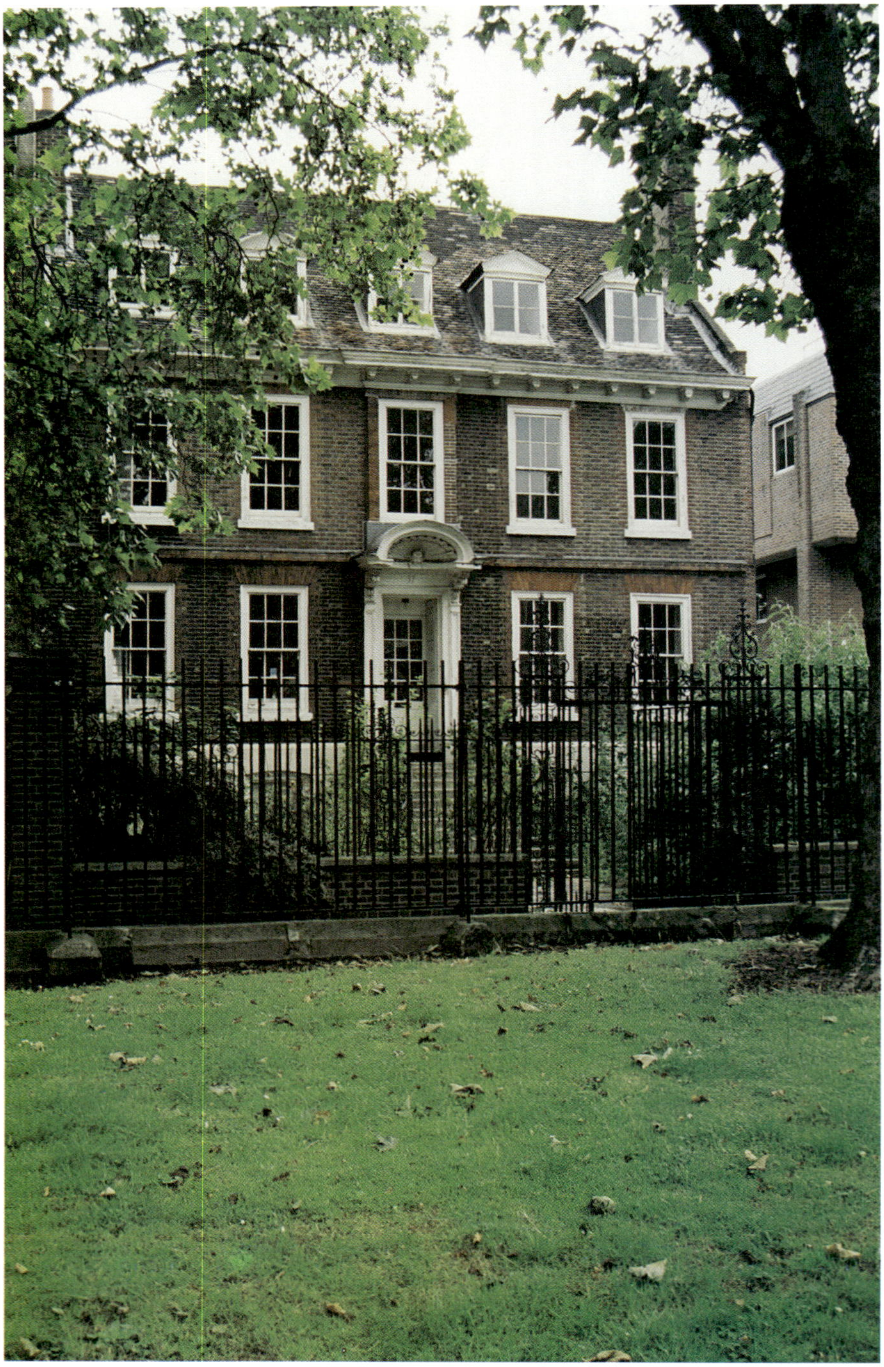

36 *Front elevation of Dormer Sheppherd's house in Mile End Old Town, built in the 1690s. In terms of size, the house conforms to the 'Mansion Houses ... of the greatest Bigness' listed in the 1667 Rebuilding Act.*

Case Study: The Story of a Merchant's House

Chapter Four

KATHARINE GOODISON

Mile End Old Town in the parish of Stepney was a village in a predominantly rural hamlet favoured by retired sea captains and wealthy citizens whose large houses and pleasure gardens peppered the area. The location was perfectly suited for a merchant, being so close to the Thames and the City of London.

Mile End Town stands here built with many good houses inhabited with divers sea captains and commanders of ships; two East India Captains by the name of Browne and other persons of good quality.

It is to be further remarked of this parish of Stepney, it is one of the greatest nurseries of navigation and Breeders of Seamen in England, the most serviceable men in the Nation; without which England would not be England. For they are its strength and wealth.[1]

EARLY OWNERS

Dormer Sheppherd[2] was a London merchant aged around forty when he bought some land on the east side of what was called Mile End Green from the late Arthur Browne. It was here around 1694 that Dormer Sheppherd built a five-bay red brick four-storey house set within a plot of land.[3] *Illus. 36, 38*

Very little is known about Dormer Sheppherd but he was described as a merchant and was married in Clerkenwell in 1681. He also had a son, Amos, who was called to the bar.[4] When Dormer Sheppherd built his house, it was in a rural and leafy setting surrounded by fields and orchards[5]. It must have looked very similar to the setting shown in the anonymous painting illustrated here. Dormer Sheppherd sold the house and adjoining land to Dame Mary Gayer in October 1712.[6] *Illus. 37*

Mary Gayer had married Sir John Gayer in India. He was the Governor of Bombay for the East India Company, the main

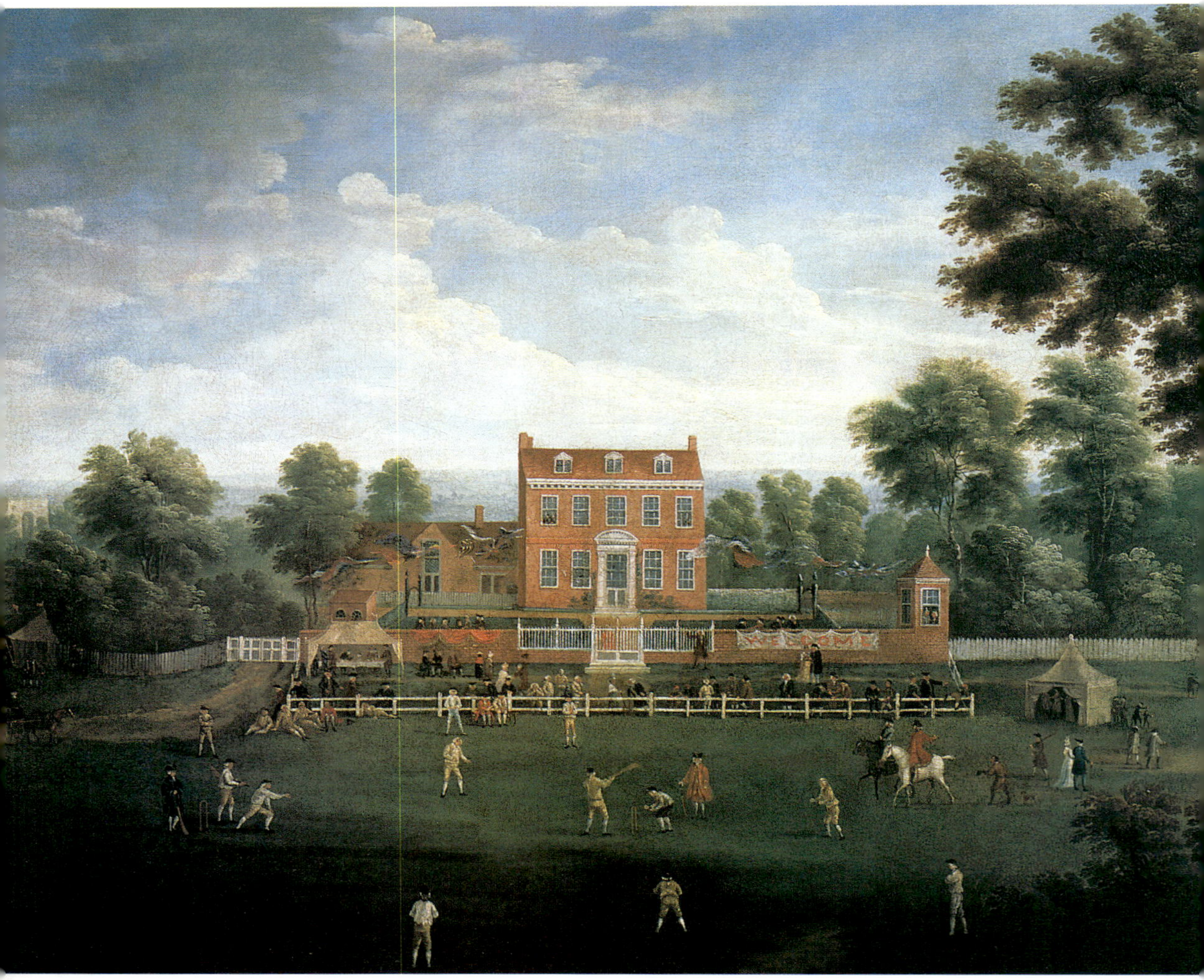

37 *This anonymous mid-eighteenth-century oil painting depicts an early eighteenth-century house in a rural setting. It is still wrongly labelled 'Kenfield Hall'. We reproduce it here because it evokes well the appearance and original environment of the Stepney Green House.*

Illus. 129 trading and mercantile company of this period. He made his money through his family and City connections as well as by trading in India, through the East India Company. Both he and Mary Gayer were imprisoned in the company's offices in Surat in India from 1700 to 1710 as a result of the tussles between the Old East India Company and the New East India Company.[7] Sir John Gayer died in Bombay Castle in the spring of 1711,[8] and by 17 April 1712, Mary Gayer was back in England proving Sir John's will.[9]

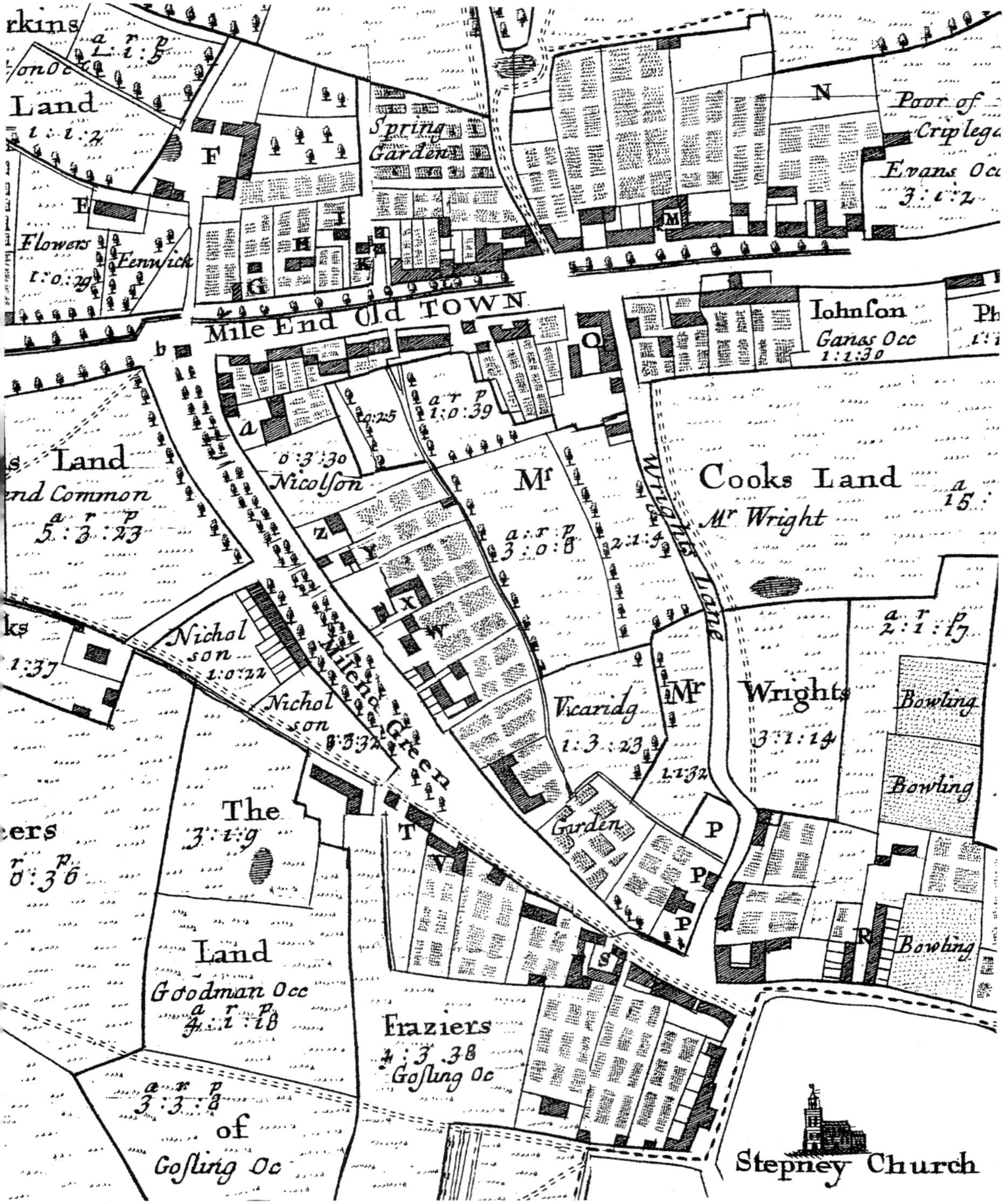

38 *This detail from Joel Gascoyne's map shows Mile End Old Town in 1702–04. Dormer Sheppherd's house is marked 'Z'.*

She was very wealthy, inheriting the bulk of Sir John Gayer's estate. On her return to England and a rich widow, she needed somewhere to live. Presumably she must have known about Mile End Old Town and maybe even the house itself through her undoubtedly good connections with merchants and the East India Company. The setting does seem rather remote for a woman in her late forties, having recently returned from abroad and planning to build a new life. It is likely that she also had a central London location at this point and she could have used the Stepney Green house as a suburban 'villa' retreat.

By 1716, five years after the death of her husband, she had remarried,[10] passing her possessions onto her new husband, Archibald Hutcheson, who interestingly also owned much land in the parish of Stepney.[11] He was a Member of Parliament, and being an economist, he wrote various papers on the South Sea Bubble finances.[12] On her marriage, Mary Gayer retained a small fortune of £10,000 in bonds, a selection of precious jewels, her name and her title.[13] It is not known when she sold or leased the House, and there is no mention of it in her will dated 1727.[14] It is likely that it passed to her husband as part of her marriage dowry and it was then sold or leased to its next owner, described as a 'mariner and a gentleman' Captain Edward Randolph, another merchant.[15]

The exterior and the interior of the house demonstrate various phases of works. The building works and the interiors were done by Dormer Sheppherd at the end of the seventeenth century. When Mary Gayer bought the house at the beginning of the eighteenth century, she must have felt it was not smart enough for her status and class, so she set about seriously enriching it. This certainly involved the removing of some of the fixtures and fittings that Dormer Sheppherd had put in previously.

THE EXTERIOR OF THE HOUSE

Illus. 36 The exterior of the house is typical of high class mercantile architecture after the Great Fire and shares many architectural similarities with other houses of this period for example, the 1670 *Illus. 16* Botolph Lane property within the City of London and Fenton House in Hampstead dated 1693, also believed to have been built for a London merchant. At that time houses were arranged symmetrically and the entrance door is therefore in the middle of the main facade, flanked by equal numbers of sash windows, spaced into groups. The group over the door is usually emphasized by a pediment or decorative brick work. At the widely projecting eaves there is a boldly carved modillion of varying degrees of richness.

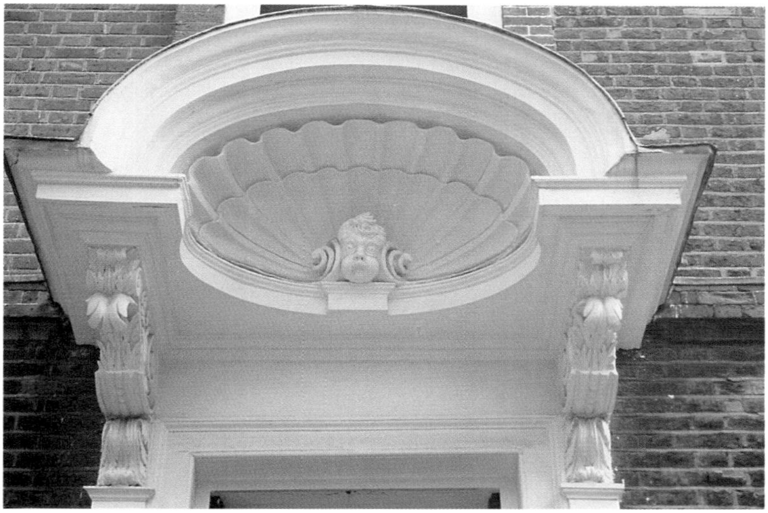

39 *Detail of shell hood over the front door of the Stepney Green house. The concave scallop shell had become a popular motif in the early years of the eighteenth century. The house of Robert Clayton illustrated on p.31 boasts an early example of this decoration.*

There is a plain projecting band, or string course, running between the two principal floors. The chimneys are gathered together in large solid stacks. The attic rooms are lit by pedimented dormer windows. There are many examples of this kind of architecture throughout the United Kingdom, though unfortunately in London a great many examples of this type of house have been destroyed.

The façade was built by Dormer Sheppherd in classic post Great Fire of London style, yet its elements reflect those appearing on buildings built prior to the Fire Prevention Acts of 1707 and 1709. The projecting modillion cornice is made of carved wood and the fashionable sash windows have the sash box exposed and set flush with the face of the external brickwork. The arch is a flat brick arch and the bond of the façade brickwork as it meets the window void is neatly finished off by introducing quarter bricks. As an extra decoration the bricks forming the window jamb are red stocks showing up against the different coloured stocks on the rest of the façade. The body of the brickwork was originally beautifully tuck pointed.*

* Tuck pointing was used as an illusory form of pointing when very thin putty joints between bricks was not possible. The mortar was mixed with brick dust to match the brick colour. It was then applied, used proud, then sanded back to the brick surface, thereby disguising the thick joint. This joint was then scored and a strip of white line putty was stuck on, resulting in an imitation joint.

The appearance of the original doorway is not known, but it is likely that this feature was upgraded by Mary Gayer. The shell hood is supported on a cantilevered doorcase of carved wood. Wooden pilasters are underneath. There are many examples of this kind of decorative embellishment surrounding front doors as the shell hood on houses in Lawrence Pountney Hill dated 1703 and in Sherborne Lane, both in the City of London.[16]

Illus. 39
Illus. 40
Illus. 41

Often decorative heads were added. Similar style heads also exist on the houses in Queen Anne's Gate, London and are dated to

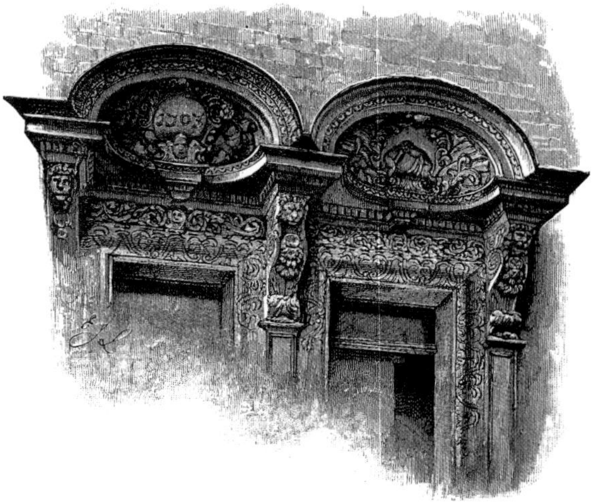

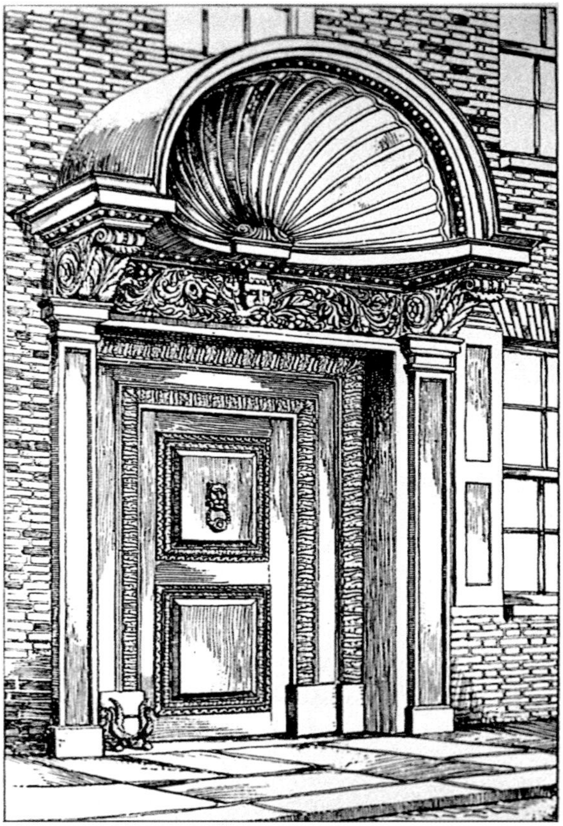

40 (above) *Detail of the front façades of houses in Lawrence Pountney Hill showing similar shell hoods.*

41 (right) *This drawing of a shell hood in Sherborne Lane in the City is a striking visual record of a property that no longer survives.*

Illus. 42 & 43 1700–05. The Stepney shell hood and puffing cherub are made of stucco. This being a house with great maritime associations, I like to think that the puffing cherub was there to blow a fair wind bringing merchants and cargo swiftly and safely back home to London.

There was a public footpath immediately in front of the house, so for enclosure Mary Gayer erected the fine iron railings. She commissioned Robert Bakewell, the leading early eighteenth-century blacksmith, and pupil of Jean Tijou, to design them. His stamp still survives on the railings. It is possible that she knew Robert Bakewell through her family, as he worked in Derby and her family were from Chesterfield in Derbyshire. *Illus. 44*

The designs of the railings contain many of Bakewell's characteristic motifs. The most striking is Mary Gayer's monogram 'MG' in typical Bakewell mirror style above the overthrow. There are also similarities of the terminal brackets, the finials, the upright fringes and the linear patterns to other examples of Bakewell's work such as Penshurst Place. *Illus. 45*

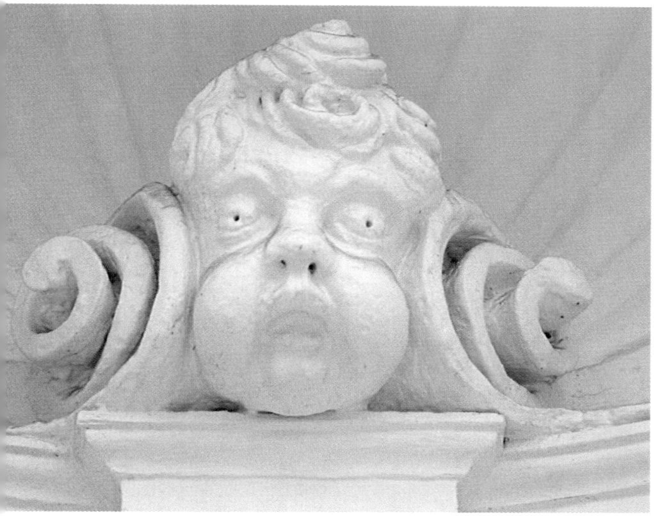

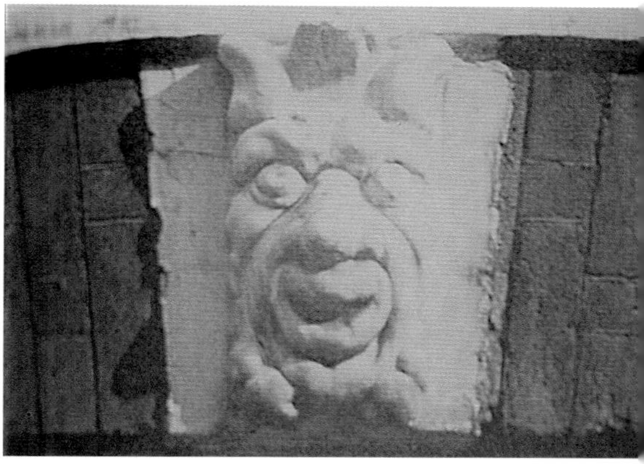

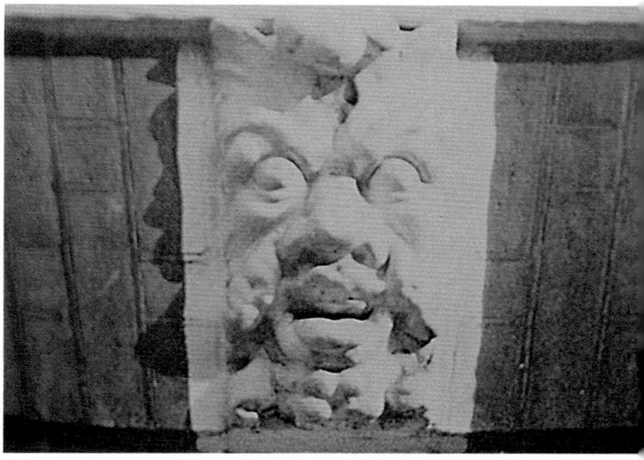

42 & 43 *The detail on the left shows the stucco head of a puffing putto over the front door of the Stepney Green House. This may be compared to the detail on the right showing the stucco heads used on a house in Queen Anne's Gate in Westminster.*

THE INTERIOR OF THE HOUSE

The staircase was a major component of the house and contained characteristic elements of staircases of the period. In the Stepney House, it ran from ground floor to the first floor only. It occupied a large stair hall space at ground and first floor level. It was a conspicuous display of wealth linking the two most important floors. The service basement and the attic top floors were linked by a lower-status back staircase out of sight. The principal reception rooms and mercantile trading rooms were on the ground floor and the important master bedroom was on the first floor. This hierarchy of front stairs and back were characteristic of larger mercantile houses of this period.

The staircase was commissioned by Mary Gayer probably replacing an earlier staircase, as the wall to the left of the staircase *Illus. 46* was moved to make room for the new design. This resulted in the central stair window being off centre. The staircase was made of walnut and pine patterns. It had delicately carved tread ends and inlaid wood. Each tread had three differently patterned balusters.

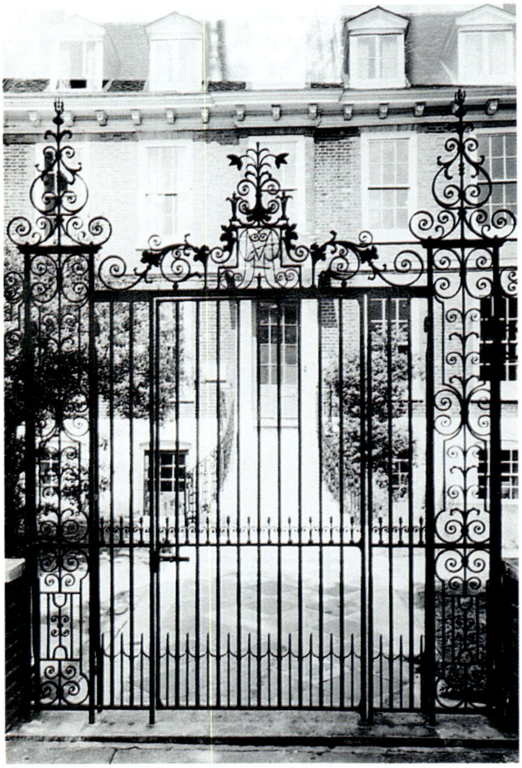

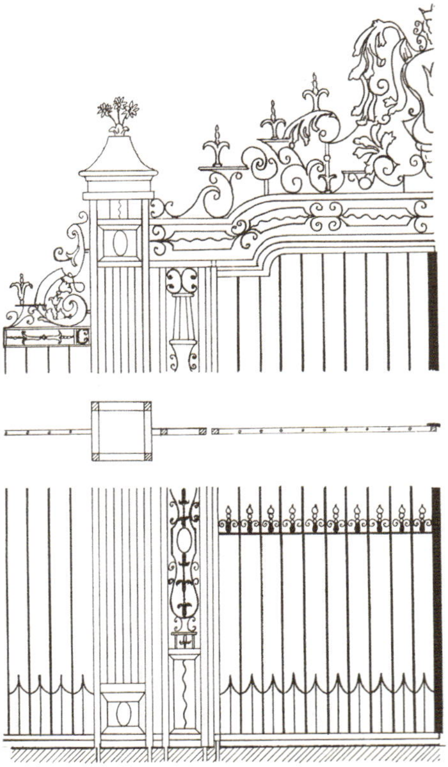

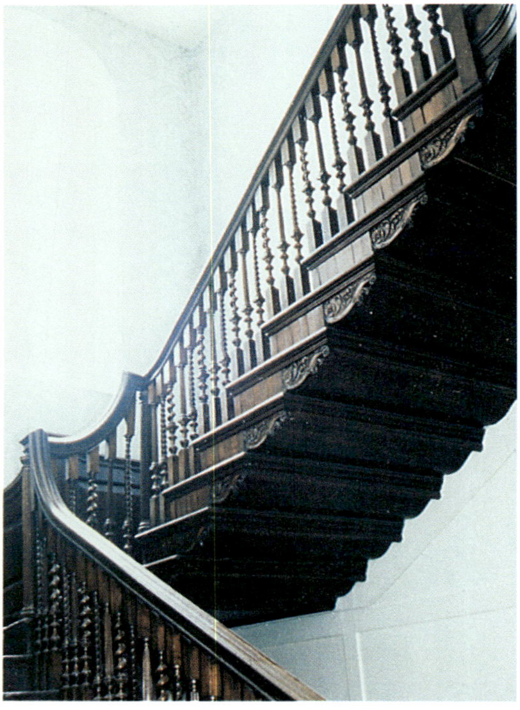

44 (top left) *Detail of the ironwork railings by Robert Bakewell. Notice the monogram of Mary Gayer in the overthrow. This is typical of much of Bakewell's work.*

45 (above) *This drawing shows some of Bakewell's motifs. It was compiled by S. Dunkerley for his 1988 publication 'Robert Bakewell Artist'.*

46 *The main staircase in the Stepney Green house.*

The stairs were of ample width and in short flights with half landings, again fashionable in this period. Unsurprisingly, there are other similar examples of staircases in houses in Spitalfields, a fifteen-minute walk from Stepney. *Illus. 47*

In keeping with the passion for enrichment so vividly evoked by Gordon and Philippa Glanville (pp. 13 and 16), Mary Gayer also commissioned a mural for the stair well. This was an age when wall and ceiling paintings were fashionable (see p. 12), particularly those with allegorical or classical subjects. Many painters were coming from the continent, like Antonio Verrio and Louis Laguerre, whilst home talent was led by James Thornhill or indeed Robert Robinson. At present it is not known who painted the mural, though it is certain that Mary Gayer commissioned it as she upgraded the staircase. *Illus. 48*

Sadly, the mural did not survive and was probably removed or destroyed in 1907, when the house became a craft school. However, there is a tantalising description of it made by a journalist in 1878 when visiting the house when it was a home for aged Jews:

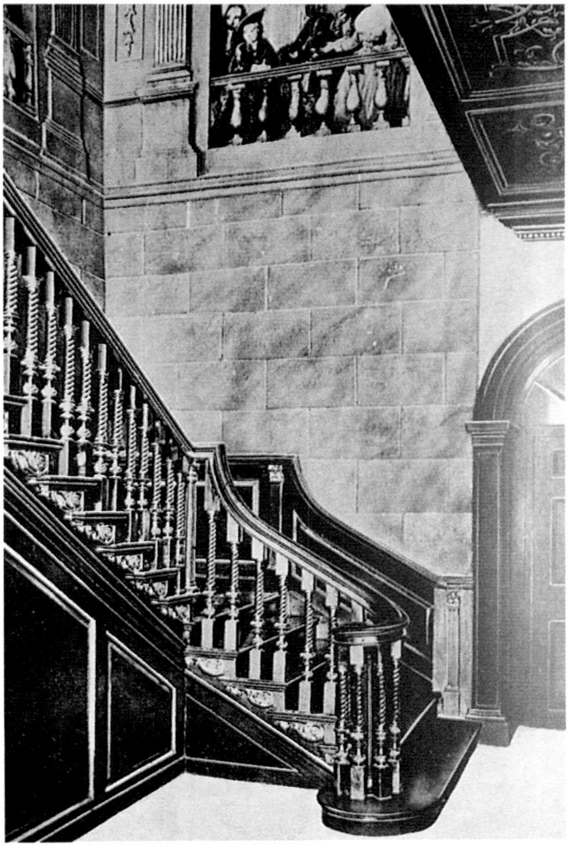

47 *This staircase and mural at 75 Dean Street are now destroyed. They may give some indication of the original appearance of the painted staircase at Stepney Green.*

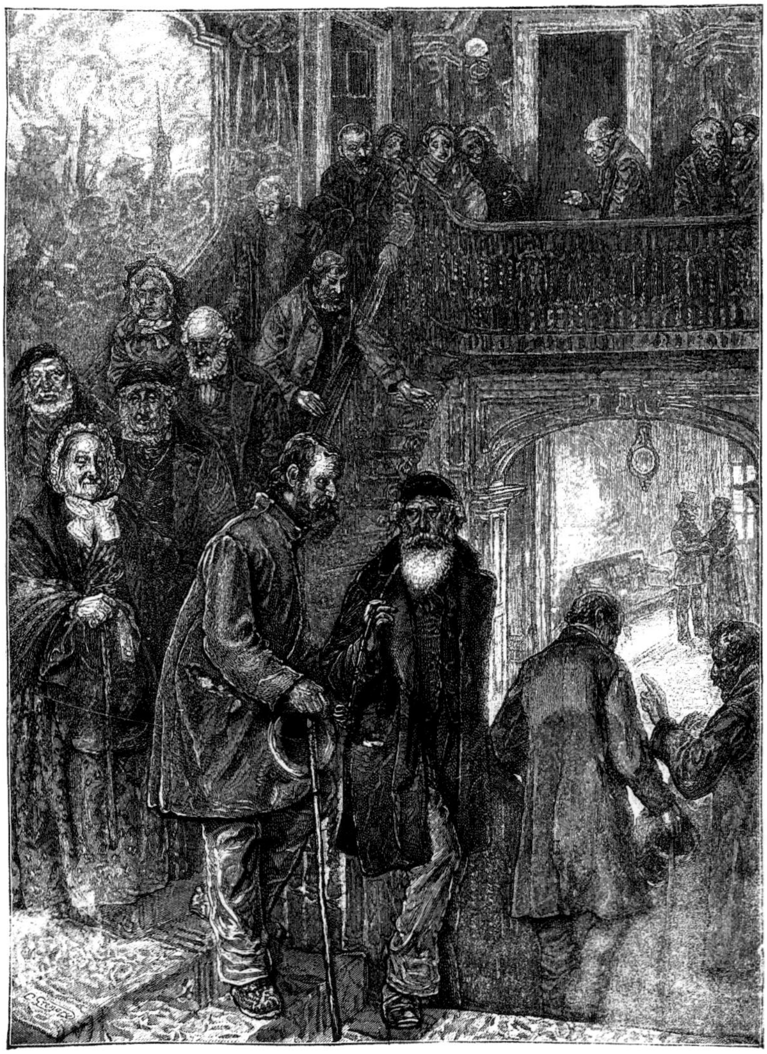

48 *This illustration comes from the magazine 'The Pictorial World' for 23 November 1878. At that time the house was used as a home for aged Jews. The description that accompanied the picture is reproduced in the text below. It does not entirely account for the Chinese looking figure discernible in the mural.*

so we pass through the hall again and up the fine old staircase, the walls of which are adorned with smoke blackened paintings. On one side seems somebody like Queen Dido embarking on board a boat; there also seems to be a gentleman who carries a Mercury's wand in his hand, but we should not like to commit ourselves to either conclusion. The ceiling is also painted in the same style, so we don't know but what some day when the canvas is cleaned the work of a Verrio may be found beneath the coating of grime and smoke.[17]

Dormer Sheppherd installed soft wood panelling in the principal rooms. Mary Gayer retained it. There is a subtle gradation in the panelling between the different rooms, demonstrating a

Illus. 49

hierarchy. The panelling in the main reception rooms was grained with a thin and fluid wash to look like walnut.

Mary Gayer replaced most of the fireplaces and they are of predictable design for the early eighteenth century, all made of marble and most are quite simple. The largest fireplace has an additional division of mantle and overmantle reflecting the higher status of the room in which it was found. The blank space in the overmantle probably had a painting or mirror in it. The high quality undercut carving compares favourably with the tombs of the period. *Illus. 50*

Mary Gayer's commissioning of the railings, front door, staircase, mural and fireplaces demonstrates her ambition to upgrade her house in a way that echoed the greatest aristocratic houses of the period although on a smaller scale. She deliberately set out to employ the best known blacksmith of her age, the finest joiner working in walnut and an unidentified but clearly fashionable muralist. Stonemasons were producing monumentally designed fireplaces but on a miniature scale. A visitor processing through all the principal spaces of the house could not have failed to notice the obvious flaunting of her wealth. It is interesting to speculate that Mary Gayer was following the contemporary fashion for demonstrating title and wealth through architecture, with the

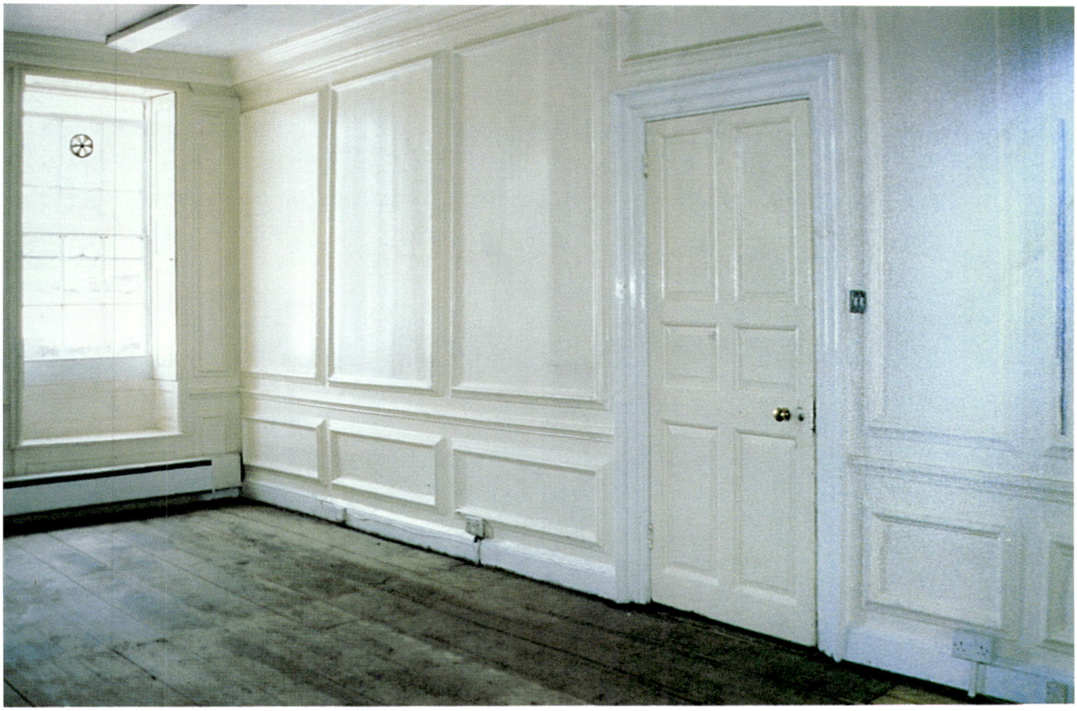

49 *Panelling in a ground floor room, Stepney Green.*

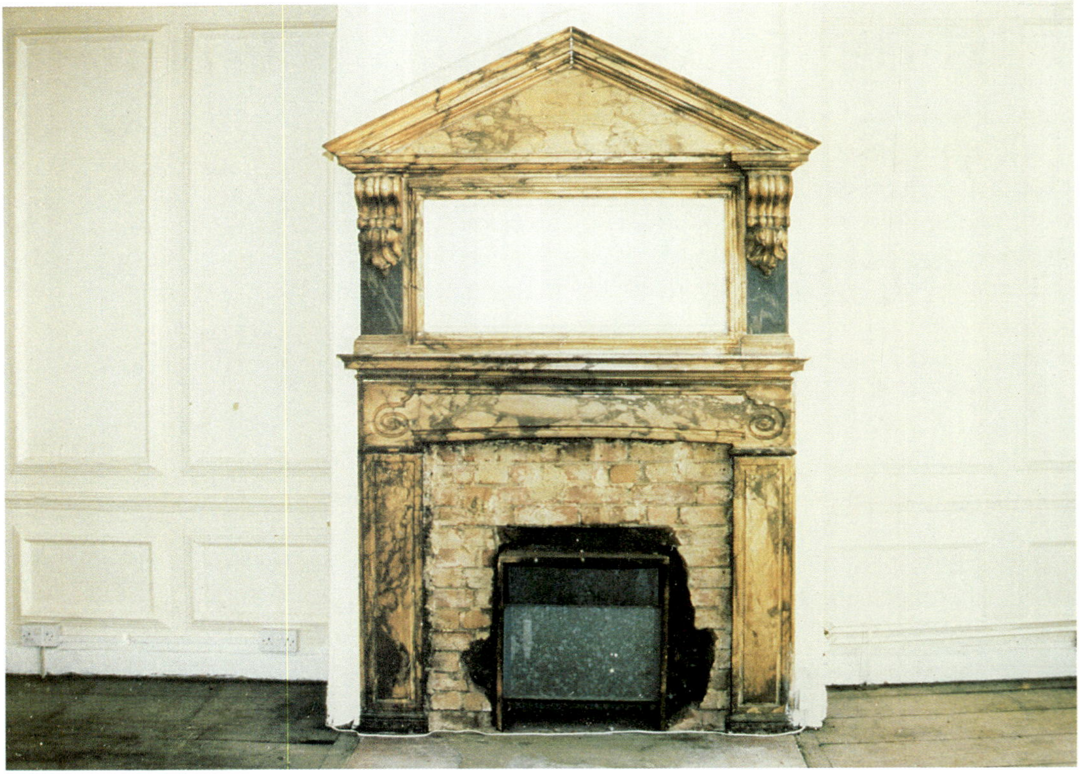

50 *This detail shows a fireplace in the Stepney Green house, situated on the ground floor.*

purpose of the house being 'on show' to virtuosi travellers and unexpected guests.

Perhaps the most tantalising thought is, having spent all this money and energy on the house, she then moved to Southampton Row, in the 'Town'[18] (see David Mitchell's essay *The Three Londons*). Did she and her husband continue to use the house as a weekend retreat? Did she leave the house due to her dislike of the rural East End suburbs, or did her successful MP husband insist that she be closer to the cut and thrust of political life in Westminster?

Furnishing the London Merchant's Town House

Chapter Five

ADRIANA TURPIN

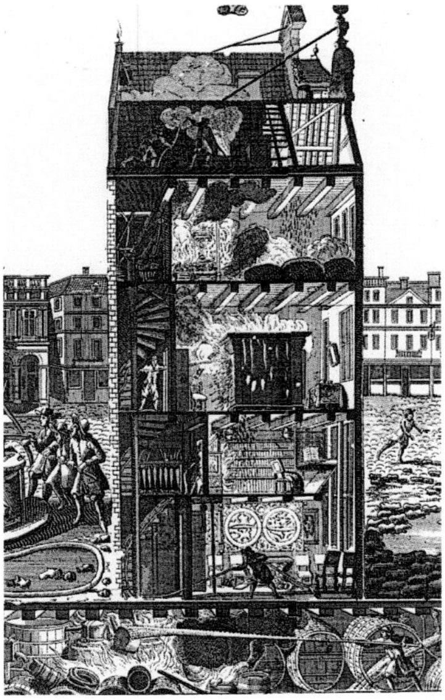

51 *John Lofting, 'A New draught and description of the fire engine' (detail), c. 1720, which shows the interiors and furnishing of a typical London house, with the bedchamber, study or closet and parlour. (See p. 187 for a larger reproduction of this house.)*

In 1683, Dudley North, Levant merchant and youngest son of Sir Dudley North, rented a large house in Maiden Lane, which he then set about furnishing. He is said to have spent some £4000 on the house; one example of his purchases is thought to have been the magnificent silk embroidered bed, once in the North family seat of Glemham Hall.* If the bed was acquired by Dudley North, it would make it one of the few documented examples of merchants' furniture to have survived.[1] Unfortunately there are no bills for its purchase, nor does the style of the bed fit easily into a purchase of the 1680s.[1] The question remains, however, whether it would have been considered appropriate for a merchant to have furniture of this extravagance.[2] This instance is typical of our lack of knowledge of what furniture merchants had in their houses and the difficulties in tracing surviving examples to answer that question. On the other hand, there are many surviving inventories which can be used to create a picture of mercantile interiors, the changes that took place in their furnishing and the range of furniture they acquired. The

Illus. 52

* Dudley North's biographer, a younger brother, the Honourable Roger North, described the state apartments as being richly furnished, but then left empty (see Illus. 52). Nonetheless, it is possible that, when intending to seek political office, he furnished his large house in a suitably grand manner and would have commissioned this bed.

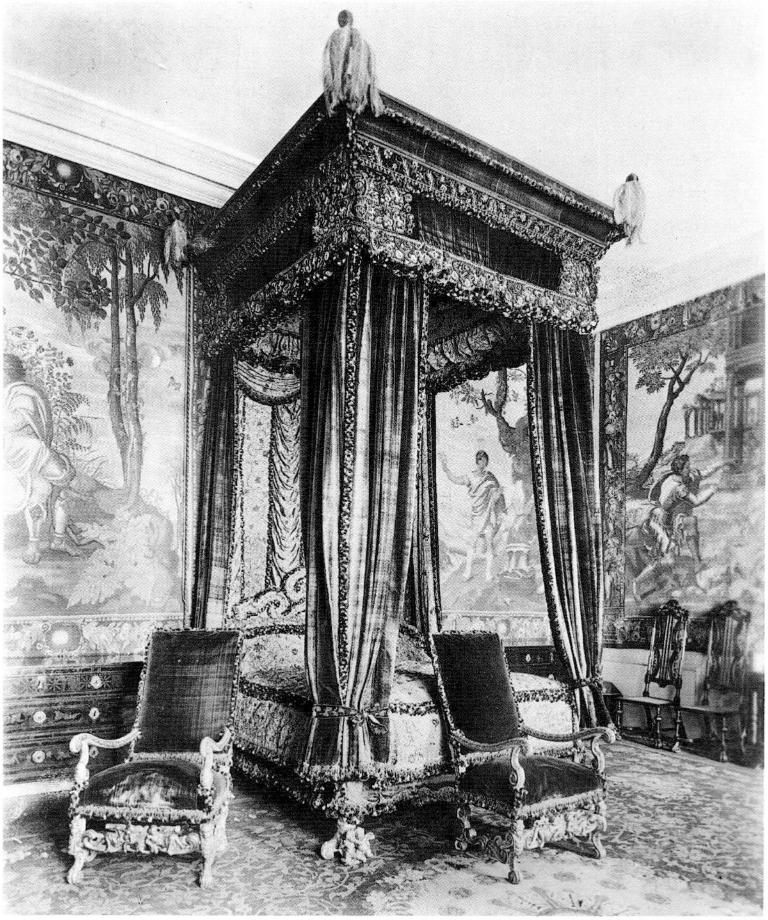

52 *The bed from Glemham Hall in embroidered silk, either made for Sir Robert North for his London house or possibly acquired by his son for Glemham c. 1700. Although documented as coming from a merchant's family, it cannot be shown that it was in the London house. It does not appear in the 1684–87 bills relating to the first furnishing of the house, and, although it could have been bought later, it seems that Dudley North moved back to his brother's house in Covent Garden because of the dirt and dust from the neighbouring goldsmiths' foundries.*

descriptions these documents provide widen our understanding of a subject which to date is dominated by the survival of furniture from country houses.[3] The analysis of the contents of merchants' houses can also be used to show what would be considered appropriate for their position and status and to determine whether or not it differed greatly from the furnishing of great aristocratic houses.

This study is based on some forty inventories of high-income merchants.[4] One group is taken from the Orphans' Court Records (1660–1720, Appendix II). Rooms were valued in their entirety; the only individual items that were valued separately were items of silver and jewellery. The second group consists of the Directors of the South Sea company, whose houses were inventoried in 1720 and 1721 (Appendix I). These, unfortunately, have very few valuations. The range in the number of rooms and the contents varied enormously among the merchants, as did their wealth. However, for the most part the houses were not large and were built vertically, as shown in illus. 51. This survey is concerned with only the richest among these merchants: Sir Joseph Sheldon's estate, for example, was valued at £12,764 while Sir Jonathan Dawes's, even higher at £22,366 16s. 6d., included £15,885 worth of silks and textiles in stock and his ships' cargoes.[5] Even here, however, there are discrepancies in the level of furnishing, and it must be assumed that there were reasons why merchants of considerable wealth, such as Nicholas Bonfoy (1619–72) were not concerned in display. Nicholas Bonfoy had no household goods to mention in his house, although a great deal of his fortune (£8,602) came from stock or ships abroad, as well as owning city property and land.[6]

Illus. 51

THE PRINCIPAL BEDROOM

At the beginning of the period the principal bedroom was the chief room for entertainment and thus contained the important items of status. The historian Peter Earle calculated that the average value of a merchant's bedroom was about £23 3s. and at least double that for the very rich;[7] Sheldon's best bedchamber was valued at £50 7s. 6d. and Dawes at £199 10s. Bearing in mind that these figures did not represent the purchase value, possibly only half the purchase price, these are considerable sums.* Both Sheldon's and Dawes's bedrooms were hung with tapestries, which no doubt made up much of the value.[8] Sir Martin Noell in 1666 was unusual in having gilt leather hangings in his green chamber, although they were occasionally found in other rooms such as the closet, in other houses.[9] The beds were equally richly furnished. Thus, although Sheldon's own bed might have been of cloth, it had silk linings just as Thomas Davies's was of sackcloth and yellow damask. Damask increasingly became the principal wall-hanging for the most important bedchamber.† One of the earliest references to damask hangings is in the inventory of Sir Nathaniel Herne for his wife's room, but in the following decade this became increasingly common.[10] By the 1690s it was also common for the wall-hangings, curtains, beds and chair coverings to be in similar material; the substantial number of merchants who had damask furnishings indicated that even the lesser wealthy merchants could afford the rich textiles. John Cary had a damask bed in his best bedroom while John Barkstead, and Daniel Thomas had rooms hung with damask and the furniture and bed en suite.[11] Other merchants at this date might have hangings of woollen mixtures — camlet and mohair were extremely popular. The same materials appear in the 1721

* In 1721 William Tilliard gave the prices that he paid for furniture six years earlier, saying that he would value the contents of his house at £200 although he had paid £400 for them at the time.

† Damask could refer to both wool and silk, so it is not easy to determine which was meant. Thomas Williams had very little furnishing in his London house (parish of St Mary Woolnoth), but had a white thread damask bedroom in his Stratford house. The value of £17 for the room suggests this might have been a less-expensive material than silk.

inventories. Thus the principal bedchamber in Sir Theodore Janssen's town house in Hanover Square was hung in yellow damask, as was the bed; in other bedrooms he had brocadella, camlet,* chintz lined with silk or yellow cloth. Hugh Raymond's principal bed on the other hand, was furnished with hangings of calamanco† and Francis Hawes's bedrooms were hung with mohair, blue camlet and one room of crimson china (silk). However, the use of tapestries did not completely die out, as Sir John Lambert in 1720 still had tapestry hangings in his drawing room.[12] The evidence suggests that the changes between 1660 and 1720 were not so much that the fabrics changed in nature but that new fabrics such as chintzes or fabrics in lighter colours came into fashion in the eighteenth century.[13]

* Brocadella (brocatelle) was related to damask in its appearance, with raised patterns often of satin, that might be on a linen ground. Camlet originally came from the East, but from the seventeenth century was woven in Europe. It refers to fabric made of a mixture of wool, silk and hair, which was figured and patterned. A room hung with camblet (sic) together with its bed was valued in the region of £20, as in the inventories of Anthony Balam.

† Calamanco is a worsted material, which could be striped, brocaded or plain.

The contents of the bedroom generally consisted of between six and eight chairs *en suite* with the fabric of the bed or walls, a set of tables, looking-glass and stands, and sometimes a cabinet. Pictures were occasionally hung over the chimney, one of the earliest examples being the bedroom of Thomas Davies in 1682.[14] The first mention of the chest of drawers in the inventories studied appears in the inventory of Nathaniel Herne in 1680, after which they become a regular feature of most bedchambers, occasionally described as olivewood[15] or walnut. The grandest of all bedrooms in this period was undoubtedly that of the wife of Sir Nathaniel Herne, who died in 1680.[16] Not only did she have a set of four great chairs and backstools, which would have been upholstered, there were also eighteen carved ebony chairs, two sets of carved tables, stands and looking glasses and an exceptional number of cabinets made in highly fashionable materials. One cabinet was of cocus wood, there were two tortoiseshell cabinets and there were two more cabinets, one black, the other possibly walnut.** Her room must have functioned as a closet with its ivory toys, Chinese porcelain and other small items. Even so, although the quantity of objects was exceptional, the type was not — many inventories were similar, particularly in having a cabinet, whether of walnut or oriental lacquer.[17] During the eighteenth century, smaller tables or chests and less-often, a cabinet were to be found, while sconces replaced the earlier candlestands or torchères.

** Cocus wood was a highly-coloured exotic wood, fashionable for cabinets until *c.* 1680. The tortoise shell cabinets were presumably imported from Antwerp or Amsterdam as there is no evidence of English cabinets being produced in tortoiseshell. There is an Antwerp cabinet of about this date at Ham House, Richmond owned by the Duchess of Lauderdale.

CLOSETS

The grander houses in the seventeenth century had closets attached to the principal bedchamber, often with a cabinet. By the 1720s this room could be called the study, as at Sir Robert Chaplin's house in Castle Street, St Martin-in-the-Fields which contained a walnut-tree bureau with glass doors, one Japanese screen, 'seven Cartoon prints, a China jar in the Chimney', a pair of pistols, a leather stool and a flower print, the total being valued at £83.[18]

This was also the room intended to house works of art and collections. Lady Noell in 1666, Sir Joseph Sheldon in 1683, Thomas Daniels in 1704 and Francis Hawes in 1721 each had significant collections in their closets. For Thomas Daniels the bulk of items were his library books.[19]* Both he and Joseph Sheldon had other items that would be housed in the library. Daniels had a globe and two hour glasses; Sheldon also had a collection of canes, while small boxes, silver ink boxes and jewellery, such as mourning rings, diamonds and a turquoise, cornelian seals were in a small cabinet, which came to a total value of £261 3s. 6d. Francis Hawes similarly was a collector on a grand scale, with works of art creating a veritable cabinet of curiosities. Among the items listed are 'A Cup carved with Boys, Ivory, A boy in ivory, A Cane engraved with figures, A Toilet embroidered with both sides with gold ... A little Altar-piece, Gold, Seven old Rings, 4 rows of India Money, An Amber bottle, two Amber candlesticks, an Amber figure and Pedestal, An Amber Crucifix and Altar, A Parcel of Christals, 52 Emperor heads carved in box, 8 heads carved in Box, 2 Boards with several Figures pasted on them, A Cabinet painted and Silver Ornaments, An Ebony Cabinet inlaid.'[20]

* This is the only such library among the inventories studied except for Theodore Janssen's enormous collection of over 560 volumes, which was catalogued separately without mentioning where they were housed. Janssens' books included works in Latin, French and Italian, John Locke and John Milton, books of mathematics and science.

EXOTIC FURNISHINGS

Noticeably the quantity of japanned† or 'Japan' furniture becomes more numerous and more varied between 1660 and 1720 as is explained in David Mitchell's essay on p. 69. Already in 1666, Lady Noell's study or closet contained an extensive collection of oriental wares, including Japan trunks and cabinet, a tortoiseshell cabinet and much oriental china and small objects, along with hanging shelves to display them (see Appendix II).[21] In the house of John Barkstead (died 1694) there were three India cabinets in the principal bedroom, two as a matching pair and one with a matching frame in the bedroom. These continue to be found in houses of the 1720s. Lady Lambert had an India screen to accompany the black table and stand in her bedroom and an India cabinet in the closet at the house in Mincing Lane. In Sir Theodore Janssen's house in Hanover Square, most of the bedrooms had India cabinets.** Hugh Raymond's principal bedroom had three black tea tables, a japanned chest and stand, a small cabinet and stand. Francis Hawes had even more exotic furniture, in one of the bedrooms there was a 'table inlay'd with ivory and mother of pearl'.[22]

† European imitations of Japanese lacquer were called japanned, which involved painting layers of shellac, usually onto a gesso ground to get a smooth surface. Stalker and Parker in 1683 published an account of japanning techniques, the designs in which were used to decorate furniture by professionals and amateurs. (See *Illus. 65*)

** Whereas in the late seventeenth century most of the richer merchants had at least one 'Indian' cabinet in the principal bedroom, Janssen and Richard Houlditch were the only two merchants to have a significant quantity of lacquer cabinets.

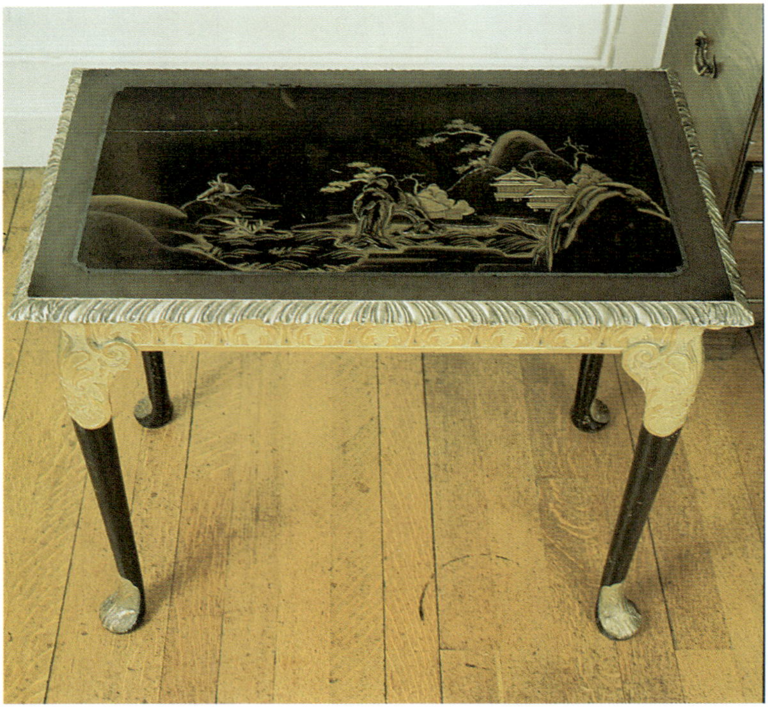

53 *A carved and gilt side table c. 1715–20 with re-used Japanese lacquer for the top. The carving of the table is similar to that produced by the workshop of James Moore (active between c. 1700 and 1726) and shows the high quality of furniture bought by a London merchant.*

Thomas Williams in 1694 had not only an 'India cabinet' but also a 'Japan cribbitch board' in one of the bedrooms (in his country house not in London), one of the first examples of these small pieces of oriental work. Oriental items increasingly appear in the dining room, parlour or drawing room, in many merchants' houses. Thus Anthony Balam had six Japan covered chairs and a Japan table in his withdrawing room in 1691, while Charles Barnard in 1710 had two round japanned tea tables in his dining room. The table illustrated with its lacquer top and carved and gilded base reflects this taste for oriental wares, which predominates in all the merchants' houses.

Illus. 53

DINING ROOM AND PARLOUR

The inventories clearly depicted the differing types of chairs found in the two reception rooms in seventeenth-century merchants' houses, variously described as withdrawing room, parlour or dining room. The chairs were clearly of less significance and value in these rooms than in the bedroom: for instance there were no 'easy' chairs or upholstered chairs as in the principal bedroom; instead there were cane chairs (generally with cushions), chairs with matted bottoms, 'Dutch' chairs and 'Turkey' chairs. Turkey chairs had been popular from the middle of the century and their presence

Illus. 54 & 55

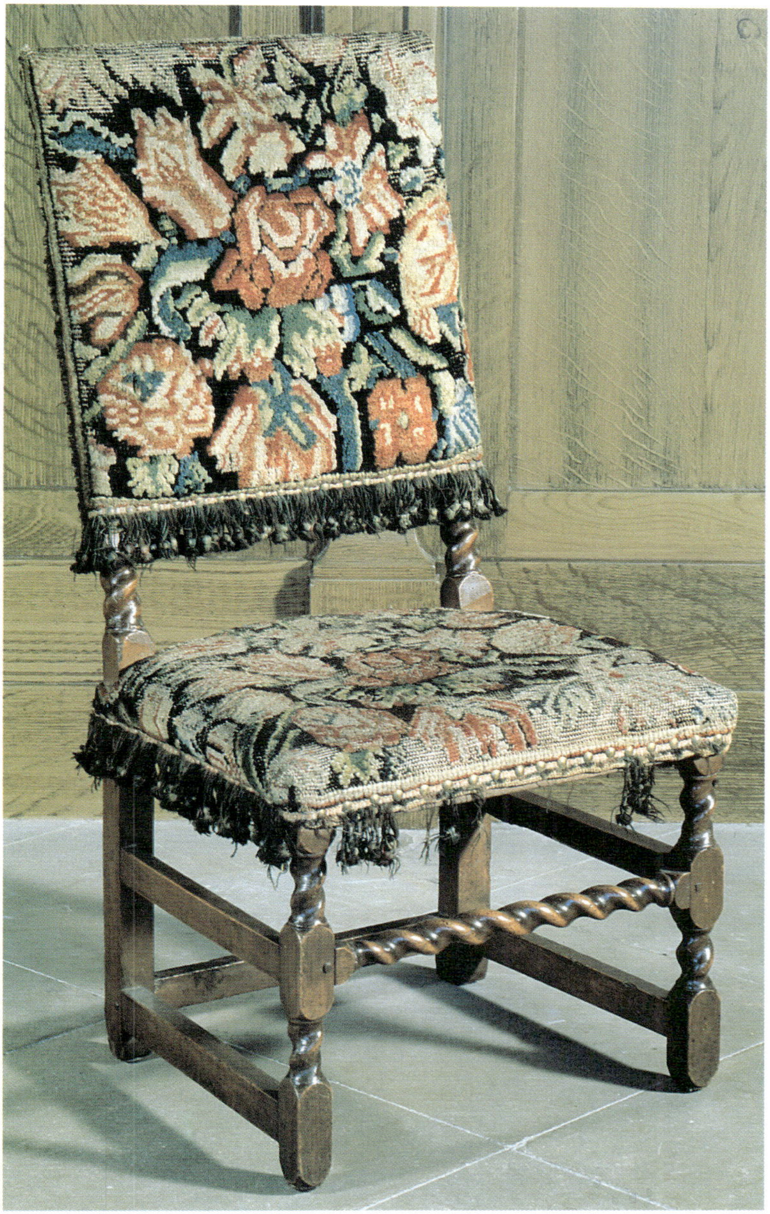

54 *A turkey work chair showing the course knotting characteristic of this material, c. 1680, when these are still described in the merchants' inventories, especially in the dining room and parlour.*

continued until the 1680s. In 1666 Sir Martin Noell had 'Turkey chairs' in both his parlour and dining room. John Smith and Thomas Davies furnished their parlours only with turkey chairs. Nathaniel Herne's inventory listed them in his two dining rooms (see Appendix II), where they were described as 'high turkey chairs' and 'old turkey chairs'.[23] In the South Sea directors' inventories two merchants, Robert Chaplin and Francis Hawes had sets of leather turkey chairs in their parlours. This suggests the possibility that the term came to refer to the lower back rather than to the material.[24] *Illus. 51* In this case the chairs illustrated in the Lofting print could be of this type of leather chair, rather than the puzzling depiction of an interior with very old fashioned furniture.

The other two types of chairs, cane chairs and 'Dutch' chairs appeared in the 1680s and continue to be present in all rooms, especially the parlour and dining room up to the 1720s.[25] Cane chairs with cushions were the most common type of chair of the seventeenth century and the large numbers that appear in merchants' inventories confirm the extent of their production.[26] The inventories suggest that these continued to be fashionable much later than is sometimes suggested by furniture historians. The high backs and simple forms of these chairs are found in an illustration *Illus. 55* of a parlour *c.* 1710 confirming the presence and type of cane chairs described in the merchants' inventories. What 'Dutch chairs' refers to has been the subject of some confusion, but the general consensus is that they were not Dutch but rather rush-bottomed chairs — often described as matted-bottomed — which would have been covered with cushions, perhaps concealing the seating and thus appearing as if upholstered.[27]

Small tables for entertaining or gaming might be found in the dining room and the parlour. When these were not oriental lacquer or japanned, they were generally walnut. Richard Houlditch's back parlour in 1720 with its seven walnut chairs, India cabinet, japanned tea table, oval table, paper screen, writing desk, cane chair and small carpet was not untypical. In Daniel Thomas's house, the dining room contained the 'show' item — the cabinet. The writing desk seems to have become increasingly associated with the parlour by the 1720s — probably a cabinet with fall front above a chest of drawers.[28] Thus Hugh Raymond had a 'scrutore' with a glass door in his back parlour in 1720 as did Frances Hawes, Richard Houlditch, Edward Gibbon (in his common parlour) and Theodore Janssen.* It might be, therefore, that the many contemporary paintings of this period showing a room with a bureau cabinet and tea table reflect a more widespread taste for this informal combination of study and reception room than hitherto thought, and moreover, one that was found both in the town and country houses of the wealthy.[29]

* In Theodore Janssen's inventory they are called book presses with glass doors and may have been similar to the glass-fronted double cabinets made for King William III and supplied by Gerrit Jensen in 1694 now at Kensington Palace, or at Dyrham Park (now in the Victoria and Albert Museum).

ORDERING AND PRICES

We may assume that, increasingly, cabinet-makers and other craftsmen sold wares directly to their clients from their shops in the more fashionable areas of London. According to Pepys, he went to the New Exchange (Royal Exchange) to buy his wife's cabinet, and this must have been a normal way to acquire particular pieces.[30] There is only one account among those studied that mentions a payment to a cabinetmaker, when Jonathan Dawes owed John Burroughs £41 for furniture.[31]*

Many of the citizens encountered in the Orphans' Court records would have purchased their furniture some considerable time before their death, so it is not surprising to find few references of payments to cabinet-makers. The evidence on the whole suggests that houses would be furnished at the time of acquisition, or marriage, with only a few alterations or special purchases taking place thereafter. John Verney, greatly concerned about the layout and decoration of his new house after his marriage in 1693, only mentions the purchase of new pieces of furniture for his home in

Illus. 56

* John Burroughs, cabinet-maker at 'Ye Looking Glass' Cornhill, was active between 1662–*c.* 1690 and was the partner to William Farnborough, whose bills appear in the Lord Chamberlain's accounts for furniture to the crown, Hatfield House and other aristocratic houses.

55 *The Tea Table, an engraving showing a parlour with an oval table for dining, and high-backed cane chairs c. 1710.*

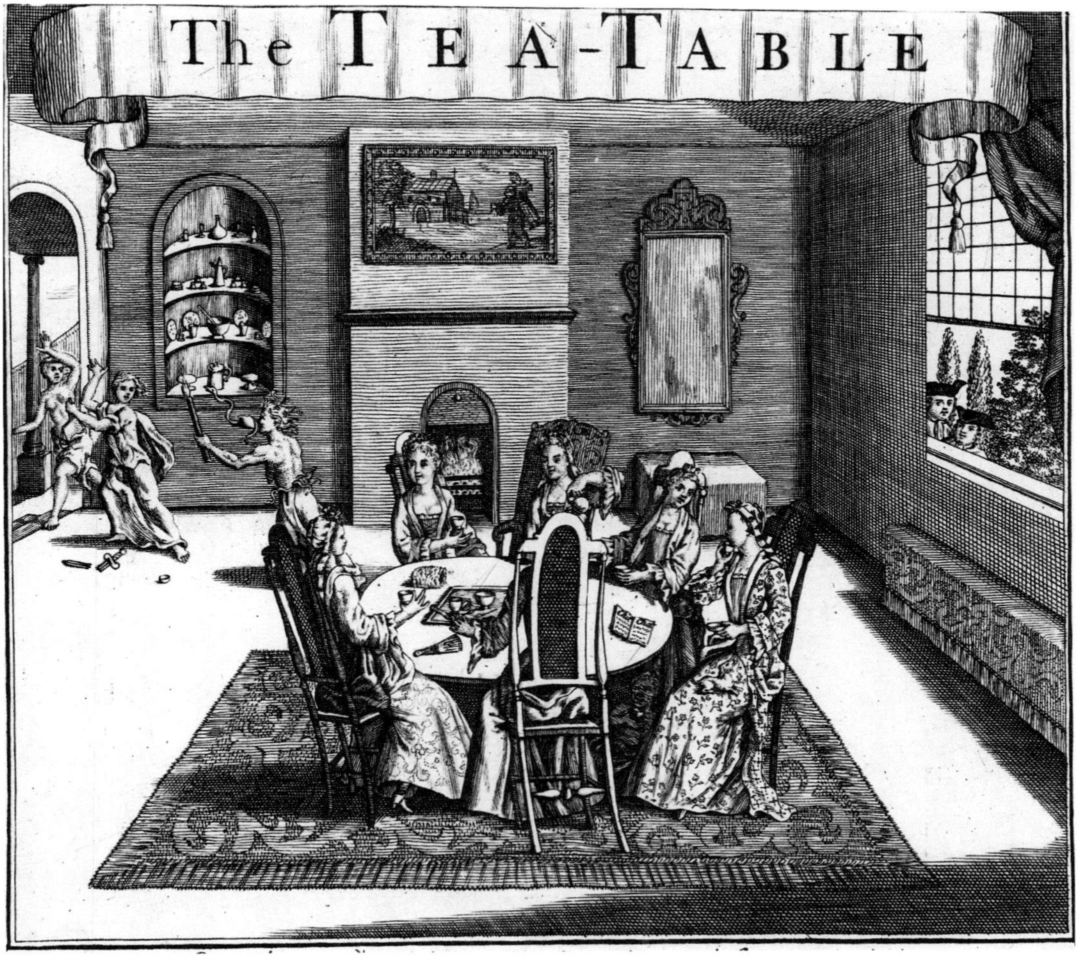

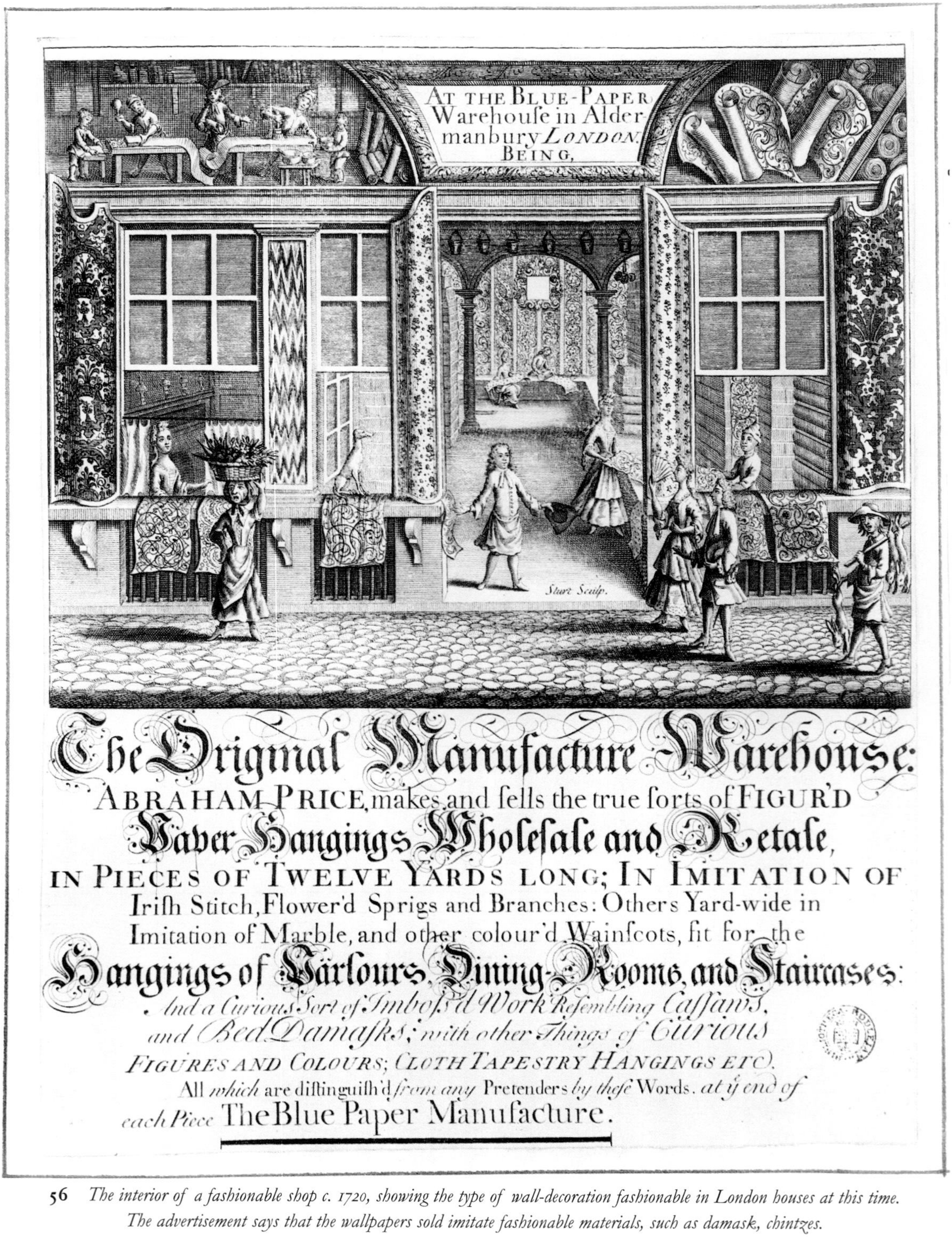

56 *The interior of a fashionable shop c. 1720, showing the type of wall-decoration fashionable in London houses at this time. The advertisement says that the wallpapers sold imitate fashionable materials, such as damask, chintzes.*

Hatton Garden — a table, stands and mirror glasses.[32] Furniture and its purchase is rarely a subject for letters. An interesting exception is the correspondence between Thomas and Jane Papillon. When in 1666 Thomas bought Acrise in Kent, his wife, Jane, wrote complaining that the country workmen were too slow and asking her husband to deal with things in London — also to bring furniture from London.[33] In 1668 twenty cartloads of furniture arrived at Acrise.

MERCANTILE VERSUS ARISTOCRATIC TASTE

In assessing the importance of furnishings in these rich merchants' houses, it is clear that similar furniture appears at the same time in both mercantile and aristocratic homes. There are two possible exceptions. One is that in general merchants would have one or possibly two rooms, richly furnished with the most expensive textiles. At aristocratic Dyrham Park* on the other hand, the inventory lists three silk damask beds and one velvet with furniture en suite and one tapestry bed, while the room hangings are equally splendid, in silk, leather, or damask.[34] This quantity is not repeated in either the merchants' houses in London, nor later in their country houses. It still leaves open the question of the grandeur of the furnishings of the principal room, and the inventory of Nathaniel Herne makes it clear that this room was extremely grand.

* The stately home Dyrham Park near Chippenham was built in 1686 for William Blaithwayt and his wife Mary Winter. Between 1691 and 1710 the size of the property was increased considerably first by a French architect called Hauduroy, then by William Talman a few years later. Most of the furniture at Dyrham dates from this period.

The second exception is the lack of floral marquetry in the merchants' houses, although we know this to have been highly fashionable between 1660 and 1700. We have some indication of the prices of this furniture — £16 for the set supplied by Thomas Pistor at Levens Hall. Might the cost have precluded their purchase? Or might it have been a question of taste?[35] Although clocks appear regularly in the hall of London houses, they are not described as being in marquetry. Interestingly, there are two such clocks given to livery companies.[36]

That merchants purchased furniture of high quality is suggested by the prices paid. Although the records are sparse, the evidence suggests that there was no great difference between prices paid by merchants and aristocrats. Thus in 1662, Robert Clayton purchased a cabinet for £56 18s. from John Burroughs,[37] not very different from the £77.00 paid by Queen Mary for an India chest.[38] In the 1690s chairs supplied by Thomas Roberts for the crown cost 10s. 8d. each, or £1 10s. for an elbow chair, £5 for upholstered.[39] Tilliard reported that the 12 cane chairs he purchased in 1714 cost £7 4s., although the upholstered set of 6 chairs and settee was certainly cheaper at £13 12s. than those in the royal accounts.

At Dyrham House there were eight Dutch elbow chairs in the front hall, three cane and one Dutch chair in the gilt-leather parlour, 12 cane chairs in another parlour, and six cane chairs with cushions in the family parlour, suggesting a style of decoration close to that found in merchants' homes. William Tilliard in 1721 listed walnut cane chairs among those items he had purchased six years ago, and valued them at £7 4s. Theodore Janssen, one of the wealthiest merchants in London, bought and furnished a house in fashionable Hanover Square in 1718.[40]* The description therefore suggests what would have been suitable for his position at this time. Thus it is interesting that there were still matted chairs and Dutch chairs in the bedrooms, walnut chairs in one room with card table, side table, and callimanco curtains. On the other hand the formal rooms were highly fashionable with crimson damask chairs, an India cabinet, tea table and ombre table in one and damask chairs and curtains in a second, which also contained two japanned tables and a japanned screen.

* The house in Hanover Square was bought for £4000 and it cost an additional £1,032 to complete the building works in 1720–21. Janssen spent £300 on upholstery. After he bought the manor of Wimbledon in 1717 for £27,000, he pulled down the existing house to build a new one in his taste. He also bought property for rental in Mayne Friar in Dorset, Queen Anne's Gate in Westminster (then called Queen Square), as well as other properties.

THE CITY IN THE COUNTRY

At Squerryes Court, Kent, surviving furniture from the early eighteenth century almost certainly reflect merchants' taste for the period under review.† The property was acquired in 1731 by John Ward (Lord Mayor in 1719) who was the nephew of merchant Patience Ward. 1719 was also the year when John Ward's son married Frances Bristow and as two sets of chairs at Squerryes Court bear the arms of Bristow and Ward, we may assume that they were made shortly after the marriage to furnish their London home. There is also a clock by Daniel Quare and Samuel Horseman which is decorated with the Lord Mayor's mace in the corners of the panelling and would thus seem to have been made during or shortly after John senior's time as Lord Mayor.[41] It shows that Quare was one of the leading clockmakers in London, the carving on the clock is very fine — evidence that merchants did not hesitate to seek the best quality available. Other items such as a Japanese cabinet on stand, chests and a very fine quality bureau cabinet could have been made for either uncle or nephew.

Illus. 57

† This pretty Kent house on the outskirts of London was built in 1680 by a London merchant — Sir Nicholas Crisp. The property was in the hands of the Villiers family between 1700 and 1731 when it was bought by John Warde. It still belongs to the Warde Family.

Although most of the interiors under discussion have been lost and are at times difficult to reconstruct, several important points emerge from this preliminary investigation. The decoration of rooms with its pending hierarchy changed from the bedroom to the parlour between the late seventeenth and early eighteenth centuries. Certain types of furniture — cane chairs for example — continue to be present (in less important rooms) some time after

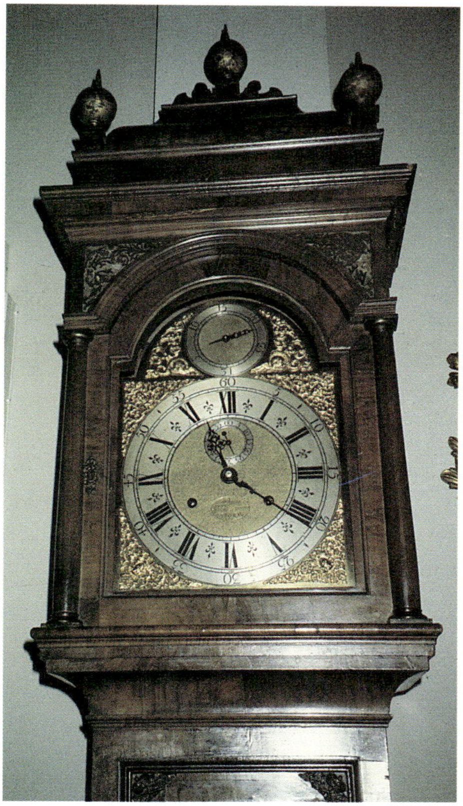

57 *Long-case mahogany clock by Quare and Horseman from Squerryes Court, Kent.*

they were thought to have gone out of use. This suggests that contemporary illustrations give a more accurate depiction than has hitherto been accepted. Finally, even allowing for the limitations of a small sample, it would seem that wealthy merchants created a luxurious but not extravagant setting for themselves, in keeping with the image they wished to present of sober but successful citizens of London.

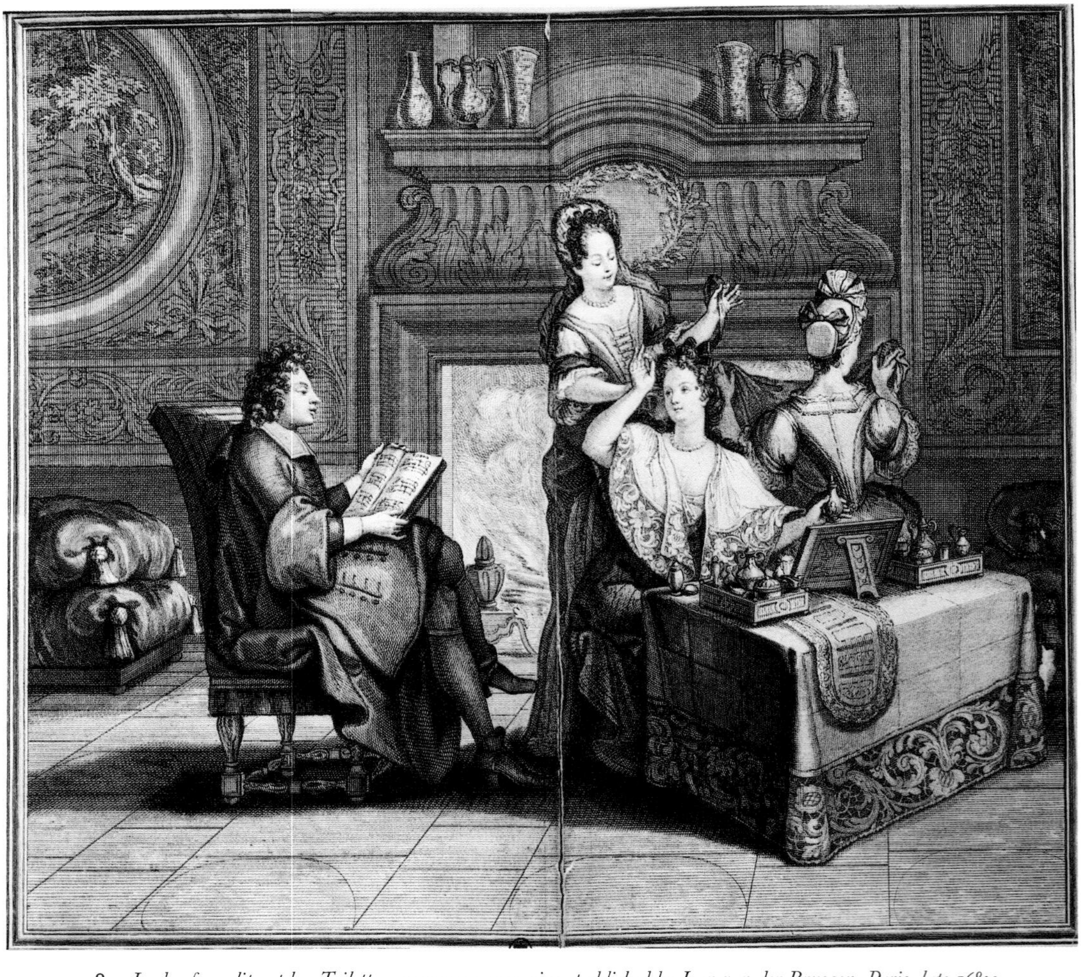

58 *Lady of quality at her Toilette, anonymous engraving, published by Jean van der Bruggen, Paris, late 1680s.*

A Passion for the Exotic

Chapter Six

DAVID M. MITCHELL

INTRODUCTION

During the second half of the seventeenth century, an increasing quantity and range of exotic commodities were landed in London by English merchants: notably, lacquer from Japan, tea and porcelain from China, textiles and diamonds from India, coffee and textiles from the Levant, and chocolate, hardwoods and tortoiseshell from the Americas. The enthusiasm for these goods resulted in a drive to produce imitations or 'counterfeyts', particularly japanned furniture and tin-glazed earthenware with patterns, and occasionally forms, derived from Japanese or Chinese originals. In addition, artefacts with purely western forms, for example in silver, were decorated with 'oriental' designs. From about 1700, comprehensive schemes in a perceived 'Chinese' or 'Indian' style were executed in the fields of interior decoration, architecture and garden design. This enthusiasm has been termed 'Chinoiserie' by modern art historians;[1] a misleading term as the decorative style exhibits a rich melange of strange forms and wild ornament, taken promiscuously from China and Japan, and from the Indies, both East and West. Seventeenth-century writers in both France and England rarely indicated a clear understanding of either the origin of Eastern pieces or the design antecedents of Western imitations, resorting to descriptions such as '*façon de la Chine*', 'Japan work' or 'the true genuine Indian work'.

The taste for exotic commodities in part resulted from an inquisitive passion for all that was new, as well as an admiration for their intrinsic properties; whether the pugilistic power of punch, the translucence and lightness of porcelain, the frothy seduction of chocolate or the bright colours and 'washability' of painted cottons. However, the nature and depth of the enthusiasm among men and women of different classes can only be explained in terms of changes in social and cultural attitudes.

SOCIAL AND CULTURAL ATTITUDES

One of the major changes was the position of women in society. Jonathan Israel argues that the erosion of 'traditional notions of virtue, family, and social roles, crucially challenging woman's existing subordinate status' was a result of the dynamic intellectual debate which in the mid-seventeenth century, 'burst upon the European scene with terrifying force ... a vast turbulence in every sphere of knowledge and belief which shook European Civilization to its foundations'.[2] Kevin Sharpe whilst acknowledging that 'scepticism, secularism and tolerance owed much ... to broader intellectual and cultural changes' stresses the influence of the Civil Wars and the Interregnum which 'systematically disrupted traditional gender roles as women wrote, prophesied, preached (sometimes naked) and petitioned parliaments'.[3]

In Restoration London, the theatre was a principal conduit to disperse some of the ideas of the 'New Philosophy', largely in a popularized version of the ideas of Thomas Hobbes. His assertion that 'there is no significant difference between one person and another', has been seen as leading to the view that men and women were driven by the same passions and appetites.[4] Indeed in William Wycherley's *The Country Wife*, Lady Fidget declared 'we think wildness in a man as desirable a quality as in a duck or a rabbit. A tame man, foh!'[5] Pepys disapprovingly noted one sign of the changing times; 'the Ladies of Honour dressed in their riding garbs ... just for all the world like men ... an odde sight'.[6]

Peter Thornton has argued that in France before 1650, women in general and the Marquise de Rambouillet in particular, led the search for *commodité*, 'questions of convenience, ease and comfort'.[7] On his visit to Paris in 1665, Christopher Wren noted somewhat acidly, 'the women as they make here the Language and Fashions, and meddle in Politicks and Philosophy, so they sway also in Architecture'.[8] A major architectural pre-occupation was the *cabinet*, a closet or dressing room opening out of the bedroom for rest, study or entertaining friends. Many of the more elaborate surviving cabinets were designed for women, a few for *femmes savantes* furnished with books and mathematical instruments, others for less cerebral natures, enchanted places for dreams of love or actual assignations, filled with exotic objects and fragrant flowers, '*un avant-goût de paradis*'.[9]

Elite women now had particular, informal, private spaces that they alone 'controlled', not only as regards their decorative schemes and furnishings, but also those who were to be admitted and the form of entertainment, including the topics for discussion and choice of the gazette or play to be read. In France, the desire among men as well as women, for private and informal spaces, and the love of *divertissements* were probably heightened by the re-imposition at Versailles of an elaborate and inflexible structure of Court life by Louis XIV. In London, although the contrast between public and private life was not so marked, it certainly existed. In the dedication to *The Plain Dealer*, Wycherley is concerned that his play should not 'languish in ladies lobbies or outward rooms', but 'may get into their closets, for what they renounce in public often entertains 'em there'.[10] Even at Whitehall, there was a desire for informality, for when the Queen entertained in the evening in her closet; 'the King himself and the duke are frequently seen there seeking relief from more weighty cares, and divesting themselves awhile of the restraint of royalty' ... and talk on any subject 'provided it be unconnected with business or state-affairs'.[11]

Before 1700, it is in such informal spaces and, in particular in the closets and dressing rooms of elite women that exotic objects were most commonly found and the new beverages consumed. In view of the connections between the City and the 'Town', described earlier in the book, this paper will investigate the level of the enthusiasm for the 'chinoiserie' among merchants and wealthy tradesmen, principally using probate inventories from the London Orphans' Court (Appendix II). The study will concentrate upon the pattern and nature of their ownership of 'oriental' artefacts or 'counterfeyts' in silver, ceramics, lacquer and textiles.

THE OWNERSHIP OF EXOTIC GOODS

For a brief period in the 1680s, London silversmiths produced plate of European form, but with exuberant flat-chased chinoiserie decoration. Virtually all these pieces were 'chamber plate', intended for the bedchamber, dressing-room or closet, rather than 'table plate' for formal dining. Much of it was gender specific, the largest single category, toilet plate, belonged to women, but the monteiths and punch bowls to men. The remainder were drinking vessels: tankards, cups and porringers which could have belonged to either sex. Charles II was supplied with 'a tankerd of gilt plate ... to carry up his breakfast in'.[12] Lady Herne, widow of the Governor of the East India Company, had a tankard in her closet as did the Queen, whose chamber plate also included two porringers, and a cup and salver, which would probably have been used to serve health-giving bouillons, also at breakfast.[13]

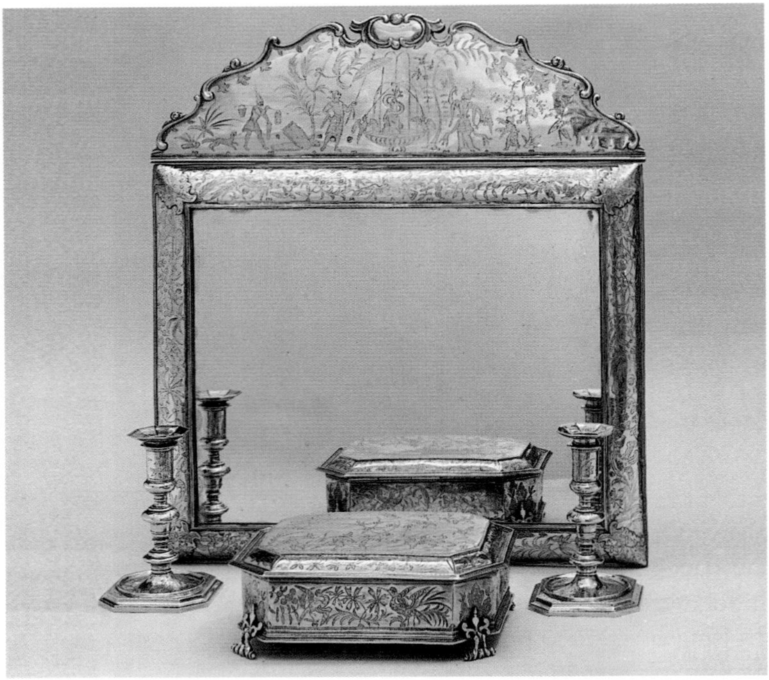

59 *The Normanton Toilet Service, silver-gilt, mark of William Fowle, London, 1683–84.*

Illus. 58 Another adoption of French manners at the Restoration was the entertaining of friends by fashionable ladies during their *toilette*,[14]

And now, unveil'd, the Toilet stands display'd,
Each silver vase in mystic order laid ...
This casket India's glowing gems unlocks,
And all Arabia breathes from yonder box.
The Tortoise here and Elephant unite,
Transformed to combs, the speckled and the White.[15]

Thus in Alexander Pope's poem, *The Rape of the Lock*, the closet inhabited by nymphs was an exotic and erotic milieu: a world reflected in the splendid toilet services fashioned by the young silversmith William Fowle between 1681 and 1684. They were of two distinct types: the first 'of Japan work' were decorated with flat-chased chinoiseries of bizarrely caparisoned figures in strange Illus. 59 imaginary landscapes; the second had cast plaquettes with scenes from Ovid's *Metamorphoses* — amorous goddesses in sensual groves, their smooth flanks burnished and the highlights of the trees chased and chiselled, in contrast to the hammered graduated Illus. 60 skies.[16]

It is unclear whether many City dames entertained in their dressing rooms but Lady Herne; Lady Sheldon, wife of a Lord Mayor; and Ruth, wife of the mercer John Barkstead all owned dressing

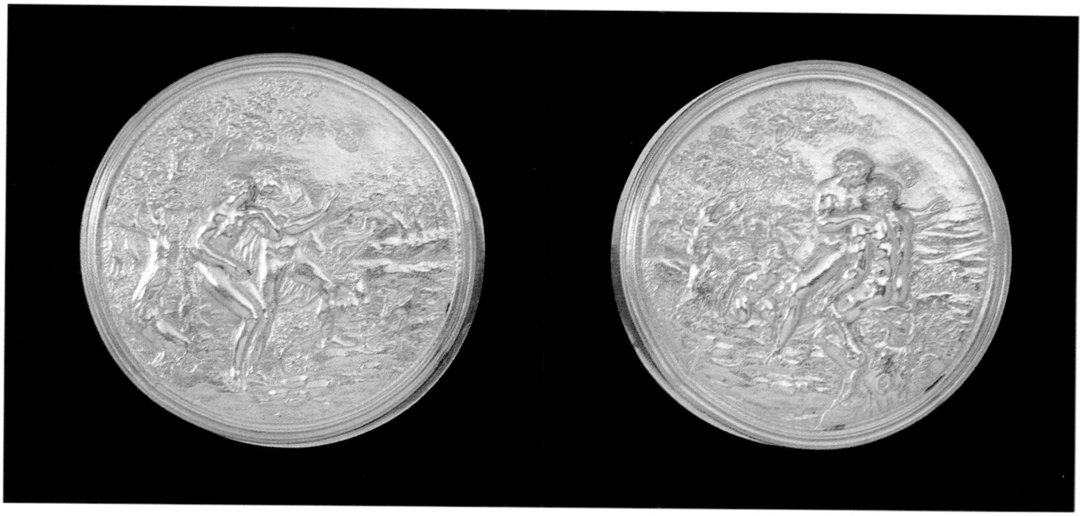

60 *Patch boxes with Venus and Adonis (left) and Hercules and Iole (right) from the Calverly Toilet Service, silver, mark of William Fowle, London, 1683–84.*

plate.[17] Others had toilet services of exotic woods such as Sarah, the daughter of the brewer Sir William Bucknall, whose finely appointed chamber included a cabinet, table and two stands, a dressing box, three brushes, two powder boxes, a little dressing box, two little round boxes and a large looking glass, all of princes wood.[18] Elizabeth, the wife of the haberdasher Thomas Peade, had a similar range of furniture and dressing boxes, but in olive wood.[19] Edward Traherne, a cabinetmaker in Covent Garden, whose customers numbered the Queen, Barbara Castlemaine and Nell Gwyn, held extensive stocks of tables, stands, cabinets, boxes, and looking and dressing glasses, in walnut, ebony, princes wood, olive wood and lacquer.[20] Among them were a number of quilted dressing boxes together with comb, powder and patch boxes, all in olive wood. Elizabeth Peade's toilet service contained, like the nymph Belinda's, a box for combs, 'the speckled and the white'. Some fine tortoiseshell combs were imported from Jamaica, but others were supplied by London combmakers such as William Cox on Ludgate Hill who also made combs of ivory, boxwood and horn.[21]

Silver punch bowls and monteiths with removable rims, some decorated with lively chinoiseries, were used to serve punch, a powerful concoction originally of arrack, water, lemon juice, sugar and spices, introduced from the East by English merchants.[22] In London, alternatives to arrack were soon found with brandy and wine being used by Hannah Wooley in her recipe of 1670.[23] Punch was drunk by groups of male friends in informal settings: closets or withdrawing rooms like the 'Painted Parlour' at Carshalton House, built for the tobacco merchant Edward Carleton. On his

Illus. 61

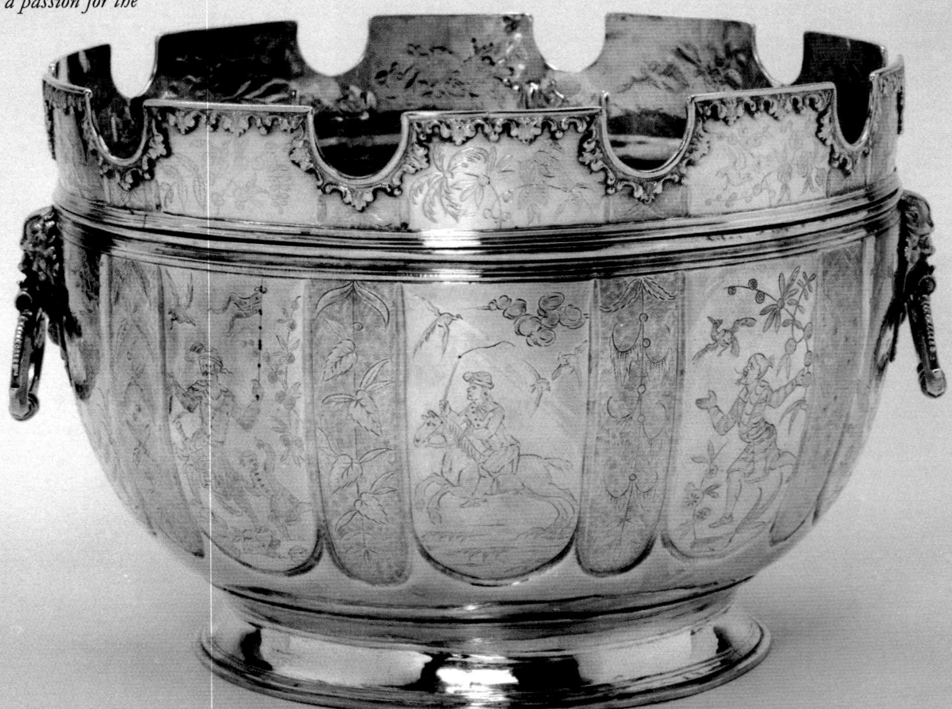

61 *The Basingstoke Trophy, a monteith with a detachable rim, silver, mark of Robert Cooper, London, 1688–89. The decoration illustrates 'a passion for the exotic'.*

bankruptcy in 1713, the furnishings of the room included 'a punch'.[24] The decoration is attributed to Robert Robinson who painted a similar room in 1696, originally situated on the ground floor of a house in the City (see p. 113 in James Ganz's chapter). This was probably commissioned for another tobacco merchant for its lively chinoiseries with subjects from both the East and West Indies include scenes of tobacco cultivation.[25]

Illus. 33, 62 & 85

Illus. 28

Illus. 87

Punch, along with the other new beverages, was also served in imported Chinese porcelains.[26] Fine pieces continued to be mounted in gold or silver, as the 'Cheney Cupps and Cheney salt-seller garnished with silver' in the London 'study or clossett' of Lady Noell (see Appendix II).[27] Food was also served in porcelain

Illus. 63

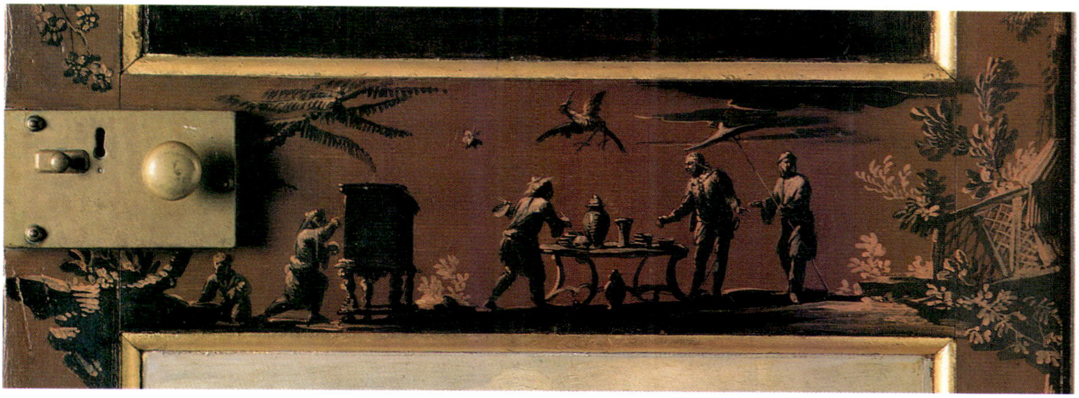

62 *Oriental figures and a table laden with oriental porcelain from the 'Painted Parlour' at Carshalton House, the decoration attributed to Robert Robinson, 1690s. This detail is found in the lively but monochrome decoration of the stiles of the panelled room. For other views of this room, see Illus. 33 and 85.*

dishes. In 1652, John Evelyn was invited to my Lady Gerard, 'where we had a greate supper, & all the vessels which were innumerable of Porcelan, which was very extra ordinarie'.[28] Porcelain for the dining table, however, is rarely found in London merchants' inventories before the end of the century. Lady Noell was unusual in owning the porcelain saltseller as well as china dishes and plates. Chocolate and tea, and sometimes coffee, were served in Ladies' bedchambers and dressing rooms during the morning, and several of the references to china were for serving these drinks:[29] for example Dorothea Scarth, wife of a prosperous grocer in Lombard Street, had twenty 'Cheney Cupps' in her chamber.[30] It is not until the next century that extensive holdings of china are found for both formal dining and for serving the new beverages. For example the 1723 inventory of the overseas merchant Alderman Robert Heysham includes plates and fruit dishes for dining as well as a punch bowl, blue and white chocolate cups, and several complete tea services. Some of these wares are described as 'burnt in China', suggesting that they were fired in the East and that the remainder were of European manufacture.[31]

Porcelain and other curiosities were also used purely for decoration. Lady Noell, whose husband was a leading member of the Levant and East India Companies and had extensive interests in the West Indies, owned a plethora of exotic goods: 'East India flower potts, Indian and Jappan Basketts, the jaw of a tiger, Jappan figures of wood, and pairs of Cheney Beakers and Waggons' [from the Dutch, *rolwagen*].[32] She also had a bird cage possibly occupied by a parrot, like Lady Herne's.[33] 'Parrat and birdcages' were made in London at this time by wireworkers such as Humphrey Dash in Crooked Lane.[34]

Illus. 64

The porcelain often found in the bedchambers and closets of elite women echoes Wycherley's association of china both with the

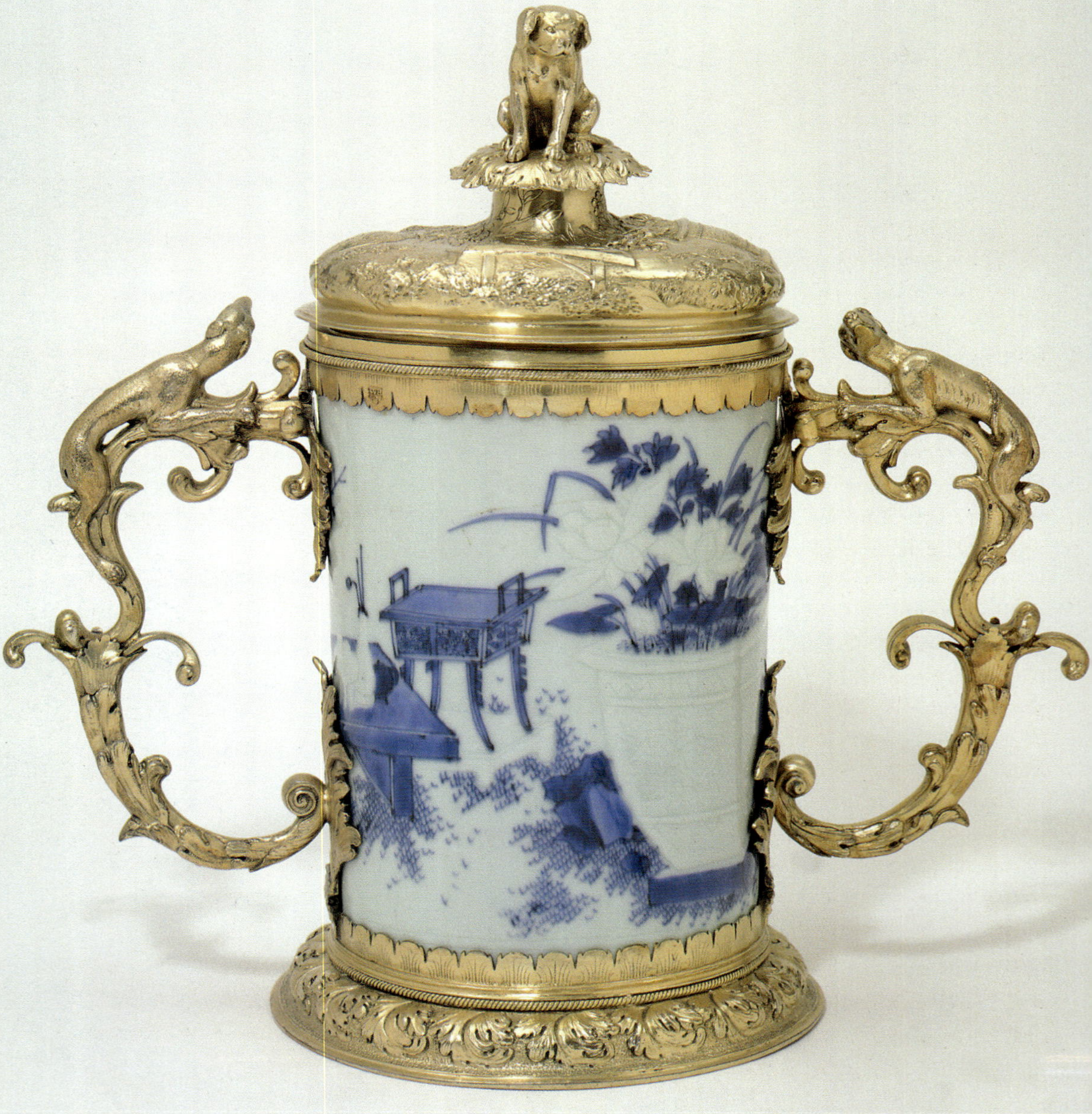

63 *Chinese porcelain jar, Transitional period, 30.5 cm high, silver-gilt mounts by Wolfgang Howzer, London, c. 1665.*

female gender and their new found sexual freedom. In *The Country Wife*, the anti-hero Horner makes lewd references to china which are taken up in *The Plain Dealer*, where the hypocritical Olivia complains,

he has quite taken away the reputation of poor china itself, and sullied the most innocent and pretty furniture of a lady's chamber . . . 'tis now as unfit an ornament . . . as the pictures that come from Italy, and other hot countries, as appears by their nudities.[35]

Nevertheless, some porcelain was found in 'public' rooms such as the dining room of the haberdasher Peter Short, 'with a parcel of China over ye Chimney and Images'.[36] 'Delftware', tin-glazed earthenware, often decorated with chinoiseries in imitation of oriental porcelain , and made in both Holland and England, was also found in London houses: Sir Thomas Davies's closet was decorated with hangings of Indian silk and 'China ware, Earthenware and some small marble statues'; Lady Noell's closet had a 'holland blew Cisterne' and 'two dozen and nine dutch plates'; whilst the Fleet Street bookseller Christopher Wilkinson had 'Dutch ware in and over the Chimney', in his parlour.[37]

Japanese lacquer was also much prized and cabinetmakers in London produced 'japanned' pieces in imitation of Eastern originals. The privy chamber of the Queen Mother, Henrietta Maria, seemingly contained both Eastern lacquer and Western japanning: 'a great China Table' and 'a Lesser Table of Counterfeit China, Two stands of the same'. She also owned 'the Indian Skreene which stood in the Queenes dressing Roome at Somersett house of six leaves'.[38] This screen was almost certainly Japanese rather than Indian. A similar confusion as to description is also apparent in Stalker and Parker's *A Treatise of Japaning and Varnishing*: the preface puffs the merits of Japanese lacquer but elsewhere they refer to 'true genuine INDIAN work'. Of the 'cutts' or patterns at the end of the book, ten have specified uses; with eight to decorate toilet boxes, brushes and mirrors, and two, the drawers of cabinets. Apart from the toilet boxes, much japanned furniture was also destined to furnish ladies' apartments,

Tea-Table, Skreens, Trunks and stand,
Large Looking-Glass richly Japan'd
And hanging shelf to which belongs
Romances, Plays and Amorous songs.[39]

In his will Lord Ossulton left his wife, 'all those pieces of silver she commonly useth in her dressing room . . . and also one Japan Table, Glass & Scritore'.[40] At Ham House, the Duchess of

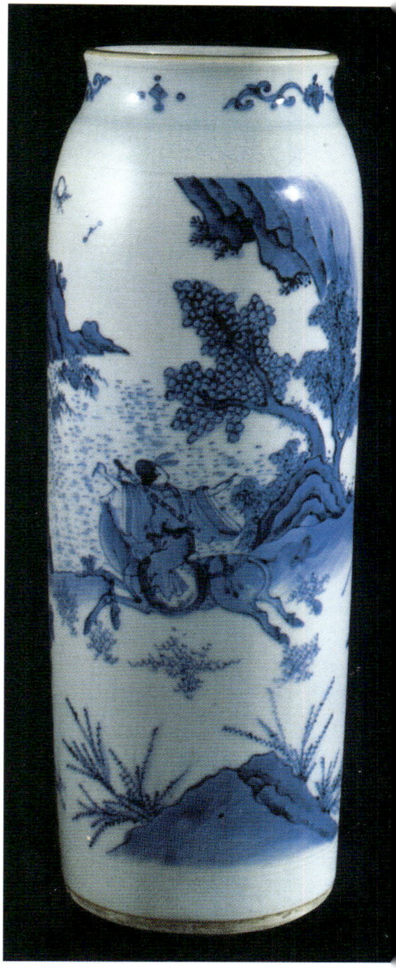

64 *Chinese porcelain 'rolwagen' or sleeve vase, Transitional period, mid-seventeenth century, 25.4 cm high.*

Illus. 65

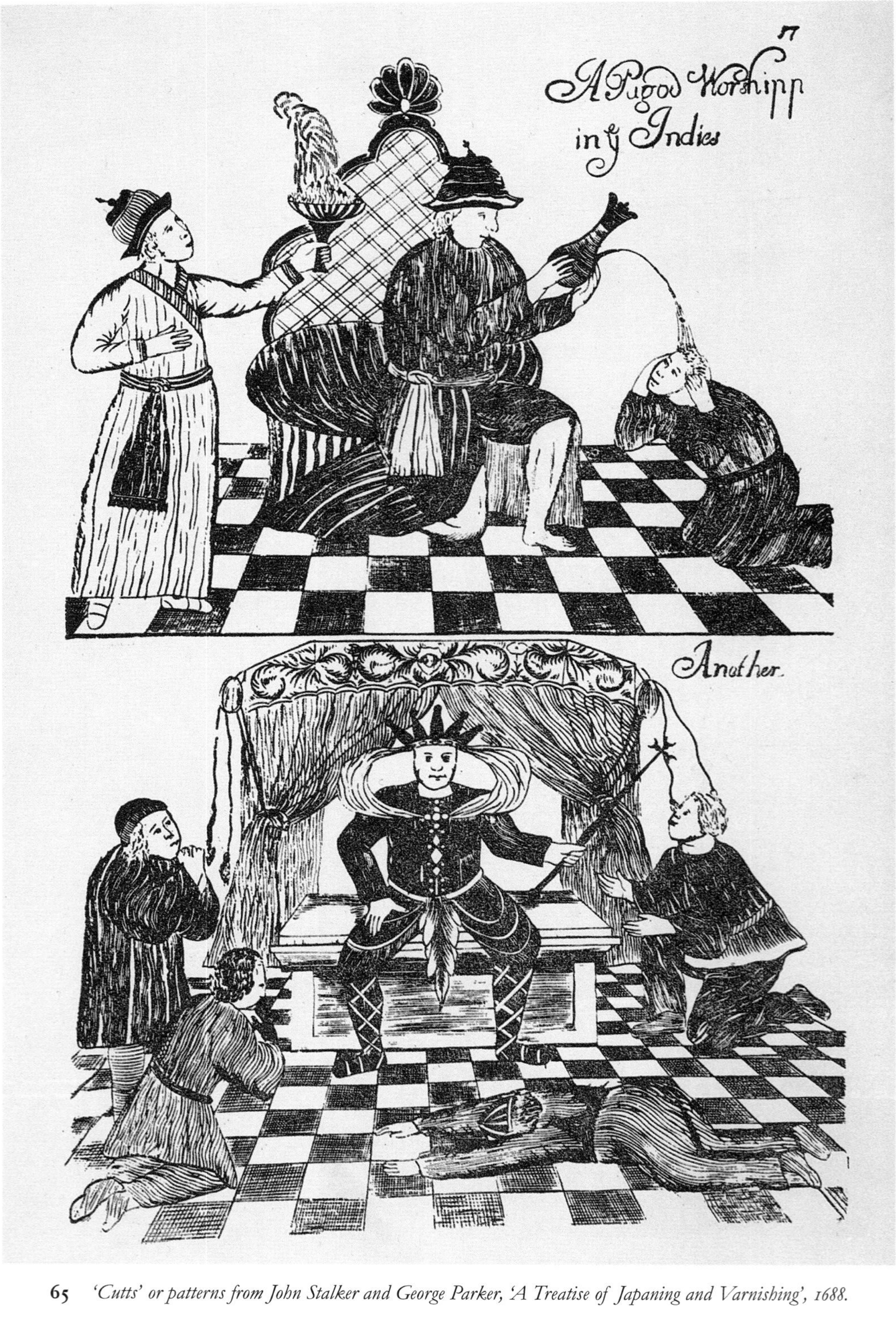

65 *'Cutts' or patterns from John Stalker and George Parker, 'A Treatise of Japaning and Varnishing', 1688.*

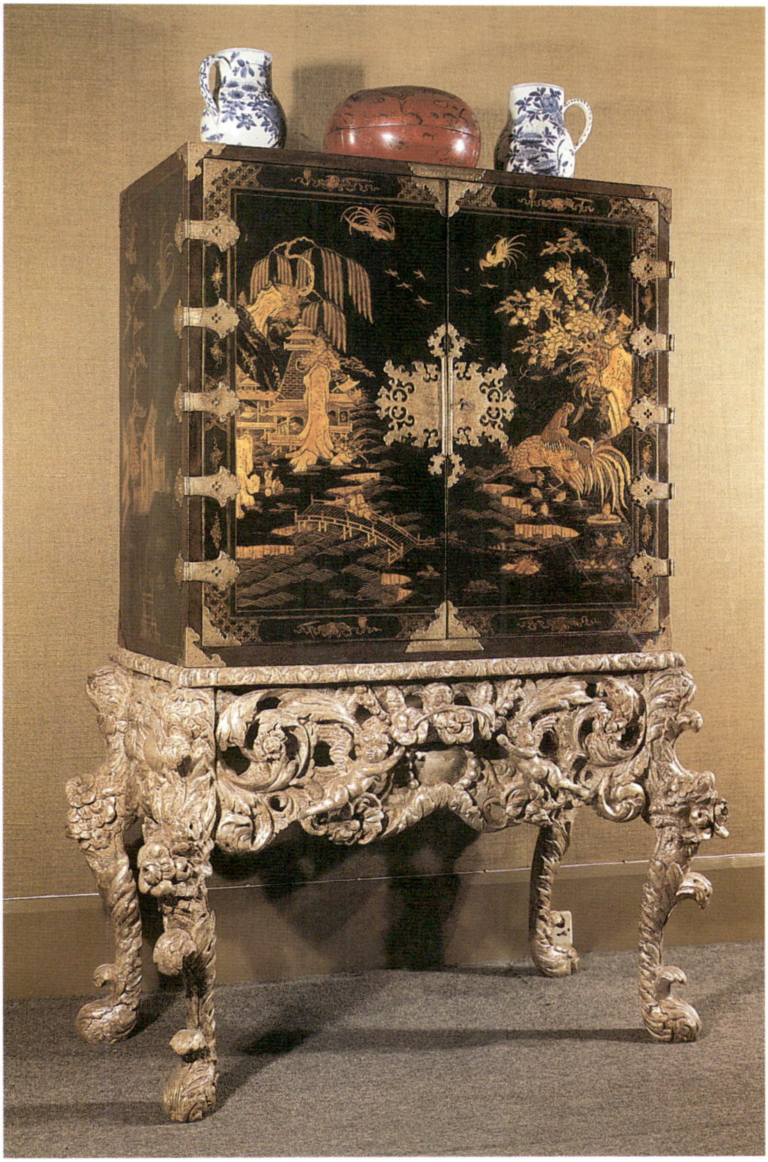

66 *English lacquered cabinet on a carved Baroque stand, probably London, last quarter of the seventeenth century.*

Lauderdale had many oriental artefacts in her apartments, along with japanned furniture presumably made in London. Still surviving are the 'six Japan'd backstooles with cane bottomes' from her private closet which have been described as 'the earliest surviving set of japanned chairs known ... no known oriental chairs look like these and they must be the fruit of a rich Carolean fantasy'.[41]

Compared with porcelain and textiles, the quantities of lacquer and japanned furniture listed in the inventories of the London middling-sort are rather limited, particularly before 1680. Prior to this date, the examples are generally from the private apartments of women and appear to be of imported lacquer: Lady Noell's closet contained a 'Jappin Cabinett', three 'Jappan Trunkes' and an 'Indian Stritore, whilst Sara Howell, whose husband was a turner with a stock of exotic woods, had a 'small India screetore' in her chamber which was hung with 'a sute of pintadoe'.[42] Towards the end of the century, lacquer and some japanned furniture was also found in public rooms: Anne, the wife of Sir Arthur Ingram who imported wine from the Canaries but also traded in diamonds from India, had a 'Jappan Cabinett & Trunke' in her bedroom, but there was a second 'Jappan Cabinett & frame' in the parlour; whilst the Levant merchant Anthony Balam's withdrawing room was furnished with six 'Japan covered chaires' and 'a small Japan Table'.[43] In 1710, the surgeon, Charles Barnard of Cecil Street in the Strand, had Indian cabinets and Japan tables as well as large China jars, beakers and bottles in his best parlour and best dining room, where the settee, chairs and window seats were covered with 'gold Atlas', a silk-satin made in the East Indies which was sometimes striped or patterned with flowers.[44]*

Illus. 66

* Charles Barnard's house also contained a 'Tea Room', a 'Beaufett' and a library of 4000 books. There are considerable disagreements over the definitions of a number of fabrics imported from the East. For the purposes of this paper, they have been taken from the book *Textiles in America 1650–1870* by Florence M. Montgomery.

In Restoration London, mercers and linen-drapers carried considerable stocks of oriental textiles, imported mainly from India, but also from China, Persia and the Ottoman Empire. The mercer, Thomas Cole who dealt mainly in silk fabrics, carried stocks of 'East India and Bengale taffety', plain and flowered 'India sattin' as well as 'Indian Gownes small & great'. Indian cottons including calicoes of fine quality which were mordant-painted and resist-dyed in India, were variously termed: painted calicoes, pintadoes or chintzes. They were sold by linen-drapers, dealing in calicoes as well as linens and fustians, like Thomas Came, Roger Gray and Andrew Kenrick who each had some twenty five lines of East India goods comprising 15 to 33 per cent of their stocks.[45] In contrast, early in the next century Richard Cocke's trade was almost wholly in Indian fabrics which constituted more than 80 per cent of his stock.[46]

Illus. 67

On 5 September 1663, Samuel Pepys wrote in his diary, 'my wife and I to Cornhill and after many trials bought my wife a Chinke; that is, a paynted Indian Callico for to line her new Study, which is very pretty'.[47] London inventories during the 1660s and 1670s rarely refer to chintz, but rather to pintado, which derives from the Portuguese, 'painted': Lady Noell's bed was of 'blew Linsey Woolsey lined with pintado' with a pintado quilt and window curtains and seat furniture 'suitable'; the country houses of John Eaton, the King's laceman had a 'Pintadoe Chamber and Clossett'; and of the

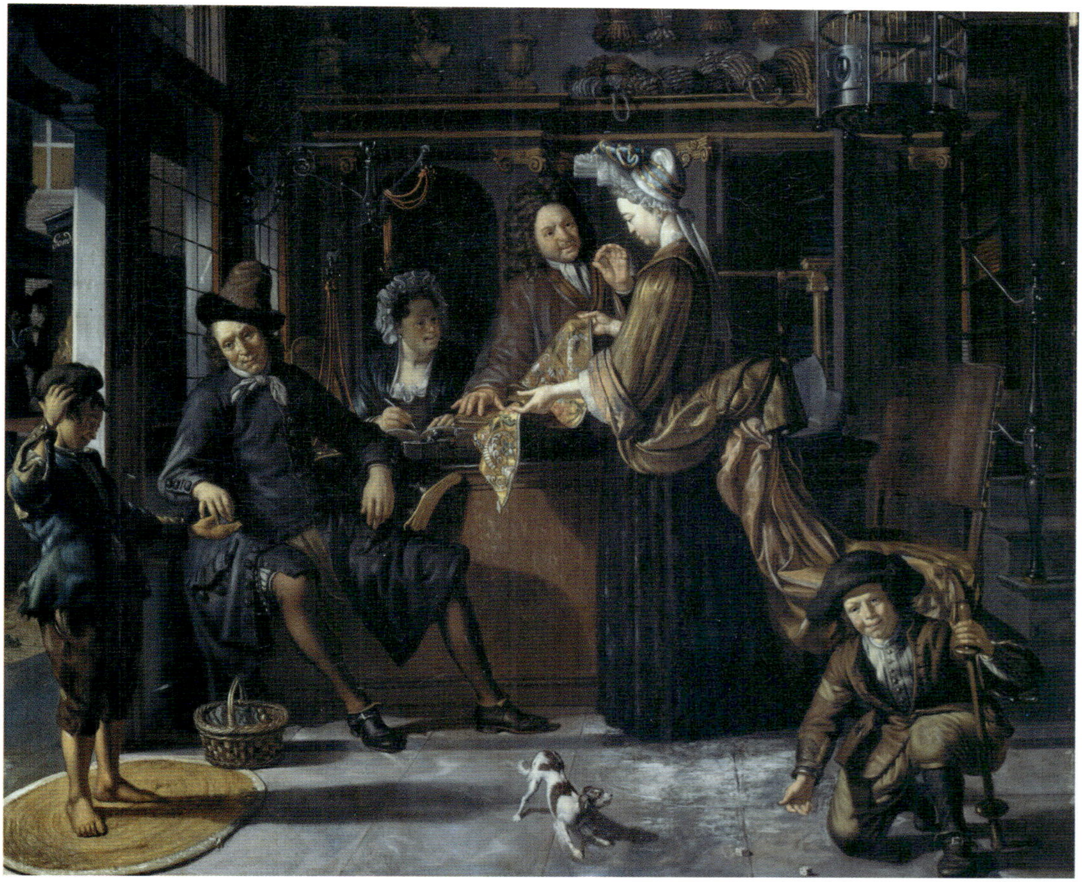

draper, John Wall Esq., a 'Pantado Roome'.[48] Subsequently, the description pintado was superseded by chintz or painted calico: the London house of Sir Thomas Davies had a 'Chint Roome' and that of Thomas Riley, a 'Callico Roome', whilst Michael Davison Esq. and Sir Nathaniel Herne owned sets of painted calico hangings.[49]

Illus. 68

Nevertheless, it would be misleading to suggest that many London houses had rooms furnished with Indian textiles. Indeed, although the apartments of the wives of City magnates often contained oriental porcelain and japanned furniture, their overall decorative schemes before 1700, like those of the aristocracy, generally remained western. For example the chamber of that lover of the exotic, Lady Herne, was hung with tapestries and the bed was of an 'imbroydered cloth furniture lined with Colloured Tabby'.[50] Such décor with eastern goods set within a western framework was commended in *Mundus Muliebris* of 1690, where the apartment was to be furnished,

67 (above) *The Cloth Shop, 1709, oil on canvas by Matthijs Naiveu. A gentlewoman is considering the purchase of a gold-brocaded silk with a swirling floral design. Seated on her left, her husband's function is to distribute money whether in alms to the beggar boy or in payment to the shopkeeper. Although set in Holland, such a scene could have been observed daily in London, at the elegant shops of smart Cheapside mercers.*

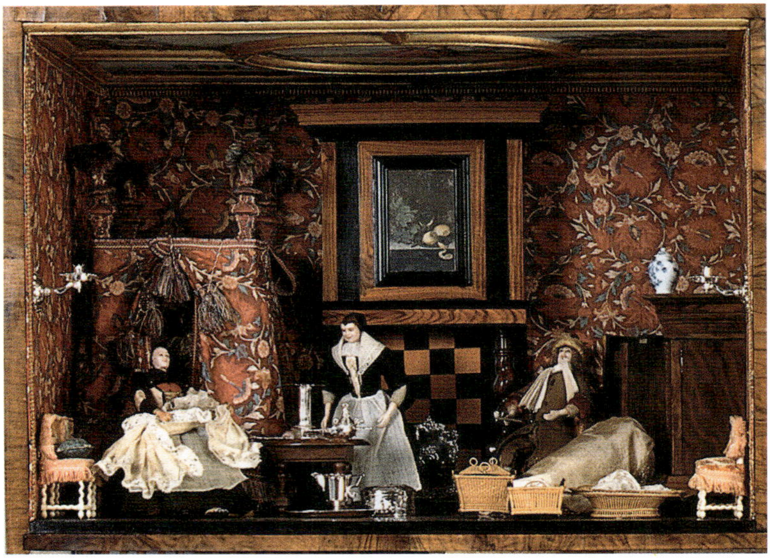

68 *Lying-in room, the doll's house of Petronella Dunois, c. 1676. This fashionable lady's bedchamber has a bed and walls hung with red chintz.*

With Morelack tapestry, Damask Bed,
Or Velvet richly embroidered[51]

Although in such a short paper detailed conclusions are inappropriate, certain general observations can be made. The enthusiasm for exotic decoration was associated with a desire for a degree of informality in private life, particularly among fashionable women, who for the first time had their own apartments where they could entertain their intimate friends. In Restoration London, it was in the chambers, dressing rooms and closets of the wives of City merchants who were also 'of the Town' — entertaining during their toilette and dining in the 'French manner' — that porcelain, japanned furniture and oriental textiles were most commonly found. Further, a significant number of these women had husbands who were major players in the Levant, East India and Royal Africa Companies.

Merchant Clients for the Painter Jan Siberechts

Chapter Seven

KAREN HEARN

In 1995 the Tate acquired a late-seventeenth-century topographical painting by Jan Siberechts, dated 1696.[1] Recent research suggests that it was painted for a London goldsmith banker by the name of John Coggs.[2] Until now, it has been thought that Siberechts's patrons were all members of the nobility. But as this, and Laura Wortley's following paper will both make clear, Siberechts seems also to have been employed by self-made men associated with the City of London, to produce paintings that showed off and celebrated their property acquisitions.[3] *Illus. 69*

The country-house-and-estate image was introduced into England in the later seventeenth century, and within forty years became

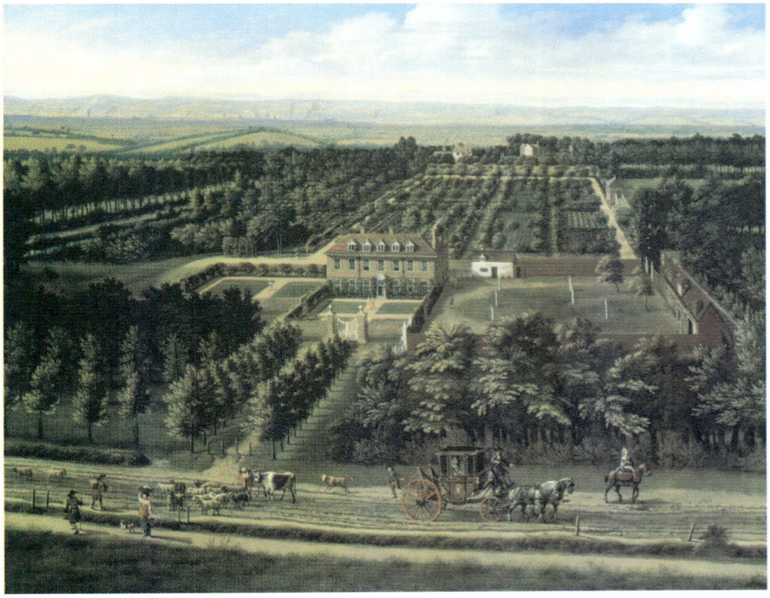

69 *'View of a House and its Estate in Belsize, Middlesex', 1696, oil on canvas by Jan Siberechts.*

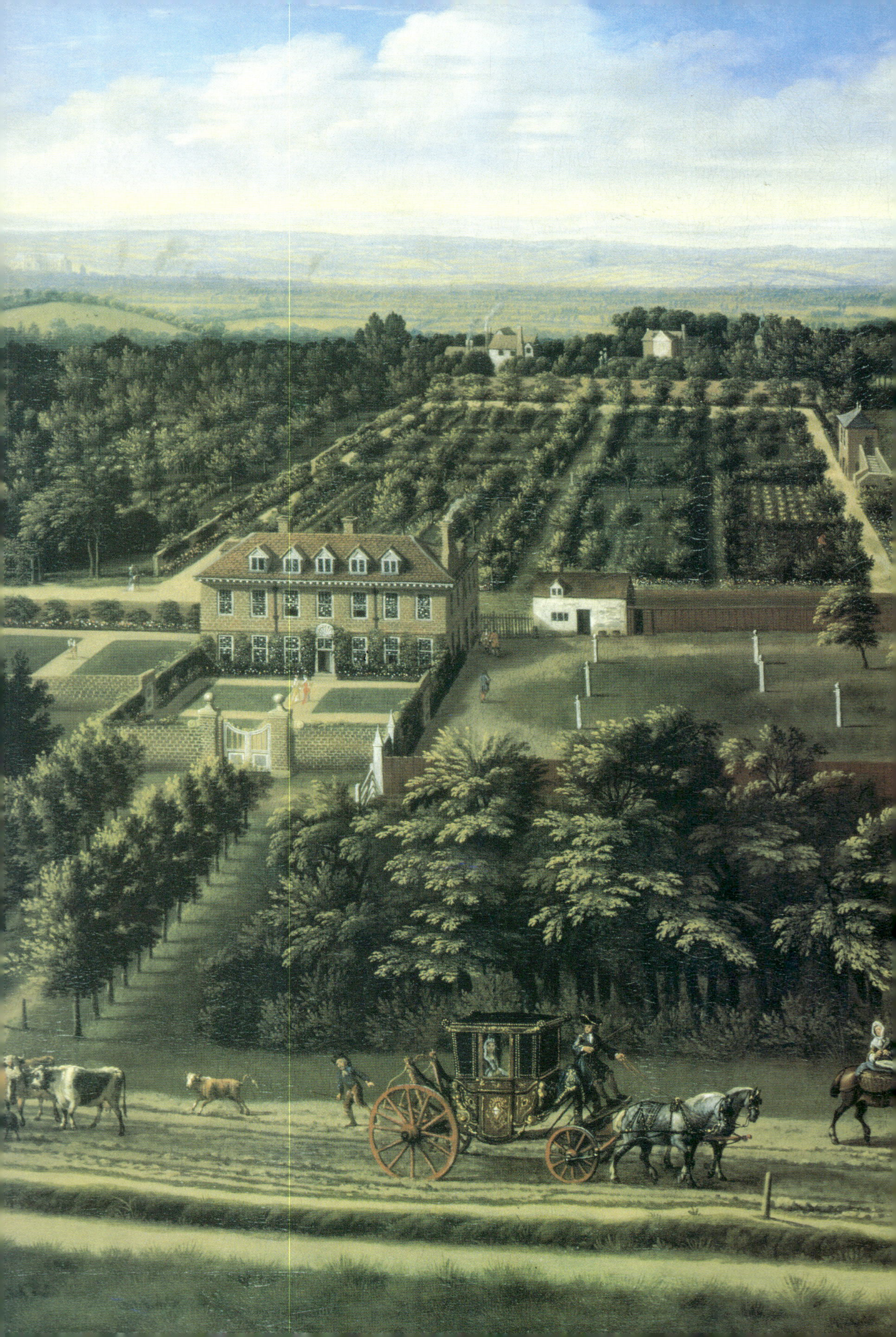

a significant local genre. Some of the earliest bird's-eye views of royal and private estates — engravings in J. A. du Cerceau's *Les plus excellents Bastiments de France* — had been published in France in 1576 and 1579. This precedent was taken up in the Northern and Southern Netherlands, particularly by the printmakers of Amsterdam and Antwerp, and the owners of landed estates became increasingly interested in commissioning engraved or painted records of their properties.* With the Restoration of the Stuart monarchy to Britain, and the return of Royalist families from exile on the Continent where they would have seen such images, market opportunities arose in England for Netherlandish painters of views. The very word 'landscape' was derived from the Dutch 'landschaap' — often written as 'landskip' in Britain. It has been estimated that at least 300 Dutch and Flemish artists came to Britain in the seventeenth century and one of these was Jan Siberechts.[4]

(Opposite and below)
'View of a House and its Estate in Belsize, Middlesex', details.

* In the first half of the seventeenth century, painted views of British royal palaces were an isolated manifestation of house portraiture. They now form a disparate group, some large and elaborate works as the Fitzwilliam Museum views of Richmond and Nonsuch Palaces, others small and less sophisticated, for example the views of Greenwich and Whitehall Palaces at Kingston Lacy House.

SIBERECHTS IN ENGLAND

Siberechts, the son of a sculptor, was born in Antwerp in 1627.[5] It is not known with whom he trained but he became a freeman of the Antwerp artists' guild in 1648 or 1649. Siberechts's Flemish works consist mainly of Dutch Italianate wooded landscapes, with

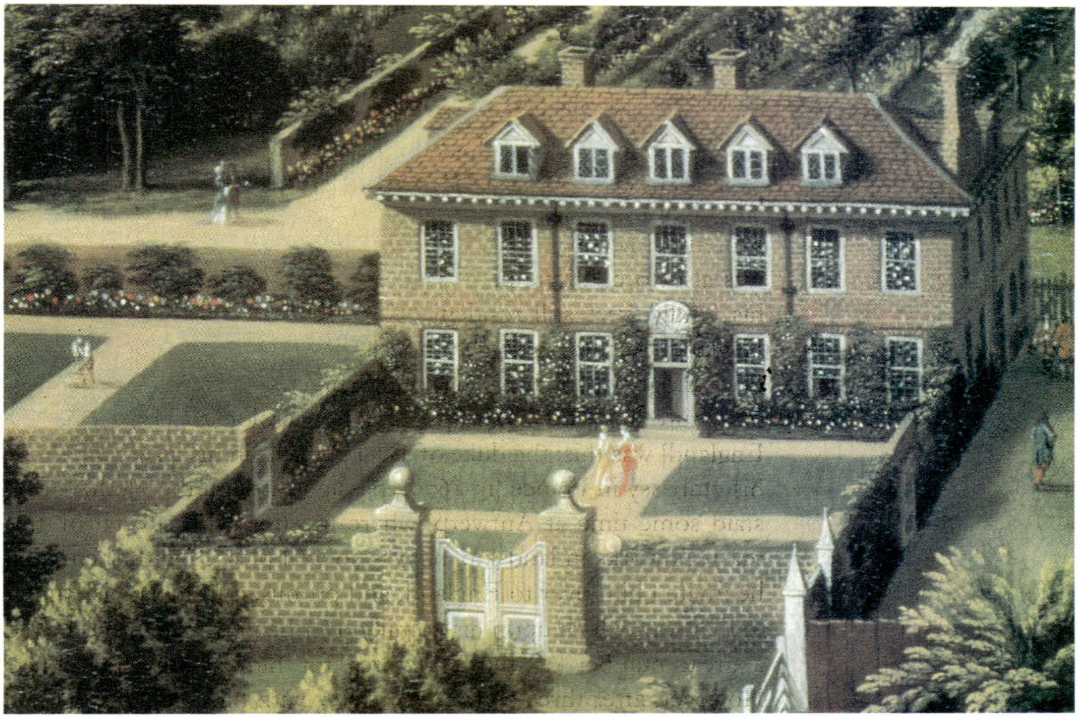

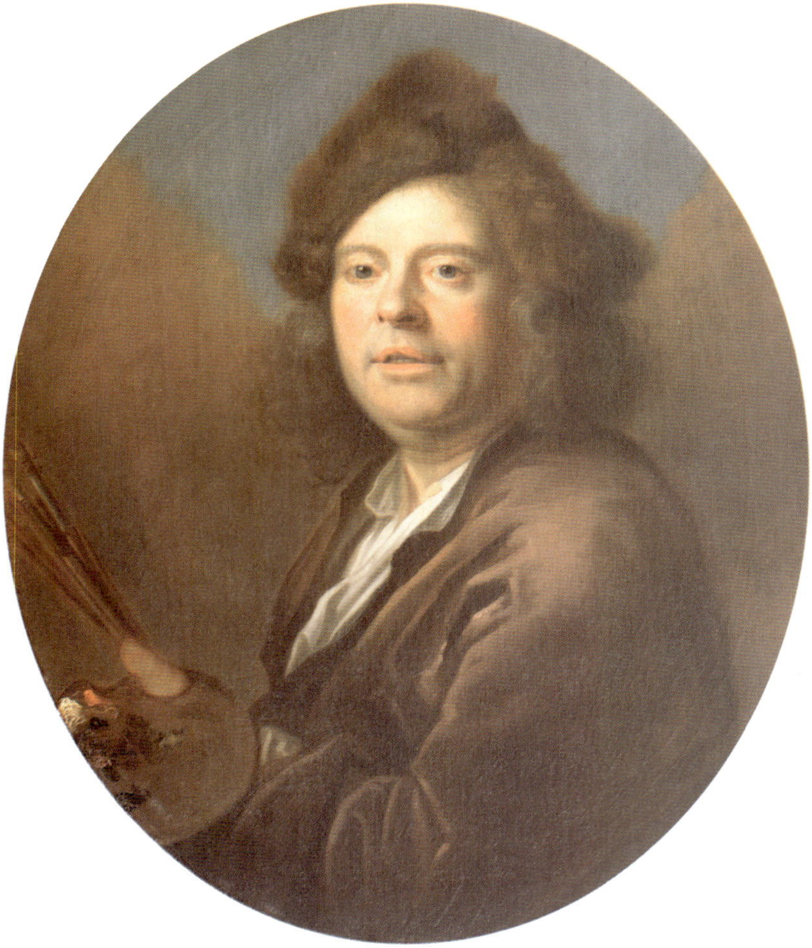

70 *'Portrait of the artist Jan Siberechts (1627–c. 1700)' by Nicolas de Largillièrre who was working in England between 1675 and 1679.*

large figures of buxom peasant girls, often wading through rivers, sometimes accompanied by rustic carts — a type of work which he was also to continue producing in Britain. In March 1672 he and his family were still resident in Antwerp, but by 1674 he was in England. According to the (not-always reliable) author Bainbrigg Buckeridge writing in 1706, 'John Sybrecht ... was a close imitator of nature in all his landskips ... The occasion of his coming [to England] was this: the duke of Buckingham, in his way home from his embassy in France [in 1670], passing through the Netherlands, staid some time at Antwerp, where meeting with several of this master's works in landskip, he was so well pleased with them, that he invited him over to England, and promised to make his Painter in that way; which upon his coming over he performed; and he did a great number of those pictures for him at Cliveden-house: However, after three or four years stay with him, he left him, and performed several pieces for the *nobility and gentry* [my italics] of England, among whom he was for some time in vogue'.[6]

Siberechts's own appearance is known from a painting by the French artist Nicolas de Largillière.[7] None of the works that Siberechts painted for Cliveden is traceable today. George Villiers, 2nd Duke of Buckingham (died 1687) was a powerful patron and a keen builder and garden-maker. So, like many artists and craftsmen of his day, Siberechts was evidently encouraged to come to England initially by aristocratic personal patronage and by the prospect of rich commercial opportunities. *Illus. 70*

Signed and dated paintings by Siberechts of English subject-matter from the years 1674 to 1681 include a group of images for Thomas Thynne, of Longleat House, Wiltshire, and of Cheveley Park, Cambridgeshire, for Henry Jermyn, 1st Lord Dover. In the 1690s, Siberechts may have painted Bretby in Derbyshire for the 2nd Earl of Chesterfield, and he certainly made various images of Wollaton Hall, near Nottingham, owned by Sir Thomas Willoughby, subsequently the 1st Lord Middleton. These were large and substantial houses, belonging to top-level patrons. In 1694 Siberechts seems to have been summoned to Derbyshire by the Earl of Devonshire to paint old Chatsworth house before it was rebuilt. Although that picture is now lost, drawings and watercolours made by Siberechts in the surrounding area in Derbyshire survive in the British Museum, Manchester and Amsterdam.[8] According to George Vertue, writing in around September 1745, Siberechts also painted works — 'Several Landskips' — for William III's powerful Dutch associate, Willem Bentinck, Earl of Portland.[9] These, too, do not seem to have survived.[10] Thus far, it is clear that Siberechts was indeed employed by 'the nobility and gentry of England', as stated by Buckeridge.

THE TATE PAINTING

When the Tate acquired its signed painting by Siberechts, about which nothing is known before 1927, the property that it depicts was thought to be in the area of Highgate, on the outskirts of London.[11] However, that identification was problematic, for the supposed site lay at the wrong angle to Westminster Abbey, which is shown clearly on the horizon in the painting.

Roy Allen, a Camden local historian familiar with the terrain in the Belsize area of north London, proposed convincingly that the building depicted was on the western side of Haverstock or Rosslyn Hill, and thus roughly opposite the entrance to present-day Pond Street.[12] The house in question was subsequently demolished in

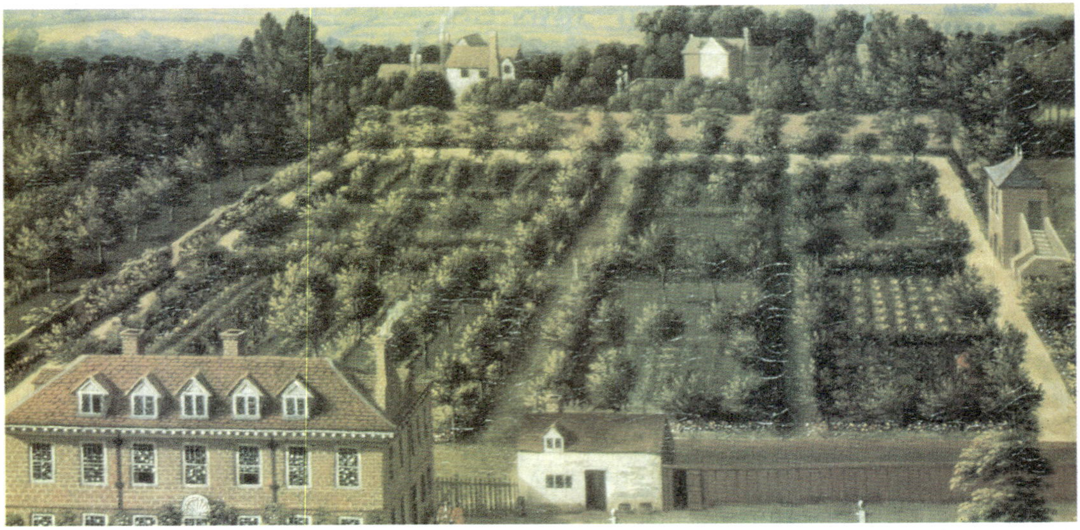

'View of a House and its Estate in Belsize, Middlesex', detail.

71 (opposite) *Map of the Manor of Belsize in 1714. This was drawn just eighteen years after Siberechts painted his view and the document confirms the topographical detail encountered in the painting.*

1770 by John Stokes, who erected another building on the site, which by 1808 was called Rosslyn Grove. In 1881 the Rosslyn Grove estate, whose freehold had reverted to the Church Commissioners, was leased to the Congregationalists who built a church on the corner of Lyndhurst Road and retained Rosslyn Grove as the manse.[13] Today, it is identifiable as the privately owned no. 11 Rosslyn Hill.[14]

Contemporaries noted how the merchants of London were acquiring the best seats in Middlesex for recreation during the summer and as withdrawing places when there were epidemics in the capital.[15]

In 1696, Belsize was four miles north of London, well out in the countryside and, indeed, Siberechts depicts the chimneys of London smoking away in the distance. During the seventeenth century, the entire Hampstead area was considered a pleasant and prestigious country retreat. In the Westminster Abbey archives, a surviving map of the whole manor of Belsize in 1714 shows the layout of a building and grounds of very similar shape to that here depicted.[16] So whoever owned the property in 1696 (the date on the picture) must have commissioned Siberechts to paint it. *Illus. 71*

Since 1317, the entire Belsize estate had been owned by the Dean and Chapter of Westminster Abbey, which probably explains why the Abbey is featured so prominently in the distance in the picture. From January 1661, the Abbey had leased it to a Colonel Daniel O'Neill (*c.* 1612–64). There were, in fact, a number of properties on the extensive Belsize estate, and O'Neill rebuilt and inhabited the main one, Belsize House.[17] The lease on the whole of

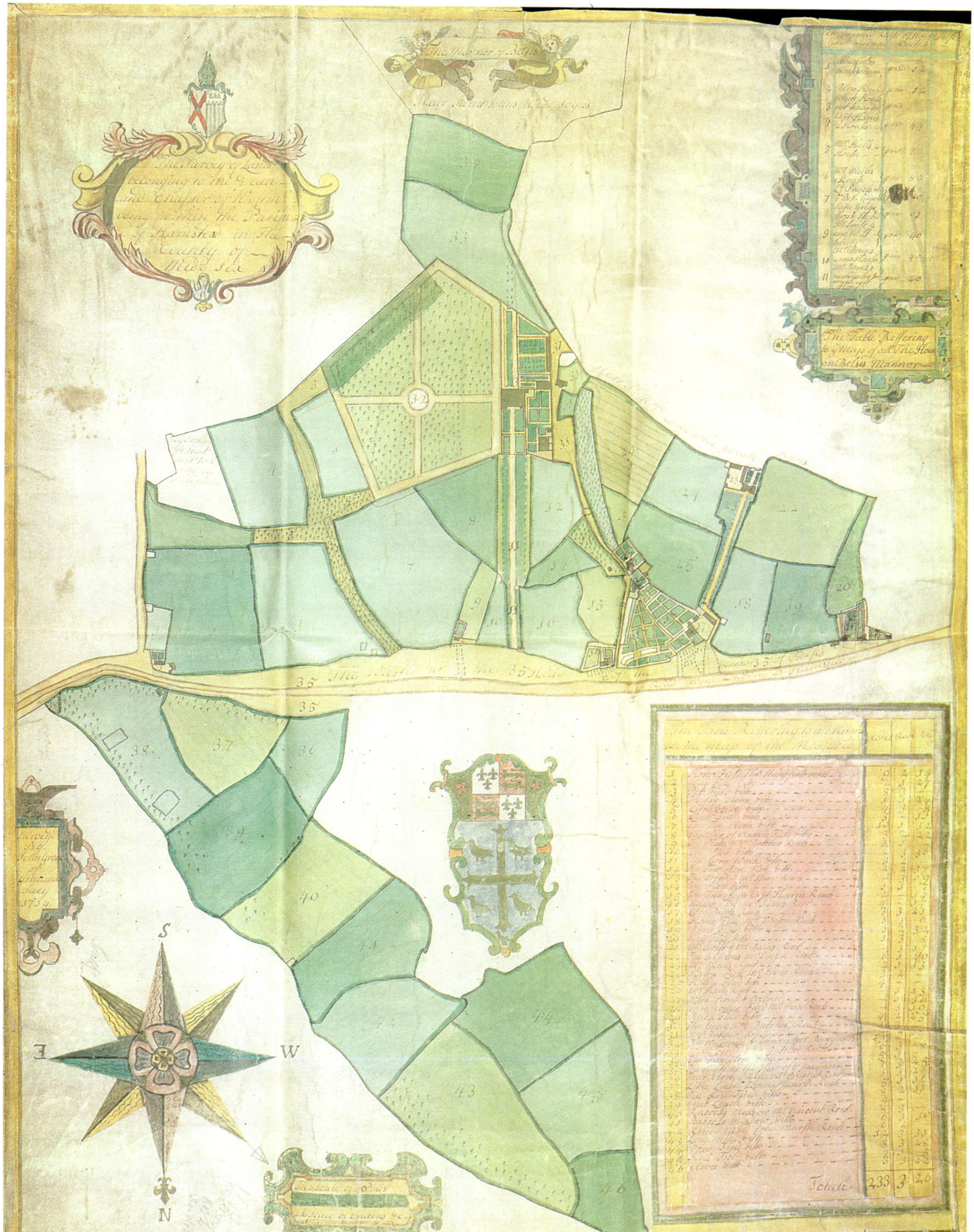
S
E
W
N

Belsize was in due course inherited by his stepson, Philip Stanhope, 2nd Earl of Chesterfield.[18] It is noticeable that Belsize House is not actually visible from the viewpoint chosen by Siberechts — presumably at the behest of his client. The property depicted in the Tate picture was the second most important one on the Belsize estate. The painting shows a brand new up-to-date, small-to-medium-sized house surrounded by trees. Evidence suggests that it is on the site inhabited 60 years earlier by the diplomat Sir Isaac Wake (1575–1632), and subsequently by Sir John Wilde (1590–1669), Chief Baron of the Exchequer.

The history of this house was recorded by John Aubrey, in notes made in about 1690:

Sir Isaac Wake: he had a fine seate at Hampsted in Middlesex, which lookes over London and Surrey, where he made those delicate walkes of pines and firres, also corme-trees, etc. — The Lord Chiefe Baron Wyld had it afterwards. His study was mighty pleasant. The lord de la Ware, who married the daughter and heire of the chiefe baron, sold this seat about 1683 to a citizen of London, who pulled it downe to build a house (1686). The Chief Baron told his cosen Edmund Wyld, esq., that Sir Isaac Wake was the first that planted pines and firres in England. E. W. might have had the study for 8 li. [pounds] per annum.[19]

JOHN COGGS, GOLDSMITH-BANKER

The 'citizen of London' who, according to John Aubrey, rebuilt the house, seems to have been the goldsmith called John Coggs or Cogges.[20] Thus, it was presumably he who commissioned the painting from Jan Siberechts in 1696. Born around 1637, the son of a yeoman also called John Coggs, of Denham in Buckinghamshire, he was apprenticed to the London goldsmith Robert Welstead for seven years beginning on 11 November 1651.[21] Coggs became a freeman of the Goldsmiths' Company on 10 December 1658. Over the period 1666 to 1702 he took ten apprentices including, on 8 May 1702, one also called John Coggs,[22] who was probably his nephew, the son of his brother Daniel, a yeoman of Denham.

Coggs was one of the new breed of goldsmiths, who kept 'running cashes' and acted as bankers to their clients. The goldsmith-bankers used the Goldsmiths' Company's formal system of apprenticeship to train new bankers.[23] The late seventeenth century was the period that saw the birth of the modern banking system.

As David Mitchell has described,[24] two distinct groups of goldsmith-bankers emerged in the mid-seventeenth century — one centred on Lombard Street, serving City tradesmen and overseas merchants and the other in Fleet Street running into the Strand, with a clientele of nobility, gentry and lawyers. Coggs came into the latter group. Few of his records seem to survive, so it has not been possible to discover whether other Siberechts's patrons were also on his books.

On 4 July 1678 Coggs married Martha Stratford (possibly a widow) at the Temple Church, just south of Fleet Street, close to his London residence.[25] There is no record that there were any children of this marriage. Martha was to die on 20 January 1697.*

John Coggs is mentioned from time to time in the Goldsmiths' Company's Court Minutes, for example in dispute with Joseph Fabian over a tankard (21 April 1682) and joining a committee regarding the will of John Perryn (18 May 1683). In 1685, he was elected Third Warden of the Goldsmiths' Company, and Second Warden in 1686,[26] the year in which, according to Aubrey, the house at Belsize was rebuilt. Coggs seems to have secured from Lord Chesterfield a lease on the Belsize property that was to run until Lady Day 1736.[27] He was clearly a man on the rise, and in 1699 he was elected Prime Warden of his Company. In 1703, Coggs was granted heraldic arms.[28]

Coggs's London address was at the sign of the King's Head opposite St Clement Danes church in the Strand,† where he was a church warden.[29] He seems first to be recorded there in 1661.[30] In a warrant of 1 March 1690, 'John Coggs ... esquire' was among a number of men appointed 'deputy-lieutenants of the City of London'.[31] On 15 January 1695, Coggs made a loan of £100 to the Exchequer.[32] From 1696 onwards, he apparently operated in partnership with a John Dann and in the same year — the date on the Tate painting — they were appointed to receive subscriptions to the Greenwich Hospital for Seamen.[33] Coggs and Dann seem also to have acted as bankers to Queen Anne, and various notes to him survive from Sarah Churchill, Duchess of Marlborough, Anne's Mistress of the Robes and Keeper of the Privy Purse. They begin: 'Mr Coggs I desire you to pay this bill ...' and are addressed to him as 'Goldsmith over ag[ains]t St Clements Church in the Strand'.[34] One of Coggs's roles was to supply the gold coins that were to be formally 'touched' by the Queen and distributed to sufferers of scrofula. Thus on 17 December 1706, the Duchess asked him to supply '200 pieces of healing gold' for the following day, 'being the last Touch for this season'; indeed during the year 1706–07 Coggs supplied 1,877 such pieces of gold, usually to be delivered to Kensington Palace, occasionally to St James's Palace.[35]

By early 1710, however, Messrs Coggs and Dann failed, and a meeting of creditors was called for 26 January.[36] Coggs died in

* At this period in England the year was considered to run from Lady Day to Lady Day; thus '1696', the year inscribed on the Siberechts painting of the Belsize property would in fact have run from 25 March 1696 to 24 March 1697.

† This was just outside Temple Bar, which was the recognized entrance to the City of London. In *A Collection of the Names of Merchants Living in and about The City of London* ['The Little London Directory'], published by Samuel Lee in 1677, 'Mr Coggs in the Strand at the Kings-head' is listed in 'an Addition of all the Goldsmiths that keep Running Cashes'.

March 1711 and was buried in St Mary's Church, Denham.* When his business collapsed, Coggs seems still to have been in possession of 'my House &c at Hampstead' (Belsize was considered part of Hampstead), and its contents — 'household Goods' — were appraised at a value of £282 12s. This was roughly the same as the value of the contents — 'My household Goods and plate' — at his property in the Strand, which were valued at £297 13s.[37] Elsewhere, in around January 1710 his 'Dwelling House in the Strand [was] Valu'd at about [£]1,100.'[38] Another document of the same date gives precise particulars of the Belsize house and gardens, and these appear to tally with the details of Siberechts's picture; the house itself is stated there to have cost £3,000 to build.[39] As Coggs's business collapsed, he mortgaged his house to one Joseph Sherwood, who after the goldsmith's death was to sell on the sublease of 'Mr Coggs his owne house', and its contents, to Lord Paget.[40]

* His name was added to the white marble wall-tablet, commemorating his sister Mary (died 1694) and his wife Martha (died 20 January 1697). The additional text describes him as 'John Coggs of London Goldsmith'. It appears that there was neither the impulse nor the money to erect a separate monument to Coggs himself.

But the year inscribed on the painting, 1696, must have been a triumphant one for Coggs. It is understandable that he would want to celebrate his fashionable, recently built country property, and his prestigious connection with the Greenwich Hospital. Such an image of his country retreat would have affirmed his prestige and success.

Stylistically, a precise painter like Siberechts might appeal to a banker because he carefully itemises every detail of the property — cabbage by individual cabbage. One might suggest a parallel with the counting and totting-up of coins! Physical examination of the painting reveals that for some areas Siberechts chose more expensive, long-lasting pigments, indicating that he was working for a patron who wanted no expense spared. The sky area, for instance, is composed of lead white with a very good quality — and thus very expensive — blue pigment called ultramarine. He also used another costly blue pigment, azurite. He was clearly working for a patron happy to pay for the best.[41]

Coggs could have displayed the painting in the house itself — possibly as an overmantel, which was often the chosen position for such pictures. Alternatively, it might have been on view at his house in the Strand, reminding Coggs of his country property. No portrait of Coggs, or of any member of his family, is known to survive. John Coggs himself does not seem to have left a will.[42] Thus all that remains today of Coggs's ambitions is Siberechts's sumptuous image of his elegant new house in a prestigious part of the countryside north of London — an enterprise in which Coggs can be seen as typifying a London City merchant.

City Merchants' Landownership around Henley-on-Thames and the Paintings of Jan Siberechts

Chapter Eight

LAURA WORTLEY

We now move from Middlesex to Henley where Siberechts executed a number of paintings and left another puzzle. The River and Rowing Museum's acquisition in 2001 of Siberechts's painting, *Henley from the Wargrave Road II*, with help from the Heritage Lottery Fund and National Art Collections Fund, prompted this institution to investigate the five known Henley paintings again. *Illus. 72* Signed and dated 1698, the River and Rowing Museum's painting depicts the town from the Berkshire bank and is probably the last of the series. Another version of this view, *Henley from the Wargrave Road I*, incorporating a study of the artist at work drawing the landscape, is indistinctly dated 169–. *Illus. 73* It probably antedates the Museum's picture and acted as a master copy, as is evidenced perhaps by the clothing hanging on the fence to the left of the composition which is omitted from the 1698 canvas, leaving small patches there completely unpainted. Meanwhile two other canvases, *Landscape with a View of Henley-on-Thames* and *Landscape with Rainbow*, depict the scene from the Buckinghamshire bank. *Illus. 74 & 75* Although the first of these is dated 1692, it is probable that both originated in slightly earlier events. Together these four paintings focus on Henley town and it *Illus. 76*

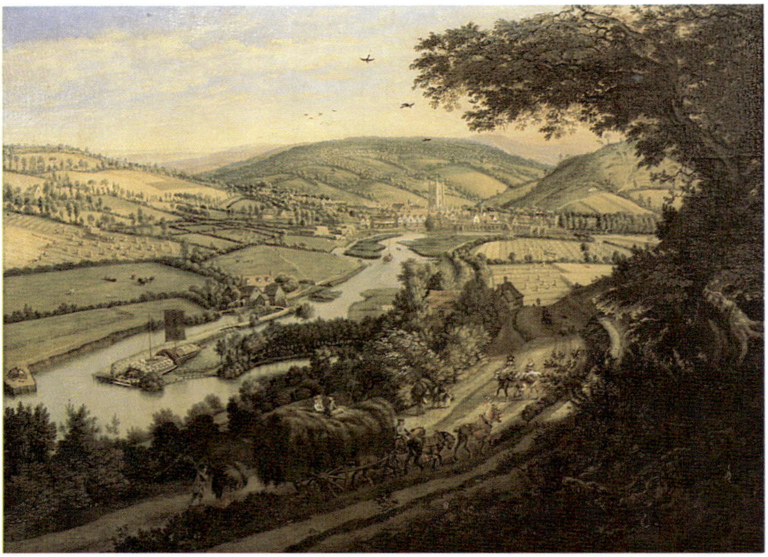

72 *'Henley from the Wargrave Road II'. This canvas is signed and dated lower right 1698 (90.2 × 120.6 cm). The view looks northwest from the Berkshire bank across the flash lock and mill towards the church and bridge. (No. 1 on illus. 76.) Two huntsmen are just visible galloping across the field to the right of the bridge. In all probability, this is not simply the last in Siberechts's Henley series but among the latest works the artist produced. Collection: River and Rowing Museum, Henley-on-Thames.*

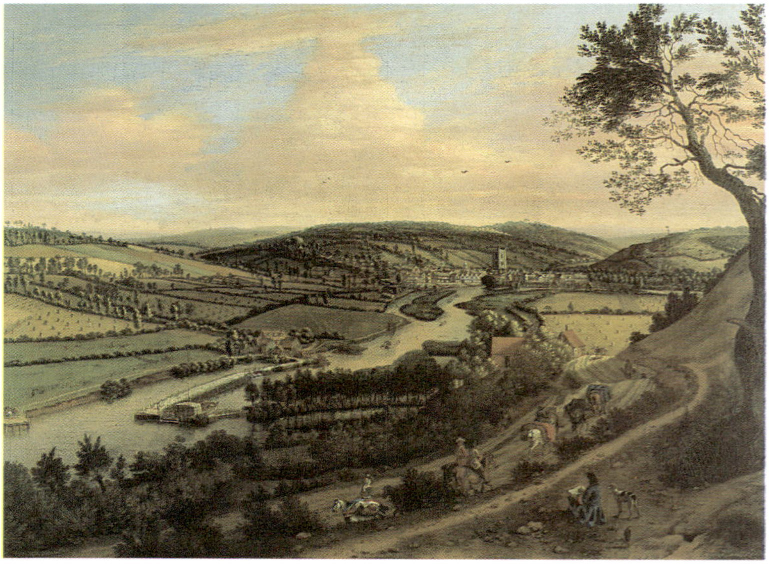

73 *'Henley from the Wargrave Road I'. This canvas is signed and indistinctly dated lower right 169– (83 × 126.5 cm). The artist depicted himself on the right hand side, seated beneath the tree drawing. This is probably the earlier of the two Wargrave Road paintings. (No. 2 on illus. 76.) Private Collection.*

seems evident as much from their subtle differences as from their obvious similarities that their origins were closely intertwined.

AN AMBITIOUS PAINTING

Illus. 77 However, the fifth view, *A Prospect of the Thames near Henley,* is orientated further downstream towards Mill End. While this painting's date, 1697, places it near the end of the sequence, it is undoubtedly the most commanding of all five in size and shape. The portrait format extends the artist's overview to encompass not just a single, enclosed bend in the river but its lengthier meanderings through a wide and fertile landscape. The artist is looking east in a foreshortened view from the Greenlands estate, where the main house was destroyed in the Civil War.[1] This painting differs strikingly from the rest of the Henley canvases, arguably the result of its mercantile rather than local connections, and for this reason it will be the main focus of this paper.

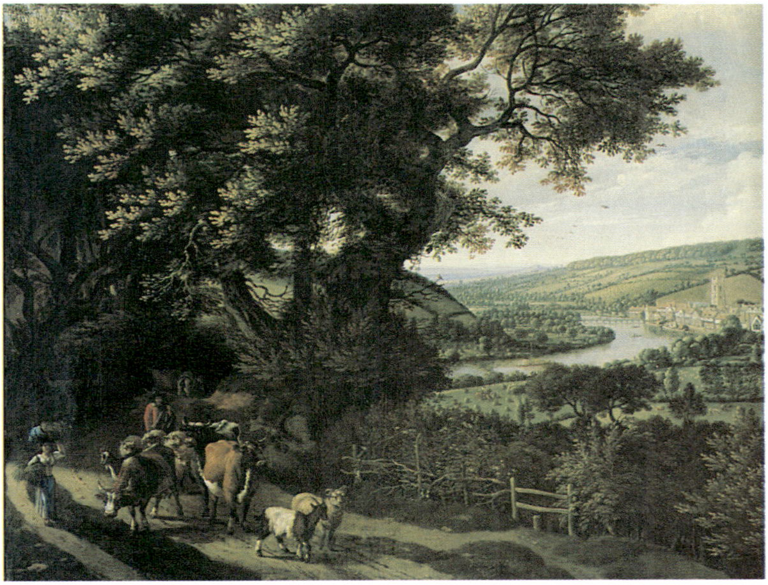

74 *'Landscape with a View of Henley-on-Thames'. This canvas is signed and dated 1692 (43 × 51 cm). Looking southeast from the Buckinghamshire bank, this is the earliest dated and smallest of the known Henley paintings (no. 3 on illus. 76). Collection: the Hon. Michael Willoughby.*

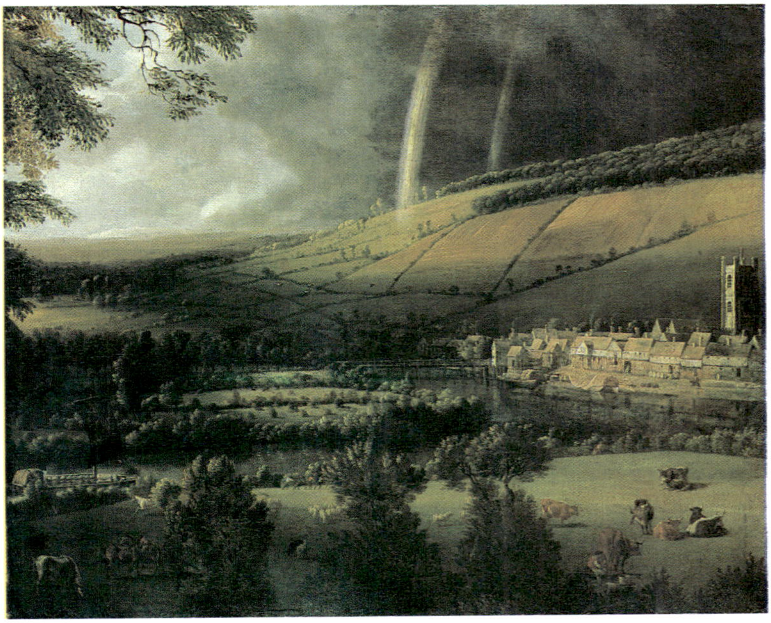

75 *'Landscape with Rainbow'. This canvas is unsigned and undated (82.5 × 103 cm). The painting offers a closer view of the town from the Buckinghamshire bank including a Western barge on the lower left being hauled upstream by a team of men (halers) as well as depicting the sort of buildings on the wharfside which would have been used by merchants trading between London, Henley and further upstream (no. 4 on illus. 76). Collection: Tate, London.*

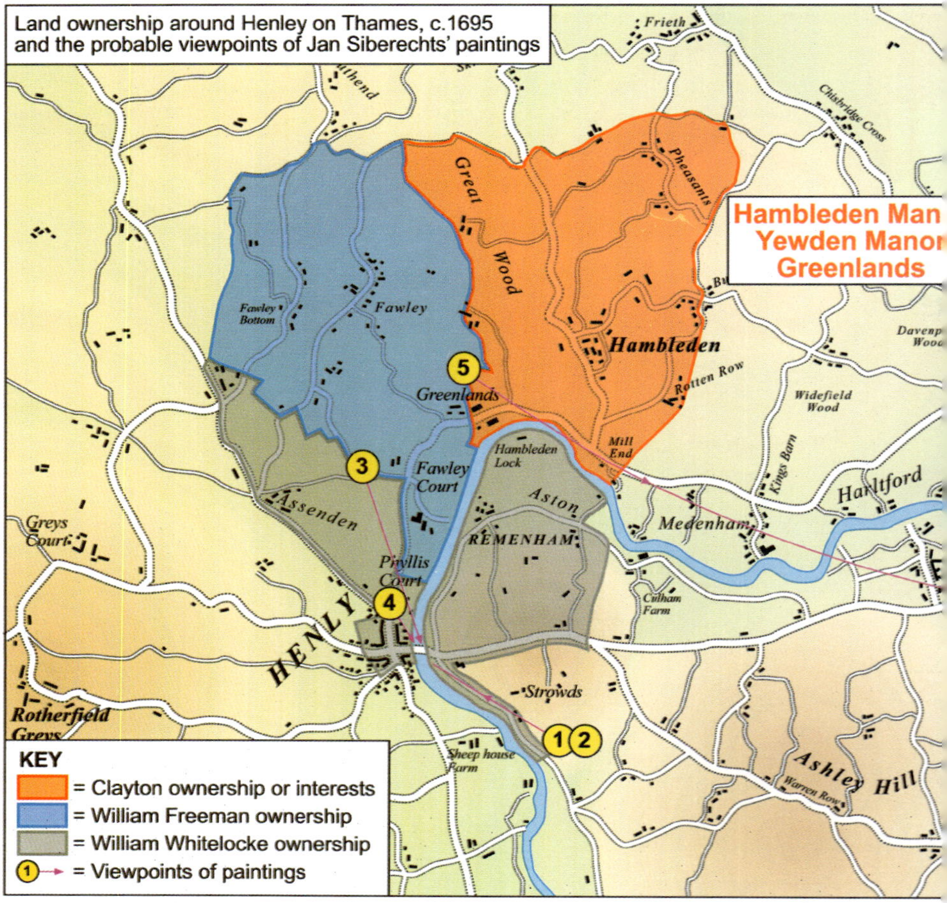

As a group, the Henley paintings pose two questions: who commissioned them, and why? The provenances of all except *Landscape with a View of Henley-on-Thames*[2] are obscure and, with their emphasis on the productive landscape and trading river, the series differs from many of Siberechts's other English paintings which celebrate the power of a single patron as personified by his country house. None of the Henley paintings features any house or estate exclusively and no single aristocratic patron for all five is evident. Instead it seems likely that the series emerged gradually out of the sometimes conflicting claims of neighbouring landowners to property, status and ultimately power. This paper will elucidate some of the complex dynamics of landownership around a town which was probably the most prosperous trading centre on the non-tidal Thames.[3] It will also argue that the wealthy City merchant Sir Robert Clayton could very well be the patron behind Siberechts's ambitious painting.

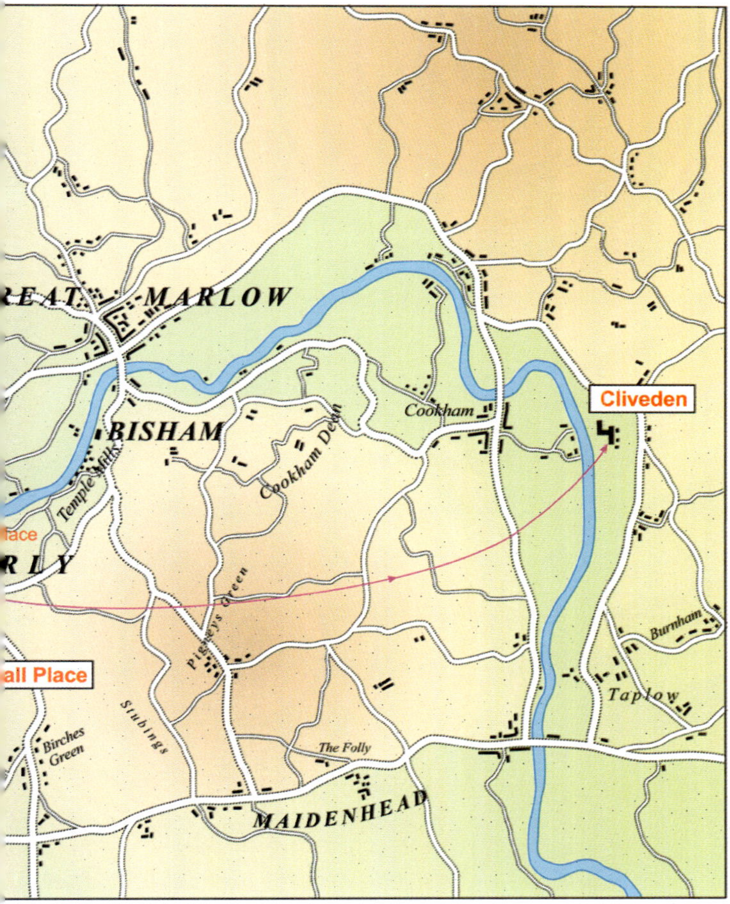

76 *This map summarizes the landownership around Henley-on-Thames c. 1695 and also indicates the probable viewpoints of Jan Siberechts's Henley paintings. This document is based on the 1786 Fawley Court Estate Map in the collection of the River and Rowing Museum and on the 1761 'Topographical Map of the County of Berkshire' by John Rocque.*

LAND OWNERSHIP AROUND HENLEY-ON-THAMES

While City merchants had owned wharves and other property in Henley town since at least medieval times, after the Civil War they became involved in the country estates. Many of these were mortgaged or had changed hands frequently over recent years, a consequence, reflected nationally, of continuing political and financial disruption. Before and during the Civil War the Whitelockes were notable owners of land close to the river and the centre of Henley. A family of eminent lawyers with both City merchant and county connections, they held Fawley Court from 1616, acquired Phyllis Court in 1632, and then the Greenlands and Yewden estates in 1651. The last two were probably bought with money Bulstrode Whitelocke came into through his third wife, Mary, widow of the wealthy vintner, Rowland Wilson.[4]* Bulstrode Whitelocke's position as a prominent Parliamentarian put him under severe financial pressure after the Restoration and from 1661, whilst looking for a sale, he

* Sir Bulstrode Whitelocke, Kt, MP (1605–75) had other City connections too. His paternal grand-father, Richard (d. 1570) was a merchant and his first wife, Rebecca (d. 1634) was the daughter of Thomas Benet, Mercer, Alderman and Sheriff of London.

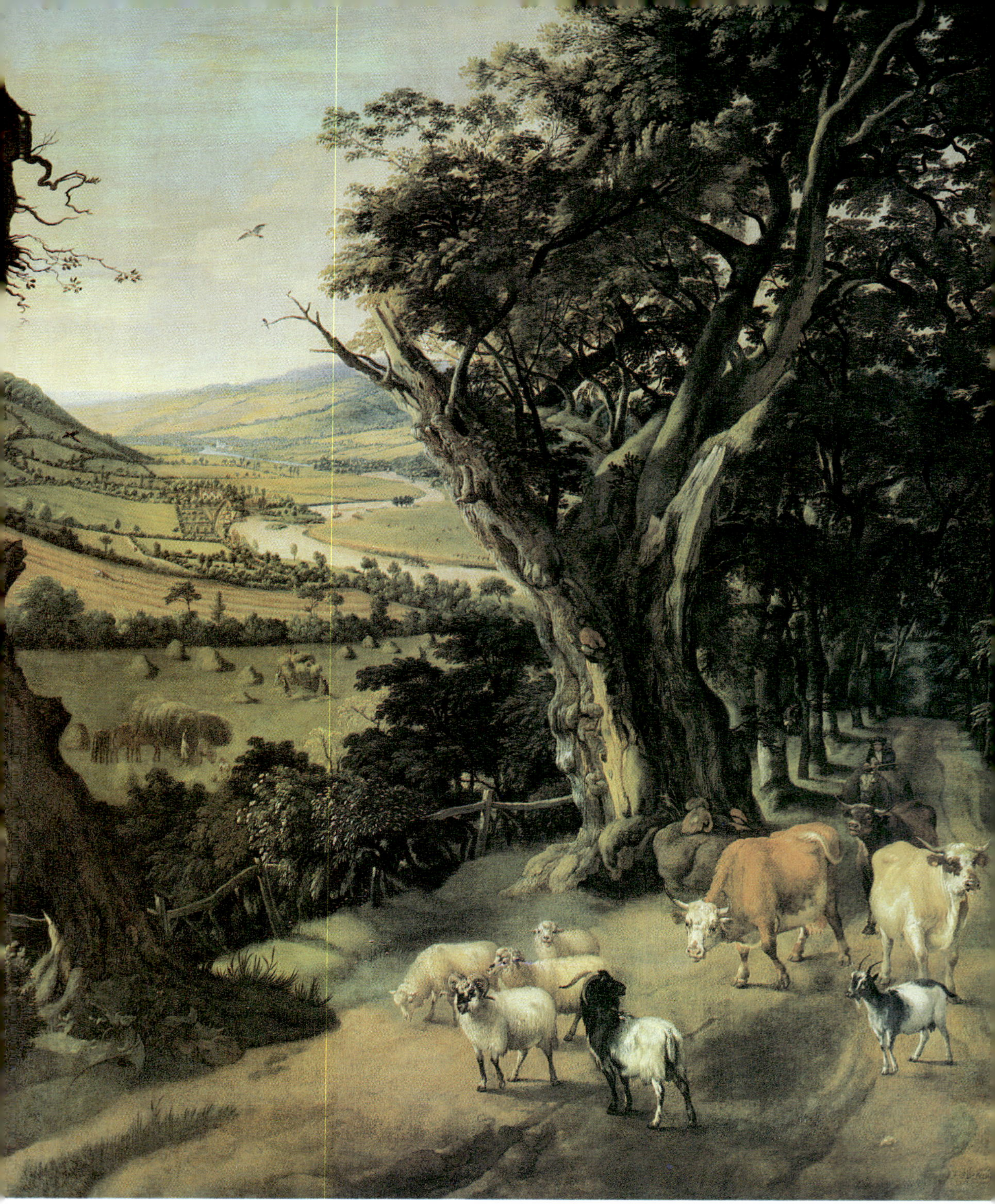

77 *'A Prospect of the Thames near Henley'. This canvas is signed and dated lower right 1697 (181.5 x 161.5 cm). Looking eastwards in a compressed and foreshortened view from the Greenlands estate, Yewden Manor and Hambleden Mill are in the middle distance with Hurley beyond (no. 5 on illus. 76). The Duke of Buckingham's mansion at Cliveden, where Siberechts reputedly first worked in England, would be just over the hills. Private Collection.*

seems to have leased Yewden and Greenlands to a succession of London merchants, among them Penning Alston of the Grocers' Company. A sale was finally concluded with the Alston Trustees in March 1668, shortly before Penning Alston's death, and the following year Yewden and Greenlands passed to Richard Chandler, who was then Master of the Haberdashers.[5]

When Bulstrode Whitelocke died in 1675, his remaining properties were divided up, Fawley Court going to the eldest son of his first marriage, James, and Phyllis Court going to the eldest son of his second marriage, William. Around 1682–83 Sir James Whitelocke, in difficulties possibly over mortgages he had raised on Fawley Court, ceded it to a merchant involved in the West Indies, William Freeman, who replaced the derelict building with a modern house completed about 1687.[6] Although this was then the most prestigious house along the Henley reach it does not feature in Siberechts's series, an omission which might well be significant.

THE CLAYTON–MORRIS PARTNERSHIP

By 1678 the Whitelockes' former estates at Yewden and Greenlands were in the hands of another London alderman, John Morris.[7] He was partner to Sir Robert Clayton, Lord Mayor of London 1679–80. The pair had expanded the money scrivener business of Robert Abbott, their apprentice-master, after his death in 1658, offering not just legal services but acting as bankers and loan brokers too.[8] They profited from the enormous demand for cash during the Interregnum and post-Restoration and, through their mortgage-based credit operation, built up a network of clients among the landed gentry which makes their ledgers read like a gazetteer.[9]* Indeed their credit and land management skills were so well-honed that in 1671 they were appointed to rescue the finances of the 2nd Duke of Buckingham.[10] Thanks to the efficiency of Clayton and Morris and contrary to popular myth, Buckingham actually died a wealthy man.[11]

Greenlands and Yewden were not the first estates round Henley on which Clayton and Morris set their sights. As early as 1671 the 3rd Earl Rivers, a Clayton client and owner of a half-share in Hambleden Manor, was trying to evade Clayton's request for first refusal on the property.[12] The scriveners already had some interests there and by 1678 the mortgage they held on Earl Rivers's share allowed them to install Robert Abbott's son in the Manor House.[13]† When Robert Abbott junior died in 1684, Clayton's brother, William, moved into the house and within two years they had bought out the half share belonging to Earl Rivers's sister-in-law.

* Sir James Whitelocke is among the many whose names appear as debtors in Clayton and Morris's ledgers although as yet it has not been possible to discover whether any of the mortgages on Fawley Court were arranged for him by them. Sir Edward Alston also appears in the ledgers but as a creditor, lending £15,000 in January 1660, which Clayton and Morris passed on to Mr Fairfax, the Duke of Buckingham's brother in law.

† Clayton and Morris apparently skated over Robert Abbott's instructions that the business should be dissolved after his death. In 1670 the younger Robert Abbott contested his father's will unsuccessfully but the family-cum-business relationship was presumably patched up in 1673 when he married Morris's niece, Susannah. The inscription on Abbott's tomb in Hambleden church refers to him as Merchant, Scrivener, 'Cityzen' and 'Late Lord of the Mannor' [sic], although the scriveners did not actually own the whole estate at that date. Abbott probably acted as agent for Clayton and Morris's interests in the Henley area, a responsibility which William Clayton subsequently assumed.

Despite these manoeuvrings it was another ten years, 1696, before the Claytons finally took over Earl Rivers's share and owned Hambleden Manor outright.[14]

Meanwhile, Morris died in 1682 leaving his cousin John Greene in residence at Greenlands and Yewden. For years Greene, a timber merchant, had profited from shipping wood from his wharves at Mill End for the rebuilding of London. Clayton, who inherited all Morris's properties, probably cleared Greene's mortgage on the estates and after Greene died in 1687 Greenlands and Yewden were divided between Greene's two underage daughters.[15]

Sir Robert Clayton owned land on the other side of the river as well, acquiring Hall Place near Hurley during the 1680s and disposing of it in the 1690s.[16] At Hurley too was Ladye Place, home of another Clayton debtor, John, 3rd Lord Lovelace, whose remaining properties were sold to pay creditors after his death in 1693.* A few miles further downstream was Cliveden, the Duke of Buckingham's magnificent new mansion, financed largely through Clayton's deft administration of the accounts and a testament to his, as much as to the Duke's, power.

* In 1695 Lovelace's properties, Remenham Manor, Remenham Farm and Remenham Park, passed to William Whitelocke of Phyllis Court in settlement of the mortgage he had held on them (see *Illus. 76*). This almost casual, old-fashioned form of mortgage between neighbours contrasted with the new style of strictly enforced mortgages which Clayton and Morris initiated.

INTERPRETING A PROSPECT OF THE THAMES NEAR HENLEY

As Karen Hearn has explained it was reputedly at Cliveden, for Buckingham, that Siberechts painted his first English views, though these have not survived. Drawing a sweeping line from Greenlands to Cliveden cuts right through the compressed landscape depicted in the fifth Henley painting across properties in which the Claytons had an active interest from at least 1671.

A Prospect of the Thames near Henley could therefore be regarded as literally turning its back on the small town concerns of the local gentry evident in three of the other Henley paintings. Instead the artist directs his gaze eastwards, not just in the direction of Cliveden but beyond that, down river, towards London, the probable destination for one of the barges in the picture and the hub of the nation's political and commercial life in which Sir Robert Clayton, a prominent Whig, played a commanding part. Indeed in December 1688 it had been he who led the deputation of peers, bishops and Aldermen of the City of London to meet William of Orange at Phyllis Court in Henley and authorize the Prince to issue a call to arms and proceed to London, thus facilitating the Glorious Revolution.[17]

It is tempting, therefore, to speculate whether the fifth Henley painting, so distinct in grandeur and scale from the others, could have been conceived by the Clayton family as a pendant to the Cliveden pictures, an upstream riposte perhaps which might even hold a clue to the lost Cliveden paintings.* Dating from 1697, a year after the Claytons became outright owners of Hambleden and too long after Buckingham's death for accusations of presumption, the commissioning of this canvas would have crowned their long process of acquisition and control in the area. In addition, the artist's enumeration of various income producing aspects of the river and countryside, regardless of seasonality, reads almost like a balance sheet while the absence of any references to hunting or leisure perhaps further emphasizes the Claytons' businesslike priorities and their rigorous maximising of agricultural and other revenue on estates over which they put their agents in control.

* The paintings Siberechts undertook for Buckingham were possibly lost in the fire that destroyed Cliveden in 1795. In any event no details of their subjects, sizes or location in the house have been traced so that they constitute a tantalising puzzle for art historians, particularly as Siberechts had a considerable influence on the development of landscape painting in England.

After the Civil War new farming methods emerged, taking more land into cultivation and reducing the national dependence on sheep. Unlike the goldsmith bankers, Clayton and Morris's business was closely linked not just to land but to agricultural systems, using drovers for instance to carry money and messages safely over long distances. Clayton also promoted balancing the acreage devoted to arable crops with the rearing of sufficient stock to produce a sustainable return on investment over the long term.[18] *A Prospect of the Thames near Henley* with its hayfields, cornfields, pasturage, woodland, orchards and stock illustrates this sort of productive agrarian diversity. The riverside mill, in which corn was ground, and the timber stacked by the wharf, awaiting transport to London by Western barge, both represent land being turned into cash through agriculture and trade. The absence of hunting suggests that whoever commissioned the painting eschewed the more usual preoccupation of such patrons, including some of those in Henley, with the chase and establishing aristocratic status. The painting thus seems to overturn the usual conventions, presenting money rather than aristocratic lineage as the ultimate source of power.

LAND ACQUISITION AND THE ART OF TOPOGRAPHY

Described by John Evelyn as 'this Prince of Citizens', Sir Robert Clayton's fortune far exceeded the other Henley landowners'.[19] Though his own country estate was at Marden Park in Surrey and he never lived in Henley himself, his brother's eldest son was brought up at Hambleden and groomed as heir to the broking business.[20] The family's vast land holdings nationally, their involvement in innumerable land transactions and their association with Buckingham and other owners of Siberechts's paintings, such as John Coggs (see p. 90) whose rent books they held, make some sort of linkage between them and Siberechts seductive, though as yet unproven.[21] Not only must bankers and artists have cultivated overlapping networks of clients among merchants and landowners, but the Claytons' immense wealth depended on their novel system of surveying and valuing distant estates accurately for mortgage, a process parallel perhaps to the topographical artist's detailed assessment of an unfamiliar landscape.

This parallel may not be altogether fanciful. Clayton and Morris could risk lending unprecedentedly large sums on mortgage because they transformed the existing, vague, estate particulars into reliable valuations. This was achieved in part by having their agents physically measure the acreage in question and record its characteristics so that the income potential could be assessed dispassionately, a practice that had not been undertaken before.[22] Clayton clearly recognized that such accurate observation could also have wider benefits for he was instrumental in persuading Charles II in 1673 to set up the Royal Mathematical School at Christ's Hospital so that pupils, particularly the future seamen, could be trained in trigonometry, navigation, cartography and drawing. Furthermore, as one of the school's governors, Clayton would have been involved in the discussions concerning the relationship between mathematics and design which led to a slight change of emphasis in studies there and added topographical drawing to the curriculum in 1696.[23] Meanwhile the portrait of Sir *Illus. 106* Robert Clayton as Lord Mayor of London, *circa* 1680, by Lorenzo da Castro, now in the Bank of England, also incorporates a bird's-eye view of Marden Dock which deserves more detailed consideration in this context.

The research presented here is part of a wider investigation into all Siberechts's Henley paintings which is still in progress. Much depends on tracing their individual provenances back to the 1690s but what has already emerged has revealed the Claytons' (and other London merchants) probably decisive influence over the landscape Siberechts was painting in and around Henley-on-Thames. Examining the area's other City connections in greater depth could add a worthwhile dimension to our future studies.

I would like to thank Jane Bowen at the River and Rowing Museum, Henley-on-Thames and Karen Hearn at Tate Britain for their interest and support.

A City Artist: Robert Robinson

Chapter Nine

JAMES A. GANZ

But why should we be so unjust to ourselves, as to think we stand in need of an excuse, for pretending to the honour of a school of Painters as well as the French, who have been in possession of it almost as long as the Italians. You know, Sir, by the many beautiful pieces you have seen of the principal masters of both nations, that if they have had their Vouets, their Poussins, and le Bruns, we have had our Fullers, our Dobsons, and our Coopers.

This passage, at once poignant and portentous, occurs in the dedication by Bainbrigg Buckeridge to Robert Child of his *Essay Towards an English School of Painters* of 1706.[1] Buckeridge's addendum to Roger de Piles's *Abrégé de la vie des Peintres* was an earnest attempt to document and commemorate the achievements of the generations of artists active in England from the arrival of Hans Holbein to the early years of the eighteenth century. While historians of seventeenth-century English art remain indebted to Buckeridge for helping to fill the considerable void with which they must contend, they cannot help but lament his decision to exclude artists still active as his manuscript went to press: 'I would not meddle with those masters that are living,' he explained, 'as well knowing that it is a tender affair, and not to be touched without running the risque of giving general offence.'[2]

One of Buckeridge's most unfortunate exclusions was the Painter-Stainer Robert Robinson (1651–1706), whose ubiquity in the City of London's art world from the mid-1670s to the early 1700s was as striking as the obscurity into which he fell after his presumed death in 1706. Like many of his contemporaries, Robinson was an artist of multiple specialties, an entrepreneur whose activities ranged from painting small easel pictures and decorative schemes to stage painting, mezzotint engraving, and print selling. The process of piecing together the details of Robinson's professional life and reconstruction of his oeuvre, begun by Edward Croft-Murray and continued by the present writer, have made it possible to put a face on a class of painter who thrived in the bustling picture trade of the 1690s.[3] Although relatively few of Robinson's easel pictures and decorative schemes have come to light, his large body of mezzotints aids in the reconsideration of his painted oeuvre. His prints also give compelling insight into the taste for art among their middle- and upper-middle class consumers, many of whom were likely to have been City merchants.

ROBINSON AND THE PAINTER-STAINERS' COMPANY

Robinson was the archetypal member of the Painter-Stainers' Company, which maintained a stronghold on the City's painting industry until the late seventeenth century. His admission to the Company by payment of a fee in May 1674, indicates that he possessed the appropriate credentials, equivalent to the completion of a seven-year apprenticeship. One could not normally obtain such credentials without servitude to a Painter-Stainer, and the supremacy of the guild during this era made it difficult, if not impossible, to gain independent experience as a painter within its jurisdiction. Robinson's admission by redemption almost certainly places his training outside the City limits, but how far outside remains a frustrating open question. There is some reason to believe that he came to London from the area around Belvoir Castle, in Leicestershire, where Edward Pierce (active 1630 – d. 1658), the painter of the Hunting Room at Wilton, was employed in the redecoration of Belvoir Castle after the Civil War.[4]

The archives of the Painter-Stainers' Company preserve an important record of Robinson's professional activity, and allow us to trace his ascension from his admission in 1674 to his election to the Livery, a position of seniority within the guild, in 1682. One of his duties as a Liveryman was to participate in regular expeditions through various zones of the City seeking to uphold standards of craftsmanship by impounding specimens of defective painting. Everything from shop signs to easel paintings fell within their purview. These search and seizure missions remained the Company's primary means of asserting its authority beyond the ranks of its membership, and occasionally provoked violent confrontations. A case in point was an incident that took place in August 1684, when the Minutes Book records that it was 'Ordered that Mr. Kneller be prossecuted [sic] at ye Charge of the Company for Assaulting Mr. Robinson upon ye search.'[5]

The Binding Book of the Painter-Stainers' Company records the apprenticeship of ten young men to Robinson between 1675 and 1699. The contract of indenture of one George Allison of St Martin-in-the-Fields, bound to him on 11 August 1692, is of

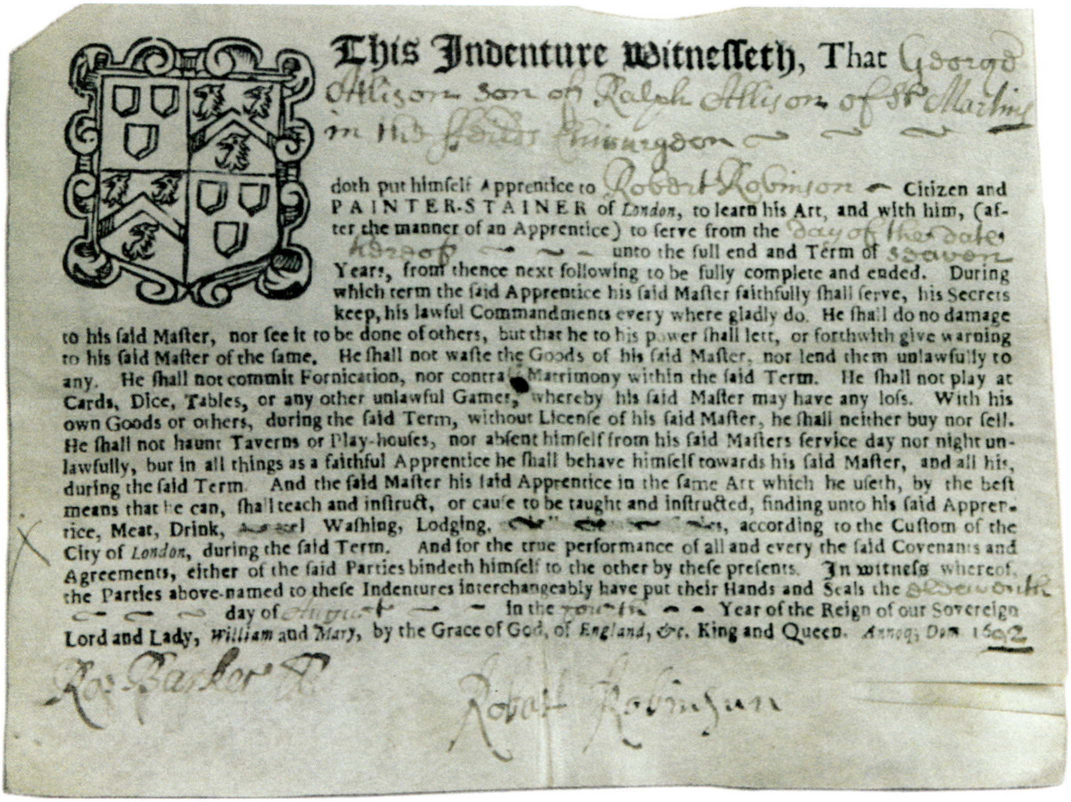

This Indenture witnesseth, That George Allison son of Ralph Allison of St Martins in the fields Chirurgeon
doth put himself Apprentice to Robert Robinson Citizen and PAINTER-STAINER of *London*, to learn his Art, and with him, (after the manner of an Apprentice) to serve from the day of the date hereof unto the full end and Term of seaven Years, from thence next following to be fully complete and ended. During which term the said Apprentice his said Master faithfully shall serve, his Secrets keep, his lawful Commandments every where gladly do. He shall do no damage to his said Master, nor see it to be done of others, but that he to his power shall lett, or forthwith give warning to his said Master of the same. He shall not waste the Goods of his said Master, nor lend them unlawfully to any. He shall not commit Fornication, nor contract Matrimony within the said Term. He shall not play at Cards, Dice, Tables, or any other unlawful Games, whereby his said Master may have any loss. With his own Goods or others, during the said Term, without License of his said Master, he shall neither buy nor sell. He shall not haunt Taverns or Play-houses, nor absent himself from his said Masters service day nor night unlawfully, but in all things as a faithful Apprentice he shall behave himself towards his said Master, and all his, during the said Term. And the said Master his said Apprentice in the same Art which he useth, by the best means that he can, shall teach and instruct, or cause to be taught and instructed, finding unto his said Apprentice, Meat, Drink, ~~Apparel~~ Washing, Lodging, ~~and all other Necessaries~~, according to the Custom of the City of *London*, during the said Term. And for the true performance of all and every the said Covenants and Agreements, either of the said Parties bindeth himself to the other by these presents. In witness whereof, the Parties above-named to these Indentures interchangeably have put their Hands and Seals the eleventh day of August in the fourth Year of the Reign of our Sovereign Lord and Lady, *William* and *Mary*, by the Grace of God, of *England*, &c. King and Queen. *Annoq; Dom* 1692

Ro: Barker

Robert Robinsun

special interest, since it is the only original document from the inception of his servitude, and bears the autograph signature of the artist.[6] Robinson's orthography is unusual; he signs his name 'Robinsun,' and this spelling appears on several of his prints and at least one of his paintings. This indenture slip also includes two interesting modifications to the standard covenant: in the list of amenities that the master is to provide his apprentice, the words 'apparel' and 'all other necessaries' were struck out. These amendments, combined with other clues in the rate books and parish records, suggest that Robinson and his family remained itinerant members of the middle class, moving among and occasionally rising to serve a more fashionable public, but never themselves rising beyond the rank of commoners.

Illus. 78

78 (above) *Contract of Indenture of George Allison, son of Ralph Allison of St Martin-in-the-Fields, Chirurgeon, to Robert Robinson, 11 August 1692 (note Robinson's signature). Allison completed his apprenticeship and was made free in 1699.*

THE MARKET FOR PICTURES

Although their names are unknown, the primary market for Robinson's easel pictures consisted of City merchants and their peers. Carol Gibson-Wood's study of probate inventories dating from 1695 to 1715 reveals the extent to which middle-class Londoners

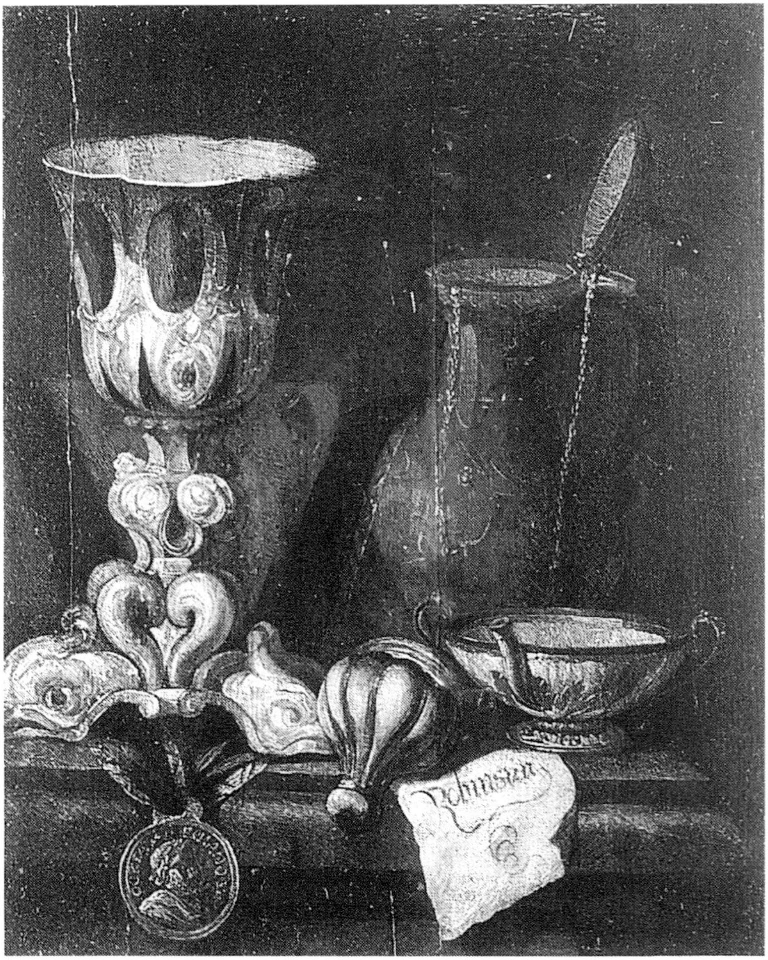

79 *'A Silver-Gilt Tazza, a Medallion, a Ewer, and a Sheet of Paper on a Ledge', oil on panel by Robert Robinson, sold at Christie's South Kensington, on 19 October, 1995, present whereabouts unknown. The silver-gilt tazza in this painted still life never existed; Robinson constructed it from motifs lifted from a series of Dutch silver designs.*

— including mercers, grocers, ironmongers, and chandlers — decorated their homes with modestly valued paintings.[7] Many of these paintings were acquired in public auctions, the best record of which is an extraordinary volume of sales catalogues dating from May 1689 to March 1692 in the British Library.[8] City auctioneers Edward Millington, Ferdinando Verryck, John Bullord and others conducted frequent sales in such popular venues as the Barbadoes Coffee-House opposite the Royal Exchange and the King's Arms Tavern in the Strand. The catalogues contain more than one hundred pictures attributed to Robinson, the majority of which are described as still lifes.[9] His banquet pieces, overflowing with fresh and candied fruits, oysters, lobsters, fish, and game, would have been especially appealing to his target audience, given the centrality of feasts and banquets to the life of City merchants.

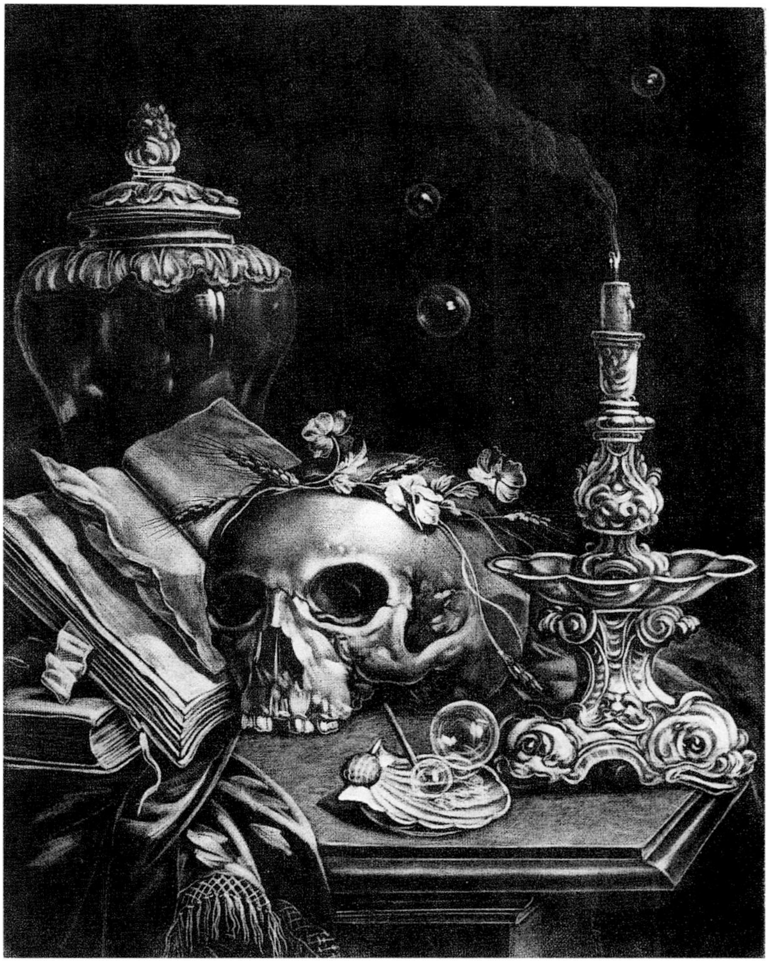

80 *'Vanitas Still Life', c. 1685–88, mezzotint with burin by Robert Robinson. The combination of objects in this mezzotint follows long-established formulas for painted vanitas still lifes.*

STILL-LIFE SUBJECTS

While Robinson's painted still lifes have all but disappeared, *A Silver-Gilt Tazza, a Medallion, a Ewer and a Sheet of Paper on a Ledge* *Illus. 79* surfaced on the London art market during the mid-1990s.[10] The modestly-scaled panel demonstrates the artist's awareness of the kinds of pictures painted by émigrés Pieter van Roestraten, Edward Collier, and Simon Verelst in a genre elevated to the heights of perfection and popularity by the Dutch. Robinson's still lifes mingle recognizably English silver articles — tankards and plates — with more ornate objects of Dutch design copied from engravings. The dolphin base of the tazza, for instance, derives from a plate in the van Vianen family's *Constighe modellen van verscheijden silvere vasen* (Artistic Models of Various Silver Vases) (*c.* 1650).[11] A *Vanitas Still Life* mezzotint of the mid-1680s incorporates an elaborate baroque *Illus. 80*

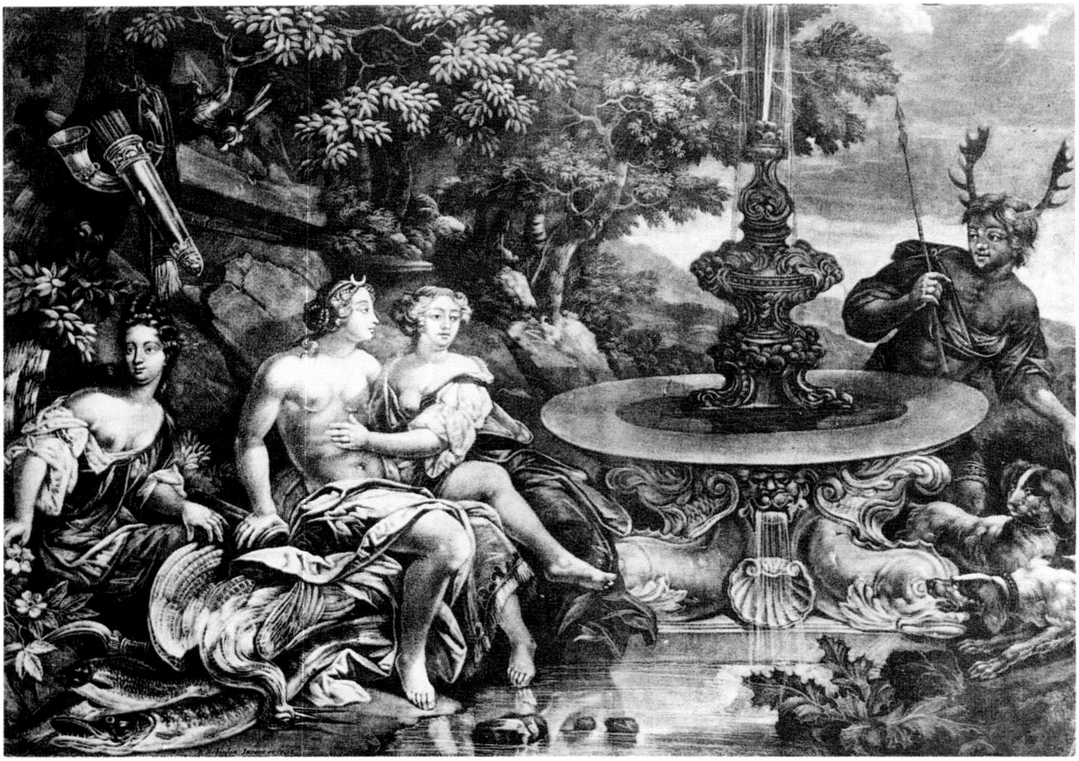

81 *'Diana and Actaeon', mezzotint by Robert Robinson. This print is composed of a number of 'stock' motifs that recur in Robinson's mezzotints. An arrangement of fish and fowl, the spoils of Diana the huntress, reflects Robinson's specialization in still life as a painter and printmaker.*

candlestick also based on designs by Adam van Vianen, and the same idiosyncratic object, a conflation of two separate plates from *Constighe modellen*, appears in a number of still lifes by Collier, suggesting either the Dutchman's awareness of Robinson's printed oeuvre, or an otherwise undocumented association between the two painters.[12] Robinson's mezzotint could be purchased at the shop operated by his main publisher, Isaac Beckett (*c.* 1653–88), at the sign of the Golden Head in the Old Bailey. After Beckett's death, this plate and many others by Robinson ended up in the hands of John Smith (1652–1743), who continued to sell impressions from them well into the eighteenth century.

LANDSCAPE SUBJECTS

Another popular genre in which Robinson specialized — the pastoral or mythological landscape — is reflected both in his mezzotints and surviving decorative schemes. One of his most elaborate mezzotints is the large plate *Diana and Actaeon*, inscribed
Illus. 81 'R Robinson Invent.'. It is characteristically eclectic in its borrowings, for while the principal figures are derived from engravings by Michel Dorigny after Simon Vouet, the dolphin fountain is again

based on van Vianen's silver designs. The composition of a vertical landscape mezzotint with a seated figure by a waterfall, also published by Isaac Beckett, bears a remarkable resemblance to a wainscot panel from a decorative scheme likely to have originated from Ladye Place, Hurley which was dismantled in 1837 and is now installed at the Henley-on-Thames Town Hall, supporting its attribution to Robinson.[13] Another of his imaginative inventions, *A Couple Strolling in a Formal Garden*, places a group of fashionable figures in a stage-like setting comprising a great ruined arch, a baroque fountain, a gondola floating in a pool, and an avenue of tall cypresses leading to a three-storied villa.

Illus. 82

Illus. 83

Illus. 84

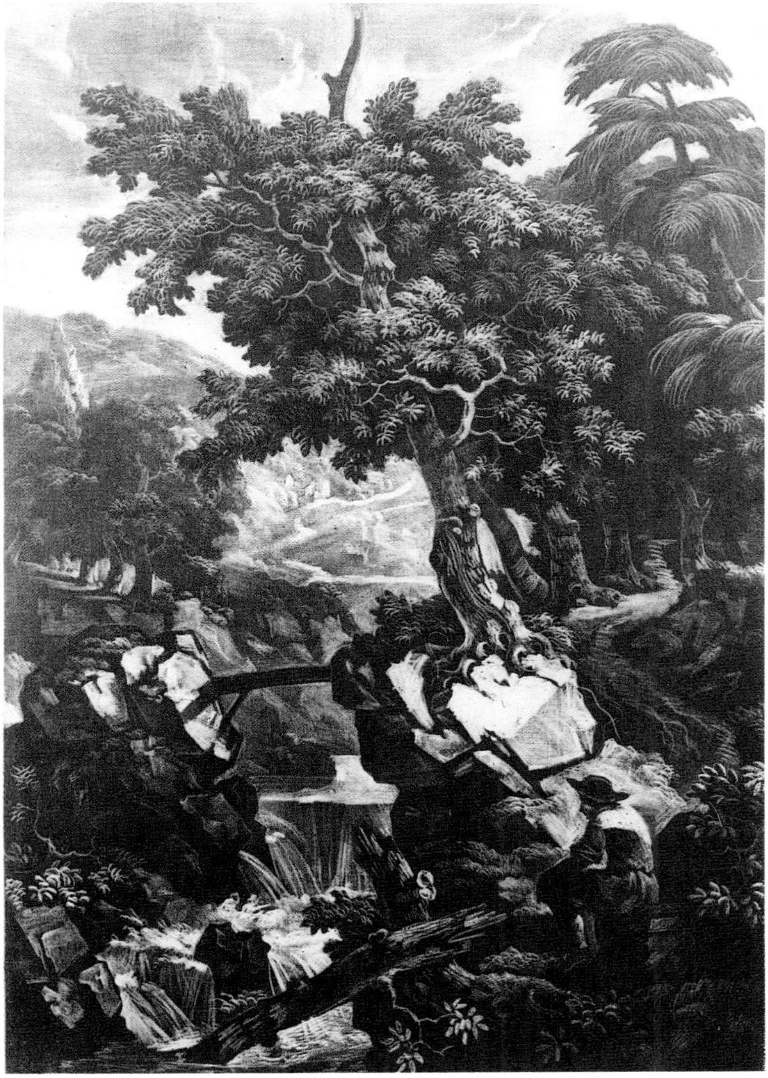

82 *'The Waterfall', mezzotint by Robert Robinson. Robinson's landscape style is heavily indebted to the Dutch, and appears to follow the lineage of Jacob van Ruisdael and Meindert Hobbema, perhaps via the landscape painter Jan Looten (John Loten) who settled in England around 1660.*

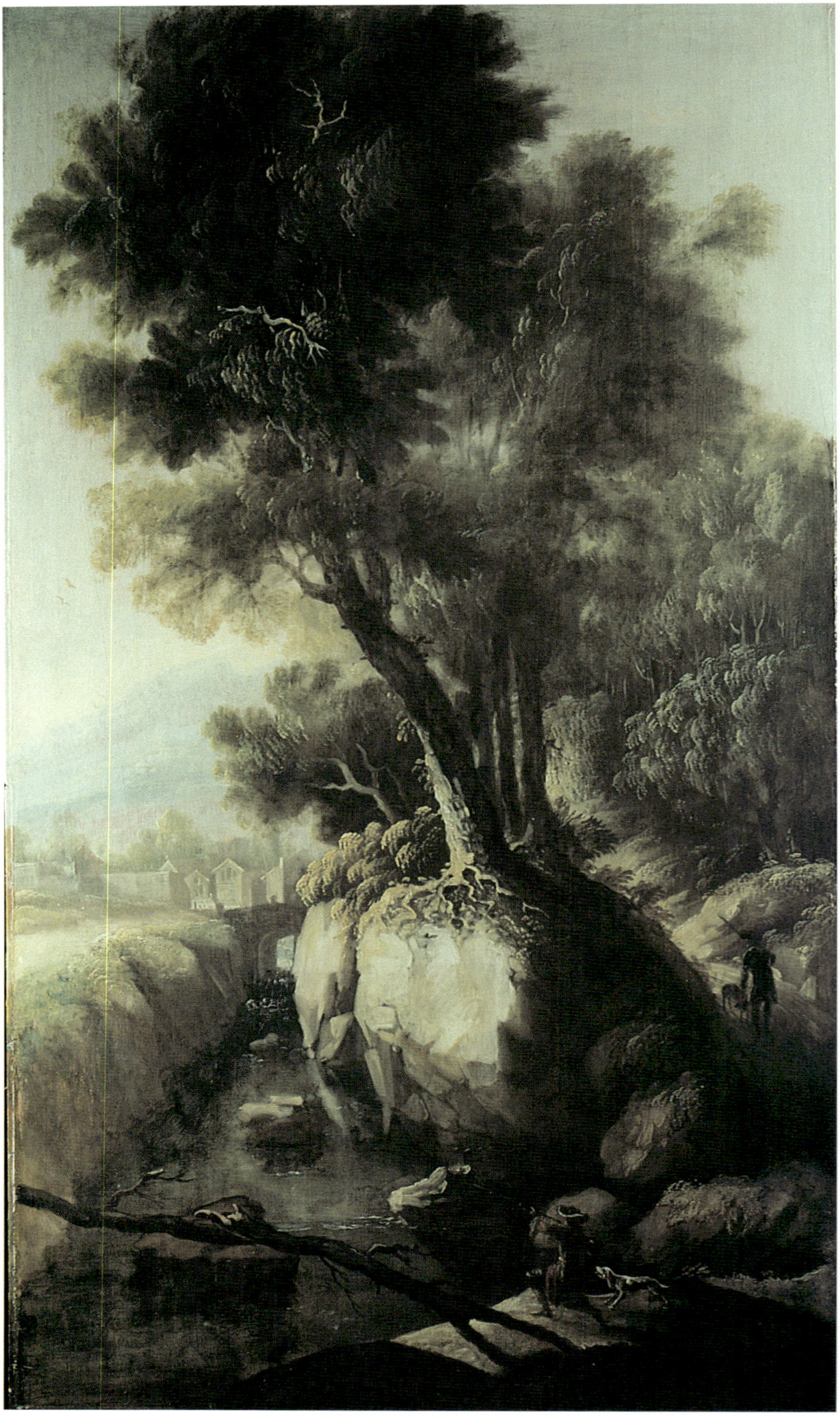

83 *Landscape by Robert Robinson, one of thirteen painted panels currently hanging in Henley-on-Thames Town Hall. There is evidence that these works originally came from Hurley Priory or Ladye Place near Henley. Laura Wortley highlights in this volume the substantial links between Henley-on-Thames and City merchants and we may one day be able to reconstruct the context for these works.*

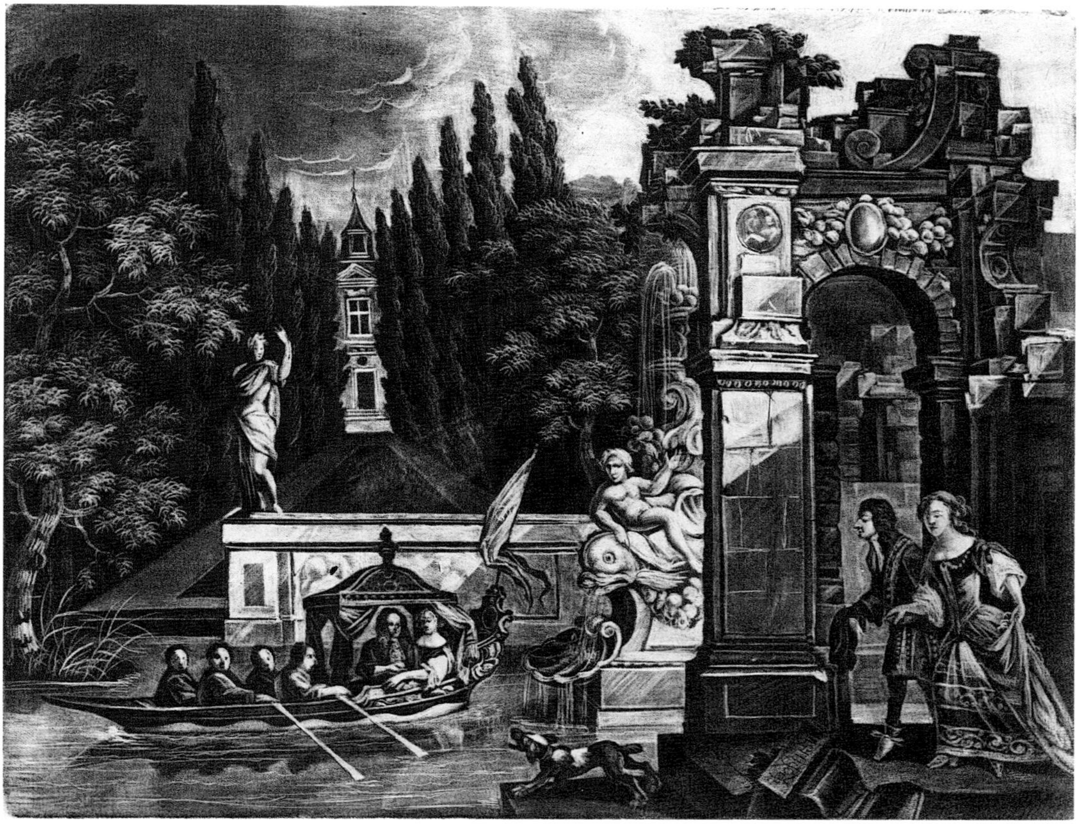

84 (above) *'A Couple Strolling in a Formal Garden', mezzotint with burin by Robert Robinson. This impression is the only one known. It is signed, with burin, on the fallen pedestal at lower right: Robinsun. This kind of theatrical 'high life' subject would have had great appeal to the merchant class.*

CARSHALTON HOUSE

The iconography of this mezzotint links it to another painted parlour outside of London in Carshalton House, a Queen Anne-era mansion located in Surrey. Some portions of the unsigned decorative scheme have been attributed to Robinson. The scheme consists of painted stiles with fanciful chinoiserie motifs and a series of wainscot panels, the most prominent of which represents a garden perspective with a tree-lined approach to a country house. *Illus. 85* In his groundbreaking studies of Robinson's decorative paintings, Croft-Murray perpetuated a false tradition that the house was rebuilt by Sir John Fellowes (*c.* 1671–1724), Sub-Governor of the South Sea Company, shortly after he acquired the property in 1716. This supposition led him to conclude that the panelling and overmantels were preserved from the old house that had been torn down.[14] More recently it has been shown that Fellowes made only minor alterations to the mansion, and that it stands much as it did when constructed beginning in 1696 at the behest of its first occupant, Edward Carleton (*c.* 1642?–1732), who vacated the premises

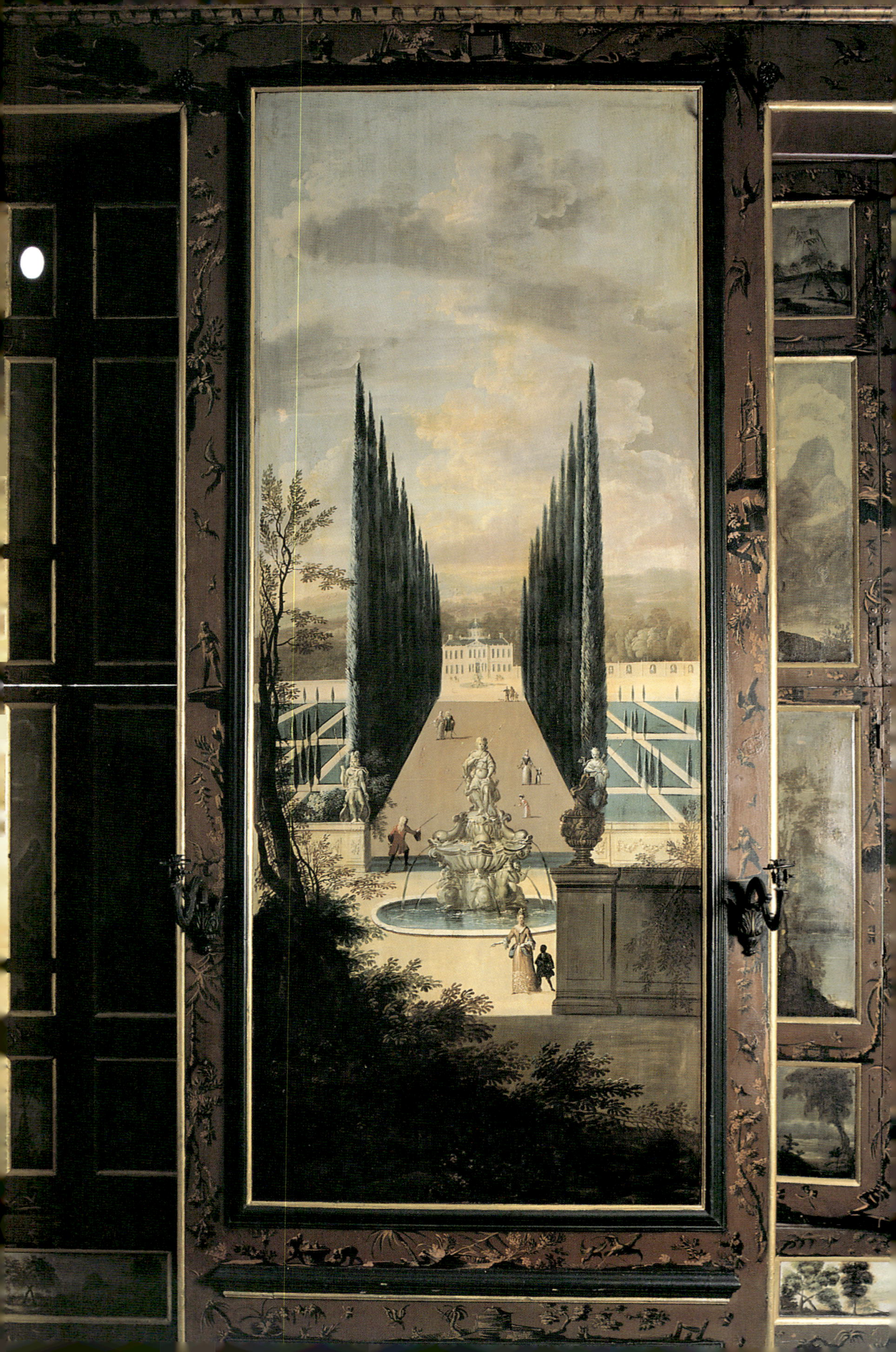

after his bankruptcy in 1713.[15] Indeed, the inventory of the house made at the time of his bankruptcy designates the room adjoining the main drawing-room on the ground floor as 'the painted Parlour.'[16]

85 (opposite) *'Garden Prospect', oil on panel by Robert Robinson, at the Painted Parlour, Carshalton House, St Philomena's School, Surrey. A local historian once suggested that this panel represented a topographically accurate view of the house in which it was painted. In fact, the idealized composition follows a long-established pictorial formula, and occurs with variations elsewhere in Robinson's oeuvre.*

THE PAINTED ROOM AT BOTOLPH LANE

Although no document has yet been found linking Robinson to Carleton or any of his business associates, Carleton's livelihood as a tobacco merchant may provide a clue to the patron of Robinson's most important extant decorative scheme, the Painted Room in the Sir John Cass's Foundation Primary School in Aldgate. The thirty-three wainscot panels were moved to the School's Boardroom in 1906 when the original dwelling containing them at No. 32 Botolph Lane was condemned. The predominant colour scheme is a dull green, with the landscapes handled in an almost monochromatic manner and the figures painted in subdued yellow and brown tones. One of the primary vertical panels is inscribed 'R: Robinson / (two lines of unintelligible characters) / 1696'. Close inspection reveals that this inscription has been repainted, as traces of the original lettering are visible through the olive background. *Illus. 86*

The primary unifying feature of the eight large panels is their lush landscape setting. Tropical vegetation includes several species of palm trees, in addition to the prominent representation of a tobacco plant. Although palms frequently appear in contemporary representations of China, they were primarily associated with South America, while tobacco is the clearest signifier of the equatorial New World. Further, the towering cliffs and rock formations depicted in several of the panels correspond with the natural features of the region, and a variety of animal life indigenous to both South America and Asia populate this resolutely exotic habitat. Among the strange beasts are snakes, iguanas, a horned giraffe, llamas, elephants, rhinoceroses, jaguars, and several fantastic species, including a race of domesticated reptiles resembling monitor lizards or crocodiles and a water-spouting sea-monster with a single tusk apparently depicting a narwhal. *Illus. 87*

Fanciful architectural elements freely combine Eastern and Western forms. The façades are ornamented with pagoda-like details, and exhibit a lack of structural logic that also suggests an improvisational approach to their design on the part of the painter. Croft-Murray found the dense cityscape in the overmantel, with its extensive lagoon, evocative of Venice, but in keeping with the South American theme, it is more likely to have been identified by contemporary viewers with Venezuela (from 'little Venice,' as it *Illus. 88*

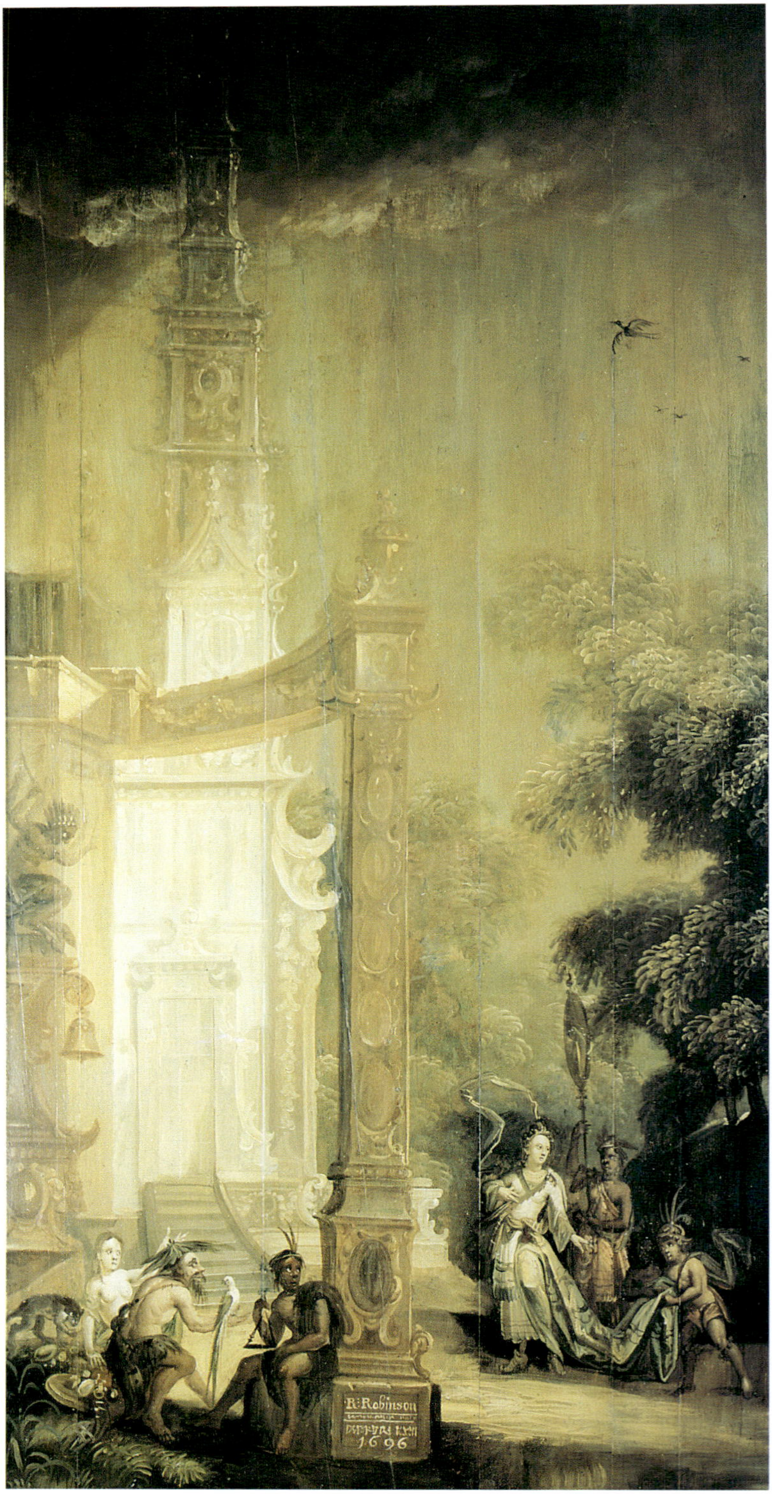

86 *'Fantastic Palace', 1696, oil on panel by Robert Robinson, from The Painted Room at Sir John Cass's Foundation Primary School, Aldgate (formerly No. 32 Botolph Lane, London). In Robinson's panels, women frequently appear as dominant figures; undoubtedly, they reflect the lore of the American Amazon.*

87 (opposite) *'Tobacco Cultivation', 1696, oil on panel by Robert Robinson, from The Painted Room at Sir John Cass's Foundation Primary School, Aldgate (formerly No. 32 Botolph Lane), London. The accuracy with which Robinson represents a tall tobacco plant suggests its derivation from an herbal or other print source.*

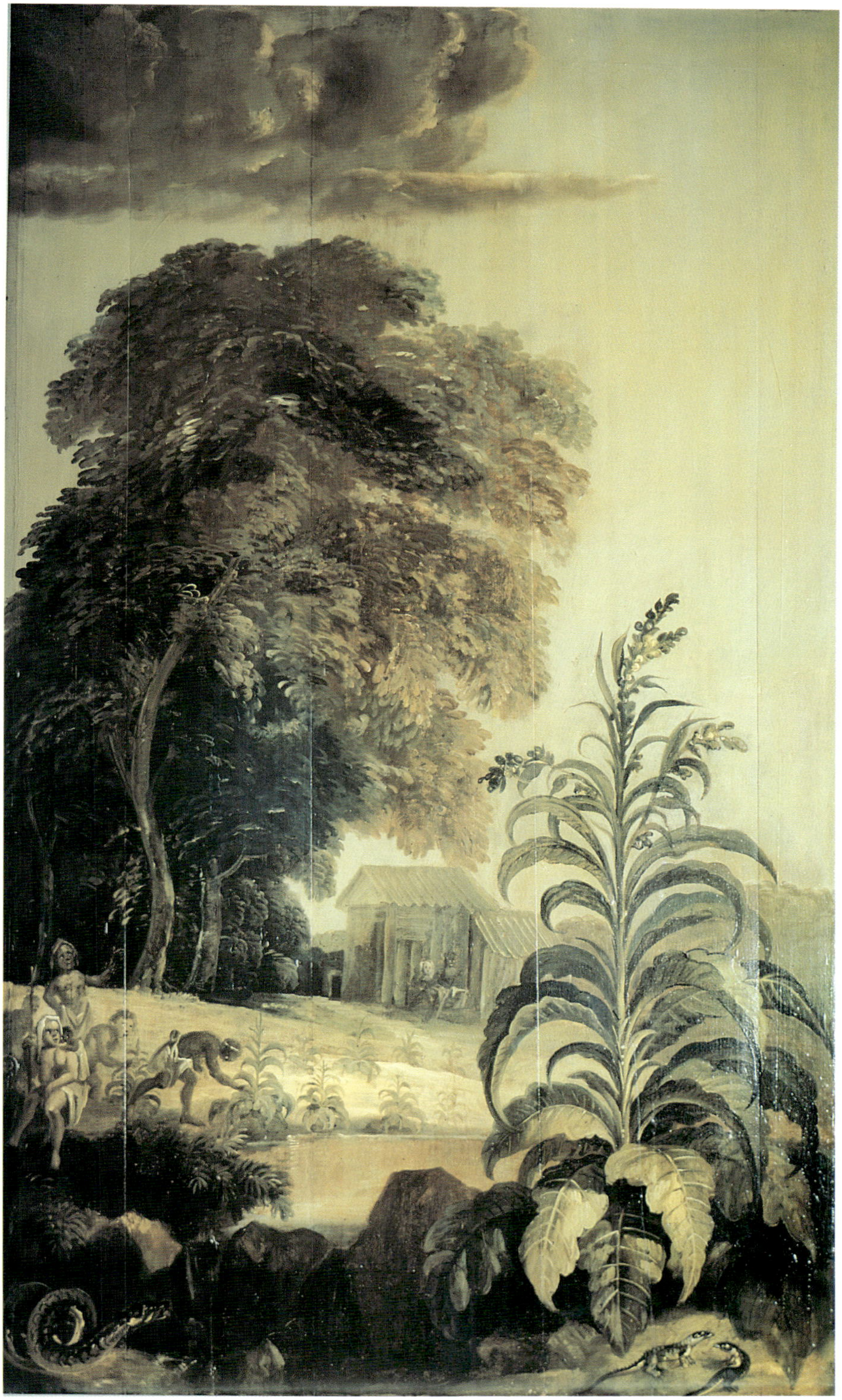

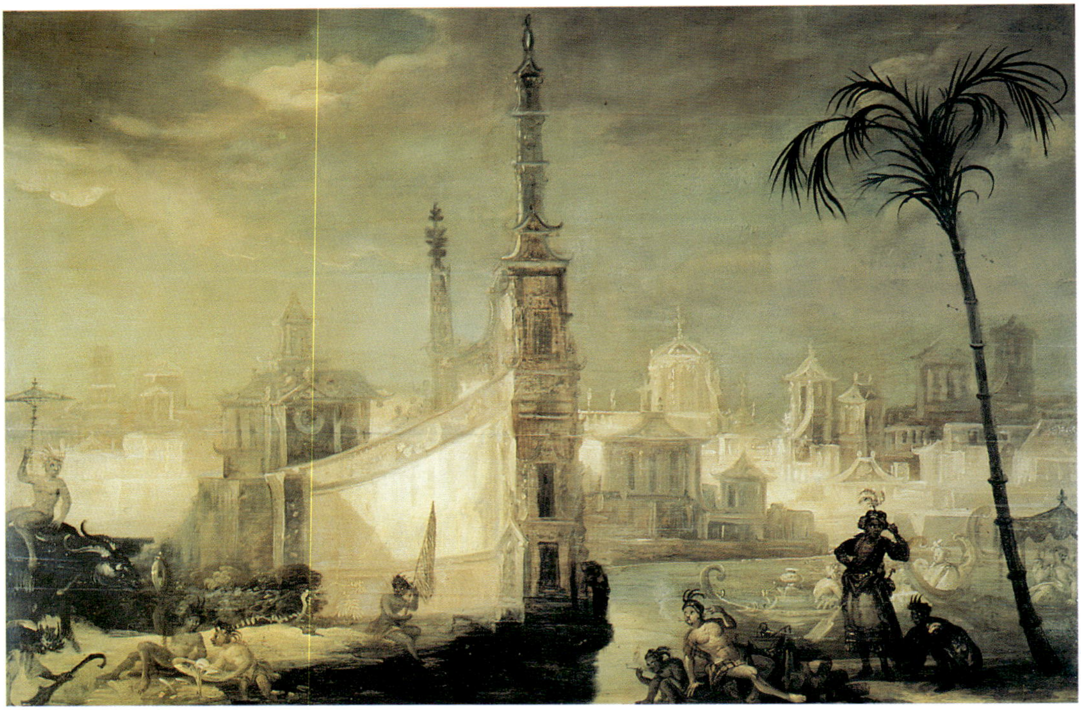

88 *'El Dorado', 1696, oil on panel by Robert Robinson, from the Painted Room (overmantel) at Sir John Cass's Foundation Primary School, Aldgate (formerly No. 32 Botolph Lane), London. In Robinson's vision of the Golden City, pastiches of Wren's architecture rise above a great lagoon, while natives smoke tobacco in the foreground.*

was named by the Italian explorer Amerigo Vespucci). Indeed, it was on the banks of a vast magical lake in the highlands of Guiana that Sir Walter Ralegh had specified the location of Manoa (El Dorado). It seems likely that Robinson intended the overmantel to represent the legendary Golden City, while the scenes portrayed in the other panels may be situated in the Delta of the Orinoco River, located in northeast Venezuela, and thought to be the gateway to El Dorado. The relatively Arcadian representation of the Orinoco Delta in this scheme, devoid of any 'savage' practices like cannibalism, was clearly meant to transform the dining room into a pleasant environment, a suitable backdrop for the civilized customs of polite society.

It is not known for whom this bold and whimsical scheme was originally painted. The archives of the Sir John Cass's Foundation held at the Guildhall Library reveal nothing of the early history of No. 32 Botolph Lane, and a study of neighbourhood tax records of the 1690s has failed to pinpoint the occupants of the house during the period in which Robinson and his apprentices executed the Painted Room (see Mireille Galinou's chapter for a range of hypotheses). It seems reasonable, given the ambition and content of the paintings as well as the proximity of Botolph Lane to the Custom House, to conclude that they were made for an individual

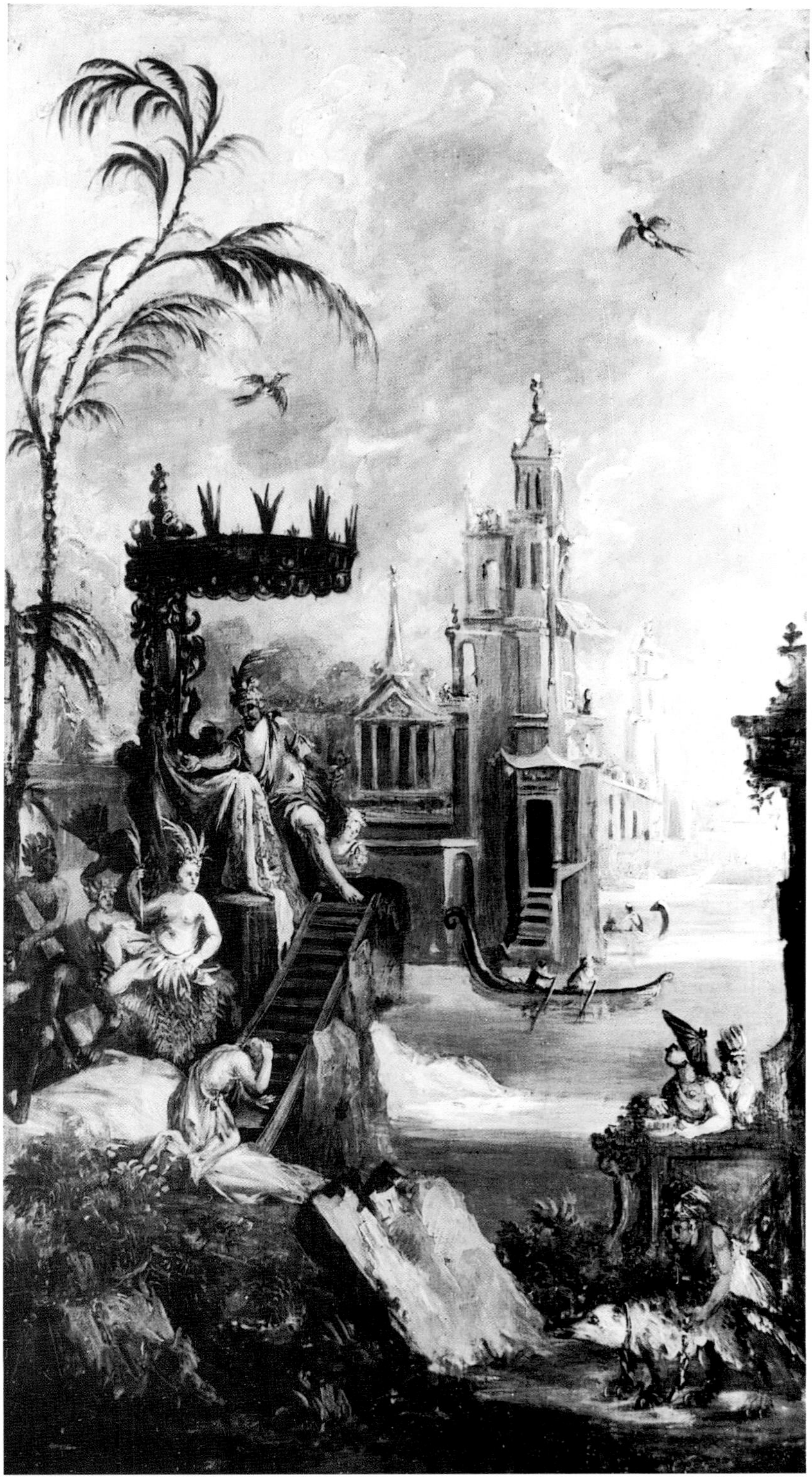

89 *'Enthroned Prince', oil on panel by Robert Robinson. This painted panel and a pendant, were part of an undocumented decorative scheme, now dispersed. Its present whereabouts is unknown.*

or family associated with international trade, perhaps a West India tobacco merchant.[17]

A pair of decorative panels, known only through black-and-white photographs, is closely related to the Cass Foundation scheme, suggesting that the latter was hardly unique, and that Robinson's production of this subject matter for merchants in and around the City of London may have been far greater than is revealed by his surviving work. One of the panels depicts an enthroned Indian prince in a cityscape with elongated, fantastic
Illus. 89 towers resembling the structures in the overmantel of El Dorado. While evoking a strange and foreign culture, the architectural elements here and in the Cass panels were clearly derived from the vocabulary of the greatest architect of the age, Sir Christopher Wren. In this way, they were grounded in the City, even as they took flight in the active imaginations of Robinson and his patrons.

Indeed, if there is an underlying theme uniting the eclectic paintings and mezzotints of Robert Robinson, it is that of the flight of fancy, and a desire for works of beauty and luxury among City merchants to decorate their gritty urban domain. An escapist urge also coloured the increasingly extravagant productions of the London stage, to which Robinson contributed scenery. Through his exotic decorative schemes, easel pictures, and widely distributed prints, he served a large and varied audience. Robinson and his fellow 'all-purpose' Painter-Stainers made vital contributions to the burgeoning art market, and the broadening and deepening of a culture of art appreciation in England after the Restoration.

I would like to dedicate this essay to the memory of Richard Godfrey, who first opened my eyes to the work of Robert Robinson.

ART IN PUBLIC PLACES

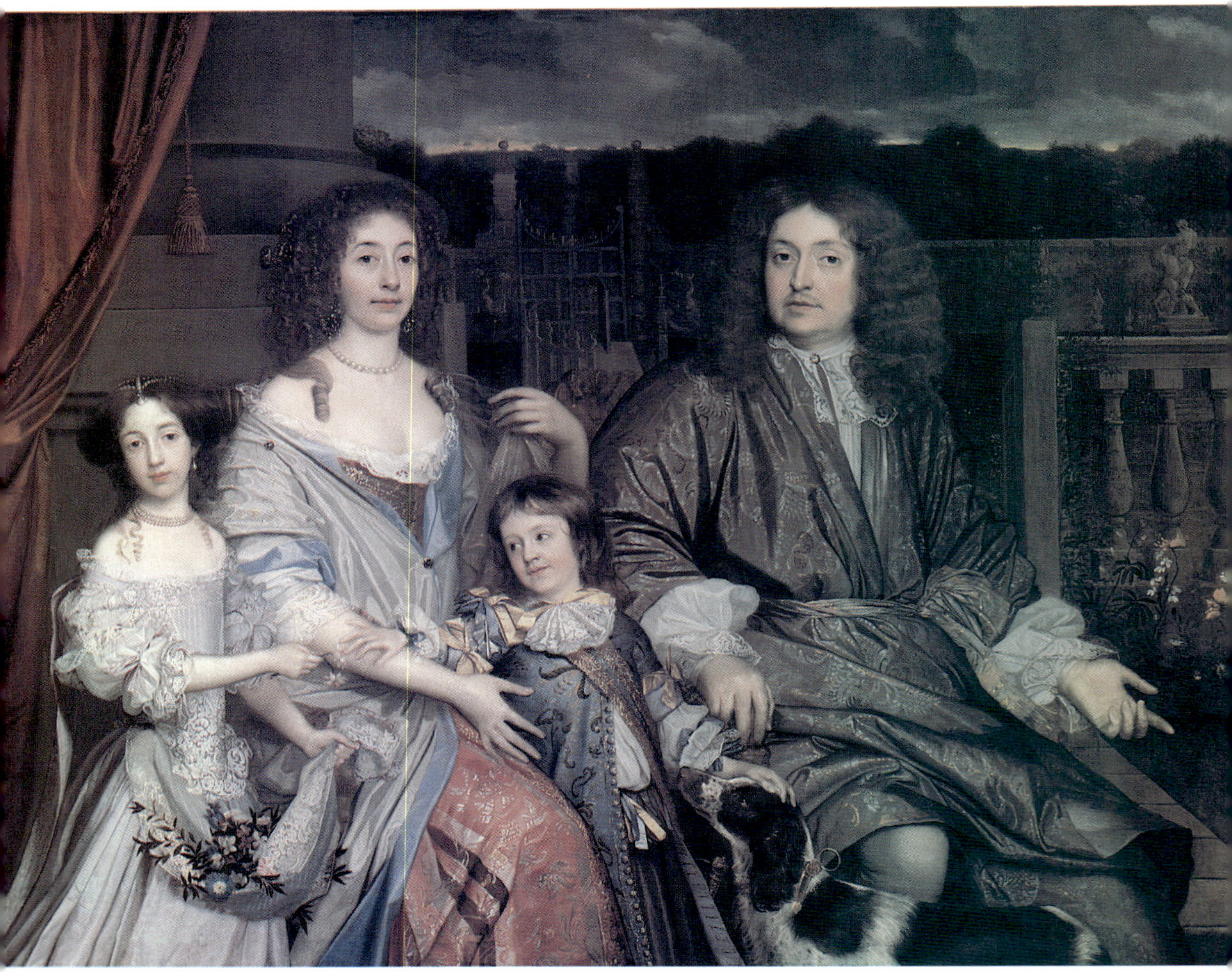

90 *'The Family of Sir Robert Vyner', 1673, oil on canvas by John Michael Wright. The portrait could be interpreted as Vyner distancing himself from the volatile nature of his business, and presenting himself and his family as country gentry. The year in which it was painted was sandwiched between two significant events in Vyner's public life. In 1672 the Stop on the Exchequer, in essence the government reneging on its arrangements with its financial backers, had almost ruined him, but in 1674 he became Lord Mayor of London.*

The Fashionable Merchant: A Case Study

Chapter Ten

VALERIE CUMMING

This essay will consider one major painting, that of Sir Robert Vyner and his family dated 1673, and a small number of other works which illuminate some of the social conventions surrounding the dress of wealthy merchants in the late seventeenth century. *Illus. 90*

A limited number of articles of clothing survive from the period covered by this book, the majority without provenance; therefore depiction and description are the main sources of evidence. Merchants were commissioning increasing numbers of paintings, some decorative, like those for the Painted Room but mostly portraits of individuals and groups. This is principally art for private consumption, though the merchants who commissioned such works almost certainly wanted a degree of approbation for their patronage of artists, and some understanding of how they had chosen to be depicted. Paintings in the halls of the major London livery companies suggest a formal sobriety of dress and a wholly masculine world. This is deceptive — such paintings present a fragment of a more complex story within which wives, and children of both sexes, also played a significant but largely unrecorded part. Hollar's prints, published in the 1640s, are the most accurate earlier depictions of female citizens of London in the early seventeenth century. *Illus. 28* *Illus. 91*

COMMERCIAL ELITE AND COUNTRY GENTRY: THE CASE OF ROBERT VYNER

Amongst the most powerful members of the merchant class were goldsmith-bankers. Robert Vyner (1631–88) was partner to his uncle Sir Thomas Vyner, and succeeded him in 1665. In the same year he was knighted, married, and acquired a country house. In 1667 Sir William Coventry noted that as soon as a successful

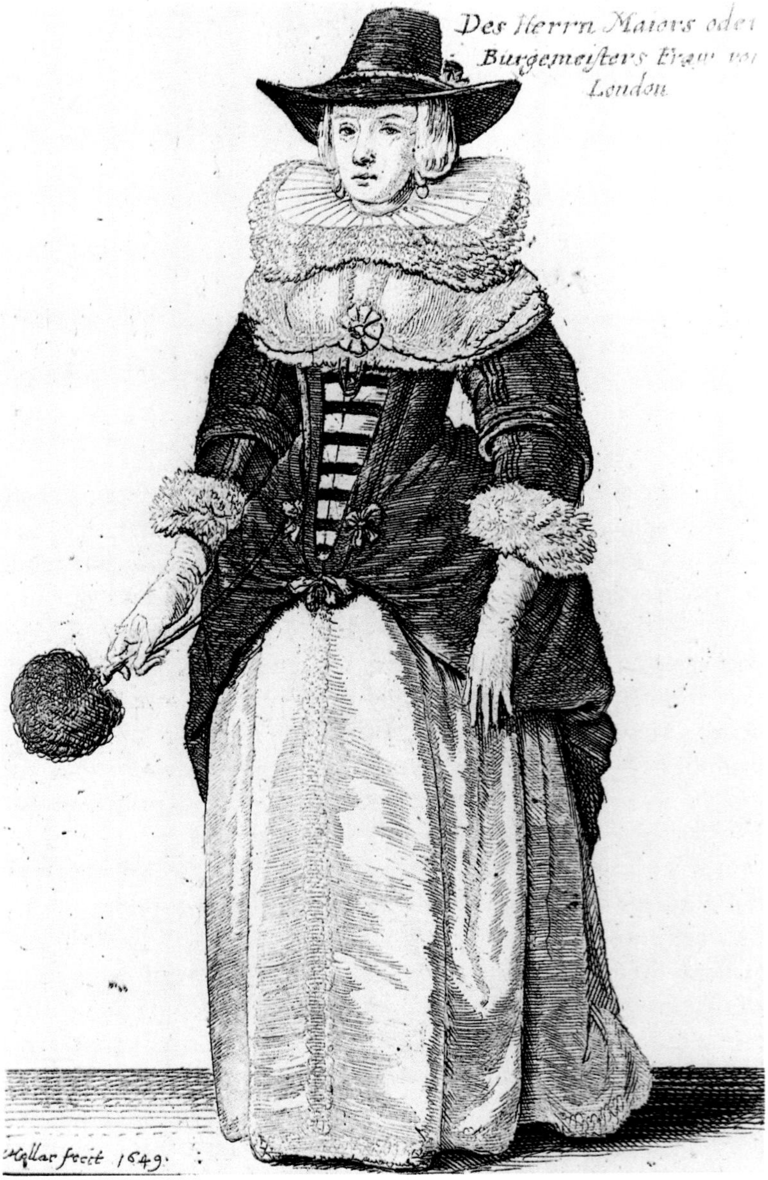

91 *'Wife of the Lord Mayor of London', 1649, etching by Wenceslaus Hollar. This is one of many prints Hollar made of English and European women. Fashion had not bypassed these civic wives, but they retained features of earlier styles of dress — the ruff, the modestly covered bosom, the broad-brimmed hat, and the plainer, darker fabrics characteristic of upright, God-fearing citizens. There was a description of Queen Henrietta Maria attending an entertainment at Middle Temple in the late 1630s dressed as a citizen's wife. Forty years later this would have been an unlikely form of disguise.*

merchant 'has a good stock of money, he presently buys an estate'.[1] In the late seventeenth century this was something of a two-way street. A pamphlet on trade and navigation published in 1695 stated that, 'The interest(s) of trade and land are the same, for the mutation frequently happens; the moneyed man today is a landed man tomorrow; and the landed man today becomes a moneyed man tomorrow'.[2] This social fluidity between London's commercial elite and established country gentry families would have been familiar to Vyner, and to a younger contemporary, John Verney (1640–1717). The latter, second son of Sir Ralph Verney of Claydon in Buckinghamshire, was apprenticed to a Levant Company merchant in 1659, setting off to Aleppo in 1662 to make his fortune in the lucrative silk trade.[3] What was considered an appropriate wardrobe for a junior merchant in the early 1660s can be assessed from what John Verney took with him — hats, caps, stockings by the dozen, socks, gloves, shoes, two white doublets, a winter suit of woollen cloth and a black silk summer suit.[4] These are discreet garments; good but not distractingly expensive or overtly fashionable. The public expression of role and status, as projected by clothing was well understood in the late seventeenth century. Samuel Pepys' diaries record his uncertainties about whether his clothing was too fine, too fashionable, too expensive for his work as a naval administrator, and there was a good deal of social satire — in both images and words in regard to excessive and/or inappropriate finery. Clothing was portable wealth, listed in inventories, sold to second-hand clothes dealers, left as surety with pawnbrokers, and regularly reported amongst stolen goods. It was a significant element in the construction of individual identity.

In September 1665 Pepys visited Vyner at his country house in Middlesex, the background for this group portrait. Pepys considered the newly acquired country estate 'a place not very moderne in the gardens nor house', but he was impressed by the long gallery, and comments 'and better or such furniture I never did see'.[5] This provides a context for discussion of the portrait and the clothing of Vyner and his family. The powerful and successful banker had chosen not to build anew — an expensive business, but to acquire an established country house. Yet his furniture was of an excellence which impressed discerning visitors. Vyner had the means, connections, and taste to provide his new family and circle of social and business acquaintances with all the trappings of a country gentleman. In 1666, the year that his son Charles was born, he became a baronet, the first rung on the ladder of hereditary titles. Interestingly he chose not to have a family portrait painted until his son was no longer in the skirts of infancy; the custom was for boys to be 'breeched', that is put into adult male garments when they were about six or so: a significant rite of passage for a male child.

Illus. 90

THE JOHN MICHAEL WRIGHT COMMISSION

The choice of artist is equally interesting. John Michael Wright* was well regarded until the sophisticated glamour of Sir Peter

* John Michael Wright (1617–94), the Roman Catholic son of a London tailor was apprenticed to a Scottish painter, but he was in Rome by about 1642 where he studied, collected engravings, paintings, gemstones, and medals. He was later attached to the household of the ruler of the Spanish Netherlands before his return to England in the mid-1650s where he sought new patrons for his work. Amongst his early sitters was Cromwell's favourite daughter, Mrs Elizabeth Claypole.

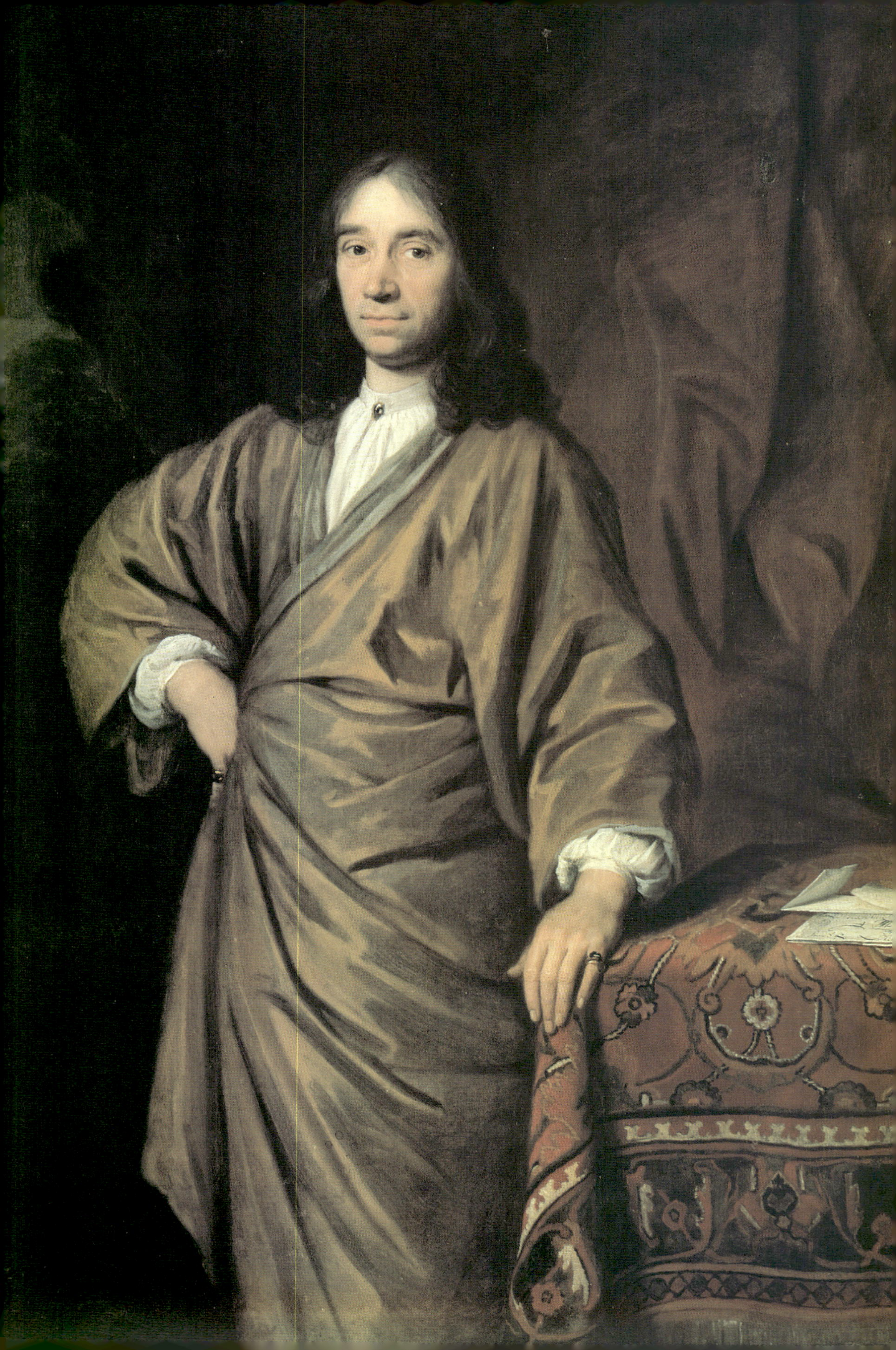

Lely's paintings defined a new courtly aesthetic and overwhelmed his competitors in the 1660s and 1670s. Wright gravitated towards City and country patrons, and in 1670 he was selected by the City Corporation to paint the twenty two portraits of the Fire Judges (See p. 145). On the selection committee were Sir Robert Vyner and Sir John Robinson, both subsequently painted by Wright. This artist's finest portraits convey the character of the sitter rather than offering a formulaic courtly gloss.[6]

In Wright's portrait we find Vyner at ease but every inch one of the men whom Evelyn called 'the greate Banquers' when he dined with Vyner and Sir Robert Clayton in June 1679, before taking them off to a meeting of The Royal Society.[7] He is not dressed in the plain cloth suit of a successful merchant, but in the informal clothes worn within the close circle of family and friends. If the identity of the sitters was unknown it would be easy to assume that they were wealthy members of the landed rather than the commercial elite. Their clothes are fashionable and expensive, tangible expressions of the impossibility of defining their role by their choice of garments.[8] Sir Robert is depicted in a fine linen shirt, possibly cambric or lawn, French fabrics which cost up to 4s. 6d. per yard when bought wholesale.[9] Shirts like that worn by him and his son could be bought readymade or might be the work of a family seamstress. The detachable lace band and cuffs are of bobbin lace, almost certainly Italian in origin. There was an English lace-making tradition by this date, but the wealthy preferred sophisticated Milanese or Venetian imports. The band and cuffs are fastened with discreet diamond and gold clasps. The pale linen, lace and stocking covering the right knee act as foils for the sumptuous Italian brocaded silk of his loose gown. This is not a dressing gown, but a garment synonymous with a gentlemanly informality — actors, artists, and writers were often painted in them. Sometimes referred to as an 'Indian gown', this description indicated the style rather than the origins of the garment or its fabric.[10] Gowns came in two weights — winter and summer, and could be purchased, from, amongst others, Henry Kirke, Indian gown seller at St Clement Danes, at a cost of between 30s. and £3.[11] Pepys hired one when he sat for his portrait, and Wright had painted the Scottish gentleman-architect Sir William Bruce in a striped silk gown in 1664. The sash that defined the waist seems to have been optional; Vyner's is of a lighter, gauzier fabric with delicately fringed ends. A plainer gown, worn by the merchant John Banckes, is seen in the first portrait painted in England by Godfrey Kneller (1646–1723) in 1676. This portrait shows the loose, unstructured

92 (opposite) *'Portrait of John Banckes', 1676, oil on canvas by Sir Godfrey Kneller. Kneller lodged with Banckes, hoping that his new patron would introduce him to influential clients in London. Banckes, described as a 'Hamburg merchant and Banker' introduced him to the secretary of the Duke of Monmouth, thus launching Kneller on a lengthy and lucrative career as the principal court painter after the death of Sir Peter Lely in 1680.*

Illus. 92

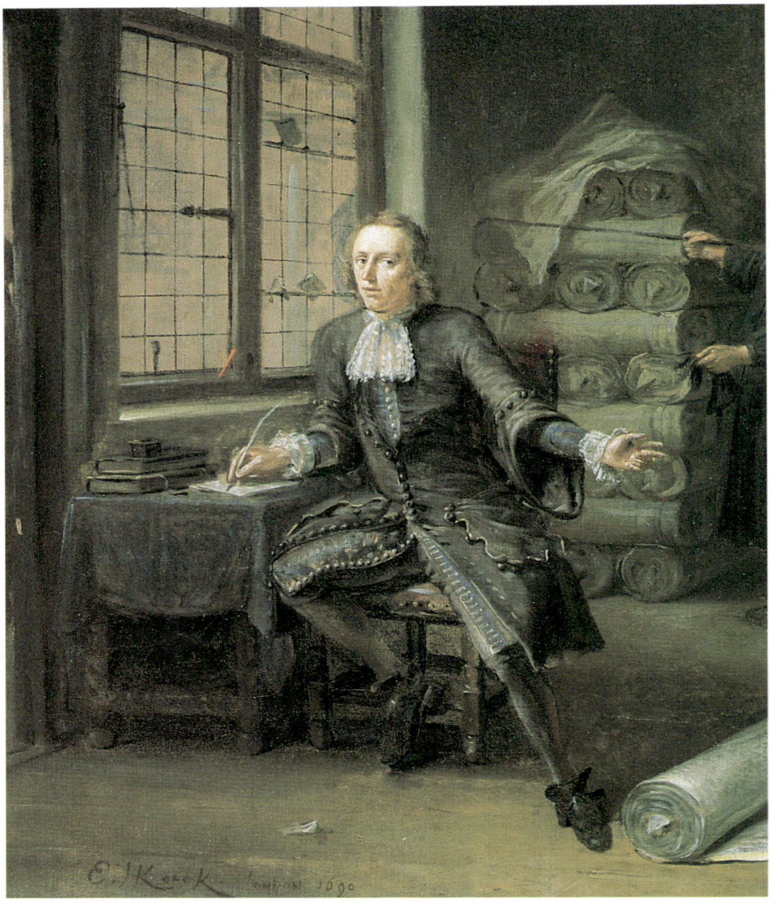

93 *'The Interior of a Cloth Merchant's, with a buyer inspecting bales of cloth', 1690, oil on canvas by Egbert van Heemskerk the Younger. This detail shows the seated merchant and is a rare depiction of a London merchant at work (see Frontispiece).*

style of the garment, and its contrasting lining, here held closed across the body by Banckes's right hand. Like Vyner, Banckes seems distanced from his business life until the inscription on the letter is read, revealing his name and profession. Unlike Vyner he does not wear a wig, an expensive accessory to male fashions which could cost anything between £10 and £20.[12]

The difference between the informality demonstrated by Vyner and Banckes in paintings intended for their homes, and the clothing they would wear for their professional life, can be seen in the painting of the interior of a cloth merchant's premises dated 1690. This genre scene provides useful information about various social groups working within the city, but the seated figure, albeit of a later date, is indicative of a style of 'business' dress which was found in John Verney's wardrobe nearly thirty years earlier. Plain but good tailoring enlivened by expensive lace at the neck and cuffs. Inventories of merchants of this period indicate that three

Illus. 93 & Frontispiece

complete suits and a range of accessories, including underclothes and nightwear were fairly typical, though a merchant who died in 1711 left five suits, seventeen shirts, and nineteen neck cloths.[13] It has been calculated that wealthy merchants with an annual expenditure of £400 to £600 per year spent about 25% of this on clothing.[14]

ROBERT VYNER'S WIFE

Sir Robert's wife Mary was the widow of Sir Thomas Hyde when they married in 1665. She brought to the marriage a daughter, Bridget, and, according to Pepys a fortune of £100,000.[15] This sum seems to have been something of a metaphor for great wealth. Evelyn writes of a merchant who 'amass'd an Estate of 100000 pounds &c.'[16] Mary Vyner was also an undoubted beauty. Pepys, something of a connoisseur of female beauty had met her in 1665, and said of Vyner's new wife —'his lady I find yet handsome, but hath been a very handsome woman — now is old'.[17] At that time the new Lady Vyner was probably in her late twenties or early thirties, but in the seventeenth century a woman was mature at twenty-five and considered middle-aged by thirty. Her choice of clothing has a studied informality. She is dressed in a fashionable French sacque — an overgown of a pale taffeta with a darker lining, but beneath is a stiffened bodice and petticoat of striped silk brocade. Stripes were popular in the late 1660s and 1670s, but the gold and silver threads used in the weave indicate that this is an expensive silk. Similar fabrics could cost up to 50s. a yard wholesale.[18] Around her shoulders, caught at the right hand side by a small gold and diamond brooch and held up in the fingers of her left hand, is a silk gauze scarf with a delicate gold thread motif shimmering in the folds. Her lace, like that of her husband, is probably Italian; such expensive laces were detached and laundered separately from the linen undergarments they trimmed. Many women kept books of domestic and medical advice and, in Constance Hall's 'Booke of Receipts' of 1672 she describes the painstaking process for washing, starching, and ironing lace, a process that might take up to three days.[19] Lady Vyner would have had servants to assist her run her households in London and in the country, almost certainly including a personal maid to help with her clothes and hairdressing. Her hairstyle of teased curls and ringlets, possibly enhanced by false hair, had originated in France in 1671. The ornaments in her hair and her earrings are of sophisticated European filigree work.

94 *'Eleanor James', c. 1695, oil on canvas by an anonymous artist.*

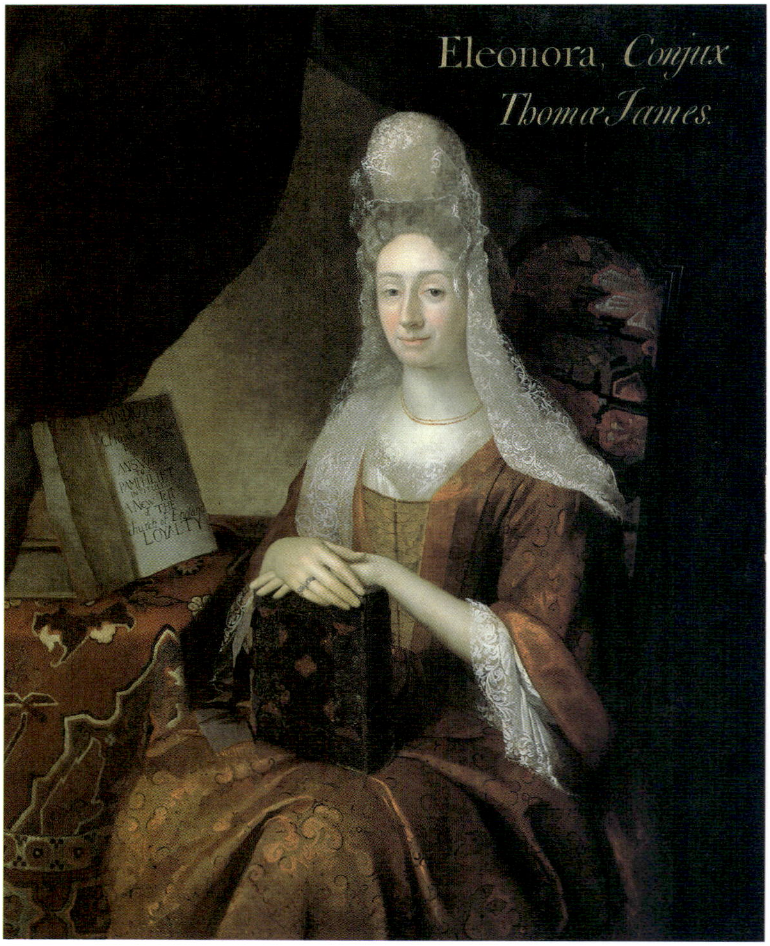

Little is known about Lady Vyner apart from her two marriages, two children, and personal wealth. Much has been published in recent years about the role of women in the seventeenth century, analysing their careers as artists, actresses, writers, and businesswomen, but the majority, of whatever social group, had domestic responsibilities. It is probable that Sir Robert Vyner belonged to that category of husband that Daniel Defoe found so dispiriting, 'The tradesman is foolishly vain of making his wife a gentlewoman ... He will ever have her sit above the parlour and receive visits ...'[20] This is certainly how a 'gentlewoman' would be portrayed, as wife, mother, and chatelaine of a country house. Nothing suggests a more public life, as we find in the portrait of Eleanor *Illus. 94* James *c.* 1695. Mrs James was the wife of the London printer Thomas James, but was known as a writer who published pamphlets and broadsheets of advice to sovereigns from Charles II to

George I. She was briefly in Newgate prison in 1689 for 'dispersing scandalous and reflective papers'.[21] Her silk brocade dress with a shift worn much higher above her breasts than was fashionable, and lace head-dress suggest modest elegance, and it is only the copy of her *Vindication of the Church of England* (1687) which hints at a formidable intelligence which found expression in writing polemical literature.

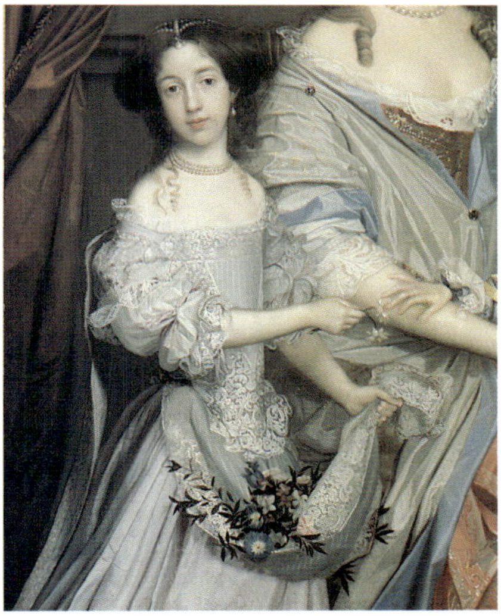

95 *Detail from 'The Family of Sir Robert Vyner', 1673, by John Michael Wright: Bridget Hyde, Vyner's step-daughter.*

ROBERT VYNER'S CHILDREN

The education of girls was lamentably narrow in the late seventeenth century, and Bridget Hyde (*c.* 1662–1734), Lady Vyner's daughter by her first marriage, is depicted as conventionally dutiful. She is dressed formally, in the manner of a miniature adult. At *Illus. 95* this date, when English portraiture often depicts adults of both sexes in a type of undress — a shirt or shift, a loose robe or a negligent swathe of rich fabric — a style associated with Lely and court portraiture, the clothing of children can offer a clearer indication of current fashions. Female children were not supposed to be informal, they were marriageable pawns and their adult physiognomy was, in part, formed by the clothing they learned to inhabit and use with grace. Bridget conforms to this pattern — her appearance is proudly adult, the only suggestion of her juvenile status is in the streamers at her shoulders, an elegant reworking of the childhood leading strings which girls retained as a sign of immature dependency until their early teens. Her hairstyle, jewellery, and clothing are those of a fashionable adult beauty. The rich

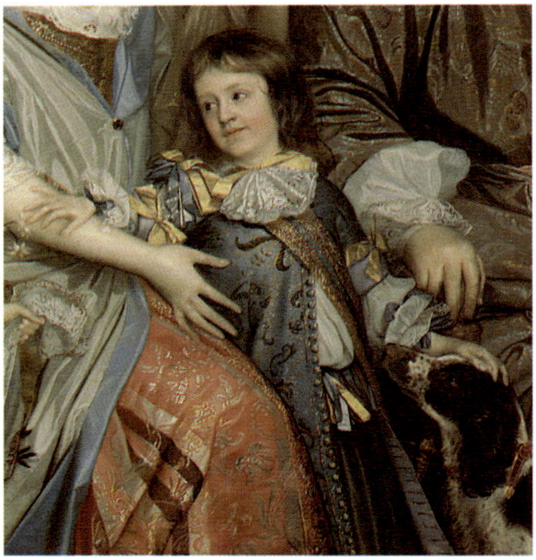

96 *Detail from 'The Family of Sir Robert Vyner', 1673, by John Michael Wright: Charles Vyner. His short-sleeved coat of brocaded silk and plain silk petticoat breeches are trimmed with an abundance of ribbons; the last could easily be of London manufacture, but the brocade, like those worn by his parents is certainly Italian.*

silk of her rigidly boned bodice and skirt, the heavily patterned lace on the sleeves, bodice and apron-like skirt panel are similar to fashions worn on formal court occasions in England and France. France was the arbiter of fashion and, by 1673, the first French fashion illustrations, a type of state propaganda for Louis XIV's luxury industries of silk, lace and millinery items, were circulating in England.

Bridget's bold, confident posture is that of a miniature adult, but her young half brother, gazing towards her, is the least self conscious member of this family group. Charles Vyner, aged six or seven, is flamboyantly fashionable. His cravat, of bobbin lace and ribbon, is similar to those seen in French portraits of this date, and his decorated sword hanger and miniature sword signify that he is being bred as a gentleman. In the 1670s there was discussion about whether apprenticeship to a trade meant that gentry sons could no longer be deemed gentlemen. John Verney's father was of the view that his son might still wear a sword, writing, 'If this were not so, the nobility, as well as the gentry, would not make their younger sons apprentices, as diverse lords have done'.[22] Obviously this was a two-way street; with a hereditary title to offer his heir, Sir Robert Vyner was raising him, dressing him, and equipping him to think of himself as an equal to the established gentry class.

Illus. 96

Detailed examination of this group portrait offers information about aspiration, social change, and the construction of identity by means of fashion and location. It is a microcosmic view of social fluidity in the 1670s. The fate of the four family members is equally instructive. In 1674 Bridget Hyde* was abducted by a cousin, but

* Bridget Hyde suffered a similar fate to that of several seventeenth century heiresses. A cousin, John Emerton abducted and married her, apparently against her wishes and those of her family. She was rescued, and the Earl of Danby became one of her supporters when Emerton instigated legal proceedings to regain his bride. The case was heard before the Court of Delegates in 1680 and again in 1682. By the time of the second hearing Bridget Hyde was married to Danby's son and Emerton withdrew, silenced by £20,000.

by 1682 she was married to the Earl of Danby's second son, Peregrine, Viscount Dunblane (1659–1729), and progressed smoothly through the peerage as her husband became Earl of Danby (1689), Marquess of Carmarthen (1694), and second Duke of Leeds (1712).[23] In 1674/75 Sir Robert Vyner was Lord Mayor of London and, despite his earlier financial setbacks, an eighteen foot high conduit placed beneath an equestrian statue of Charles II in Stocks Market in the City of London ran with claret when he was sworn in. The statue* had been Vyner's gift to the City, and was publicly unveiled in 1672 on Oak Apple Day, 29 May, the anniversary of Charles II's birth in 1630, and his restoration to the throne in 1660.[24] It can be glimpsed in the background of a design for a fan leaf which depicts the fashionably dressed but rowdy crowds of London's citizens surrounding the Chariot of the Virgin Queen of the Mercers' Company passing through Stocks Yard in 1686. Lady Vyner died in 1675 and her husband did not remarry. In 1683/4 Sir Robert's creditors had him declared bankrupt, and in 1688 Charles Vyner, heir to the baronetcy, half brother to a Viscountess, died. Two months later Sir Robert was dead. The painting remained in the Vyner family until acquired by the National Portrait Gallery. What was once art for private consumption has become a public record of fashion and social fluidity in the 1670s.

* This statue had an odd history; originally commissioned in Rome by the Polish ambassador to the Court of St James to celebrate John Sobieski, the elected king of Poland, overcoming Turkish invaders, it was acquired by Vyner who commissioned Jasper Latham to change John Sobieski's head into that of Charles II, and the head of the token Turk into that of Cromwell. Both were suitably adjusted but the turban on the head of the Turk remained on the head of Cromwell.

Illus. 97

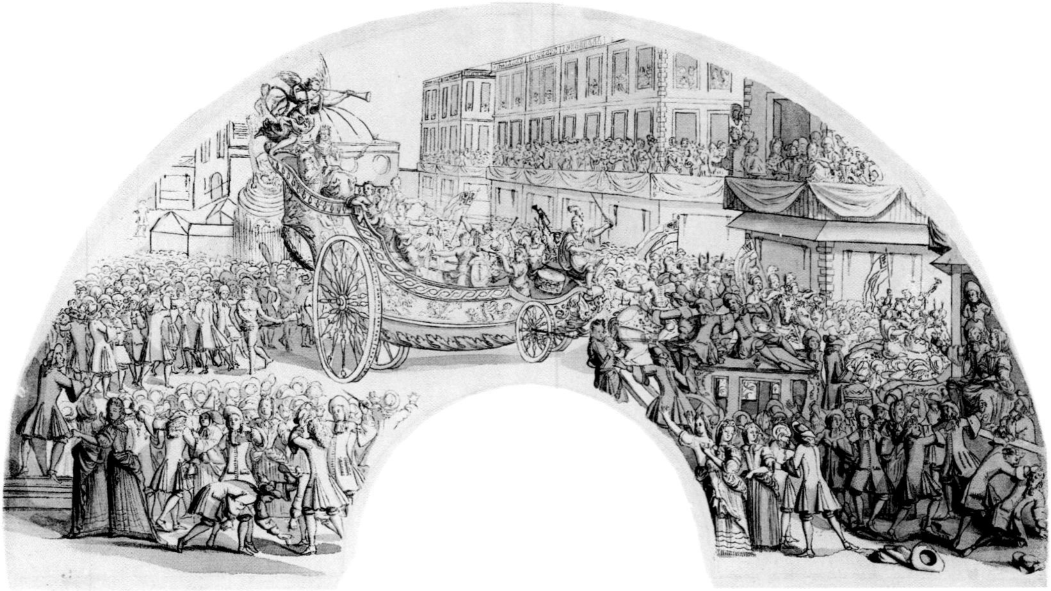

97 *'The Chariot of the Virgin Queen of the Mercers' Company, Lord Mayor's Procession, 1686'. Pen and wash drawing by an unknown artist. A contemporary, Matthew Taubman, described the Mercers' Company contribution to the procession as an 'Imperial Chariot of Roman Form'. The procession and jostling crowd are depicted outside the unfinished church of St Stephen Walbrook (in the background), very close to Grocers' Hall where the procession ended.*

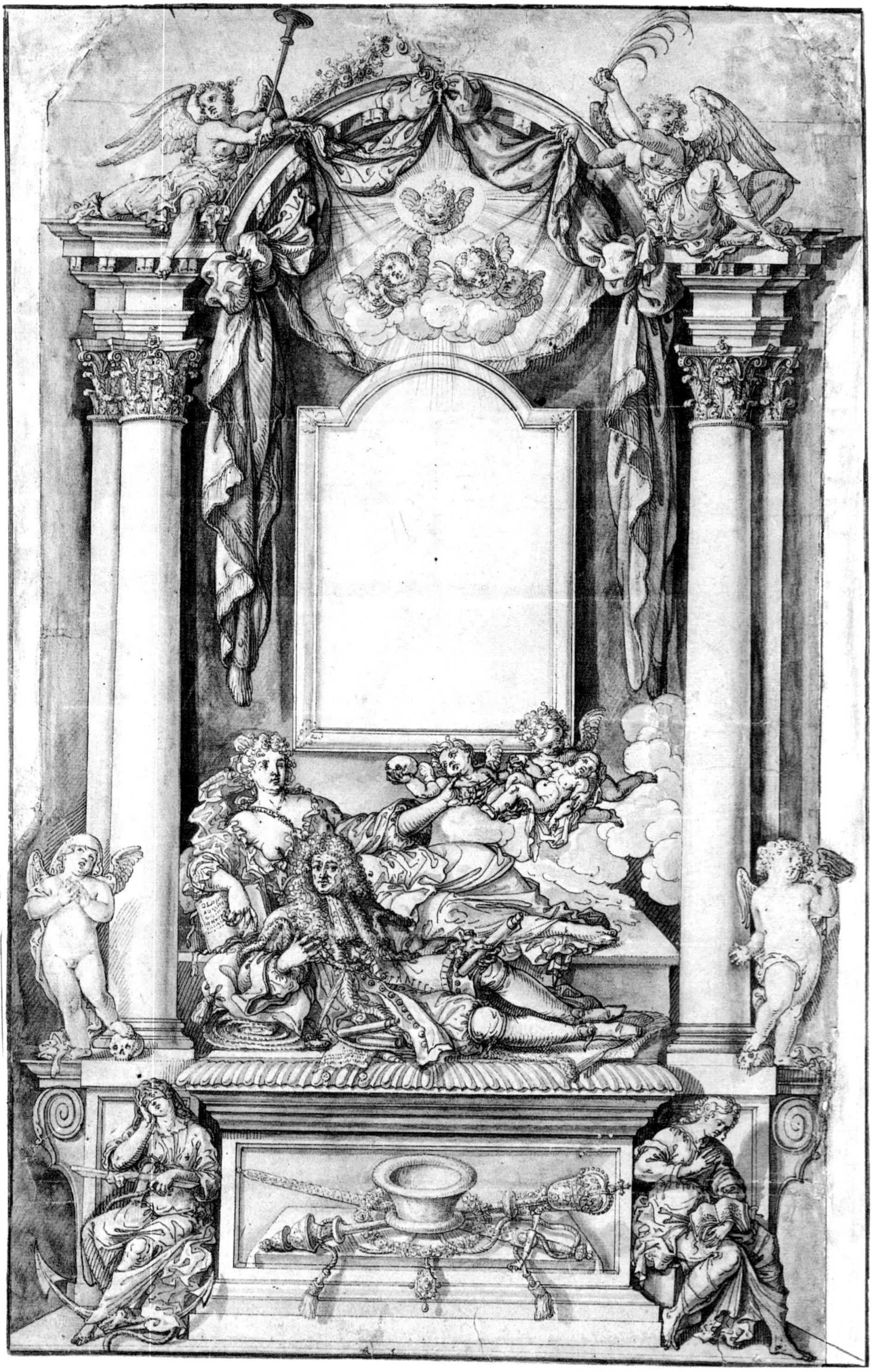

Tomb Sculpture and Dynastic Ambition

Chapter Eleven

ANTHONY HOTSON

The scope for mercantile families to rise into the gentry was a recognized part of the social scene in seventeenth-century England.[1] This paper examines two seventeenth-century families, the Langhams and the Claytons, both of whom successfully moved from trade to land. Both families commissioned noteworthy tomb sculptures in furtherance of their dynastic ambitions. The two family monuments considered in this paper frame the late Stuart period — one early, one late — and illustrate the circumstances in which *nouveau-riche* families commissioned tomb sculpture.[2]

John Langham and Robert Clayton both used their moneyed fortunes to acquire landed estates outside London. Langham acquired the manor of Cottesbrooke, close to his native town of Guilsborough in Northamptonshire. Between 1638 and 1642 he purchased various interests in the estate for a total consideration of £35,000.[3] The Cottesbrooke estate comprised some forty houses and 2,000 acres: a suitable landholding for a family aspiring to become county gentry.[4] Langham subsequently built an almshouse in Cottesbrooke, a grammar school in Guilsborough and he settled an endowment on Northampton hospital.[5] He also added to his Northamptonshire estates by acquiring the manors of Walgrave, Raunds and Quinton.[6]

Langham nevertheless remained primarily resident in London and there is no evidence that he lived for any prolonged period on his country estate.[7] The Langhams had fifteen children, of whom three sons and three daughters survived their father.[8] Five of the children died in infancy and were probably interred in the family vault in St Martin Outwich, Threadneedle Street, London.[9] In 1642 the Langhams moved to Crosby House, Bishopsgate, in the parish of St Helen's, London. Langham acquired a 99-year lease on

98 (opposite) *Drawing of an alternative proposal for the Clayton monument, attributed to the elder William Woodman (c. 1654 – c. 1731).*

Crosby House and used its great hall for his shrievalty.[10] St Helen's was close to Crosby House and was used for the family's weddings and christenings.

After the purchase of Cottesbrooke, its parish church became the main burial place for members of the family. In the early years, vault space was required for numerous children dying in infancy. Two of John Langham's sons and three of his nephews were buried at Cottesbrooke between 1642 and 1666.[11] The three nephews were encased in lead shrouds: 'lead shaped to the body and the top forms an Effigy of a child'.[12] The need for additional burial space at Cottesbrooke caused Langham to build a new burial chamber at ground level in the south transept of the church.[13] The south transept was sealed off to the nave at ground floor level and access to the chamber was by an external door. Langham was able to appropriate the south transept as a family vault by virtue of his position as lord of the manor and holder of the advowson of the local benefice.[14] After the death of the incumbent rector, Langham appointed Edward Pearce, husband of one of his nieces, to the living at Cottesbrooke in 1662/3.[15] The reorganisation of the family vault in the south transept was probably undertaken after Pearce's appointment since Langham's will, signed in 1670, refers to 'the Vault at Cottesbrooke lately made (by my appointment) . . .'.[16]

Langham died at Crosby House on 13 May 1671, aged 88. He was transported to Cottesbrooke and interred in the family vault on 7 June, the anniversary of his elevation to the baronetcy.[17] His wife's remains were also transferred from St Martin Outwich to Cottesbrooke in accordance with instructions in her husband's will.[18] Langham and his wife were the tenth and eleventh family members to be interred at Cottesbrooke. The elder Thomas
Illus. 99 Cartwright (*c.* 1617–1702) was commissioned to erect a monument to commemorate the family patriarch and his wife.[19] Cartwright had recently completed the Royal Exchange and its frontispiece.[20] John Langham's youngest surviving son, Stephen Langham, made what was possibly a final payment of £290 for the monument in 1676.[21]

Illus. 100 The Langham family monument was erected thirty-five years after Sir John served as sheriff and twenty-five years after the death of his wife. During the intervening period fashions had changed dramatically. By the late-1660s most moneyed men wore periwigs rather than shoulder length hair, and lace collars had replaced plain bands. Sir John's sculpted bust is similar in outline to a portrait painted *circa* 1650 when he was sixty-seven years old and
Illus. 101 had been expelled from office. Dame Mary's facial likeness and tied

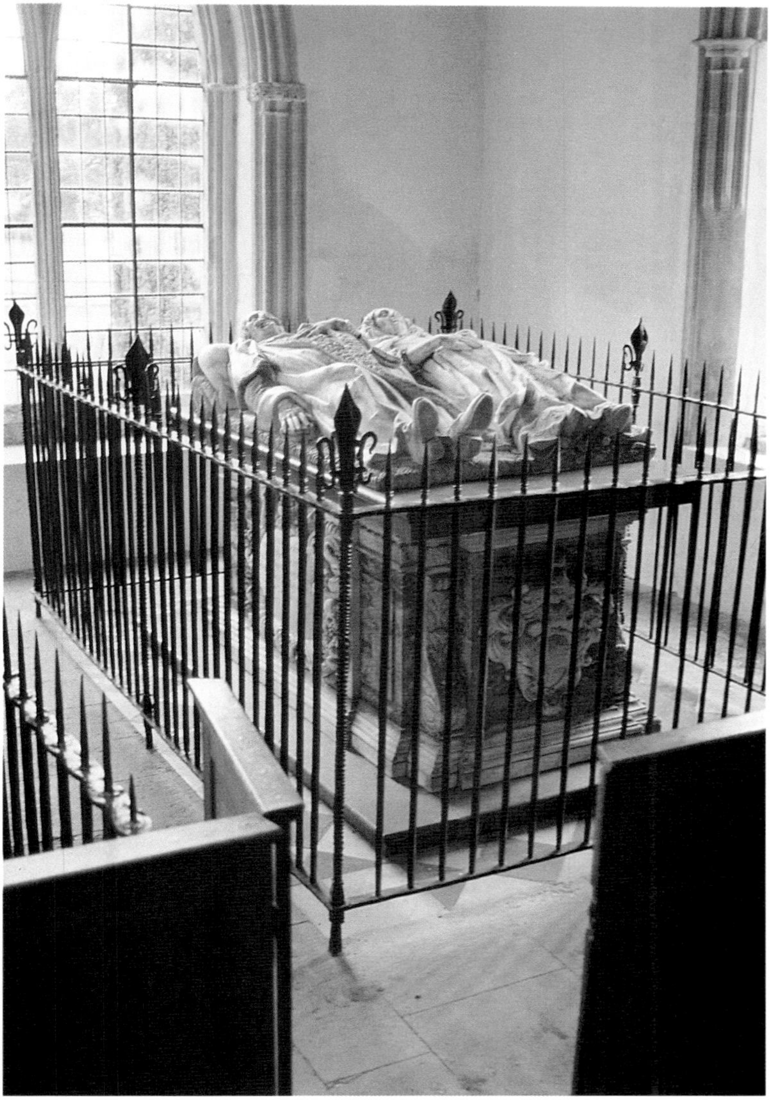

99 *Langham family monument, Cottesbrooke, Northamptonshire. The free-standing monument was erected behind the family pew and above the main family vault. Later generations of the Langham family could enter the church through their private door (now blocked) and walk by the monument on their way to the family pew. Sir John and Dame Mary are portrayed as full-length effigies recumbent on an altar-tomb.*

hood follow the outline of her portrait painted in 1650 when she was fifty years old.[22] *Illus. 102*

There is an account of John Langham wearing his aldermanic robes and regalia in The Hague in May 1660 when he was part of the deputation of sixteen commissioners and other officials, who met the exiled King after the Declaration of Breda. Sir John took his eldest son with him and both were knighted by the King in The Hague:

Alderman Langham met the King at the Hague in his Furgown and gold chain: his majesty asked what venerable man that was, and upon hearing his name said

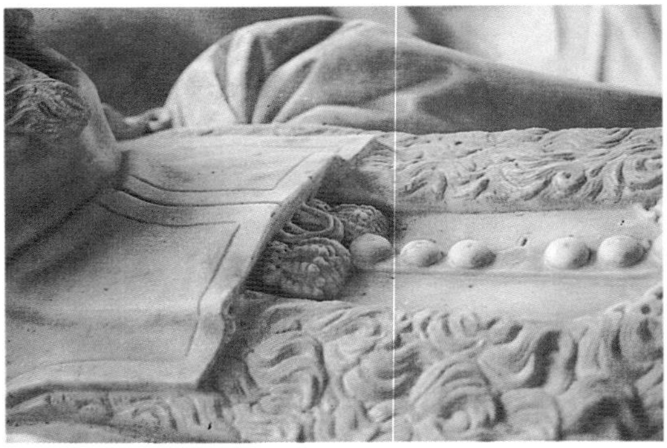
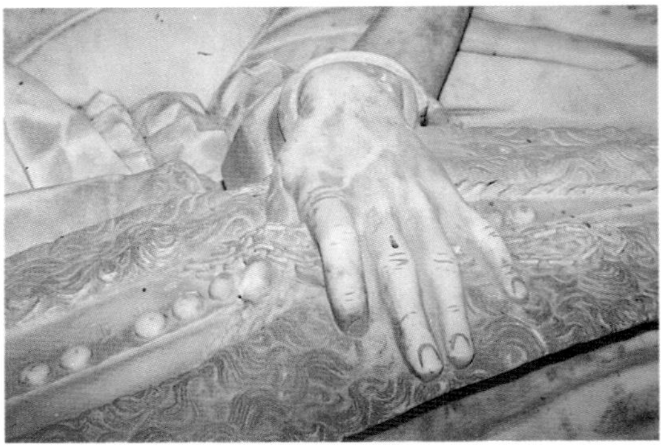
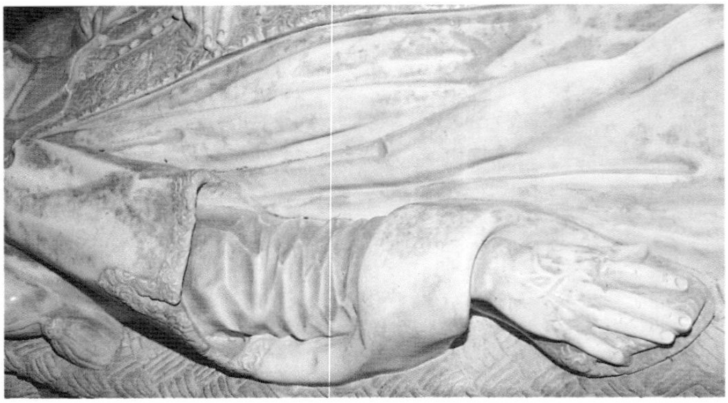
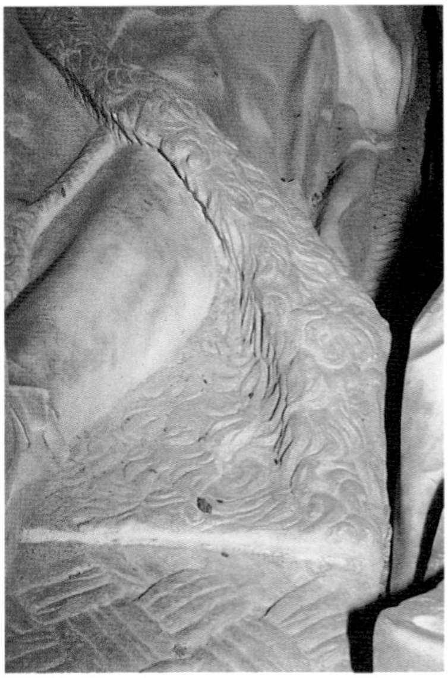

100 *Sir John Langham is represented in his aldermanic robe and regalia. He is wearing a plain band tied with tasselled band-strings. His left hand clutches his chain of office and his right hand rests on the hanging sleeve of his robe. The hanging sleeve on his left side is pulled across his robe. The edges of the robe are fur-trimmed with a fur lining inside. Dame Mary Langham is portrayed with a hood tied under her chin and a jewelled pendant. Her bodice is waisted, her sleeves ruffled with bows at the elbows. Her right hand holds a rose and her left arm is extended with her hand holding her skirt.*

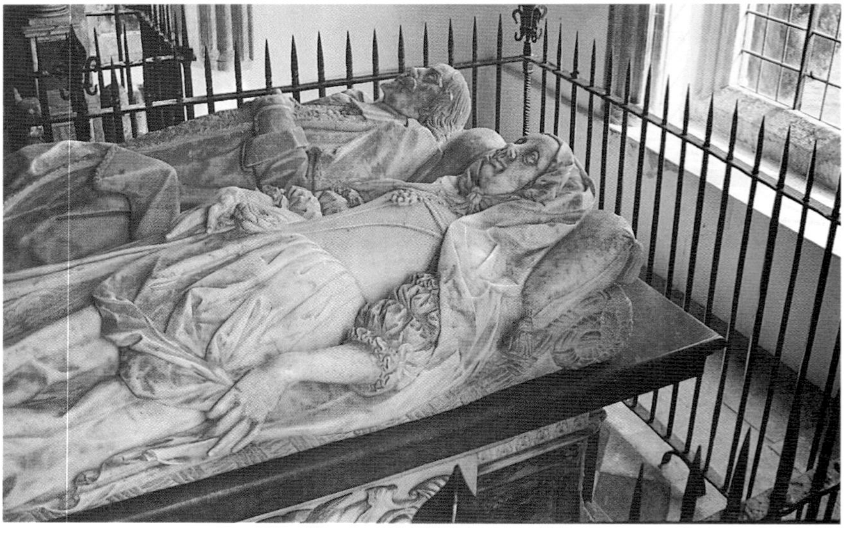

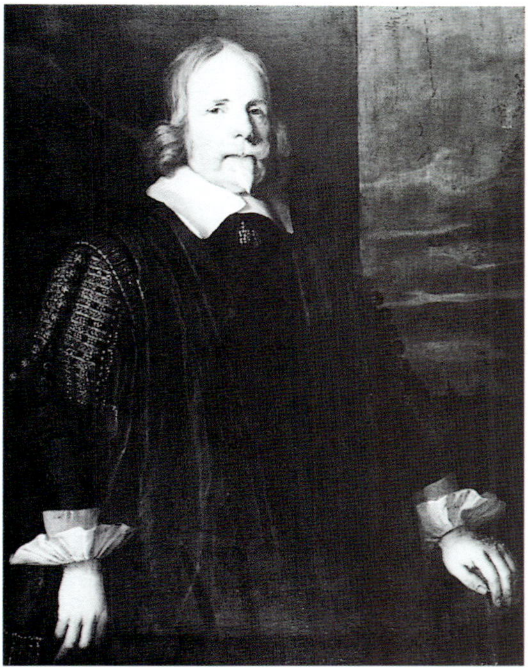

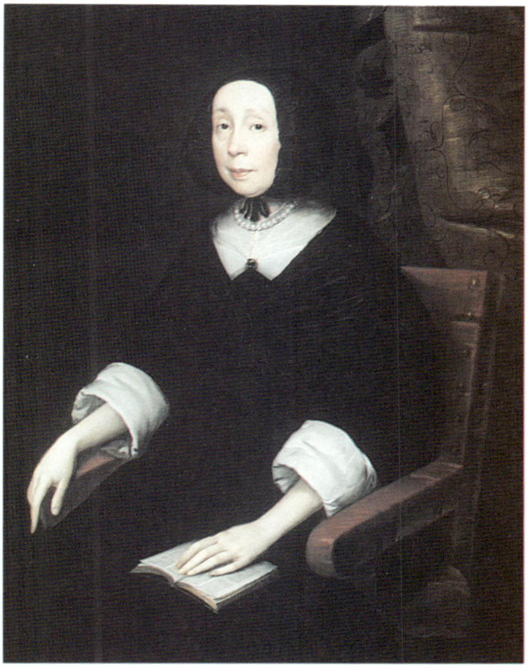

101 & 102 *Langham companion portraits c. 1650. An inventory dated 1769 attributed both paintings to 'Zoust' (Gerard Soest), although they may have been by different hands. A vignette in John Langham's portrait depicts two ships, reflecting the source of his fortune. John Langham is styled 'Kt and Bart' in an inscription on his portrait, but this must have been added later since he received his knighthood and baronetcy at the time of the Restoration in 1660. The dress in Dame Mary's effigy differs from that in her painted portrait. She did not live to see the Restoration, but her effigial dress appears to be post-Restoration with its ruffled sleeves and bows, and a petticoat with an elaborately embroidered hem.*

'I am more obliged to that man's purse than any Private man in England,' and then Knighted him and his son, James, who was with him.[23]

Sir John's aldermanic effigy symbolizes his governmental status. It need not, however, be interpreted as a reference to his unhappy experience as alderman and sheriff during the Civil War. It seems more likely that his family regarded it as evocative of his triumphal reinstatement in 1660, aged seventy-seven.

Robert Clayton pursued similar dynastic objectives to that of John Langham.* Clayton acquired the manor of Marden, near Godstone, Surrey, in 1672/3. He had just completed his year in office as sheriff and had been knighted. The Marden estate was relatively modest compared to Langham's acquisition comprising 1,000 acres of agricultural land and a farmhouse.[24] Clayton established a programme of improvements for the estate and built a new mansion house.[25] The diarist, John Evelyn, visited the newly completed house in 1677 and discussed the possibility of using Woldingham church, half a mile from the house, as the family church:

I earnestly suggest'd to him, the repairing of an old desolate delapidated Church [Woldingham] standing on the hill above the house, which I left him in good disposition to do, & endow it better, there no[t] being above 4 or 5 inhabitants in the Parish besides this prodigious rich Scrivenor.[26]

* His commercial landed interests are discussed in Laura Wortley's chapter on p. 93.

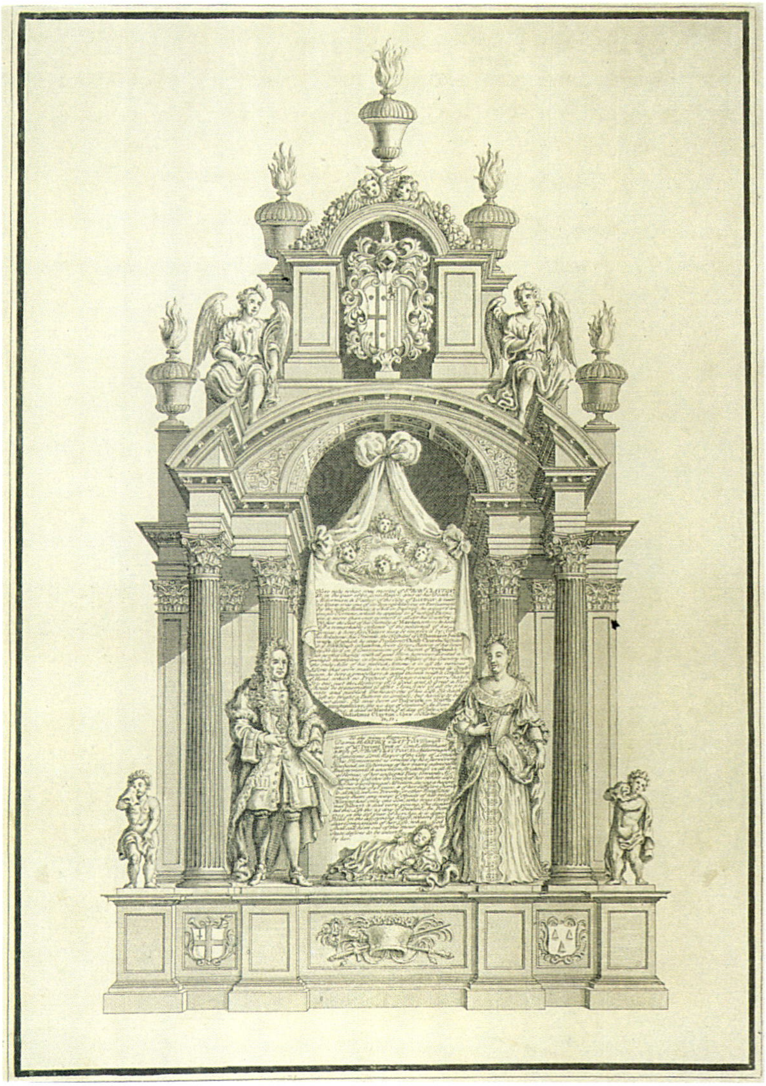

103 *Engraving of the Clayton family monument by E. Kirkall. The monument is signed by Richard Crutcher (c. 1660–1725) and it is his magnum opus. The monument comprises a trio of figures: Sir Robert and his wife, Dame Martha, are standing life-size figures half-turned towards each other. Between them at their feet is the recumbent figure of their one and only child, who died an infant. One of Clayton's nephews inherited the estate.*

In the following year Clayton took possession of the manor of Bletchingley, Surrey, which was four miles from Marden.[27] Although Bletchingley's church was further from Marden, it was larger and associated with a more prestigious estate. Clayton therefore decided not to renovate the dilapidated Woldingham church and settled on Bletchingley as his family's church. He was able to secure space for a number of burial vaults for his family. Clayton's wife, Dame Martha, died in December 1705 and was buried at Bletchingley. At the same time provision was made for an 'adjoyning vault' for her husband.[28] Clayton's younger brother Thomas, who lived in Bletchingley, died in 1707. Thomas was buried in the same area of the church beneath a flagstone.

Sir Robert commissioned Richard Crutcher (*c.* 1660–1725) to erect his family's monument after the death of his wife.[29] In Sir Robert's will, dated 1707, he makes reference to the monument he is erecting in the south west chancel of the church: *Illus. 103*

... and for the payment of such yearly and other Summs and ... of money as shall be either fitt convenient or necessary for the cleaning repairing and amending when as often as need shall be the Monument which I am now erecting for my self and my late dear wife ... in the South west chancel of the church of Blechingley.[30]

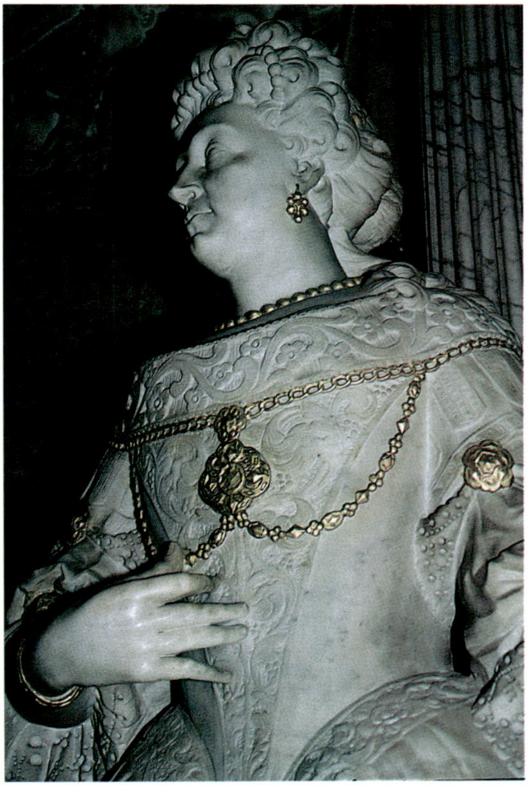

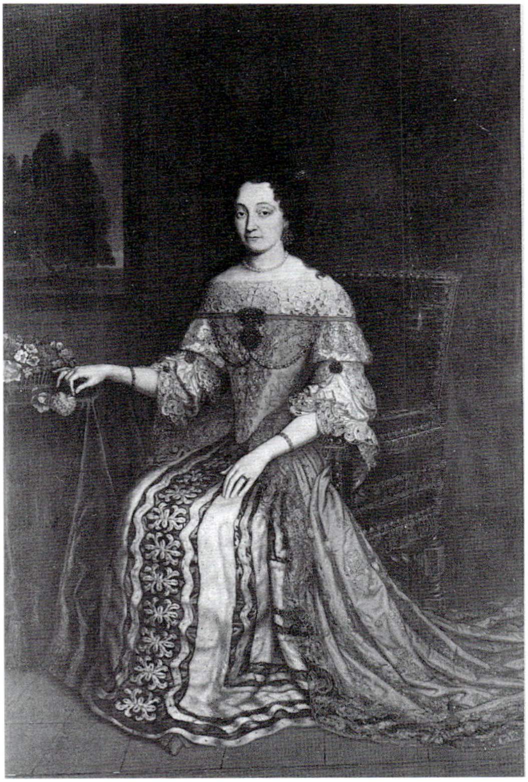

104 & 105 *Detail from the Clayton Monument: Dame Martha's effigy closely follows the signed portrait of her by Lorenzo da Castro (fl. 1672–1700). The portrait is dated 1680, when Dame Martha was 38 years old and the Claytons were holding court as Lord Mayor and Lady Mayoress. Details of her costume and her mayoress's regalia are faithfully reproduced in her effigy. Dame Martha is wearing a rigid bodice with a broad lace collar masking her décolletage. Her trained skirt is opened at the front to reveal a richly brocaded petticoat. The tiered effect of the sleeves is constructed from lace ruffles, ruched smock sleeves and ribbon bows. Her regalia includes a chain-band around her shoulders, a pendant, and chains attached to the pendant. She is wearing a mass of additional jewellery: pendent earrings, a pearl necklace, jewelled clasps on her sleeves, and bracelets on her lower arms. Her hair is tightly curled and entwined with pearls. A coiled ringlet falls on her left shoulder.*

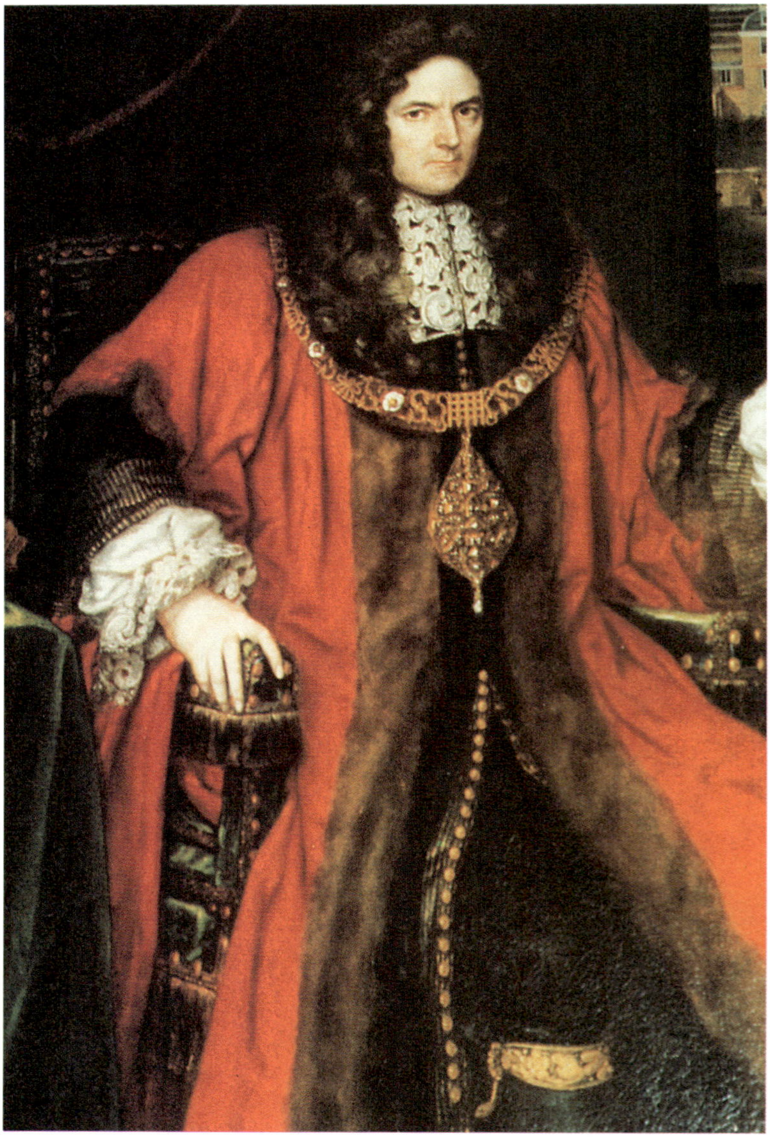

106 *Lorenzo da Castro was one of a number of artists who painted mayoral portraits of Sir Robert Clayton, but da Castro's portrait does not appear to be the source of Crutcher's mayoral effigy of Sir Robert.*

The effigy of the Claytons' infant in the Bletchingley monument was pre-dated by an earlier memorial at Ickenham church in Middlesex. The marble memorial at Ickenham is of a recumbent child in swaddling clothes. The Claytons had spent most of 1665 outside London to escape the plague, and the child was born while they were staying in Sir Robert Vyner's country mansion, Swakeleys, near Ickenham.[31] The inscription on the memorial notes that the infant 'dyed ye 16th of August 1665 within a few hours after his birth' and refers to 'Sr Robert Clayton Knight'.[32] This suggests

Illus. 90

that the memorial was completed after 1671 when Clayton was knighted.

A drawing of another proposal for the Clayton family monument at Bletchingley has been identified.[33] Geoffrey Fisher has attributed the drawing to the elder William Woodman (*c.* 1654–*c.* 1731) by comparing drawings in the same hand with his monuments.[34] Woodman's drawing and Crutcher's executed design follow a common design brief. Both are standing wall monuments with effigies of the three principal figures framed by an elaborate architectural surround. Both designs portray Sir Robert in his mayoral regalia, both incorporate a large City insignia centrally placed on the monument's base, and both have arms of the Corporation of London and the Drapers — Clayton's livery company — on either side of the base. The architectural surrounds are of the Corinthian order with columns supporting an elaborate entablature.

Illus. 98

Illus. 98 & 103

Notwithstanding the common design brief, there are important differences between the two designs. In the Woodman design, the principal figures are flanked by two Virtues: Hope on the left supporting an anchor, and Faith on the right reading a bible. The reclining figure of Dame Martha is dressed, like the Virtues, in antique classical robes representing the third Virtue of Charity. Her bare breast offers love and succour to their infant child held aloft by putti. Dame Martha was well known for her charitable works and this aspect of her reputation is strongly articulated in Woodman's design.[35] In Crutcher's design, Dame Martha's supporting role as Lady Mayoress is emphasized rather than her role as a philanthropist.

Woodman's effigy of Sir Robert makes reference to his role in commerce as well as his 'Station in the Government'.[36] Sir Robert's reclining figure bears his mayoral regalia, but he is also surrounded by the tools of his trade as a scrivener and money-lender: documents, ledgers, pen and ink. The Crutcher design focuses solely on Sir Robert's public office and makes no references to his trade as a mortgage lender. The Drapers' arms are included in both designs, but by the late Stuart period this would have been interpreted as a reference to Sir Robert's civic standing, rather than his trade. Clayton's trade had proved to be particularly contentious. Bletchingley had been repossessed from the estate of the second son of the Earl of Peterborough.[37] Clayton's subsequent repossession of Helmsley in Yorkshire from the estate of the late Duke of Buckingham proved to be even more controversial.[38] It is perhaps not surprising that Sir Robert decided not to be represented as a scrivener in Bletchingley parish church.

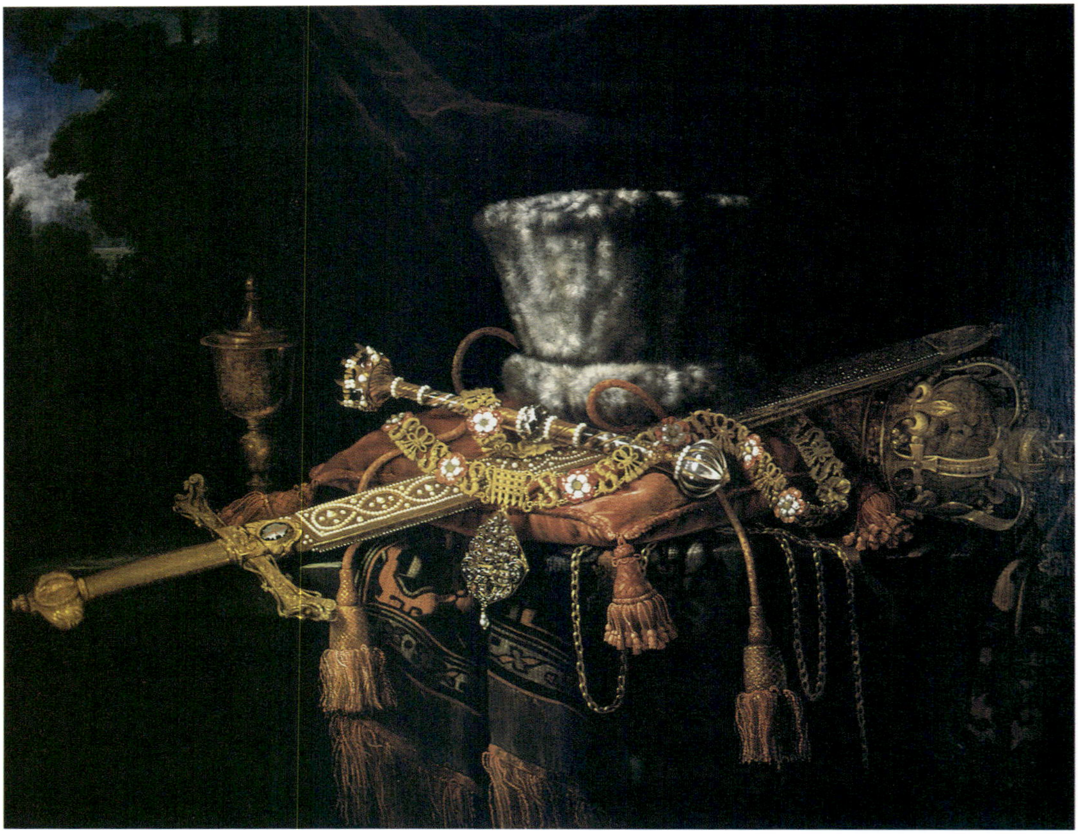

107 *Still life of City insignia attributed to Pieter Gerritsz van Roestraten (1630–1700).*

A further key difference between the designs is the realism of the Crutcher effigies and the idealization of the Woodman effigies. The Crutcher effigies are intended to be historically accurate portrayals of Sir Robert and Dame Martha at the time of their mayoralty in 1679–80. Dame Martha's effigy is a sculpted replica of her mayoress's portrait by Lorenzo da Castro (op. 1672–1700). Sir Robert's effigy is not a replica of his da Castro portrait, but he is represented in official robes in the style that was worn at the time of his mayoralty. The dress styles of Sir Robert and Dame Martha in the Woodman effigies are modernized. Sir Robert is portrayed in robes that were fashionable at the time he died. Dame Martha's flowing dress could be interpreted in two ways. Firstly, as classical drapery in which she is portrayed as the Virtue of Charity alongside the other two allegorical figures of Hope and Faith. Secondly, as a fashionable dress commonly worn by upper-class portrait sitters in the Queen Anne period. Sir Robert's chosen design was carried out in 1707: it represents him and his wife as they were in 1680, some twenty-five years earlier when he was at the pinnacle of his career, with no concessions to later changes of fashion.

The City insignia that formed part of the design brief of the Clayton monument had featured elsewhere. A late-seventeenth-century still-life painting, attributed to Pieter Gerritsz van Roestraten (1630–1700), illustrates the regalia worn by lord mayors — the collar of esses with its pendent badge and jewel. It also depicts the various insignia that accompanied the Lord Mayor and Court of Aldermen at official functions — sceptre, sword of state in its scabbard, the mace, cap of maintenance and chains of office. The sword and sceptre are crossed with the cap of maintenance above and a loving cup to one side. A similar arrangement of the City insignia was published in Wallis's 'London Armory' in 1677. Wallis's insignia design is the earliest of its kind to be found in the City's print archives and it may have been influenced by the Roestraten still life.[39] *Illus. 107*

Clayton served as vice-president of the London Workhouse in 1680 and John Riley (1646–91) was commissioned to paint a mayoral portrait of Clayton for the courtroom of the workhouse.[40] Riley's portrait included an upended sword and mace behind the lord mayor's chair. As the painting is currently being restored we reproduce here the print that was published after the Riley painting.[41] From the 1680s City insignia became commonplace in mayoral portraiture. The portrait of Clayton hung at the London Workhouse was framed with three carved oak panels attributed to Grinling Gibbons.[42] The panels were carved with the City's insignia: 'the Sword of State, Mace, and the Cap of Maintenance and shields of Arms and other ornaments.'[43] The Riley portrait of Clayton and its frame were transferred to the Corporation of London when the workhouse was demolished in 1831. The frame was re-varnished and glazed in 1899 and, in 1930, the painting was restored and re-framed.[44] The old panels survived the Second World War, but were in poor condition and their current whereabouts is unknown.[45] *Illus. 108*

The elaborate inscriptions on the Clayton monument seek to vindicate his moderate Whig politics and his moneyed wealth. The inscription, 'Non vultus instantis tyranni', at the foot of Sir Robert's effigy is taken from a verse of Horace's *Odes*:

Iustum et tenacem propositi virum	*Not the depraved ardour of urging citizens,*
non civium ardor prava iubentium,	*not the glare of the threatening tyrant,*
non vultus instantis tyranni	*Shakes from his steady mind*
mente quatit solida . . .[46]	*the just man who holds to his purpose.*[47]

The verse sums up Clayton's political stand at the high point of his career as Lord Mayor of London during the Exclusion crisis. On

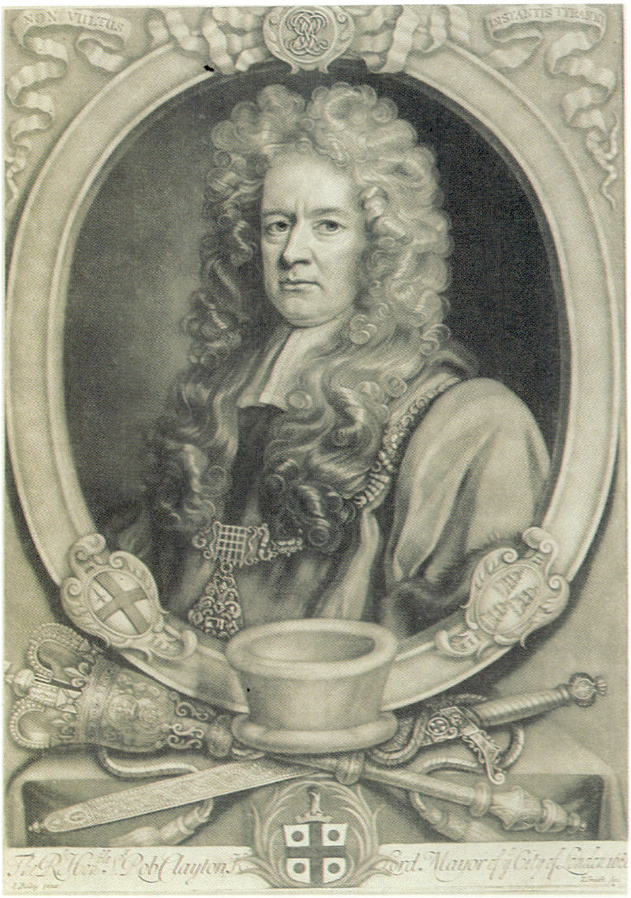

108 *John Smith (1652–1743) published a mezzotint of Riley's mayoral portrait of Clayton. The memorial plate was probably commissioned by the Clayton family and printed at the time of Sir Robert's death. Smith's mezzotint included the motto from Horace's* Odes *above the Riley portrait and below the portrait he depicted the three emblems from the base of the Clayton monument: City insignia, City arms and arms of the Drapers.*

the one hand he had to contend with the radical nonconformists and London mob — 'the depraved ardour of urging citizens' — and on the other hand he faced Charles II — 'the glare of the threatening tyrant'. The Whig principles set out in Clayton's lengthy epitaph include references to the rights of property, not to mention the 'just means' by which he made his fortune. Reference is also made to his belief in constitutional government and — within limits — a tolerant Anglican Church.

The presentation of Clayton's legacy was a truly multi-media affair encompassing portraiture, sculpture and print. For both the Langham and Clayton families, tomb sculpture nevertheless proved to be a key medium through which they could express their dynastic ambitions. A significant number of moneyed families of the late Stuart period followed in this tradition, albeit with variations on the theme exemplified by the Langham and Clayton families.

First Art Commission for Guildhall

Chapter Twelve

'... pictures be taken by a skilful hand & kept in some publique place of the citty ...'

VIVIEN KNIGHT

This essay examines the commission which the Court of Aldermen — comprising the City's grandest merchant elite — gave in 1670 for portraits of the judges who were assessing the property and compensation claims arising from the Great Fire of London.* The story of the commission, the fateful restoration scheme of 1779, the damage the portraits sustained in the Second World War and the ultimate de-accessioning from the Corporation's collection of all but two of them (*Illus. 109 & 110*), was told by the late James L. Howgego.[1] There are few facts to add to his comprehensive account; however, little has been done to place these portraits within the artistic context of their time and this is what this chapter will attempt to do.

* Before 1670 there are no references to any paintings in the Guildhall itself. In 1607 the Court of Aldermen had granted the Freedom of the City to John Cobbold, an artist from a distinguished Norwich family of gold and silversmiths: 'John Cobbold Painter so that he first give to this City the Kings Majesty's Picture in a fair table, to remain with the Lord Mayor for the time being shall be made free of this City by redemption in the Company of Painter Stainers' (Aldermen's Repertory 16 April 1607 fo. 7/8b). Nothing more is known of this picture.

FASHION FOR CELEBRITY PORTRAITS

Suites of portraits of illustrious men and beautiful women had been assembled in Italy and the Low Countries since the Renaissance.[2] In England, full length portraits of kings and queens had decorated the long galleries of great Elizabethan and Jacobean houses. Collections of commemorative portraits were also made for other reasons.[3] During the second half of the seventeenth century, a rise in the standard of living and the prestige accorded to the arts by the Restoration court led to an increase in the

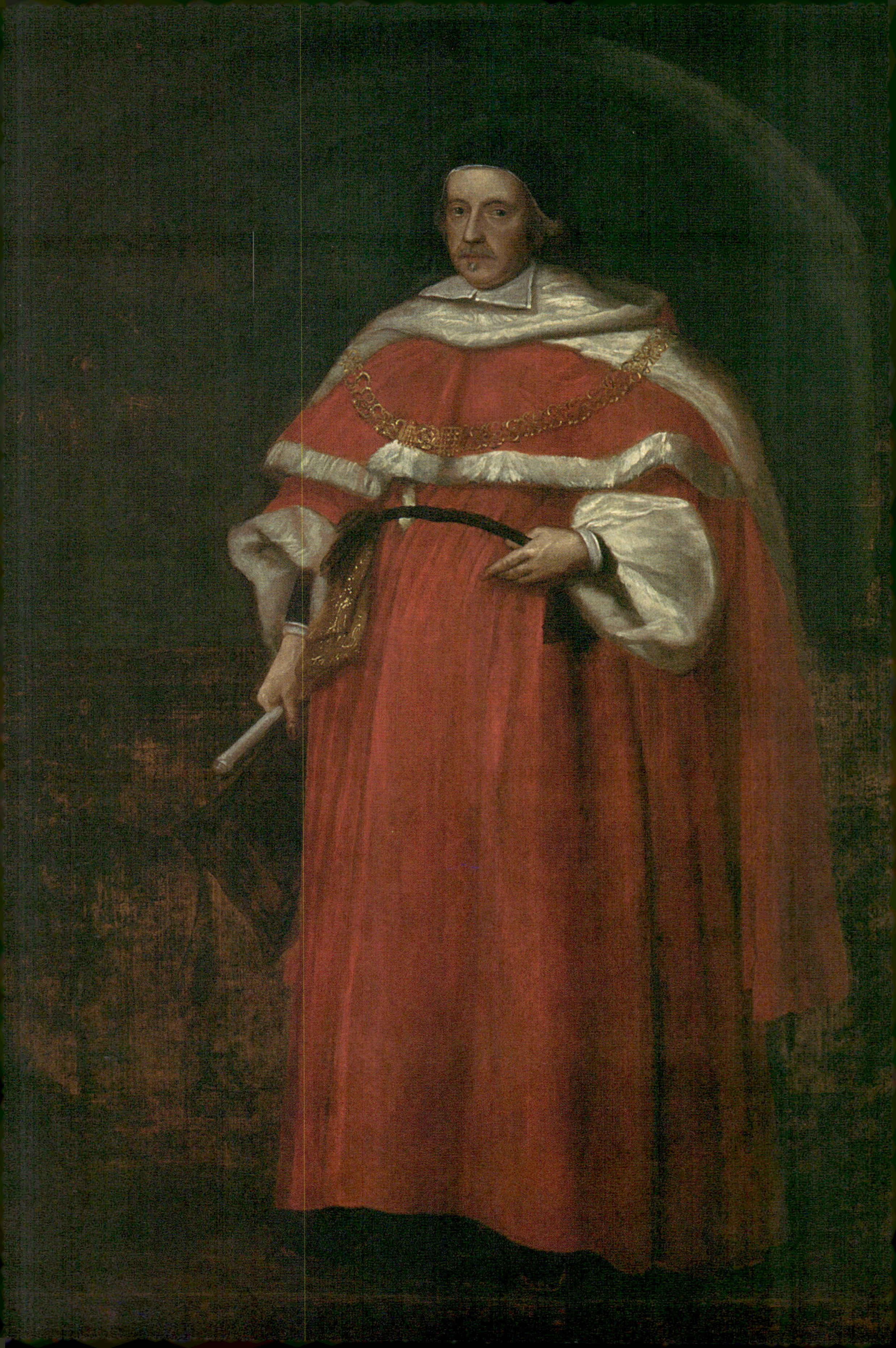

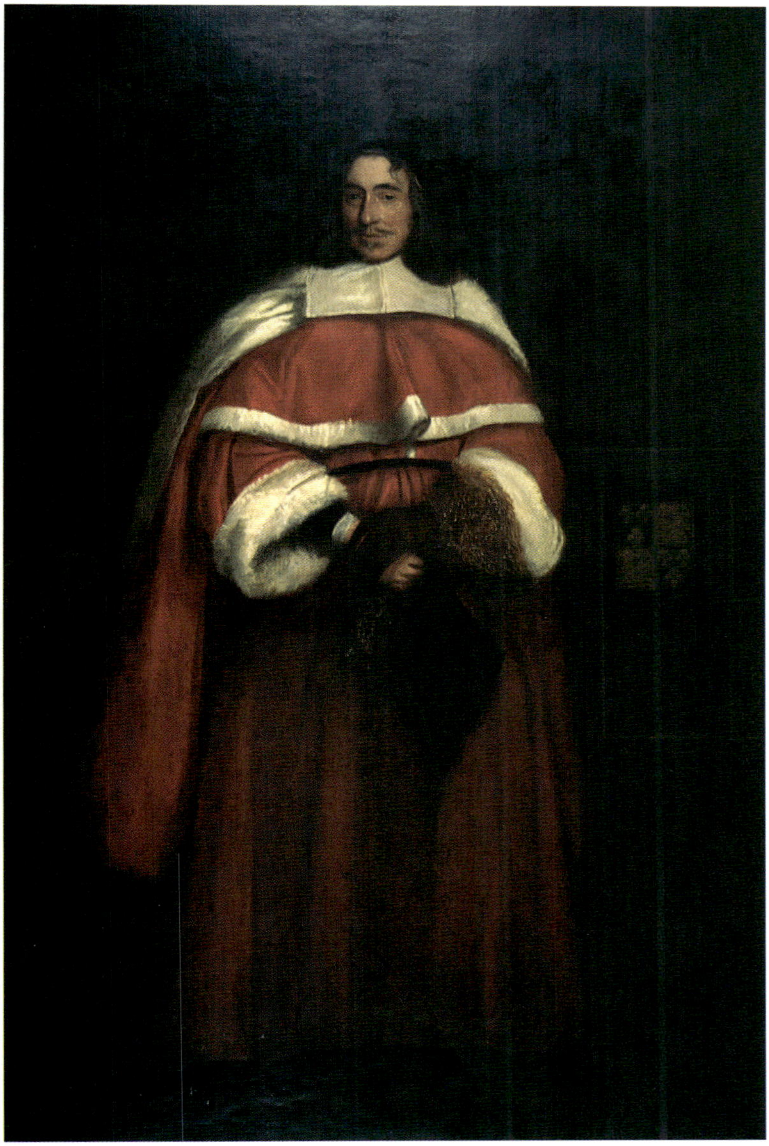

109 (opposite) *Portrait of Sir Matthew Hale, Chief Justice of the King's Bench, c. 1670/1, by John Michael Wright, oil on canvas.*

110 (this page) *Portrait of Sir Hugh Wyndham, Judge of the Common Pleas, c. 1670/1, by John Michael Wright, oil on canvas.*

production and popularity of portraits,[4]* which became important status symbols. From the mid-1660s onwards there was a positive fashion for sets or series of portraits, perhaps commemorating a significant event or associated with the building or restoration of an individual house. Rather than arising from a tradition of municipal or civic portraiture, such as that which had existed in Norwich since the mid-sixteenth century,[5] it was not until 1800 that the City of London commissioned its first mayoral portrait (Alderman Boydell). Even today only one further mayoral portrait

* Art historian Katharine Gibson has described the unprecedented popularity of portraits of Charles II: 'our most frequently depicted monarch before the benefits of photography. There are 1000 paintings of the King, 400 portrait engravings and some 60 or so works of sculpture'. On 27 July 1676 Wright wrote to Sir Walter Bagot: 'I am told the King will sit to my great picture for the Citty this next moneth …'. Presumably 'the Citty' referred to somewhere other than the Guildhall, as there are no references in Court of Aldermen minutes to such a commission.

has entered the collection this way, that of Dame Mary Donaldson, commissioned from Richard Stone in 1985 to commemorate her as the first female Lord Mayor. The origins of the Corporation's present-day collection lie instead in a set of portraits along the lines of those series which were assembled in court and aristocratic circles in the second half of the seventeenth century. Not only was the Fire Judges commission a response to this climate of fashionable taste, it also demonstrated the Aldermen's own taste and status in a highly visible and public manner.

THE 'FIRE JUDGES' COMMISSION

A Commission had been appointed to decide how to rebuild the City in October 1666, a month after the Great Fire; Parliament passed the first Rebuilding Act the following February. So that rebuilding would not be delayed or impeded by disputes between landlords and leaseholding tenants (on whom the obligation to rebuild was placed), a court of senior judges, the Fire Court, was also established to settle the inevitable claims. Eventually numbering twenty-two judges, this Court sat at Cliffords Inn from 1667 to 1672, its proceedings obviously of intense interest to the Court of Aldermen. On 19 April 1670 they resolved that:

in contemplacion of ye favour & kindnesse of ye right honoble Sir Orlando Bridgeman, kt. & barrt., lord keeper of the great seal of England, and the Justices of ye K(ing)s Bench and common pleas & barons of the exchequer to ye state of this citty in & about ye act of parliament & ye execucion of it for erecting a judicature for determining of differences between landlord & tenant, doth think fitt & order that their pictures be taken by a skillful hand & kept in some publique place of the citty for a gratefull memoriall of this good office.[6]

On 28 April the Court ordered the Recorder and Sheriffs to inform the judges of this decision and to ask them to sit for their portraits. No further references appear in the minutes for five months, until the meeting of 27 September 1670, when:

Mr Wright, Mr Houseman, Mr Haies and Mr [name omitted] being recommended unto this Court as skilfull Masters to draw the pictures of the right honourable the Lord Keeper, the Justices of both benches and Barons of the Exchequer ... It is thought fit and ordered that Sir John Robinson, Sir Robert Hanson, Sir Robert Vyner and Sir Joseph Sheldon or any three of them doe informe themselves and consider which one or more of the said Masters to employ in that work and make agreement with him or them for doing the same accordingly with all convenient speed.[7]

Were Robinson, Hanson, Vyner and Sheldon selected as the sub-committee because they had nominated the four artists? Had one or more of them been the originator of the scheme in the first place? In the absence of surviving background papers to the meetings of the Court of Aldermen at this period it is impossible to tell. However, they were also put in charge of the commission resolved upon the next day, 28 September 1670, when it was recorded that the Court

doth think fit and order that good peeces or pictures be obtained of his Majesty and His Royal Highness the Duke of York and that the same be placed where the Judges are intended to be in Guildhall ... as some Remembrance of their Royal Favours and encouragements to the work of rebuilding the City.[8]

Virtually twelve months passed with no further reference to the scheme, but portraits were evidently being painted at a speedy rate[9] because on 5 September 1671 it was 'ord that the lower part of the windows of the Guildhall shall be made up so far as shall be required for placing the Judges pictures which are now ready for that use.'[10]. Two days later, the Court ordered 'Prince Rupert's picture to be put up in Guildhall', but nothing more is heard of this.[11] On 14 December 1671 the sub-committee reported to the Court: *Illus. 111–112*

We have agreed with Mr. Lilly for the pictures of the King and Duke of York to pay him one hundred pounds And for the pictures of the Lord Keeper and the Judges which were done by Mr Wright wee have agreed to allow him XXXVI li. per picture which for the 14 pictures amounts to £504, although his common price hath always been £40 for pictures of whole length and for these hee demanded more in regard of his extraordinary expenses in painting the same upon Bed Tickin (which are usually done on canvas) and priming them on both sides double for strength and substance. Also Mr Wright the Herald Painter's bill for painting the Judges' Coates of Arms and inscriptions of their names at Xs apiece amounts to £6. 10s. And we also certify that wee agreed with Mrs Ashfield and Mrs Flushier for doing the frames of the Judges' pictures (...) at £12 a peece and £15 a peece for the Kings and Duke of Yorkes, eight of the Judges were done by Mrs Ashfield which amounts to £96 and five by Mrs Flushier which with the other to amounts to £90 (besides one formerly paid for to Mr Norris).[12]

We now know the names of the chosen artists: Sir Peter Lely (1618–80), the most important and successful painter of the restoration court, and one of his principal competitors John Michael Wright (1617–94). We also learn that Lely was paid £50 for each full length portrait (which seems something of a knock-down price, since his price for a half-length was recorded in October 1671 as £30, and at the time of his death only nine years later his regular charge for a full length was £80); and Wright £36, although this too was below his normal price, particularly as the Guildhall portraits were painted on a more durable support.*

* Restoration of the portrait of Sir Matthew Hale (*Illus. 109*) in 1990 revealed that it had been painted on linen with a herring bone weave, i.e. a support that corresponds with Webster's *Dictionary*'s definition of bed ticking. It is not clear whether it had been primed on both sides, because all the portraits were lined in 1779. However, instead of being paid more than usual for this support, Wright was paid less. Presumably the Aldermen had been able to negotiate a lower price for quantity.

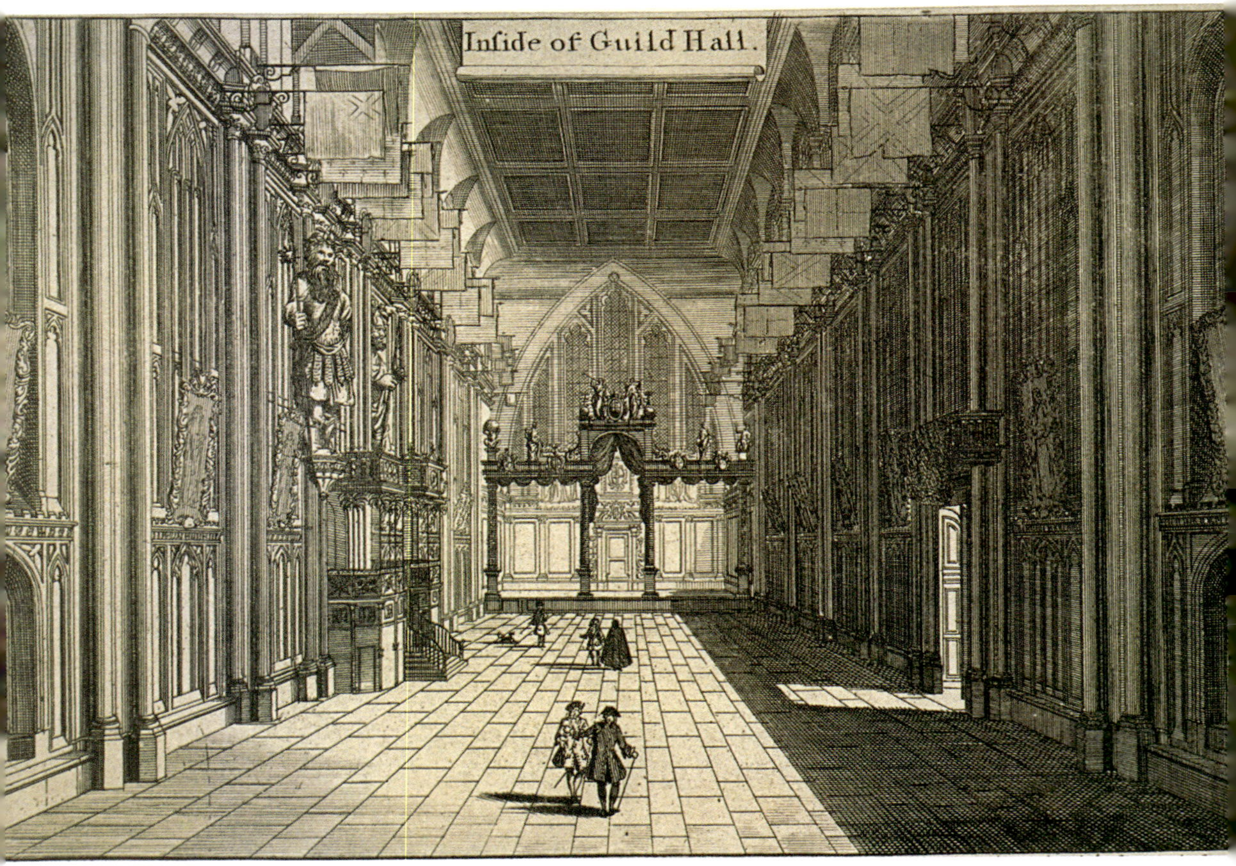

111 *Interior of the Guildhall looking East, 1724, engraving. This is the earliest visual record in existence showing the original arrangement of the Fire Judges paintings along the lower half of the windows.*

It is not known whether Wright employed assistants on the Guildhall commission and the devastating restoration and over-painting of the surviving portraits mean it is impossible to distinguish different hands. Nevertheless, he completed the fourteen whole lengths in as many months (i.e. between September 1670 and December 1671, when he was paid), and may even have finished them by September 1671 when the windows of Guildhall were blocked up. The portraits evidently gave satisfaction, since Wright was paid for the portraits of three further judges in November 1672 and on the same day was ordered to copy an existing portrait of Sir Samuel Browne, who had died. In 1674 he was commissioned to paint Heneage Finch, Earl of Nottingham and in 1675 he was paid for three more, bringing the total to twenty-two. All were framed in matching but not identical pine auricular or Sunderland frames, a style which was fashionable between the 1660s and the 1680s. John Evelyn went to view the series before its completion recording in his diary, 'I went home, turning in, as I

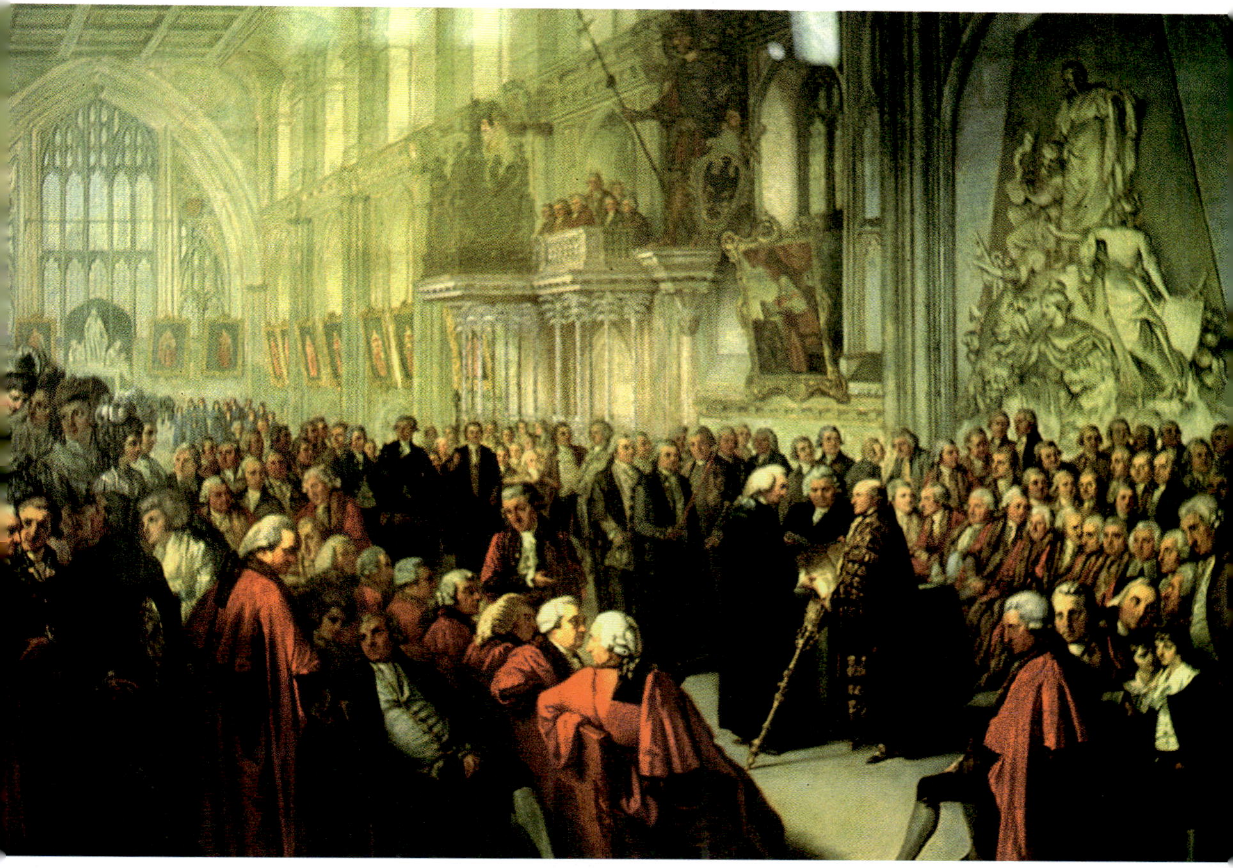

went through Cheape side to see the Pictures of all the Judges and Eminent men of the Long Robe newly painted by Mr Write, and set up in Guild-Hall costing the Citty 1000 pounds [sic; Evelyn was mistaken]; most of them are very like the persons they are made to represent, although I never took Write to be any considerable artist.'[13]

112 *The Ceremony of Swearing In Alderman Nathaniel Newnham, 8 November 1782, by William Miller, oil on canvas. In 1803, John Nichols recorded: 'when the Guildhall was repaired in 1779, all the portraits (except the modern ones) were in so bad a condition that it became a matter of doubt whether they were to be restored to their places or committed to the flames'. The portraits were restored and this painting, executed a few years later, shows them rehung.*

PRECEDENTS FOR THE SERIES

Evelyn had himself been associated with a commemorative series of portraits which may have set a precedent for the Fire Judges. This was the collection assembled by Edward Hyde, Lord Clarendon (the Lord Chancellor), for the great mansion which he built in Piccadilly between 1664 and 1667. It followed renaissance models in containing the portraits both of famous historic figures and of contemporaries.[14] Clarendon received some of the older portraits as gifts and was able to acquire some originals by Van Dyck at sales, but most of his collection comprised copies of existing portraits

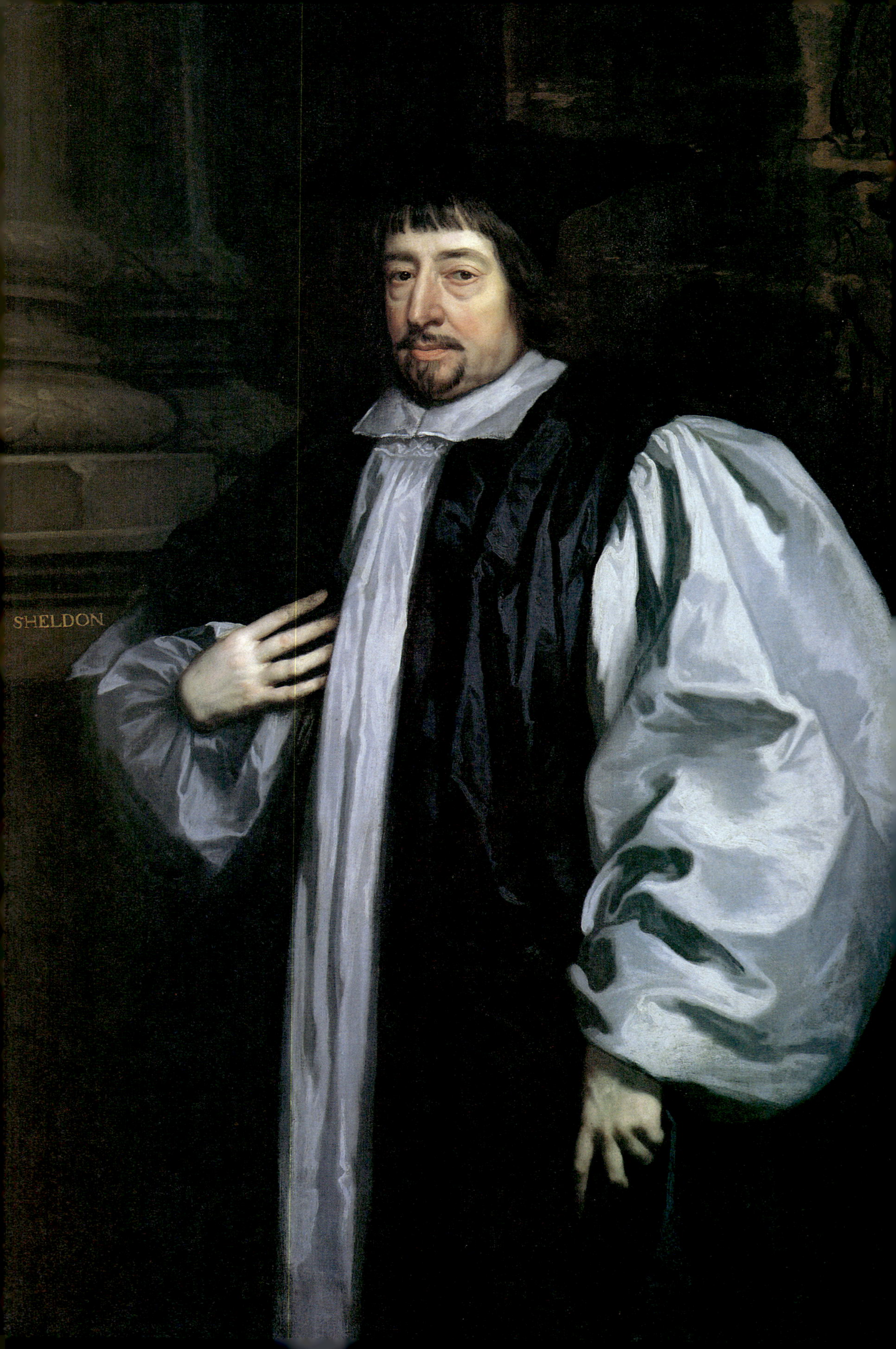
SHELDON

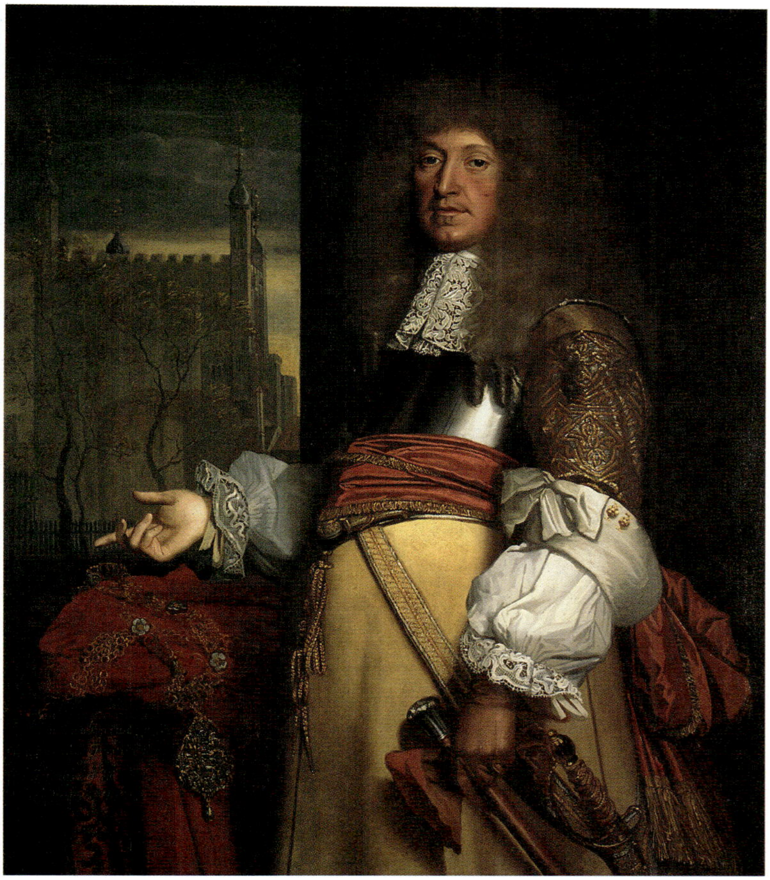

113 (opposite) *Portrait of Gilbert Sheldon, Archbishop of Canterbury, c. 1665, Studio of Sir Peter Lely, oil on canvas.*

114 *Portrait of Sir John Robinson, c. 1672, by John Michael Wright, oil on canvas. It had hitherto been assumed that Robinson's portrait was painted to commemorate his mayoralty in 1662. However, the weather vanes shown in the painting were only installed in 1669 and the style of the wig is datable to 1672–74. It is probable that the portrait was painted after the Fire Judges commission, perhaps in 1672 when Sir Robert Vyner, Robinson's colleague on the sub-committee, commissioned both his family's group portrait (Illus. 110) and that of Prince Rupert from Wright.*

elsewhere and original portraits of his contemporaries, which he commissioned from Lely and his studio from the mid 1660s. They were all half length (roughly 50 x 40 inches)[15] and had gilded Sunderland or other auricular frames.[16]* The portrait which Clarendon commissioned *c.* 1665 of his old friend Sir Gilbert Sheldon (*Illus. 113*), Archbishop of Canterbury and uncle of Alderman Sir Joseph Sheldon, offers a direct link between Clarendon's collection and the Guildhall commission.

Another very well known series was that of the Flagmen of Lowestoft, commissioned by the Duke of York for his apartment at Whitehall.[17] The set depicted the officers who had served under the Duke to defeat the enemy at the opening battle in 1665 of the second Dutch War and comprised thirteen three-quarter-length portraits by Lely. The Flagmen were probably modelled on an earlier series depicting Lord Vere's Commanders.[18] We may infer that Alderman John Robinson was aware of the series because of the similarity in both the pose and the costume of his own portrait,

* In a letter to Pepys (12 August 1689), Evelyn wrote: 'When his designe was once made known, anybody who either had them of their owne or could purchase them at any price, strove to make their court by these presents; by which means he got many excellent pictures of Vandyke, and other originals by Lely and the best of our modern masters' hands.' As late as March 1667 Evelyn sent Clarendon a list of 42 further sitters to be included, not long before Clarendon fell from grace and fled to France. On 20 December 1668 Evelyn dined with Clarendon's son, recording in his Diary: 'I dined with my *Lord Cornbury* at *Clarendon house*, now bravely furnish'd; especialy with the Pictures of most of our antient & modern *Witts, Poets, Philosophers* famous & learned English-men, which Collection of my L: Chancellors, I much commended, and gave his Lordship a Cataloge (sic) of more to be added.'

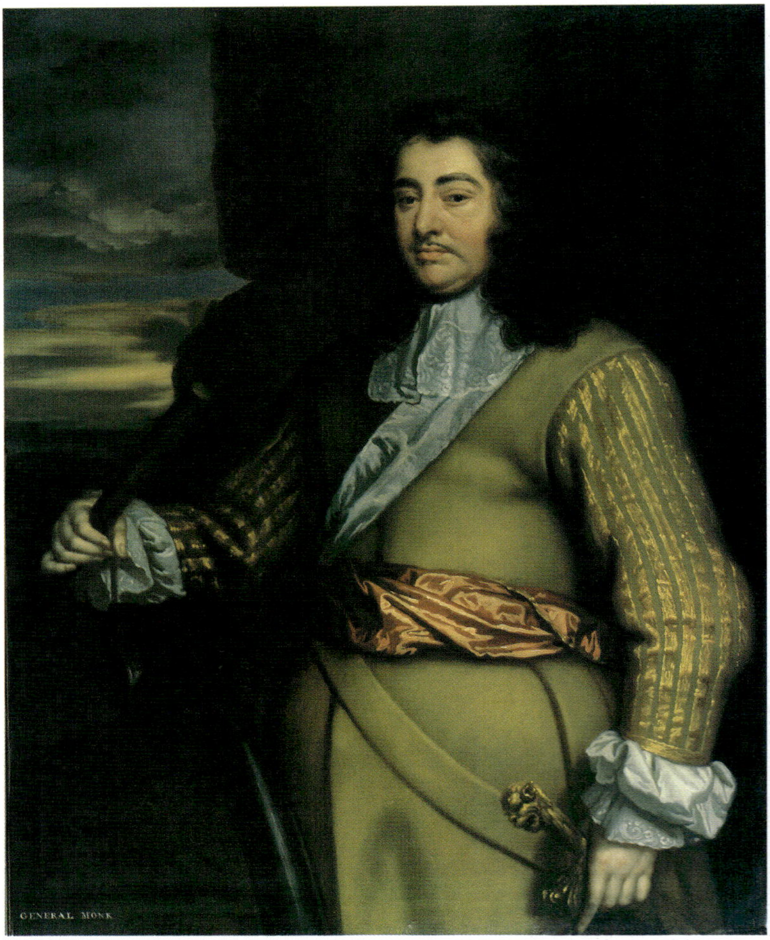

115 *George Monck, 1st Duke of Albemarle, c. 1665–66, Studio of Sir Peter Lely, oil on canvas. This is a replica of Monck's portrait by Lely, one of the original 'Flagmen' paintings now hanging at the Queen's House in Greenwich. In this small world, Robinson and Monck were at least acquainted. John Evelyn, who also knew Robinson, recorded on 15 December 1665: 'I din'd at the Sheriffs of Lond. with the Duke & Duchess of Albemarle & Lieutennant of the Tower, where was a mighty feast.'*

116 (opposite) *Portrait of Sir Joseph Sheldon, 1678, by Gerard Soest (1600–81), oil on canvas. Soest also painted Fire Judge Sir Richard Rainsford in 1678, a copy of which is in the National Portrait Gallery.*

as Lieutenant of the Tower of London (1660–80) by John Michael Wright with some of the Flagmen's portraits — in particular with that of George Monck, Lord Albemarle. A firm royalist, Robinson was a figure of some influence in the move towards the restoration of the monarchy[19] although Pepys described him as

Illus. 114 & 115

a talking, bragging Bufflehead, a fellow that would be thought to have led all the City in the great business of bringing in the King ... [nor is there] any man that could have kept the City for the King thus well and long but him — and if the country can be preserved, he will undertake that the City shall not dare to stir again — when I am confident there is no man almost in the City cares a turd for him, nor hath he brains to outwit any ordinary tradesman.[20]

Monck on the other hand was a hard professional soldier who had been genuinely responsible for bringing Charles II back to England. If we are to believe Pepys on Robinson's character, it is tempting

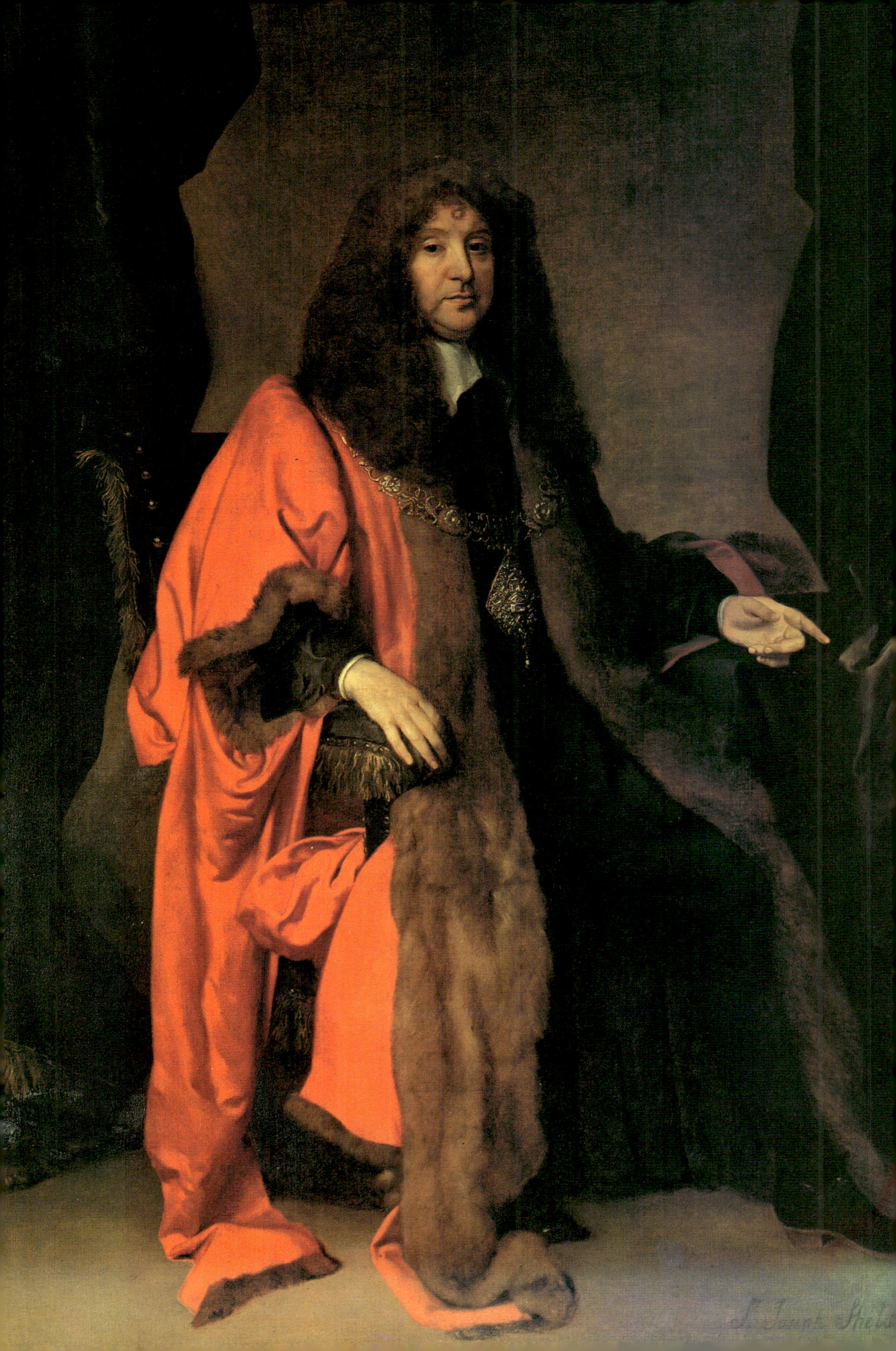

to think that boastful vanity may have led him to be portrayed in the same mould. Furthermore, while retaining the same format, his own portrait is slightly larger!

Sets of portraits of beautiful women were also very popular from the mid-1660s onwards. The principal scheme was that of the 'Windsor Beauties', ten half length portraits of the leading and most beautiful women at Court, painted 1666–68 by Lely for Ann Hyde, Duchess of York. It is not now known how they were framed[21] but the 'Althorp Beauties' which they inspired — painted by Lely and studio for Robert Spencer 2nd Earl of Sunderland from the mid-1660s for his newly remodelled house — retain the 'Sunderland' frames so named in the nineteenth century because of the Earl's fondness for them.[22]

SIR PETER LELY, TRENDSETTER

The name common to all the series mentioned above is that of the most fashionable and successful painter of his day, Sir Peter Lely. Unsurprisingly, according to George Vertue, he was the Aldermen's first choice, but 'he would not wait upon the Judges in the City to paint them wherefore Wright had them to do'.[23] Without further documentation we cannot know with certainty, but the long gap between the Aldermen deciding on the scheme in April and only considering four recommended artists in September suggests that a hiccup of this sort must have occurred. We know from Pepys that Lely was 'a mighty proud man ... and full of state',[24] but also that he did wait upon his more important patrons.[25] We also know that by this time the demand for series of portraits and copies of royal portraits was so intense that Lely only painted the head, the rest of the figure, the draperies and background being undertaken by assistants. It is therefore quite possible that he and his studio were simply too busy to undertake to produce fourteen full-length portraits at this time.[26]

So whose was the missing name in the list of artists considered by the Court on 27 September 1670? If Lely had already turned down the Fire Judges job at some date between April and September his would not have been the fourth name, alongside 'Mr Wright' (John Michael Wright), 'Mr Haies' (John Hayls) and 'Mr Houseman' (Jacob Huysmans). Further, why would the minuting clerk not have been able to grasp Lely's very well known name on this date, when he had no difficulty with it the following day? Perhaps the missing name was less familiar, and a harder one to spell. A possible candidate for the fourth man could be Gerard Souest, (approximately pronounced 'Zerst'), chosen by the

Drapers' Company to paint Sir Joseph Sheldon in 1678. Their records show how hard it was to grasp his name — the Company's clerk spelled it 'Zeux (a limner)'.

Illus. 116

CONCLUSION

All the evidence — circumstantial though it is — shows that the Aldermen had elevated models before them when they commissioned the first ever paintings for Guildhall. Commemorating those involved in enabling the City to rise anew from the ashes of the Fire was like commemorating the Flagmen who had inflicted their decisive defeat on the Dutch only the year before. Like Clarendon and the Earl of Sunderland, the Aldermen had a building needing to be appropriately beautified (Guildhall had been extensively damaged during the Great Fire and was newly restored). A direct link with Clarendon's collection existed in Sir Joseph Sheldon, while Sir John Robinson must have known Monck's 'Flagmen' portrait. The same fashionable style of frame as had been used by

117 *Unveiling The Coronation Luncheon at Guildhall, 1937, by Frank O. Salisbury. The Fire Judges had been hung in the old Council Chamber from 1886 and were transferred to the Gallery in 1909. They can clearly be seen here along the top of the walls, their gilded frames now painted brown.*

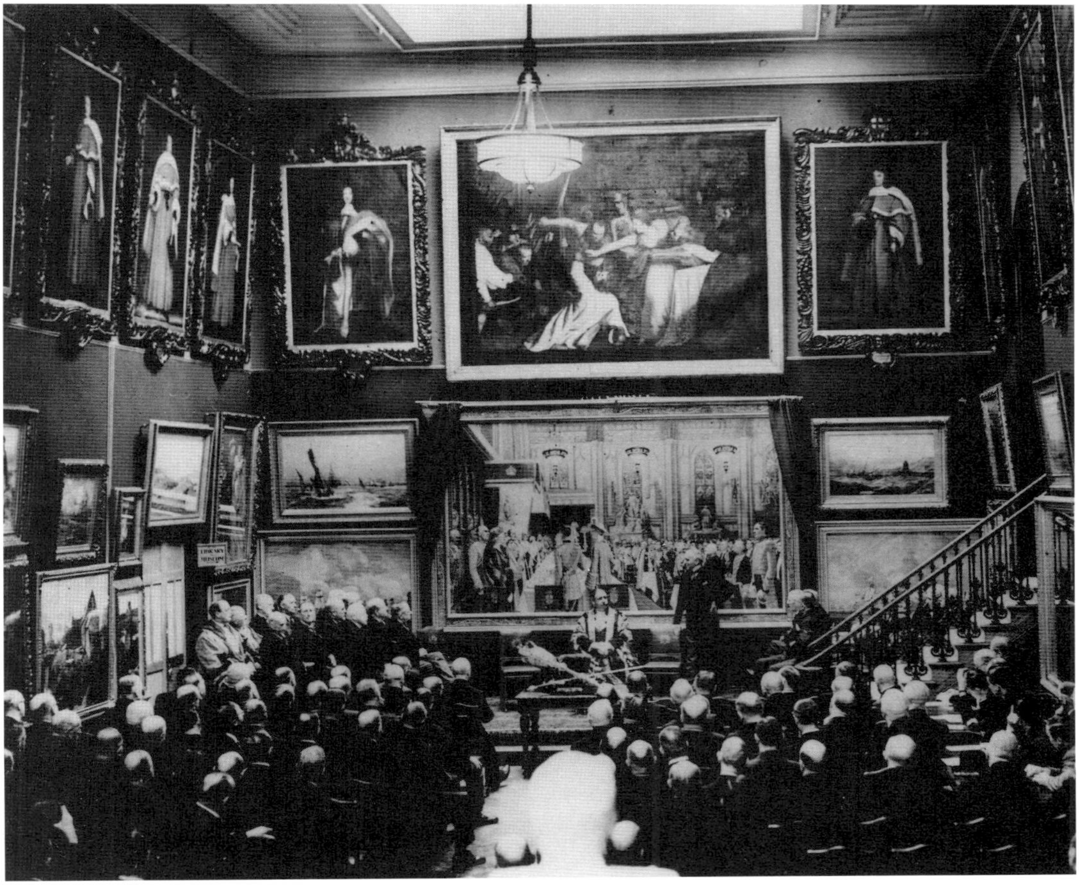

Lord Clarendon and Lord Sunderland was employed both for the Fire Judges and the two royal portraits, showing that all the portraits were conceived as a single series, at the forefront of contemporary taste. And while the Flagmen, Clarendon's portraits, the Windsor Beauties and the Althorp Beauties were all three-quarter length (roughly 50 x 40 inches), the Court of Aldermen proclaimed their magnificence by going one step further in having the Judges portraits as full lengths of 87 x 60 inches to which the large, fleshy shapes and the proportions of the Sunderland style of frames were even better suited. Though sadly now dispersed and some destroyed, the Fire Judges series formed an extraordinary document of grand patronage by City Merchants boldly embellishing the unique institution to which they belonged. *Illus. 117*

A DAY IN THE LIFE OF A MERCHANT TAYLOR

A Realistic Fantasy

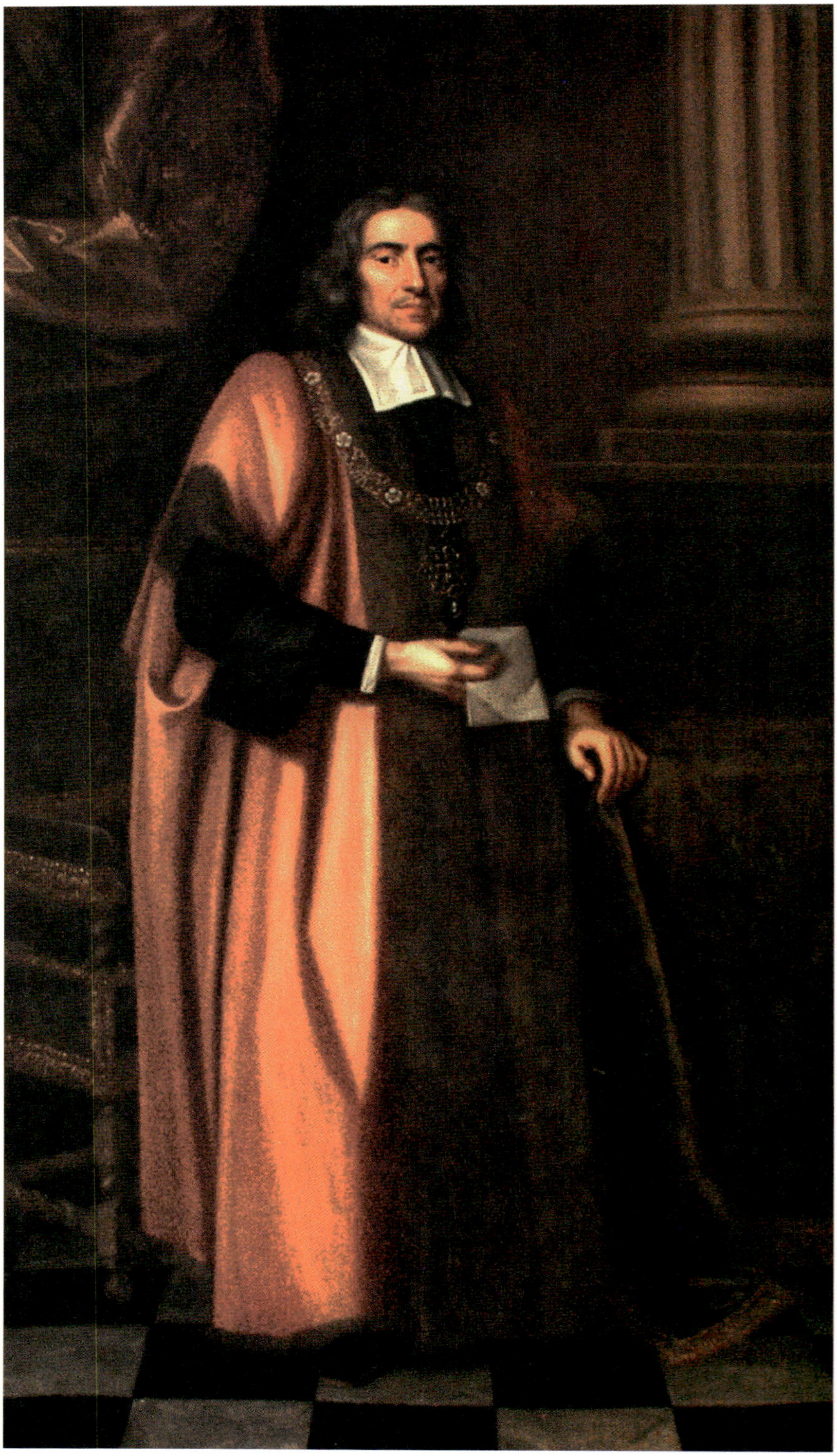

118 *Full length portrait of William Turner, 1675, by Mary Beale, oil on canvas. This portrait, executed two years after the present account, shows William Turner wearing his mayoral chain of office. In 1675, Turner had sold the business beside St Paul's and moved to Warwick Lane; he furnished his new dwelling handsomely but without extravagance.*

A DAY IN THE LIFE OF A MERCHANT TAYLOR

Chapter Thirteen

Sir William Turner 1615–1693

'a sober, considering man'

Pepys' *Diary*

ANN SAUNDERS

Sir William Turner stirred in his bed; it was the morning of 1 November 1673 and he was almost two months past his fifty-eighth birthday. It was more than eleven years since the King had knighted him.[1]

It was very early, not yet light, and he lay warm and comfortable under a coverlet and two stout blankets of Yorkshire wool, and let himself drift in and out of sleep. It was a small luxury; once up, it would be a long and busy day. He was, thank God, under his own roof.[2]* His house in Cheapside, opposite the Mercers' Hall and the street called Old Jewry, was one of the first to be rebuilt after the dreadful Fire. He had intended it to be an example to the whole City, to demonstrate that, even after so complete a catastrophe, determination and sheer grit, true grit — Yorkshire grit — can pull you through, can drive you to rebuild on the ruins, and to build better than before.

* His own roof. I am uncertain where this was in 1673, but it was probably over his shop on the south side of St Paul's Churchyard. For the purpose of the paper, I have left him at 73 Cheapside, the house opposite Old Jewry, where he is said to have kept his mayoral year in 1668.

Illus. 119

He had been Lord Mayor in 1668, a hard year. Being a bachelor — for which too he thanked God — he had been entitled to a gift of £400 from the King and he had claimed it. His Majesty had laughed, said he didn't know where to find the money, but had

Illus. 118

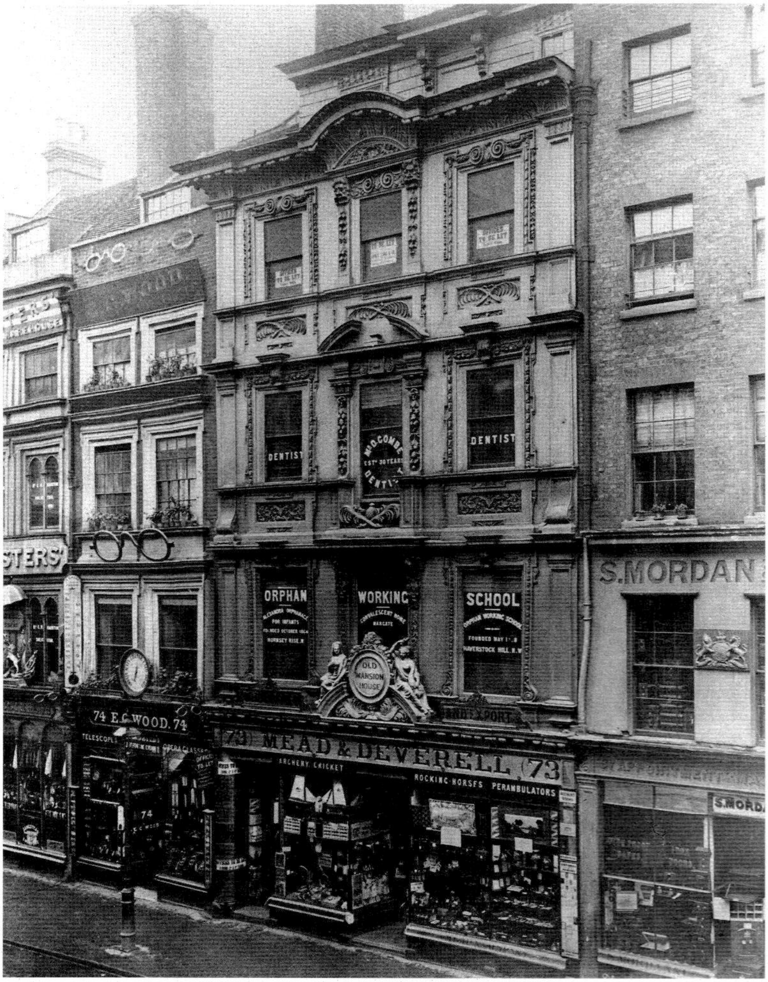

119 *This Henry Dixon photograph records the house of William Turner at 73 Cheapside in 1883. Traditionally, the house was attributed to Wren, and was certainly one of the first to be rebuilt after the Fire. In the 1840s, Thomas Tegg, man of letters and bookseller, had his premises there; it was only demolished in 1929.*

given it all the same, and he, William Turner, had given it all to the City, to go towards the rebuilding of Guildhall which would soon be getting a fine new roof. He had kept his mayoral year soberly enough, not that he was averse to feasting and merriment, but because the emergency was such that prudence and restraint were the only wise measures. He had gone by water to Westminster for his swearing in as Mayor. There had been no pageant but he had permitted the Company one small extravagance — sky-blue plush caps for the oarsmen of his barge — and they had looked bravely as they went along the Thames on a grey day in late autumn.[3] Nevertheless, he had given a grand dinner, with over £300 spent on the meats and with oysters in plenty, and he himself had looked grand too, wearing a gown of sable velvet trimmed with gold buttons and loops, and with a grey squirrel mantle about his shoulders.

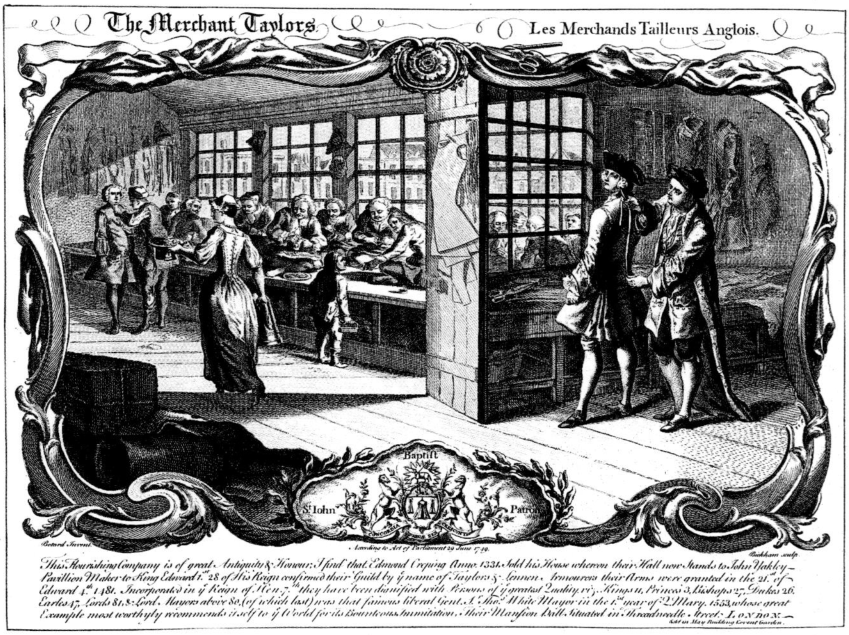

120 *This 1749 print by Louis Philippe Boitard shows the interior of a Merchant Taylor's workshop. On the right is the foreman, 'the best workman in the shop . . . who takes measure when the Master is out of the way, cuts and finishes all the work, and carries it Home to the Customer'.*

Altogether he had spent nigh on £100 on his clothes, and the saddle and furnishings of his horse had cost him more than £50 — it was a good beast that he had ridden, now safe in the stable, and that had been another £28 — he could not stop reckoning — but it had all made a grand show.[4] And it was not only the lofty ones that he had entertained — he had given not one but two dinners to those who were not on the Livery. The freemen — the Bachelors' Company, they called themselves — the fellows who did the cutting and pinning and tacking and stitching — he had feasted them as well as he had done the lords, and they had revelled in it.

Irritating thoughts began to impinge on his mind — how his predecessor in the mayoral chair, Sir William Bolton, a fellow Merchant Taylor, had greedily insisted on the impoverished Company giving him his full allowance of £100 when they could scarce afford it; and had then dipped his fingers in the City funds, had taken nigh £2000 of the money given to help the Fire sufferers.[5] Well, Bolton had disgraced himself and his Company, though they still allowed him to sit on the Court, but he, William Turner, had done better by the Merchant Taylors and would do more that very day once he was up and about.

He lay warm for another few minutes. He could hear the household beginning to stir and Nan, the youngest of the four maidservants, riddling at the ashes to light a fire in his room where he conducted business.[6] He thought he could hear her singing in a

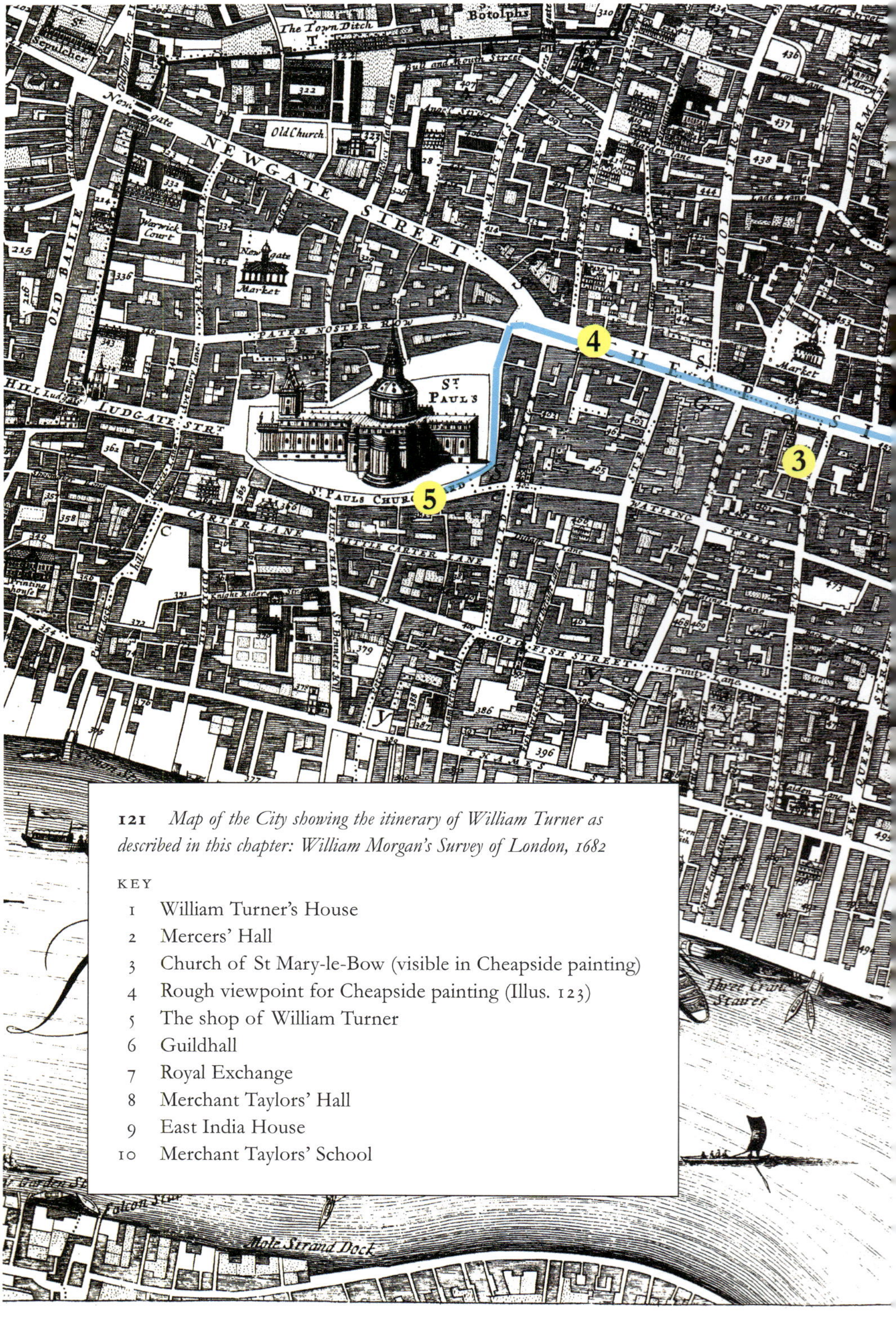

121 *Map of the City showing the itinerary of William Turner as described in this chapter: William Morgan's Survey of London, 1682*

KEY

1 William Turner's House
2 Mercers' Hall
3 Church of St Mary-le-Bow (visible in Cheapside painting)
4 Rough viewpoint for Cheapside painting (Illus. 123)
5 The shop of William Turner
6 Guildhall
7 Royal Exchange
8 Merchant Taylors' Hall
9 East India House
10 Merchant Taylors' School

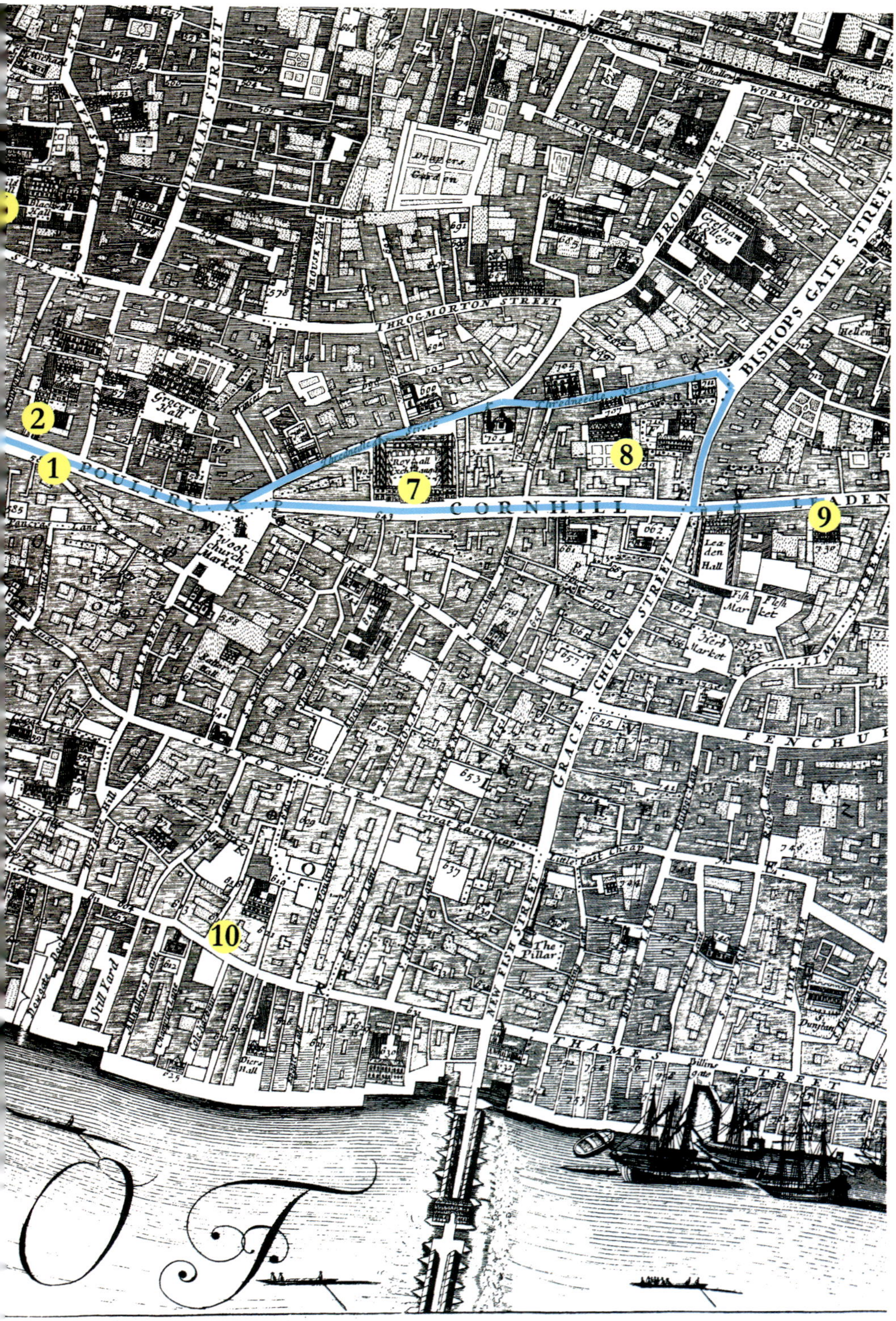

1
2
7
8
9
10
COLEMAN STREET
THROGMORTON STREET
BROAD STR.
BISHOPS GATE STREET
WORMWOOD
Drapers Garden
Gresham College
Grocers Hall
POULTRY
CORNHILL
Wool church Market
Leaden Hall
Fish Market
Flesh Market
Herb Market
GRACE CHURCH STREET
NEW FISH STREET
The Pillar
Still Yard
THAMES STREET

small voice, an old song with a plaintive tune, about a girl from the north come up to London and sighing to be home again. He knew that feeling. Home was Kirkleatham near the north Yorkshire coast, cold, but the air was clean, not like London; and a man could see and walk for miles across the moors.

But it was no use complaining. London had done well by him, and he by London, he told himself. He remembered how he had come up, a raw lad in his mid-teens, and had been apprenticed to Master Jerrard Gore, Merchant Taylor, who had taught him well how to serve a customer and how to measure cloth and assess its quality. It was in the sale of cloth, rather than in the making of garments, that money was to be made — unless you could get a Government contract, that is. He had become free of his Company, and had dined in its fine old Hall with the great model ship hanging from the roof beams. In that ship, three singers, attired in pale blue silk like luxuriously apparelled mariners, had serenaded the King, Scots Jamie, in 1607. He, William Turner, had not been born then but old Merchant Taylors still remembered the feast, which had cost over £1000, and the rare delicacy of potatoes had been served to the guests, while Master Ben Jonson had written welcoming poems and songs.[7] Those had been the days!

Frontispiece, Illus. 67

Illus. 120

But then it had all gone sour with the quarrels between Jamie's son, Charles, and his Parliament. He had remained in London through the war years, keeping his head down, not getting involved. Three of his name, though no relatives of his, had got contracts and made fortunes from making uniforms and boots for Cromwell's men — and had sent one load out to Ireland of such poor quality that the troops refused to accept the gear.[8]

Those wars had taught the young to be saucy, however. Sir William began to fidget in his bed, remembering how, as Mayor, he had been invited to dine with the Lent Reader of the Inner Temple, but had been advised to come as a mere citizen without his sword borne in state before him, since the Temple precinct was outside the City's jurisdiction. He had sent word that he would certainly come, but in such state as befitted the Lord Mayor of London — 'I will bear up my sword and see who dares take it down'. The student lawyers had dared — two of them judges' sons, moreover — and there had been a scuffle and general fracas and a good dinner spoiled. Sir William had complained to the King, who had promised to adjudicate in the matter, but had done nothing. There was no way of knowing it, that November morning, but ten years later the City would have its revenge on the Temple — but that is another story.[9]*

* The revenge came ten years later, when a fire broke out in the Inner Temple and the Corporation turned away its fire engines when the inmates still refused to acknowledge the City's authority.

Sir William got out of bed and washed his face and hands. He put on his banyan, a loose wrapping gown that had become fashionable and which he liked for it was very comfortable. He went down to his room for business, where the fire was alight and drawing well, drank some ale and munched a piece of bread; folk talked about the new luxury drinks of coffee and tea, and no doubt he would hear more of them at a noontime meeting he must attend, but he preferred well-tried, honest fare. He planned the day ahead as he put on his shirt carefully, pulled on his breeches and stockings, and settled his coat on his shoulders. First, he would walk up to his shop, the Golden Fleece, on the south side of St Paul's Churchyard,[10] and see how matters were going there and how the cloth was displayed; he had long since ceased to work as a tailor — there was more money to be made out of the sale of French silks and luxury goods. He had great confidence in his staff and their foreman — there were half a dozen of them and a couple of boys — but it was as well to keep an eye on how things were going.

Illus. 121

Nothing was happening yet at St Paul's. The great cathedral was still in ruins. He had heard from his friend Robert Hooke that *his* friend, Dr Christopher Wren, had great plans for it, but that the dean and canons were contentious; he hoped the King would intervene soon — whatever you might say about the royal family — and there was plenty that you *could* say — young Charles — well, not so young now — was a good monarch for all his frivolous exterior and his love of the theatre and, Sir William feared, of actresses.[11]* Anyone who had been in London in those dreadful days when the Fire had raged to consume everything, would remember how Charles had kept his head when most others, including Tom Bludworth, the fool who was Mayor that year, stood by dithering and wringing their hands, the doo-lally lot. Charles had taken charge and God had helped him by sending rain in the early hours of Thursday morning after four days of devastation.[12] Once the new cathedral was under way, whatever form it might take, Sir William would rebuild his shop in the churchyard. Now, it was little better than a booth, though it still turned a pretty penny, but he had plans for it. His foreman told him that his kinsman by marriage, Samuel Pepys, who was doing well in the Navy Office, though his father had been a poor and unsuccessful tailor, had been in the previous day to buy cloth for a new vest, coat and breeches, and had paid for it on the nail.[13]† Sam Pepys was a good fellow, Sir William thought, and perhaps he himself should have a new suit of clothes, but plain-cut and sensible, like himself.

Illus. 122

* Turner seems to have been particularly harsh towards prostitutes. After his death, a rather rude poem was published, *Good Sir W—knock: The Whores Lamentation for the death of Sir W. T.* It refers to the ladies as

A Jolly Troop and wondrous
Tender-Hearted
All with thy Favours graced,
Some Whip'd, some Carted.

† Turner's elder brother, John, was married to Jane Pepys, the daughter of the diarist's cousin. It was she who offered her house in Salisbury Court to the diarist when he was operated on for the stone, and she nursed him back to health afterwards. John Turner, a lawyer, became Recorder of York in 1662 and King's Sergeant in 1669.

Illus. 123

He began to walk back along Cheapside, past his own front door, reflecting how, when he had finished his year as Mayor, they had wanted him to serve a second term. He was not having any of that — one year of office had cost him enough — the quantities of oysters those fellows could eat![14] Yes, shellfish were cheap enough, but in such mounds! Who was that giant he had heard of in the French tale? Gargantua or some such name? Well, the Frenchman would be nothing beside his fellow Aldermen.

As he walked, he wondered what was going on in the City in the way of tailoring. He knew that there was some secret stitching in hand to provide the King's brother, the Duke of York, with a suit in which to meet his new bride when she reached these shores.* The Duke's first wife was dead — Anne Hyde, a commoner like himself but a handsome woman and well able to bear herself in royal circles. She had borne eight children, brave lady, the last when she was dying herself of some inward cancer, but only two had survived, two little girls, Mary and Anne. He knew the Duke for a stout fellow and a true experienced sailor, and he knew Sam Pepys had great respect for His Grace — but now the Duke had turned Catholic and all was in a pother. Sir William himself was firmly Protestant — not a fanatic like those who had caused so much

* In 1671, Anne Hyde, wife to James, Duke of York, and mother of the future Queens Mary and Anne, died. Two years later, the Duke decided to marry again. He sent Henry Mordaunt, Earl of Petersfield, as his representative. Mordaunt inspected the Princess Mary of Modena on 18 September 1673, and reported favourably on the young girl. James signified his willingness though it took a letter from the Pope to persuade the Princess to agree to the marriage. They were married by proxy on 30 September and Mary set out, accompanied by her mother, reaching Dover on 21 November. The proxy marriage was confirmed before witnesses and was considered legal.

122 *We have grown used to the images of the devastation left by the Great Fire. This account of William Turner's day restitutes to this vast and well known episode some of its poignancy. This detail from Hollar's panorama of London after the Great Fire of London focuses on St Paul's Cathedral where, in the churchyard, William Turner had his shop.*

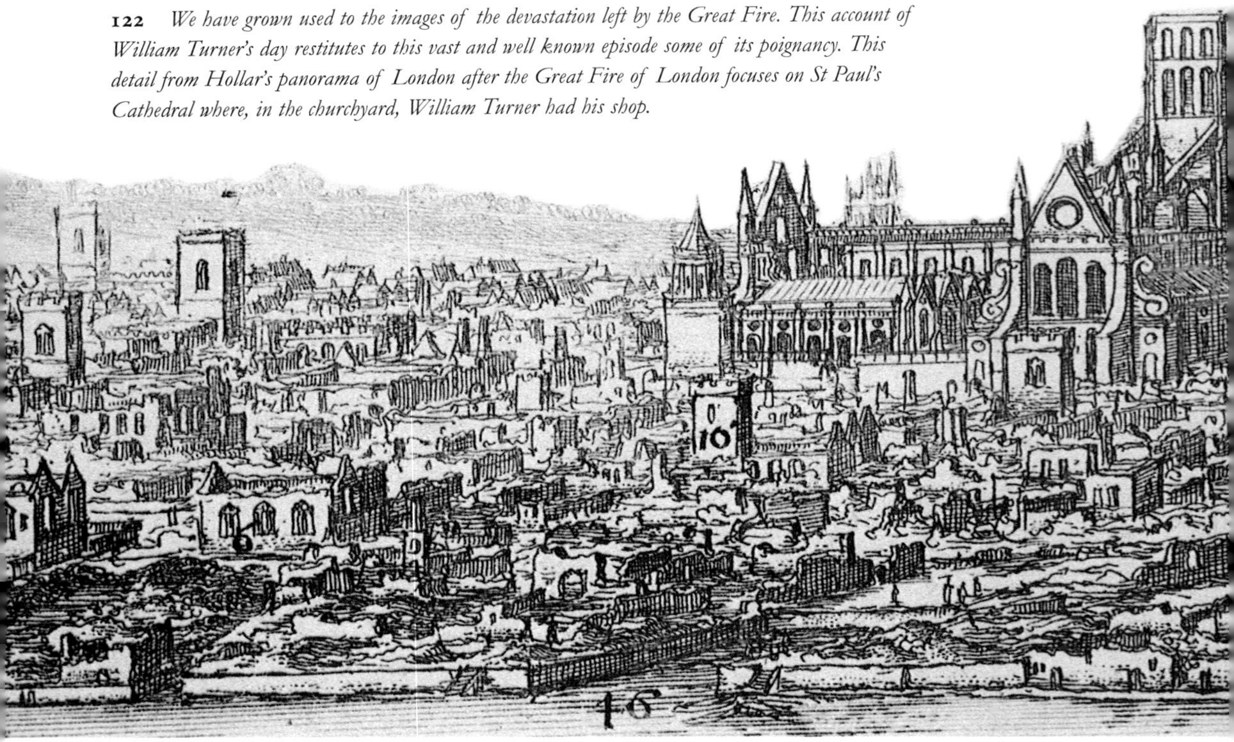

grief — but one who kept his own chaplain – he paid Dr Coventry £7 10s. each quarter — and was very willing to let a quiet group of like-minded friends come to his house to read the Bible and pray together. And he would join them — he was no lover of elaborate ceremony, and was glad that the little princesses had been made wards of the state to be brought up as true members of the Church of England.

But now they would have a stepmother, for the Duke was married by proxy to an Italian princess whom he had never seen. Sir William thanked God that he had never had a mind to marry — women were a nuisance, always wanting this or that, and his nephews, his brother's sons, were good lads, welcome to his money when he was done with it, though he had no intention of going before his time, and meant to be still richer when that time came.*

His thoughts went back to the Duke and the wedding clothes. He had to admit he was curious, intrigued. What would a man of forty wear, to meet an unknown fifteen-year-old coming from Modena in Italy who, it was said, had no wish to marry but longed to enter a convent? The Duke would need to impress the lass at first sight. Sir William did not know who was doing the making, though he guessed it was some foreigner whom the Duke

Illus. 124

* He certainly died a rich man and Kirkleatham still benefits from his generosity. His Hospital flourishes, providing fortunate old age pensioners with homes, and the school building which his nephew and heir erected in accordance with Turner's will still stands, no longer a school but a local museum with particular enthusiasm for children's activities. There is a handsome display of church plate, given by Turner, which is still used once a year for communion at Easter. The family mansion was, lamentably, demolished in the early 1950s; nothing survives but the stables. A school for disabled children is on the site.

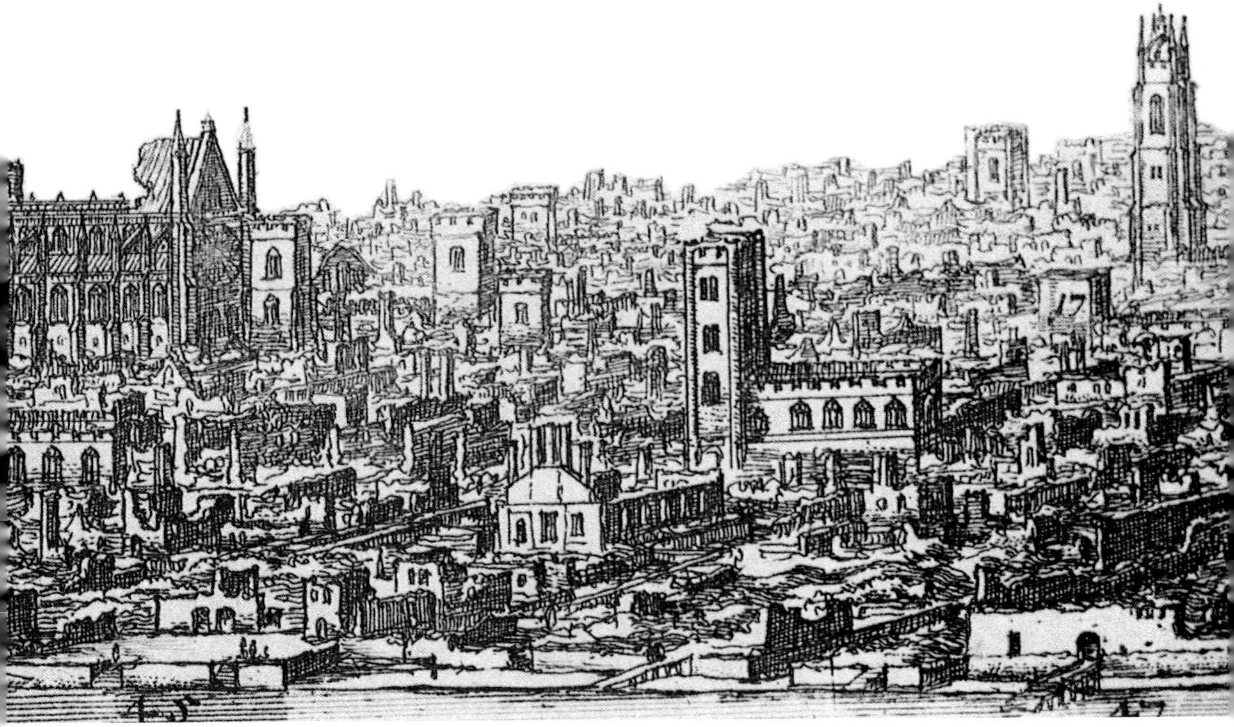

123 *This view of Cheapside as rebuilt after the Great Fire comes from a c. 1730 anonymous painting. It bears witness to the determination and sacrifice of seventeenth-century Londoners like William Turner in the face of seemingly insuperable odds.*

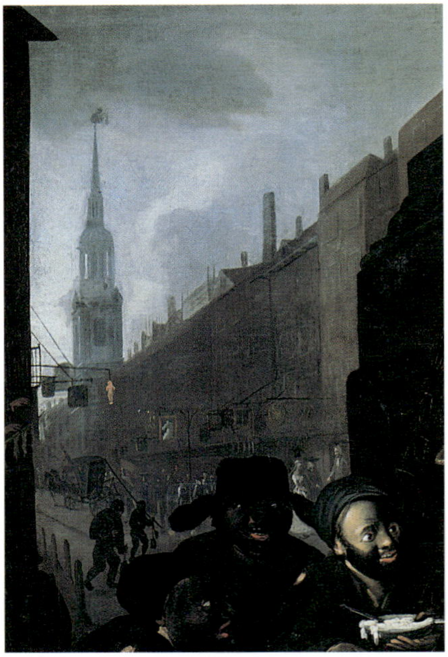

favoured, some fellow with fancy cutting skills, but he had heard that it was to be embroidered all over and that *that* work was being done in London. Quite right too. English fingers stitched skilfully. He wished he knew where the work was being done — he would like to be able to make an excuse and drop in casually, just to see; he felt a professional interest. He hoped the Duke would cut a good figure for he felt sorry for the little lass — a playmate for the Duke's daughters rather than the mother they lacked. But there were other matters to be considered.

He was beginning to hurry. He passed the Royal Exchange, built up again in only three years after the Fire. Poor Ned Jarman had worked himself to death over that and eight other Company Halls; Tom Cartwright had finished it with Christopher Wren's blessing. It was a noble building and a tribute to the Londoners' determination to get back on their feet. It was well done, though he had heard that the Mercers had almost bankrupted themselves over it.[15]*

Illus. 126

By now, he had reached his own Company's Hall, the Merchant Taylors, one of the oldest and proudest in the City. He had been saddled with the Treasurership for the rebuilding; a responsibility but an honour as well, and it gave him a chance to indulge his interest in architecture. He had picked Thomas Lock, Joseph Lem and Joseph Avis for the rebuilding, honest, experienced workmen, but now it was time for a little adornment.

Illus. 125 & 127

* Before the Fire, Edward Jarman (or Jerman) was a great pageant master for the City; after it, he literally worked himself to death, rebuilding eight Company halls and the Royal Exchange. Thomas Cartwright (d. 1702), took over much of the work after Jarman's death and completed it successfully.

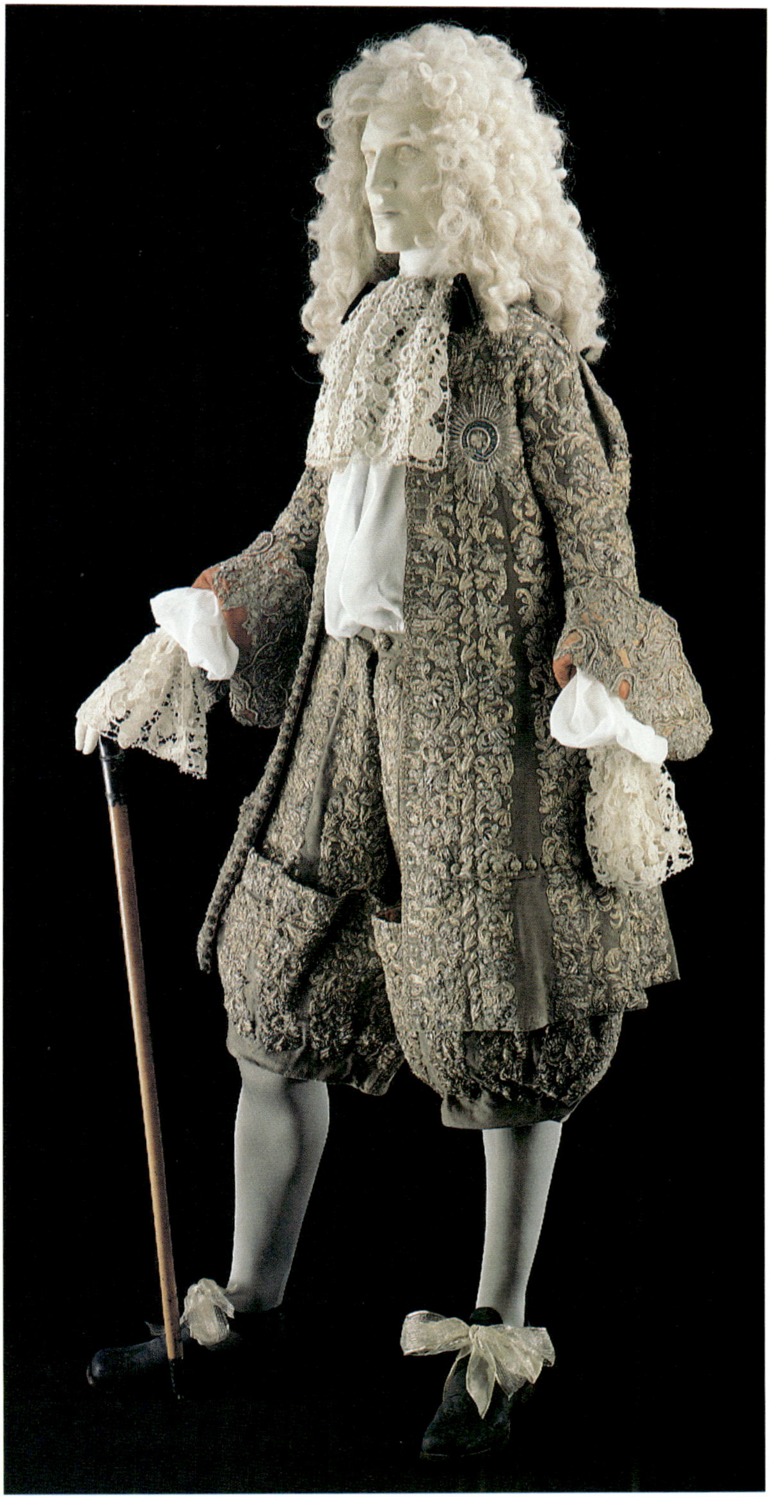

124 *Marriage suit worn by James Duke of York (1633–1701) in 1673. It consisted of coat, breeches, vest, saddle and bridle, and became the perquisite of Edward de Carteret, son of the Governor of Jersey, where the clothes remained, though now only the coat and breeches survive. We do not know who made the suit, but we can calculate that there was less than eight weeks for the work, so it can hardly have been made anywhere but London. It is of wool, worked all over with spectacular silver embroidery. There is no evidence that Sir William took any practical interest in garments — that is pure imagination — or that he could tailor, sew, or embroider himself.*

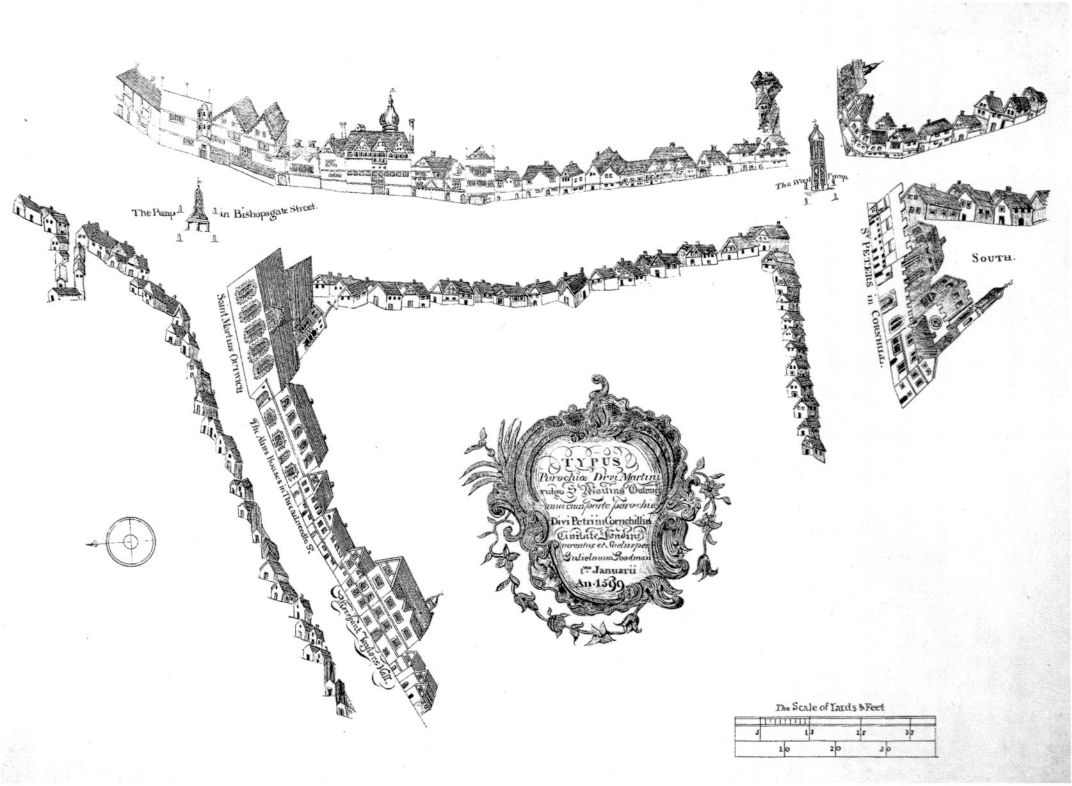

125 *View of the parish of St Martin Outwich, attributed to William Goodman, showing Merchant Taylors' Hall and the almshouses in 1599. From an 1824 lithograph by Whishaw after the lost original.*

He was meeting Robert Hooke at the Hall. A strange little man, Sir William thought, a mathematician, bent with poring over books, though he had been straight enough in his youth. Hooke was said to be churlish, awkward, quick to take offence, but Sir William had always got on well with him. As a favour, Turner had asked Hooke to design a screen for the Hall;[16] the sketch had been drawn out fairly by George Sawley — £3 well spent — and now Mr Whiting the joiner had estimated it would cost £200 to construct. Well, the Company had £100 in hand, since the last Master had put down cash for the rebuilding rather than holding a grand dinner, sensible man, and the work was complete, just in time for Lord Mayor's Day. Hooke wanted to view the finished work, and approved of it. The Hall kitchens were active again and had even managed, in 1667, to put on a dinner for the whole Livery under an improvised, temporary roof.[17] Now the staff provided Sir William and his guest with a light meal — a couple of stout slices of game pie and a luxury — timely enough in November — of a dish of stewed quinces served with cream. They ate in the parlour, the first room to have been put to rights and afterwards walked in the garden;

Hooke made suggestions for a fresh laying out of the ground for the better pleasing of the Company, promised a sketch, and agreed another meeting with Sir William at the Company's school in Suffolk Lane. The play yard there needed attention. The school had been burnt though the books had, by the courage and diligence of the headmaster, Dr Goad, and by God's good grace, been saved. The volumes had been entrusted to the safekeeping of Nathaniel Withers, a past Master to the Company, since his house in Seething

Illus. 128

126 *South West Prospect of the Royal Exchange, as rebuilt after the Great Fire. Engraving by William Sherwin, 1674.*

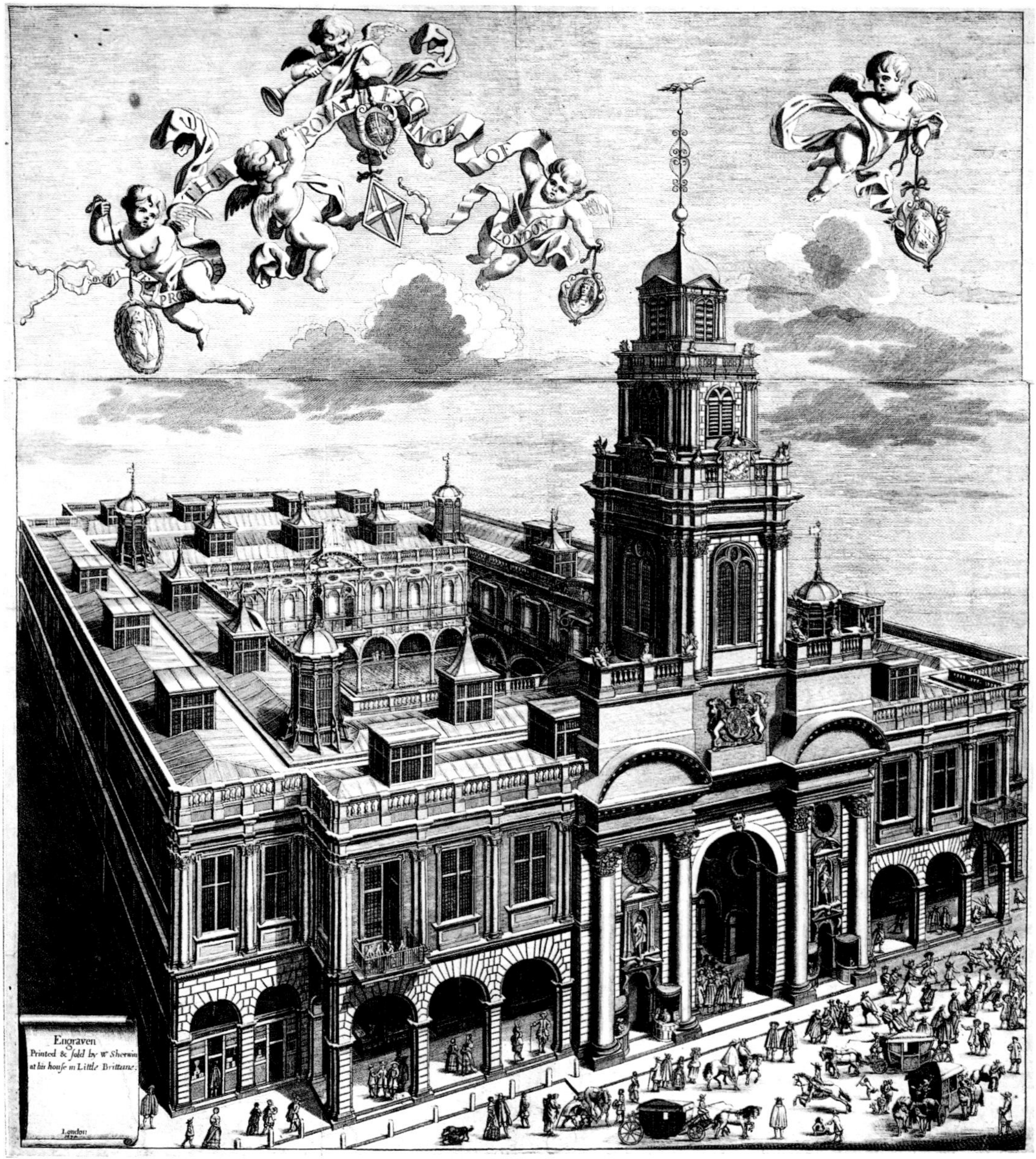

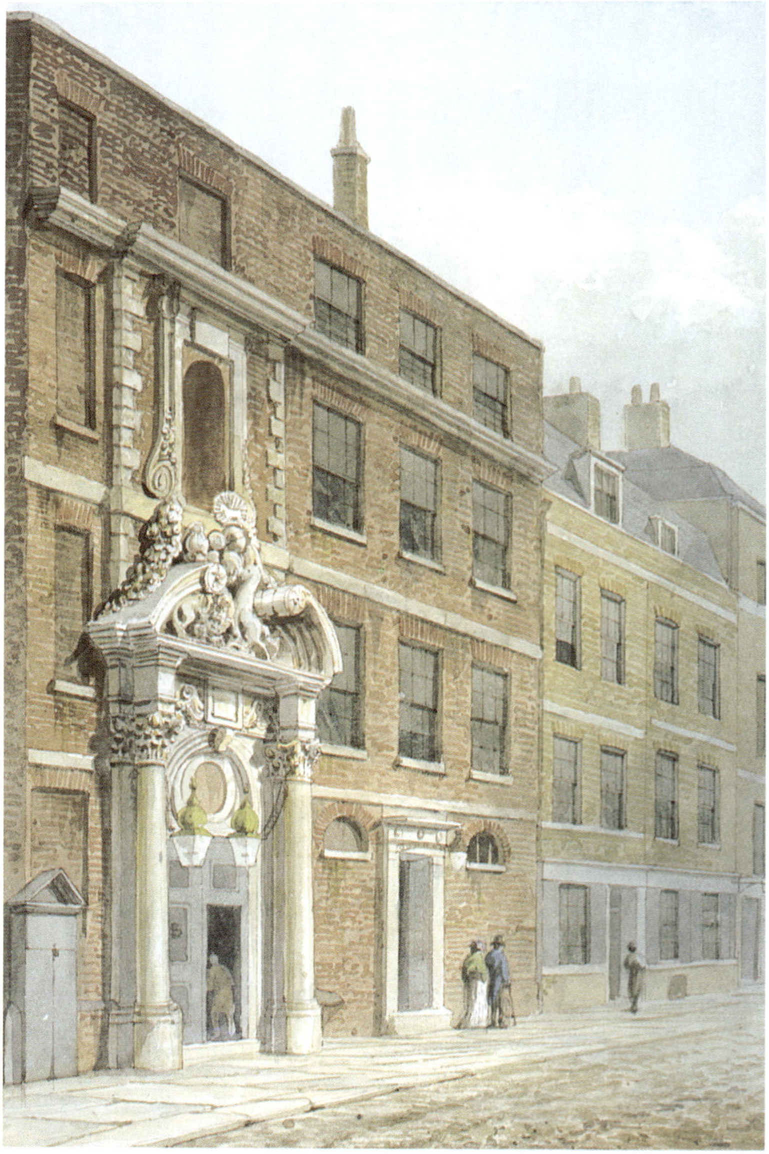

127 *View of the Merchant Taylors' Hall in Threadneedle Street as rebuilt after the Great Fire. Watercolour by George Shepherd c. 1810.*

Lane, near to Samuel Pepys, was one of the few to be spared by the Fire. Withers had taken a fancy to the books, had been loathe to part with them. It had needed a Court order, and the threat of mayoral intervention, to get the volumes away from him, but they were safely in the Hall now, waiting to be restored to the school when building was completely finished.[18]

There might be trouble over that too — there were times when Sir William felt that his life was made up of coping with other people's troubles. The new school had been designed by Hooke —

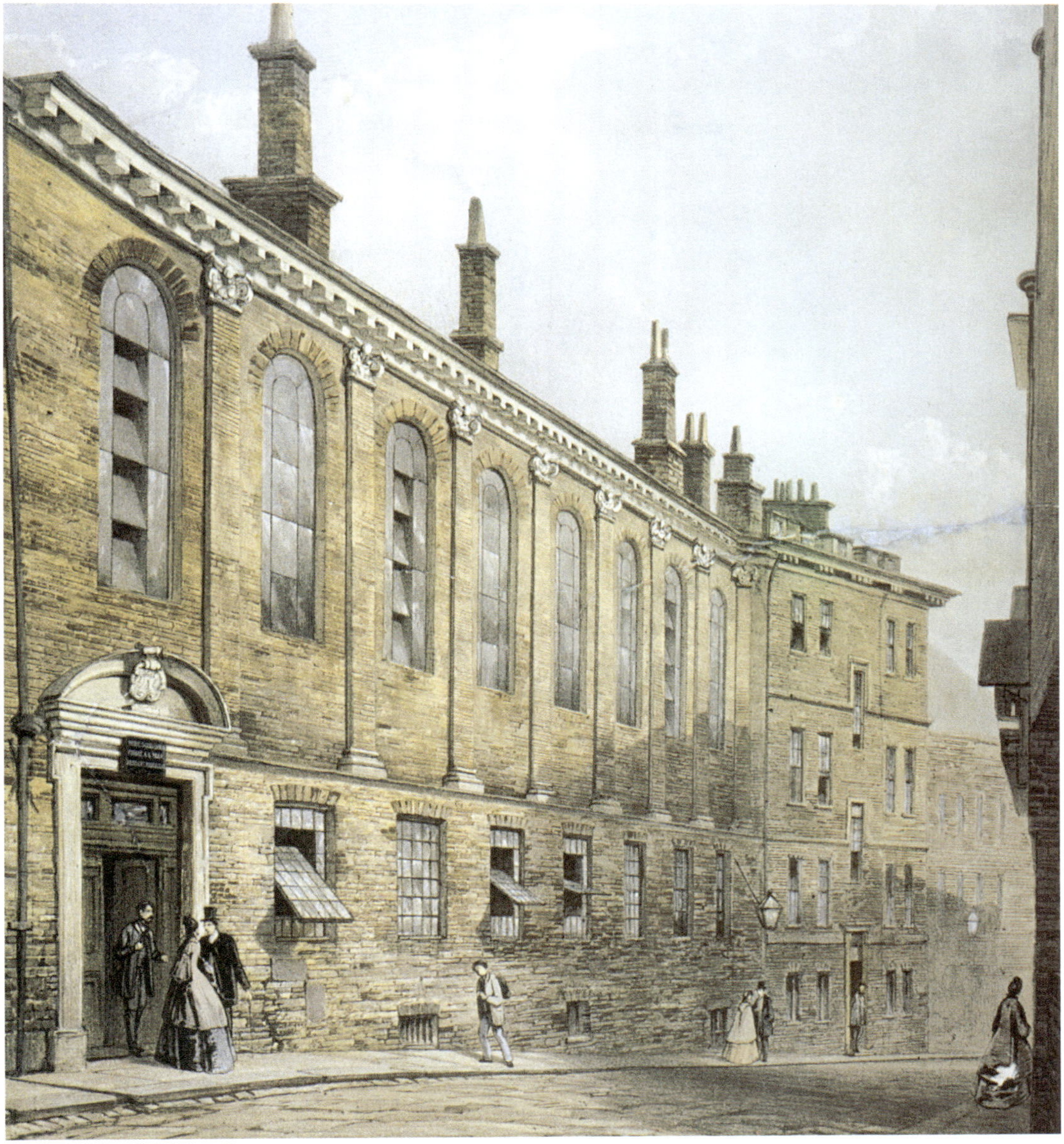

128 *View of Merchants Taylors' School in Suffolk Lane. Coloured lithograph by James Fahey, 1864.*

his friend Dr Wren had made some suggestions — but Patience Ward, a man who had had to be put in prison for contempt before he would do his duty and become a Merchant Taylor, was trying to encroach on the school yard which, goodness knew, was small enough.[19] Ward knew that he would soon become an Alderman and would be in the running for the mayoral chair; he would need a large room for official entertaining, but Turner was determined that he should not have it at the school's expense. The children had little enough room for play, nothing like the freedom of his own childhood away in the North Riding between the Cleveland Hills and the sea, and he was going to be sure that these poor urchins should not be cheated of a yard, or even a foot of their playground. He said farewell to Hooke and returned to the Hall for a brief Court meeting. Since it was a Friday, it was not the full Court — only Sir William Pritchard, the Master for the year, the four wardens — good fellows all — and a couple more like himself, zealous to be sure that all went well with the Merchant Taylors. There were four apprentices to be sworn in. One of them was a thin little fellow in a threadbare coat, not fit protection against November weather, but he carried himself well. Turner asked a few questions of the man who was to be the boy's master. The lad was fatherless; there were five younger children and their mother struggled to support them as a washer woman. Sir William had had much to do with the Court of Orphans — he knew poverty when he saw it. Not a case for the Company's Poor Box, installed fifteen years earlier, he thought. He felt in his pocket for a half-guinea, gave it to the boy's master and told him to see the child was properly equipped. It was a tailor's duty to look smart and well turned out, he said, and the boy was to come back to the Court the next Friday to present himself.[20] The master looked an honest man, but half a guinea was a temptation, and one needed to keep an eye on things.

But now it was past noon, and time for him to join the Commissioners of the East India Company. *Illus. 129* He had served in the previous year, and knew they wanted to consult him over raising more money. These were trying times; we were at war with the Dutch for the third time in twenty years, and much of it was due to rivalry over trade in far-off parts. But the goods imported were too valuable not to struggle for them; a shipload of spices and pepper and nutmeg could yield a pretty profit, and there was still more to be made from the brilliant fabrics that had begun to come from India. How well those fellows wove and dyed the cottons![21] Even he, William Turner, experienced cloth merchant that he was, felt amazed.

And now the Company was beginning to trade with China. Dangerous work, but fine goods to be brought home. Blue and white porcelain, rugs and carpets, spices and ambergris, one good voyage could set a man up for life. Turner was eager to do business. He was already rich and was planning his great undertaking — the foundation of an Almshouse, Turner's Hospital it was to be called, at Kirkleatham. It would benefit the entire neighbourhood there, for — even if he had spent his whole adult life in London — his

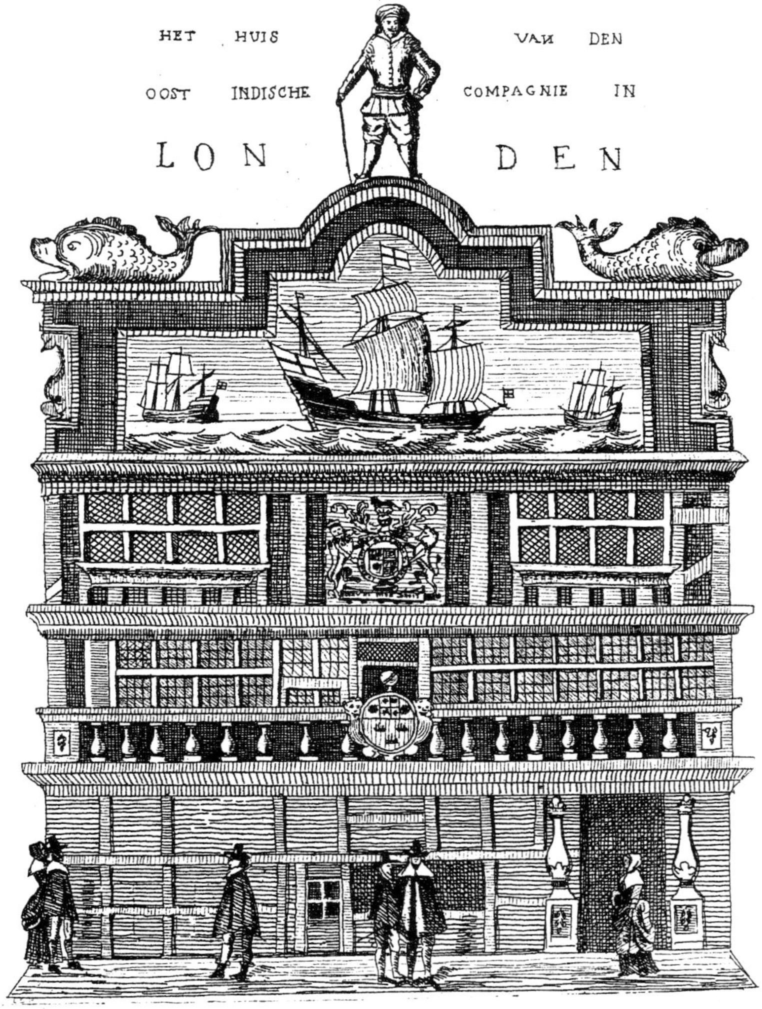

129 *View of the Old East India House in Leadenhall Street, etching. Between 1648 and 1726 the Company was based in the extraordinary house of Sir William Craven (Lord Mayor in 1610). This unassuming print is inscribed 'from a painting in the possession of Mr Pulham of the India House, 12 inches by 8'. This is fascinating because it shows that some merchants possessed painted portraits of their work premises, in this case the work of a Dutch artist.*

heart was with his birthplace where he intended his final resting-place should be. Plans were already underway, but first he must make certain that the money was in hand.[22]

The meeting over, he stopped to talk genially to his friends. There was talk of setting up another company for trade with Africa and Sir William would be ready to subscribe to that too, and to take shares in any venture. He knew that sometimes you had to risk money if you wanted to make it.

The November day was short and it looked like rain. Sir William turned his back on the East India Company headquarters. The house in Leadenhall Street had once been the home of William Craven, a Merchant Taylor like himself, and Lord Mayor in 1610. It had escaped the Fire and was still one of the most magnificent in the whole City, its Great Hall paved with squares of blue and white marble and a great gilt beam across it, supporting the figure of an angel. Craven's son, now made a lord, had sold the house and had moved to a new mansion in Drury Lane, where he had given shelter to the King's aunt, Elizabeth of Bohemia, the Winter Queen they called her. It was said that Sir Henry Wotton wrote poems for her, celebrating her beauty, but it was William Craven, a Merchant Taylor's son, who had done all any man could to make her comfortable till she died. Now the East India Company had the old mansion — times change.[23]

And you must change with them, thought Sir William, hurrying home briskly. It was four o'clock and he was eager to sup. He expected company beside that of his chaplain, Dr Coventry. He had invited John Moore, recently Warden of the Grocers' Company, an Alderman like himself, knighted the year before, and bound to be Lord Mayor one day. They were much of an age, Moore some five years younger than Turner, of the same attitude when it came to religion, but willing to support the Stuarts as the best available arrangement when it came to government. Plain men both, inclined to good works, but determined to have money to make those good works into realities. Sir William meant to be worth more than £50,000 before he died.[24]*

* Sir William made up his accounts regularly. On 1 January 1689, he recorded he was worth £50,040, adding beside the entry, 'Blessed be Almighty God that has blest me with this estate'.

Sir John, who came from Appleby Parva in Leicestershire — another country lad once, come up to London — was, Turner knew, planning the foundation of a school there. There was something to be learnt from him, how to safeguard one's good intentions, and how to see the work out fairly.

He had told Mr Peach, his cook, to prepare a tempting meal — a roast goose, some slow-cooked venison, a dish of stewed rabbits.[25] He would have had fish, too — a sturgeon had they been in season — but the weather was stormy and there might be nothing fresh. But there would be a custard, and sweetmeats and kickshaws, and a jar of ginger in syrup. And plenty of good wine — Mr Lovelace, his steward, well paid at £6 the quarter, would see to that. He had time to make himself neat before his guest arrived.

They supped well in the warm parlour and talked long of all they planned to do. Like himself, Sir John was childless, though married; again, like himself, the heirs would be nephews. Well, that was the way life went.

The guest departed. Dr Coventry read prayers to the household. Sir William went to his bed and slept the sleep of a just man.

Notes

NOTES TO INTRODUCTION

CLRO	Corporation of London Records Office
GL	Guildhall Library
LMA	London Metorpolitan Archives
PRO	Public Records Office
THLHL	Tower Hamlets Local History Library
VCH	Victoria County History (see Bibliography)

[1] Hancock, pp. 9–10.
[2] William Schellinks, *The Journal of William Schellinks' Travels in England 1661–1663*, trans. Maurice Exwood and H. L. Lehman, Camden Fifth Series, vol. 1, Royal Historical Society, London, 1993.

NOTES TO CHAPTER ONE: The Three Londons

[1] Evelyn 1652, pp. 108–09 and 111.
[2] [Anonymous], *The Character of England. As it was lately presented in a letter, to a Noble Man of France*, London 1659, p. 27.
[3] [Anonymous], *A Character of France. To which is added Gallus Castratus or an Answer to the late Slanderous Pamphlet, called The Character of England*, London 1659, p. 32.
[4] *Gallus Castratus*, p. 11.
[5] Sorbière, pp. 12 and 16.
[6] Magalotti, p. 197.
[7] Barbon, p. 2, quoted in Spence, p. 1.
[8] See Bimbenet-Privat & Mitchell.
[9] Larry Klein Paper 'The Talk of the Town: Cultural Origins of an Eighteenth-Century Commonplace', given at The Economic and Social History of Pre-Industrial England seminar at The Institute of Historical Research, University of London, on 16th March 2001.
[10] [Steele], 1715.
[11] For example, London, Public Record Office, C104/124 pt.1, Invoyce, Novemb. Ye 12th 1687, for £2447 16s. of silver sent to Fort St George in East India to purchase diamonds on behalf of Richard Viscount Lumley, Sir Thomas Fowle [goldsmith-banker], Mr John Cholmley [merchant], Mr Ambrose Isted [merchant], and Mr John Da Costa [Sephardic merchant].
[12] Whyman 1997, pp. 16–22.
[13] Hunting, pp. 83–110.
[14] Whyman 1999, p. 67.
[15] Jessop, volume ii, 250–51, quoted in Whyman 1999, p. 72.

NOTES TO CHAPTER TWO: The Art Market and Merchant Patronage in London

[1] Gregory King, author of *Natural and Political Observations 1696*, cited in Charles Wilson, *England's Apprenticeship 1603–1763*, 1965, pp. 228–29: Earle 1989; Museum of London 1985.
[2] Carswell, p. 221; South Sea Inventories.
[3] Gibson-Wood 2002.
[4] Ormrod, pp.167–86; Meadows, p. 217.
[5] Ogden, p. 86; Cartwright, 1987.
[6] Pepys, vol. 1, p. 298.
[7] Pears, p. 58–59. Ogden pp. 87–89.
[8] Ogden p. 88. Meadows, p. 328, Chartres pp. 281–84 cited by Cowan; Meadows p. 19; Montias, pp. 145–93.
[9] Lugt; Ogden; Gibson-Wood, pp. 493–94.
[10] Ailesbury, p. 179; Ogden, p. 91.
[11] Ogden, p. 88, Coleman, p. 179, Holmes, pp. 432–33.
[12] Friedman p. 14.
[13] Tillemans, p. 24.
[14] Fox, p. 19.
[15] Crawford, p. 179.
[16] Mitchell 1995, pp. 18, 30–31.
[17] See Isaac Fuller entry in Waterhouse.
[18] Brewer, p. 109.
[19] Gibson-Wood 2003, pp. 504–09.
[20] Saunders 1991, pp. 24–25; Friedman, p. 14.
[21] Vertue, passim.
[22] Glanville, 'From the buffet to the cabinet of curiosities'; Parry.
[23] Griffiths.
[24] Shaw, pp. 402–06.
[25] Lauderdale.
[26] Oman; Schroder, cat. 4; Forbes.
[27] Hooke.
[28] Discussed in Moore, cat. 78; Tillemans, p. 22; Tate Gallery 1987, cat. No 29.
[29] Whyman 1997, pp. 16–31.
[30] Millar 1997, pp. 518–27
[31] Ingamells & Ford.

NOTES TO CHAPTER THREE: Merchants' Houses

[1] Mrs J. H. Riddell was the married name of Charlotte Elizabeth Cowan (1832–1906). The critic E. F. Bleiler argued that she was one of the most popular women authors of the nineteenth century; he was apparently responsible for organising the reprint of some of Mrs Riddell's work in the 1970s, principally her ghost stories.
[2] Riddell, 1885, vol. 1, Chapter III, p. 66.
[3] CLRO, P.D.163.1, p. 7.
[4] Misson, p. 292.
[5] Hyde, p. 18.
[6] CLRO, P.D.163.1, p. 5.
[7] Cooper, p. 116.
[8] Cooper, p. 139.
[9] Mills & Oliver.
[10] Hancock 1995, p. 11. The dynasty/circle with its roots in the seventeenth century is the Boyd Circle. It started with Augustus Boyd (1679–1765).
[11] John Schofield, who kindly agreed to read this essay, commented that the Botolph Lane property was a courtyard house like the fifteenth-century Crosby Hall (e-mail of 6 October 2003).
[12] Riddell, vol. 1, p. 60.
[13] Ogilvy, p. 28.
[14] Facsimile with notes in *A to Z Restoration London*.
[15] The letters which accompany the map entries stand for Farringdon Without (A), Farringdon Within (B) and Castle Baynard (C). The following houses have been indexed: Thanet House (A31); the houses of Thomas Bludworth (B3), Sir John Frederick (B51), Sir Thomas Davis (B34), Sir Robert Clayton (B52), Nathaniel Herne (B54), Henry Tuke (B55), Samuel

Barnardiston (B61), John Lawrence (B67), Robert Vyner (B85), the Dean of St Paul's (C5), Sir Joseph Sheldon (C7), Sir Patience Ward (C38), Thomas Papillon (C54), Sir George Waterman (C57), Sir Robert Clayton (h39) and John Morris (h39).

[16] Mills & Oliver, vol. I, pp. 11 and 17.

[17] Samuel Beak; Mr Boldt; John Eaton; Hen. Goodhew, John Hamford, Joseph Hayward & Daniel Wagfield; John Johnson; Mr Parker; Edward Sanders; Mr Scowell, Mr Shilgrove, Mr Winefield are listed under 'Buttolph lane' in the trade directory

[18] *The Tobacco Contractors: A Brief Directory* in Price, pp. 105–10

[19] CLRO, Sir John Cass's Foundation Archives.

[20] 3 December 2002 e-mail from John Wells, Department of Manuscripts, Cambridge University Library, where the Phoenix Archive is kept.

[21] Hatton, vol. I, p. 242.

[22] Jeffery, p. 13.

[23] Baker, p. 149.

[24] Cherry 1993.

[25] Cherry 1993, p. 97.

[26] Cherry 1993, p. 98.

[27] Hare, p. 9, suggests the black and white marble floor is characteristic of the work of Nicholas Stone.

[28] Survey of London, XV, pp. 23–30, Pares & Taylor, pp. 75–107.

[29] Survey of London, ibid, p. 30.

[30] Hancock, p. 94.

[31] Platt, pp. 39 ff.

[32] Metcalf, p. 100.

[33] Quote from John Stow in Metcalf, p. 96.

[34] Kew Palace is currently being restored by English Heritage. The work has encouraged extensive research into the house, though this research will only be become available when the house reopens in 2006. I am most grateful to Suzanne Groome and Lee Prosser for their help.

[35] Bold.

[36] Bold, p. 79.

[37] Donald.

[38] Cluett, p. 18/V.C.H. Surrey, vol. IV, pp. 181 ff.

[39] Thomas Godfrey (died 1623) had twenty children by his two wives. See Nichols.

[40] DNB.

[41] Foster, under Godfrey.

[42] Michael Birks' notes 'The Lushingtons of Norton Court' were kindly lent to me by the current private owners of Norton Court. I am very grateful to them for granting access and for their help with this project.

[43] CLRO, P.D.163.1

NOTES TO CHAPTER FOUR: Case Study: The Story of a Merchant's House

[1] Stowe 1720, 2, pp. 47–48.

[2] The spelling 'Sheppherd' varies in source documents, reflecting phonetic spelling. Thus 'Sheepheard', 'Sheperd', 'Sheppard' and 'Sheppherd' appear, all referring to the same Dormer Sheppherd. Shortly before going to press, new information emerged about Dormer Sheppherd. These new facts have been incorporated to the biographical entry on p. 195.

[3] London Metropolitan Archives (LMA) MDR 1712/4/20

[4] For Dormer Sheppherd's marriage, see Guildhall MS 10 091/29. For Amos, see Lincoln's Inn Admissions Register 1420–1893, Oct 22, 1703.

[5] For background information on the detailed and informative Gascoyne map reproduced here, see Ravenhill.

[6] LMA: MDR 1712/3/118.

[7] British Library, EIC Records, G/21-40 1595–1800.

[8] British Library, L/MAR/B/115B 1710–12. John Gayer is still alive on 9 February 1711 and must have died soon after for Mary Gayer to have returned in time to prove his will.

[9] National Archives PRO PROB 11/526 sig 70.

[10] Tower Hamlets Local History Library (THLHL) MSS 6696, 1715

[11] THLHL MSS 6696 and 6697.

[12] Sedgewick.

[13] See note 8.

[14] PRO PROB 33/2 1733–33 and DEL 10/100.

[15] LMA; X024/15 (1720–29)

[16] There is another illustration of the shell hood in LMA prints and drawings SC/P2/CT/01/1282 as well as a delicate watercolour by T. H. Shepherd in Guildhall Library (Department of Prints and Maps).

[17] In *The Pictorial World*, 23 November 1878.

[18] See note 9.

NOTES TO CHAPTER FIVE: Furnishing the London Merchant's Town House

[1] The bed hangings were Lot 77, Sale of Important Furniture, 30 November 2001, Sothebys, London. Stylistic comparisons were made with the Venetian Ambassador's bed at Knole (*c.* 1688) and a bed of 1696 at Belvoir Castle.

[2] This has been extensively discussed by, among others, Horwitz and Hunt. Grassby 1994, pp. 115–18, discusses the concepts of gentility and the London merchant's expenditure.

[3] Earle, pp. 290–98 and Grassby 1994, pp. 335–41: both discuss the furnishing of the London merchants' houses.

[4] Earle analysed over three hundred inventories in the period under discussion. This essay covers a much smaller sample, and only discusses the richest inventories. I am grateful to David Mitchell, who gave me references to several merchants of importance not listed by Earle.

[5] Grassby 1995, pp. 245–46, argues that Sheldon was in fact much richer than the records account for, with huge loans to corporations, which were not included in his estate at his death.

[6] CLRO, Orphans Court Inv. 975. Bonfoy was a Clothier and became an alderman. He was also well-connected as both his brother and cousin (Sir Thomas Davies) were merchants.

[7] Earle, p. 290.

[8] CLRO: Orphans Court Inv. 809, Sir Jonathan Dawes, Fishmonger (died June 1672) and no. 1730, Sir Joseph Sheldon, Grocer (died 1683). Ten years later, Joseph Sheldon's bedroom had two large tapestry hangings, a cloth bed with silk linings, table, stand and glass together valued at £29 03s., while 'the lady's chamber in Mr. Parry's house' seems to have been given the same value, with twelve smaller tapestry hangings. He also had a wardrobe with a considerable number of tapestries in it, the total being valued at £104 09 01.

[9] CLRO: Orphans Court Inv. 500 and 659, Sir Martin Noell.

[10] CLRO: Orphans Court Inv. 1591, Sir Nathaniel Herne. Also see Appendix II.

[11] CLRO: Orphans Court Inv. 2264, Anthony Balam, Fishmonger (died 1691–92), no. 2261, John Barkstead, Mercer (d. 1694), no. 2593, Daniel Thomas, Mercer (d. 1704); no. 2503, John Cary, Salter, (d. May 1701) had a damask bed in his

mohair hung bedroom, which was valued at £82 6s. John Barkstead's best bedchamber was valued at £94 1s. and Daniel Thomas's green damask room at £86.

[12] South Sea Directors, vol. 2, Sir William Lambert.

[13] Earle, p. 293 argues that the materials grew lighter in the eighteenth century, but given the continuity of both mohair and damask as furnishing fabrics, the only significant change is in the less-frequent use of tapestries, although even these appear in the bedrooms in the early eighteenth century with calicoes and plaids in the lesser rooms.

[14] CLRO: Orphans Court Inv. 1602.

[15] For example Cary, see note 11.

[16] CLRO: Orphans Court Inv. 1591.

[17] A less wealthy merchant such as Anthony Balam nonetheless had two Japanese cabinets and a small amount of plate in his bedroom, which was valued at £113 3s. 6d., whereas the other rooms were only estimated at between £14 and £18.

[18] South Sea Inventories, vol. 1, Sir Robert Chaplin.

[19] CLRO; Orphans Court Inv. 2593, Thomas Daniels.

[20] South Sea Inventories, vol. 1, Sir Francis Hawes.

[21] Sir Martin Noell, see note 9.

[22] It is difficult to imagine this as an English piece of furniture; it may have been imported from Antwerp or even southern Germany, where this combination of materials was very popular in the early eighteenth century.

[23] The description of '*high* turkey chairs' implies the higher backs which came into fashion in the 1680s. The fact that turkey chairs no longer appear in the richest houses after this date coincides with petitions from the turkey workers to protect their industry. Bowett argues on p. 77 that turkey chairs continued to be made until the end of the century, although in decreasing numbers and Earle on p. 386 (footnote 43) shows that turkey work chairs continued to be present in inventories but in increasingly small numbers until 1710. However, as they are not found in the richest houses, this suggests they were no longer considered fashionable.

[24] In general, chairs of the early eighteenth century would have had high, possibly arched backs and not the squat, cubic forms that were typical of the mid-seventeenth century.

[25] Cane chairs are described in every inventory after 1680. Dutch chairs, on the other hand, were much less frequently described. Only two parlours were furnished with Dutch chairs. On the other hand, the principal bedroom of John Cary's house, inventoried in 1702, had 6 Dutch matted chairs, 2 cane elbow chairs and 3 crimson damask cushions.

[26] See Bowett, pp. 84–93 and 260–71. He cites the Case of the Cane-Chair makers of 1690 made to parliament in which they reckon that 72,000 cane chairs were produced per annum.

[27] 'Dutch chairs' with matted bottoms appear in the 1718 Boughton inventory, p. 9. I am grateful to L. Wood for this reference as well as for discussing her evidence for this definition of 'Dutch' chairs.

[28] The terminology for writing furniture no doubt reflects the change from a fall-front desk to a desk with cabinet above. The term 'scritoire' appeared for the first time in 1690 referring to a square writing box on legs, similar to the French 'bureau Mazarin', in the bills from John Guilbaud to the Great Wardrobe. (PRO; L.C. 5/42 p. 344).

[29] See Saumarez-Smith, p. 171 for a portrait of the Gough Family by William Verelst showing this combination of bureau cabinet and tea table. Sir Henry Gough was a Director of the East India Company from 1735 to 1752.

[30] Pepys' Diary, vol. 9, pp. 405–06. Elsewhere Pepys refers to the cabinet maker Mr Norris from whom he bought a set of frames (Beard & Gilbert, p. 654).

[31] Beard & Gilbert, p 133.

[32] Whyman 1999, p 62–63.

[33] Papillon, pp. 100–02.

[34] Dyrham inventory 1703, Gloucestershire Archives, Cheltenham.

[35] Nor do they appear in the lesser rooms in country houses, being reserved for the more important rooms. For an account of Thomas Pistor, see Turpin.

[36] A clock with floral marquetry case was given in 1683 to the Grocers' Company and the Vintners' Company has a similar one, given by John Channon, Master in 1704.

[37] Gilbert and Beard, p. 136.

[38] British Library: Add.Ms. 5751: Accounts of sums paid to tradesmen on the death of Queen Mary. The sum was owed to Jan van Collema, one of the principal merchants supplying Queen Mary with luxury goods.

[39] PRO: LCO 5/43

[40] Veale, p. 273.

[41] The partnership between Quare and Horseman lasted from 1701 to 1726, so the date of *c.* 1719 fits.

NOTES TO CHAPTER SIX: A Passion for the Exotic

[1] *The Oxford English Dictionary* for 1971 gives the earliest reference in English to *Harper's Magazine* in 1883.

[2] Israel, Radical, pp. 83 and 3.

[3] Sharpe, pp. 17–18.

[4] Jensen, p. xiii.

[5] Wycherley 1675, Act V, scene IV.

[6] Pepys, vol. 7, p. 162, 12 June 1666. For miniature of Frances Teresa Stuart, later Duchess of Richmond and Lennox, in a riding habit, see, MacLeod & Alexander, p. 96.

[7] Thornton, pp. 7 and 8.

[8] Quoted in Thornton, p. 10.

[9] Mérot, p. 105.

[10] Wycherley 1677, Dedication to my Lady B.

[11] Magalotti, p. 178.

[12] The National Archives (NA): PRO, LC5/107 Jewell House Warrants 1660–85, f. 90, 10 July 1662.

[13] CLRO, Orphans Court Inv. 1591, Sir Nathaniell Herne, 31 March 1680, (hereafter, Inv. Herne 1680).

[14] For detailed discussion see Bimbenet-Privat & Mitchell 2003.

[15] Alexander Pope, *The Rape of the Lock*, London 1714, Canto I.

[16] For detailed discussion see, Mitchell 1993, pp. 386–400.

[17] Inv. Herne 1680; Orphans Court Inv. 1951, Sir Joseph Sheldon, 15 September 1681; Orphans Court Inv. 2261, John Barkstead, 18 July 1694.

[18] Orphans Court Inv. 1324, Sir William Bucknall, 26 October 1676.

[19] Orphans Court Inv. 1685, Thomas Peade, 24 February 1679/80.

[20] Orphans Court Inv. 1177, Edward Traherne, 26 November 1675. Also see Lindey.

[21] For examples of Jamaican combs see Alcorn, no. 78. Snodin & Styles, p. 134, no. 29. For London combmakers see; Orphans Court Inv. 1920, William Cox, 14 November 1682, and Inv. 177, Laurence Pickering, 14 February 1701/02.

[22] For punch see Brown & Schwartz, pp. 45 and 46.

[23] Wolley, p. 155.
[24] Galinou.
[25] Ibid. For a panel in the V&A attributed to Robinson see, Snodin & Styles 2001, p. 134, no. 30.
[26] Orphans Court Inv. 1608, Symon Snow, 14 June 1680, vinegar maker in Shadwell. 'China punch bowles and beakers' are listed in his wife's chamber.
[27] Orphans Court Inv. 500, Sir Martin Noell, April 1666 (hereafter, Inv. Noell 1666).
[28] Evelyn, vol. 3, p. 60.
[29] For further discussion see Mitchell 2004.
[30] Orphans Court Inv. 2266, Phillip Scarth, 12 November 1695. His trade goods totalling £1589, included tea and coffee as well as the raw materials for perfumery, musk, civet and ambergris.
[31] Orphans Court Inv. 3263, Robert Heysham Esq., 6 & 11 March 1722/23.
[32] Inv. Noell 1666.
[33] Inv. Herne 1680.
[34] Orphans Court Inv. 1901, Humphrey Dash, 1 November 1682.
[35] Wycherley 1677, Act 2.
[36] Orphans Court Inv. 1968, Peter Short, 28 November 1681.
[37] Orphans Court Inv. 1602, Sir Thomas Davies, 1680, (hereafter, Inv. Davies 1680); Inv. Noell 1666; Orphans Court Inv. 2221, Christopher Wilkinson, 6 September 1693.
[38] NA: PRO, SP78/128, Queen Henrietta Maria inventory, November 1669.
[39] Anonymous, *Mundus Muliebris or The Ladies Dressing-Room unlock'd, And her Toilette spread*, London 1690.
[40] NA: PRO C104/116 Pt II, will of 'John, Lord Ossultone', 9 October 1694.
[41] Thornton & Tomlin, p. 84 and Fig. 87.
[42] Inv. Noell 1666 and Appendix II. Orphans Court Inv. 355, Richard Howell, 20 September 1667, his stock included 'boxwood, cocus, greenewood, speckled wood and lignumvitae'.
[43] Orphans Court Inv. 1832, Sir Arthur Ingram, 31 October 1681. Orphans Court Inv. 3364, Anthony Balam, 17 March 1691/92.
[44] Orphans Court Inv. 184, Charles Barnard Esq., 19 December 1710.
[45] Orphans Court Inv. 124, Thomas Came, 3 December 1673; Orphans Court Inv. 2033, Roger Gray, 15 June 1686; Orphans Court Inv. 2208, Andrew Kenrick, 2 March 1690/91.
[46] Orphans Court Inv. 3013, Richard Cocke, 3 October 1714.
[47] Pepys, vol. 4, p. 299.
[48] Inv. Noell 1666; Orphans Court Inv. 90, John Eaton, 4 November 1670; Orphans Court Inv. 878, John Wall Esq., 6 September 1672.
[49] Inv. Davies 1680; Orphans Court Inv. 2213, Thomas Riley, 11 March 1692/93, wine merchant; Orphans Court Inv. 1226, Michael Davison Esq., 18 July 1676, merchant trading with both the East and West Indies; Inv. Herne 1680.
[50] Inv. Herne 1680.
[51] See note 39.

NOTES TO CHAPTER SEVEN: Merchant Clients for the Painter Jan Siberechts

[1] Acquired with assistance from the National Art Collections Fund and the Friends of the Tate Gallery (now called Tate Members).
[2] See Hearn.
[3] Much rewarding new research is being carried out on non-Court ownership of paintings in London, for example, Gibson-Wood 2002, pp. 491–500.
[4] Rubinstein, 1994.
[5] The only monograph devoted to this artist remains Fokker.
[6] Buckeridge, pp. 425–26.
[7] See Cassidy, pp. 415–16.
[8] Stainton and White, pp. 155–56; see also Rubinstein 2004.
[9] Vertue, 'Notebooks V', p. 52, where the signature 'J. Siberechts. 1676' is also transcribed; as '1676' predates Bentinck's arrival in Britain, at least some of these works may have been collected rather than commissioned by him.
[10] I am grateful to Derek Adlam and David Onnekink for confirmation of this.
[11] Letter from Mary Vaughan, and unknown author's response, *Country Life*, 2 January 1959, p. 152.
[12] Letter to Mr John Richardson, 25 June 1994, supplied to Tate Gallery 1996, and letter to Tate of 29 September 1996; subsequently *Newsletter of the Camden History Society*, no. 167, May 1998, p. 3.
[13] *Victoria County History*, vol. IX, pp. 51–53, 57.
[14] Department of Environment, 'List of Buildings of Special Architectural or Historic Interest: London Borough of Camden', Part 2, 'Streets J–End', May 1974, p. 405; *Camden History Society Newsletter*, no. 122, November 1990, p. 2.
[15] Cliffe, p. 5.
[16] The Muniment Room, Westminster Abbey, WAM 12450, no. 17; Allen.
[17] For Belsize House itself, see Knight, pp. 60–67.
[18] The very Earl whose palatial house at Bretby in Derbyshire Siberechts is thought to have painted.
[19] Aubrey, pp. 272–73. Sir John Wilde, or Wylde (1590–1669) was Chief-Baron of the Exchequer. His daughter became the wife of Charles West, 5th Baron De La Warr (*c.* 1625–87) and the couple did indeed inherit Wilde's house (PRO E 179/143/370 m.43.d).
[20] First proposed *Victoria County History*, vol. IX, p. 51 and confirmed by subsequent research.
[21] Goldsmiths' Company Apprentice Book 2, p. 45, entry dated 7 November 1651, as stated in letter of 7 October 1996 from David Beasley, Librarian, London Goldsmiths' Company (hereafter 'Beasley').
[22] On 8 February 1703 the younger John was turned over to a Painter-Stainer called John Stevens, but became a freeman of the Goldsmiths' Company in 1709, and was elected to the Livery in 1712, according to Beasley (see note 21). It is not clear whether he is to be identified with the 'John Coggs Mathematical Instrument Maker, at the Globe and Sun against St. Dunstan's-Church in Fleetstreet' mentioned on the 1721 title page as vendor of *The Description, Nature and General Use, of the Sector and Plain-scale* .... This Coggs was still operating in the Fleet Street area in the 1730s, according to John R. Millburn, *Adams of Fleet Street, Instrument Makers to King George III*, Aldershot, 2000, p. 15. According to Heal, p. 127, 'John Coggs (Jnr) Goldsmith, London, died in 1751'.
[23] See Stephen Quinn, in Mitchell, p. 61; Quinn's diagram entitled 'The "Gold" Boys Network: apprentices turned bankers' shows Coggs's place as an early trainee of Robert Welstead, fig. 28, p. 62.
[24] Mitchell, p. 9 ff.
[25] See Squibb, p. 72.
[26] Hilton Price, pp. 40–41; and 'Beasley' (note 21).

[27] British Library Add. MS 38464, folios 65, 98.
[28] College of Arms Grants 5 92 (letter from Timothy Duke, Chester Herald, 7 August 1998).
[29] See *Calendar of State Papers: Domestic: William and Mary, 1694–95*, ed. William John Hardy, London 1906, p. 462 where on 8 May 1695 a pass was recorded 'for Daniel Auber and Martha, his wife, two French protestants, and Daniel Obery, a German, to go to Harwich or Gravesend for Holland, on the recommendation of John Coggs and Thomas Kirkham, church wardens of St. Clement's.'
[30] Westminster Archives Centre, Poor Rates receipts, St Clement Danes, B.1325. For the year 1661 John Coggs paid 4s. 4d.; for 1662 and 1663 6s. 6d.; for 1664, 1665, 1667, 7s. In the St Clement Danes Surveyors Accounts, B.5, he is listed in April 1678 living in the ward of Temple Bar, which seems to be associated with the 'Dutchy Liberty'. In the same accounts in April 1681, and for subsequent years, he is listed as living in the same Liberty, in 'Essex Streete'. Essex Street had been laid out in the grounds of old Essex House by Nicholas Barbon in 1675, and runs south from the Strand, from just opposite St Clement Danes church.
[31] *Calendar of State Papers: Domestic: 13 February 1689 – April [sic]1690*, ed. William John Hardy, London, 1895, pp. 487–88 (the list also included Sir Robert Clayton).
[32] *Calendar of State Papers: Treasury Books: January 1693 – March 1696*, vol. 10.2, ed. William A. Shaw, London, 1935, p. 913.
[33] *London Gazette*, 6 July 1696. As a result, a few papers relating to Coggs's business, especially towards the end of his career, have survived among papers relating to the Greenwich Hospital in the British Library (Add.MSS 38,464 and 38,465).
[34] British Library, Add MS 61420.
[35] Ibid.
[36] *The Manuscripts of the House of Lords 1710–12*, vol. 9, new series, London, 1949, p. 5, 'Cogg [sic] Estate Act'.
[37] British Library Add. MS 38464, folios 39, 65v.
[38] Ibid, fol. 39.
[39] Ibid fol. 98; quoted extensively in Hearn 2000. Coggs also owned 'A Farme at Denhame in the County of Bucks', the place of his birth, fol. 106.
[40] PRO C.10/519/57.
[41] See Jones R., pp. 38–41.
[42] The will of his brother Daniel Coggs, 'of the parish of Denham' was proved in October 1722, leaving property in Denham and at Uxbridge in Middlesex to his two sons Daniel and John Coggs (PROB 11/587 sig. 90).

NOTES TO CHAPTER EIGHT: City Merchants' Landownership around Henley-on-Thames and the Paintings of Jan Siberechts

[1] Establishing an exact viewpoint for this painting is difficult since the topography is compressed to incorporate the river bends between Hambleden and Hurley in one eastward sweeping view (see No. 5 on illus. 76). Siberechts similarly 'shifted' local features in relation to the River Trent for his painting *View of Nottingham from the East*, *c.* 1700 (The Castle Museum, Nottingham).
[2] The painting is believed to have entered the collection of the Willoughby family shortly after it was painted.
[3] The town developed as a trans-shipment point for river freight between Oxford and London because of difficulties in navigating the higher reaches. The early involvement of London merchants in Henley is considered in detail in Peberdy.
[4] Spalding 1990 Contemporaries, pp. 425, 438–44, 446-447, & 482–83. Bulstrode Whitelocke's purchase of Greenlands is noted in Spalding *Diary* 1990, p. 272.
[5] Richard Chandler was one of the Alston Trustees alongside Penning's brother, the wealthy physician Sir Edward Alston MD (1595–1669): See Spalding 1990 *Diary*, pp. 727 & 739, n. According to Petrie, p. 13 & Appendix, it was Robert Chandler, a relation of Richard, who took over the property in 1669.
[6] The William Freeman who rebuilt Fawley Court had a father of the same name whose career is touched on by Tyack, p. 130. Hancock 2002, p. xxxiv n.75, discusses in greater detail Sir James Whitelocke's financial affairs in relation to Fawley Court, which Freeman had leased from 1679, and notes that Sir James had on occasions mortgaged the rents on the property while his father was still alive. William Freeman senior had links to the Royal Africa Company in which Sir Robert Clayton also had an interest, see Melton 1986, p. 91.
[7] The estates were apparently conveyed to John Morris by Richard and Winifred Chandler and Edmund and Sarah Harrington, see Petrie, p. 13 and private papers of late W. E. Snell, 1970 (private collection).
[8] Robert Abbott (1610–58) was Robert Clayton's uncle and the growth of his business in Cornhill is related in Melton 1986, pp. 44–57. Further details of his family and property are recorded in Abbott, pp. 31–39.
[9] Sir James Whitelocke is listed in Clayton and Morris's ledgers: Guildhall Library, Clayton Papers 6428. Sir Edward Alston also appears in the ledgers: Guildhall Library, Account book for the Duke of Buckingham, Clayton Papers 15818.
[10] Full details of Clayton and Morris's business, including their accounting systems, mortgage practices and management of their clients' estates and other interests are given in Melton 1986.
[11] Melton's elucidation of Clayton's handling of Buckingham's finances refutes the enduring allegations that Clayton swindled Buckingham out of his fortune (Melton 1986, pp. 198–99).
[12] Earl Rivers's correspondence with Clayton is in the Bodleian Library (Clayton Papers, MS Eng Lett. c. 201, no 71).
[13] Melton 1986, p. 70.
[14] *Victoria County History*, III, p. 48. Clayton concluded the transactions concerning Hambleden Manor in 1696 after the 3rd Earl Rivers's death. He had in fact held a mortgage on the 3rd Earl Rivers's share of the estate since 1668 and bought the half share held by Earl Rivers's sister in law, Annabel Howe, in 1686.
[15] Greene had previously owned Mill End Wharf alongside Yewden Manor: Petrie, pp. 13–14. Morris's will (Surrey History Centre, Clayton Papers, 2246/1) specified a particular bequest of £1500 for Clayton to use within three years for paying off all or part of Greene's mortgage on Yewden Manor and Greenlands. Greene's will subsequently named Sir Robert Clayton and Robert Abbott, 'my brother in law' though previously deceased, as two of his three executors (Stanton p. 88), which suggests that Clayton retained effective control over this property after Greene's death.
[16] Hurley Parish pp. 2–3.
[17] Clarendon, p. 224, reads: 'Dec.13, Thursday [1688] We went to Henley: the Prince came hither likewise, and lay at Mr Whitlock's . . .'. Holborrow, pp. 288–89, supports the identification of the meeting place as Phyllis Court. This incident is probably relevant to several of Siberechts's other Henley paintings.

[18] Clayton's close involvement with agriculture is described in Melton 1986, pp. 12–14 & 20.
[19] Evelyn, IV, p. 185.
[20] Robert Clayton, William Clayton's eldest son and Sir Robert's nephew, attended All Souls, Oxford, but died abroad while on the Grand Tour in 1698: Melton, 1986, p. 208. Some of his letters relating to this journey are in the Bodleian Library (Clayton Papers, MS Eng. Lett. c. 309).
[21] Melton 1986, p. 221 & n. This author notes how the scriveners acted on behalf of Coggs and other goldsmith-bankers in collecting and recording payments for them.
[22] Melton 1986, pp. 158–80.
[23] Sloan, pp. 104–05 and *Dictionary of National Biography.*

NOTES TO CHAPTER NINE: A City Artist: Robert Robinson

[1] Quoted from the third edition of 1754, published in facsimile by Cornmarket Press, 1969, not paginated.
[2] Ibid.
[3] Croft-Murray, 1955, pp. 174–79; Croft-Murray 1962, vol. I. pp. 46–47, 223–25; and Ganz 2000.
[4] On this issue, I refer the reader to Chapter 2A of my dissertation, 'Robinson's Origins to 1675,' pp. 17–22. Copies have been deposited in the British Museum Print Room and in the Paul Mellon Centre in London.
[5] Guildhall Library MS 5667, vol. 2, part 1, fol. 289.
[6] CLRO, CF1 146, October 1699.
[7] Gibson-Wood 2002, pp. 491–500.
[8] Pressmark 1402.g.1. The contents of these catalogues are described in Gibson-Wood 2002; Ganz, 2000, pp. 48–59; and Ogden, p. 126.
[9] A complete list of paintings by Robinson recorded in the London auction catalogues appears in Ganz 1998, p. 98.
[10] It was sold at Christie's South Kensington, 19 October 1995, lot 403, as by an unidentified Follower of Pieter van Roestraeten.
[11] On van Vianen, see Ackley, pp. 204–05. The candlestick base is modified from plate 25.
[12] The candlestick is copied from plates 23 and 25 of *Constighe Modellen.*
[13] The paintings were previously installed in the Henley-on-Thames post office. Their attribution to Robinson was first suggested by Mrs. M. J. Hamilton-Bradbury, in an unpublished paper 'The Paintings Now in the Town Hall Previously in the Post Office, Research Notes on their Attribution,' a copy of which was kindly provided by the River & Rowing Museum in Henley-on-Thames.
[14] Croft-Murray 1962, vol. 1, p. 224.
[15] Jones, pp. 9–10.
[16] Typescript of the 1713 inventory in the Surrey Record Office, p. 5, kindly provided to me by Andrew Skelton.
[17] This suggestion was first made by E. W. Tristram who restored the room in 1913, p. 75.

NOTES TO CHAPTER TEN: The Fashionable Merchant: A Case Study

[1] Earle, p. 152.
[2] Whyman 1999, p. 38.
[3] Whyman 1999, p 42.
[4] Ibid., p. 48.
[5] Pepys, VI, p. 215.
[6] Stevenson & Thomson, pp. 22–23. Wright's career is presently being reassessed in a doctoral thesis, but this catalogue provides the best illustrated survey of his work currently available.
[7] Evelyn, IV, p. 170.
[8] Cumming, p. 105, and Ribeiro, pp. 82–84 discuss the clothing worn by the Vyner family in this painting.
[9] Earle, p. 286 provides a table of the wholesale prices of textiles between 1671 and 1701.
[10] Swain, p. 11. A surviving example of this type of gown, worn by William III, is in the collections of the Rijksmuseum, Amsterdam.
[11] Ibid., pp. 11–12.
[12] Arnold, pp. 14–15.
[13] Earle, p. 284.
[14] Ibid., pp. 269, 281.
[15] Pepys, VI, p. 215.
[16] Evelyn, IV, p. 96.
[17] Pepys, VI, p. 215.
[18] Earle, p. 286.
[19] Quoted in Crawford & Gowing, pp. 102–03.
[20] Earle, p. 164.
[21] National Portrait Gallery Online Catalogue entry for Eleanor James.
[22] Whyman 1999, p. 47.
[23] Evelyn, IV, pp. 354–55.
[24] Murdoch, pp. 207–12. This article discusses the fan leaf and places it within the context of late seventeenth-century City ceremonial.

NOTES TO CHAPTER ELEVEN: Tomb Sculpture and Dynastic Ambition

[1] Tawney, p. 17.
[2] A larger number of late Stuart moneyed men is examined in my doctoral thesis, which is currently in preparation (Courtauld Institute of Art).
[3] Langham MS, Microfilm copy of family records held by Northamptonshire County Record Office, Acc. 1973/M 198, page numbers 1–583 ascribed by author to microfilm frames, pp. 47–48.
[4] Langham MS, p. 50; Mingay, pp. 9, 19; Wilson and Mackley, p. 18.
[5] Langham MS, p. 60.
[6] Langham MS, pp. 50, 60.
[7] Langham MS, pp. 48, 91.
[8] Inscription on Langham monument.
[9] Langham MS, p. 54.
[10] Langham MS, p. 48.
[11] C. Eaton, 'Transcription of Cottesbrooke parish register', Northamptonshire Records Office, 1983.
[12] Langham MS, pp. 80–81.
[13] Will of John Langham, PCC Duke 79, PRO 11/336, Public Records Office.
[14] Bridges, I, p. 555.
[15] Langham MS, p. 18.
[16] Langham will, op. cit.
[17] Eaton, op. cit.
[18] Langham will, op. cit.
[19] Gunnis, p. 87; White, p. 17.
[20] Gunnis, p. 87.
[21] Clayton ledger, Guildhall Library, cited by Gunnis, p. 87.

22 National Trust, Guide to 'Dunham Massey, Cheshire', 1995, pp. 54–55.
23 Langham MS, p. 59.
24 Lambert (1929), pp. 277–78.
25 Evelyn, v, 16 September 1700, pp. 425–26.
26 Evelyn, iv, 12 October 1677, pp. 121–22.
27 Manning, iii, p. 313.
28 Inscription on Clayton monument.
29 Inscription on Clayton monument.
30 Will of Robert Clayton, PCC Poley 165, PRO Prob 11/495.
31 Melton 1986, p. 69.
32 Inscription on Clayton infant's monument.
33 Leeds Museums and Galleries, Henry Moore Institute, Acc. LEEAG. PA. 1999. 0008.
34 G. Fisher, Conway Library, Courtauld Insitute of Art, unpublished note dated 25 September 1998.
35 Dr John Sharp's Easter sermon, April 1680 in Granger, xxxvi, p. 55; Evelyn, iv, 18 November 1679, pp. 185–86.
36 Clayton will, op. cit.
37 Evelyn, iv, 18 November 1679, pp. 185–86.
38 Cokayne, ii, p. 394.
39 Guildhall Library and Museum, 16th Annual Report 1914, AN 21.3.3, p. 17.
40 Guildhall Art Gallery, no. 96. Transferred from London Workhouse to Corporation of London in 1829.
41 O'Donaghue, p. 444; Griffiths 1989.
42 Guildhall Art Gallery file on Riley.
43 Guildhall Art Gallery file on Riley, typed sheet headed 'John Riley (1646–1691)', p. 2.
44 Frame restored by W. Rutley in 1899, portrait restored by Bennett in 1930, Note in Guildhall Art Gallery file on Riley.
45 'The 3 panels of carvings were taken to Swallowfield. These were badly damaged, but most of the pieces were tied up in a parcel attached. RR 693.' Typed report in Guildhall Art Gallery file on Riley.
46 Horace, *Odes*, iii, iii, lines 1 to 4.
47 English translation, John Newman's letter to author dated 30 June 2001.

NOTES ON CHAPTER TWELVE: First Art Commission for Guildhall

1 Howgego.
2 Campbell.
3 In April 1609 Viscount Bindon wrote to Robert Cecil, Earl of Salisbury, requesting his portrait for 'the gallery I lately had made for the pictures of sundry of my honourable friends, whose presentation thereby to behold will greatly delight me to walk often in that place where I may see so comfortable a sight.' (Gibson R., p. viii).
4 Gibson K., p. 1.
5 Morgan.
6 CLRO, Repertory of the Court of Aldermen, 75, f. 160b.
7 CLRO Sept 27 1670 f. 313.
8 Ibid f. 316.
9 Wright received his first part payment of £100 on 28 February 1671, followed by further payments on 27 June, 9 October and 6 December.
10 Repertory of the Court of Aldermen, 76, f. 232.
11 There are no other references to this painting. Could it be the half length portrait of Prince Rupert in armour which Vyner commissioned from John Michael Wright in 1672 and which is now at Magdalen College, Oxford, presented by William Huggins in 1755? Was it ever hung at Guildhall and if so, for how long?
12 CLRO Repertory of the Court of Aldermen, 77, f. 43. 'Mr Wright the Herald Painter' is said to be John Michael's brother. The frame makers Mrs Ashfield and Mrs Flushier may have been the wives of the painters Edmund Ashfield (fl. 1670–1700), described by Walpole as a 'scholar' of Wright's, and Balthazar (?) Flesshier, said by Walpole to have been a frame-maker as well as an artist, and by whom a 'large piece of fruit' was in Sir Peter Lely's collection. Flesshier (whose wife was named as the frame maker of Lely's portraits of the King and the Duke of York) was perhaps one of his assistants, since a copy by him of a portrait of the King's mistress, Louise de Kerouaille, was among a group of pictures acquired from Lely's studio by Sir Thomas Isham in 1675–76. 'Mr Norris' was John Norris, a leading framemaker who worked for many important patrons and artists and shared a workshop in Long Acre with Henry Norris, presumably his father, brother or son, who was described as 'Keeper of the King's Pictures' in 1682 (I am grateful to Victoria Doran, Frame Conservator at Guildhall Art Gallery for this information). In 1689 John Norris was appointed joiner to the Privy Council, and Vertue described him as 'frame maker & picture keeper at Court in King William and Queen Anne's time.' He is recorded as making only one frame for an unspecified Fire Judge, but Victoria Doran notes that he may have made more than this as there are six whose makers are unrecorded. Frames for later pictures in the series were also made by Mary Dorrell (Sir Samuel Browne, 1672/3) and Laurence Dorvile (Heneage Finch, 1674). They may also have been a husband and wife team whose surnames have been misread.
13 Evelyn, 31 July 1673. Evelyn also made the following references to Wright in his Diary: 'Came the Earl of Northampton and the famous Painter Mr Write to visit me.' (5 April 1659); 'Went to visit Mr Wright, a Scots-Man, who having lived long at Rome was esteemed a good Painter (3 October 1662); 'Went to see Mr Write the Painter's collection of rare shells etc.' (6 May 1664). Pepys makes a single reference to Wright in his Diary: (following an account of Lely's portraits of the King and Duke of York 'thence to Wright's, the painter's; but Lord! To see the difference that is between their two works!' (16 June 1662).
14 Campbell notes that the category of 'uomini famosi' evolved in Italy and that such sets could include military heroes, philosophers, poets and politicians, with persons of the distant past placed alongside recent or even living figures.
15 The terms half-length and three-quarter-length tend to be used interchangeably for portraits of this size.
16 After Clarendon's death in 1674 his son Lord Cornbury inherited the house and paintings. In 1683 the house was sold and the collection moved to Cornbury House. There it was seen in 1729 by Vertue, who made an incomplete list of it (Note Books II p. 65). Half of the collection was secured by the Duchess of Queensberry, daughter of the 4th Earl. This passed to the Douglas family and was mostly dispersed in Earl of Home sale at Christies 20 June 1919. Gibson R. provides a catalogue of the works remaining in the collection, and the illustrations show parts of the frames.
17 Pepys recorded in his Diary seeing the heads 'all started and some finished' in Lely's studio on 18 April 1666 and they may have all been completed that year. The Flagmen's portraits were presented (with the exception of that of Prince Rupert,

which remained in the Royal Collection) to Greenwich Hospital by George IV in 1824 and are now in the Queen's House, Greenwich.

[18] Horace Vere, Baron Vere of Tilbury was the greatest professional soldier of his day. Many commanders on both sides in the English Civil Wars, including Skippon, Fairfax and Monck served under him. He began his service in the Netherlands in 1590 and became one of Prince Maurice's most trusted captains. The series of their portraits which the Prince commissioned (Mauristhuis) included one of Vere by Ravesteyn (1611). They probably inspired Vere to commission his own set of the commanders who fought under him with the Dutch against Spain. These portraits descended to the Townshend family and were dispersed at Christies in 1904. Vere's own portrait of 1629, by Miereveldt, is now in the National Portrait Gallery. See Piper, p. 362 n. 4.

[19] I am grateful to Sheila Russell and Valerie Cumming for their comments on the weather vanes and costume in the John Robinson painting (*Illus. 114*). CLRO, Biographical notes on Sir John Robinson.

[20] Pepys, 17 March 1663.

[21] The set originally hung either at Whitehall or St James's Palace and later became known as the 'Windsor' Beauties — it is now at Hampton Court. See Simon.

[22] Both Pepys and Evelyn collected portrait engravings, while another portrait painting collection formed at the time (but unlikely to have offered a model for the City's commission) was Sir John Nicholas's (1623–74) historical collection of copies of Royalist portraits at West Horseley Place. He probably formed it on Clarendon's example, and Evelyn may also have advised him. The fashion for series and suites of portraits persisted into the eighteenth century.

[23] Vertue, p. 44. Dallaway, in Walpole., vol II, p. 93, n.3 stated: 'Lely was applied to, and accepted the commission. Upon finding that the Judges would not wait upon him for that purpose, he would not compromise the dignity of the King's painter, and declined the engagement. It was transferred to Michael Wright.' Scharf also stated that Lely was the chosen artist, and that tenders were invited from other artists only after he declined the commission.

[24] Pepys, 18 July 1666.

[25] Millar 1978, p. 17 and note 30: 'to very important sitters Lely would take his equipment and set it up in their apartments'.

[26] In October 1671 a servant of Lely's told his friends the Beales that Lely still intended to 'finish' every picture himself; see Beckett, p. 21. We cannot now know how much of the Guildhall portraits of the King and the Duke of York Lely painted himself, because at some stage between 1705 (when they were listed for restoration along with the other paintings in the Guildhall) and 1778 (when they were not included in an estimate delivered by the City's Clerk of Works, George Dance, for 'cleansing and repairing the several pictures belonging to Guildhall'), they decayed or were otherwise lost; there are no records of their fate.

NOTES TO CHAPTER THIRTEEN: A Day in the Life of a Merchant Taylor

[1] What follows is based on fact, but is otherwise purely imagination. William Turner was not given the honour of an entry in the original *Dictionary of National Biography*; perhaps he may be included in the new edition. He does, however, get a proper mention in the History of Parliament, *The House of Commons 1690–1715* (2002), vol. V, pp. 708–09, and many of the details of this essay are taken from there. A most profitable visit to Kirkleatham, North Yorkshire, was made by the author on 14 July 2003. Guildhall Library (GL), MSS 5099–5113 are all concerned with Sir William, his business and his family. A copy of his will is at GL, MS 10770.

[2] GL, MS 5107/2.

[3] Merchant Taylors' Archive; GL, MS 34010/8, pp. 178–81.

[4] GL, MS 5100, unpaginated, contains much information about Turner's mayoral expenses and about his household.

[5] Merchant Taylors' Archive; GL, MS 34010/8, p. 118 and Woodhead, p. 34.

[6] GL, MS 5100 gives all the servants' names and their wages.

[7] Merchant Taylors' Archive; GL, MS 34010/4, pp. 261–83. Jonson's song, which so delighted the monarch, survives among the archives in Hatfield House. It will be published in Davies & Saunders.

[8] Edwards, pp. 31–35.

[9] Conway Davies, vol. II, pp. 970–79. Also Hope, pp. 92–93.

[10] GL, MS 29,432 gives the tithes for St Gregory and St Mary Magdalene for 1672, and gives Turner's name, though it is hard to calculate the exact location. He had as a neighbour the unfortunate Stephen Colledge, the Protestant Joiner, who was hanged at Oxford — London juries having refused to convict him — for criticising the Duke of York. A further tithe return, GL, MS 9801, Box 2, gives Turner's name again.

[11] Turner was willing to lend to the King and in fact got his money back. He provided 'rich bronze' fabric for a royal robe and was paid for it. GL, MS 5102, f. 51.

[12] Bell. Though an old book, it is still the best.

[13] See Pepys, vol. X, Companion volume, pp. 459–60.

[14] GL, MS 5100, unpaginated. The quantities of food provided are impressive.

[15] Doolittle, Chapter VII, pp. 96–110. Also see Saunders (ed.) and Collins.

[16] Hooke: frequent early entries make it clear that Turner and Hooke were on familiar terms. The previous, provident Master was Robert White.

[17] GL, MS 34010/8, p. 180.

[18] GL, MS 34010/8, p. 162 and Draper.

[19] GL, MS 34010/8, p. 351.

[20] The story of the threadbare apprentice is pure fantasy, but Sir William Turner's care for the poor was such that it is not beyond imagination and certainly apprentices were required to look smart and well turned out.

[21] Brett and Irwin.

[22] See also Cornforth. I am most grateful to Dr Christine Stephenson for telling me of these articles.

[23] Schofield 1995, pp. 194–95; Croot, pp. 43–45.

[24] GL, MS 5105, f. 39r.

[25] The menu appears on the first page of the Merchant Taylors' run of Court Minutes (GL, MS 34010/1) as a feast for the Bachelors' Company in 1562. In spite of the distance between the dates, I felt I could not do better than follow it for Sir William's imaginary meal.

APPENDICES

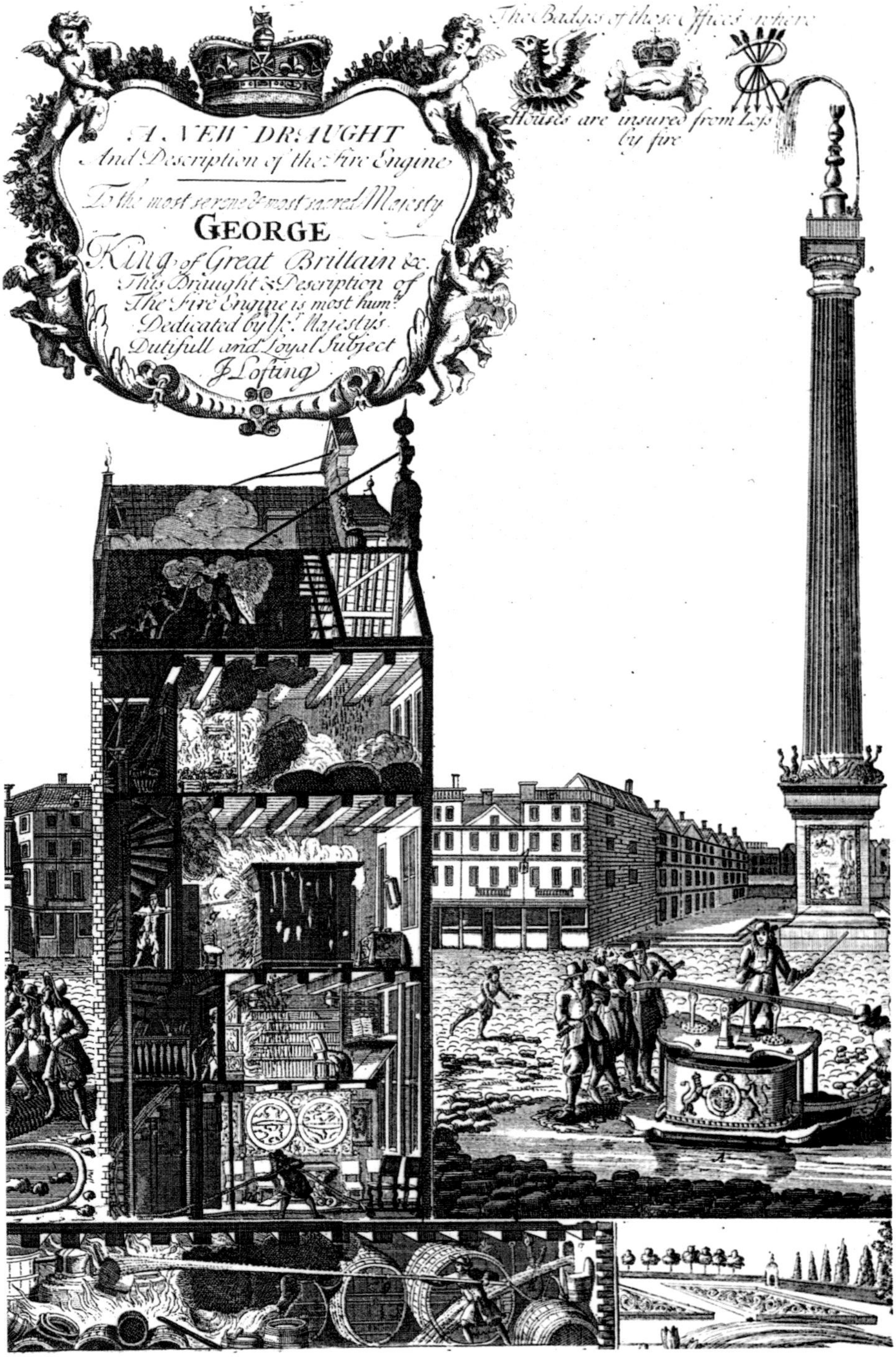

130 *John Lofting, 'A New draught and description of the fire engine' (detail), c. 1720.* *See Illus 51.*

Appendix One Sample from the South Sea Company Inventories

An Inventory of the Houſehold Goods, Linnen, and Plate, of Sir *John Fellows*, Bar^{t}. at his Houſe at *Carſhalton*, taken *March* 13, 17$\frac{20}{21}$, and are as follows, *viz.*

Numb. I.

Mr. Reeve's Room, a Wainſcot Bedſtead, Sacking, Rods, a Suit of Drugget Furniture, Drugget Hangings round the Room, a Feather-bed, Bolſter, three Blankets, one Pillow, and a Callico Quilt, a Wainſcot Cheſt of Drawers, five Chairs, and one Stool, a Pair of Iron Dogs, and a Shovel, a Blunderbuſs, and a Muskatoon, a parcel of Lumber in the Cloſet adjoining.

Numb. II.

Maids Garret, a Beach Bedſtead, Sacking, Rods, a Suit of Crimſon China Curtains, lined with a ſtriped Crape, a Feather-bed, Bolſter, two Pillows, three Blankets, and a Callico Quilt, and a Holland Quilt, printed Stuff Hangings round the Room, four Chairs, and two Stools.

Numb. III.

A Worſted Damask-bed compleat, a Feather-bed, Bolſter, three Blankets, Drugget Hangings round the Room, ſeven Cane Chairs, and four Stuffit Stools, a pair of Dogs, Shovel, Tongs, and Fender, two Tables, and a Peice of Carpetting.

Numb. IV.

An Orange-colour Camblet-bed, three Chairs, and two Stools, China Hangings round the Room, a hanging Glaſs, and a dreſſing Glaſs, a Feather-bed, Bolſter, two Pillows, a Callico Quilt, two Blankets, and a white Holland Quilt, a braſs Hearth, Shovel, Tongs, a pair of Dogs, a corner Cupboard, two Wainſcot Cheſts of Drawers, one painted Picture, and a Wainſcot Table.
Cloſet adjoining, a Perſia Carpet, ſix painted Pictures, an old Fender.

Numb. V.

A Bedſtead, and printed Stuff Furniture, a Featherbed, Bolſter, two Pillows, a Rug and three Blankets, Hangings round the Room of Drugget.

Numb. VI.

A Cloth Bed lin'd with *Perſian*, two Featherbeds, one Bolſter, eight Pillows, and two Quilts, five Chairs, a braſs Hearth, Shovel, Tongs, Fender, and Dogs, Tapeſtry Hangings round the Room, and Lumber.

Numb. VII. *Maids Garret.*

A Bedſtead, and Drugget Furniture, a Featherbed, Bolſter, one Pillow, two Blankets, and a Quilt, a Table, two Chairs, and a Cricket.

Numb. VIII. *The Gallery.*

Seventeen Chairs, a Couch, a Squab, and Pillow, an old Sattee, two *Spaniſh* Tables, and Carpets, and ſix old Cuſhions, thirty two Pictures, an old Clock without a Caſe.

Numb. IX. *Cloſet up one Pair of Stairs.*

A Couch cover'd with Caffaw, three ſquare Stools, and an old Cuſhion.

Numb. X.

A Chintz Bed lin'd with Culgee, compleat, four Pair of Callico Window-curtains, Corniſhes, and Vallance, a Featherbed, Bolſter, two Pillows, three Blankets, and a Callico Quilt, a Crimſon Damask eaſy Chair, three blue Damask Chairs, two Sattin ſquare Stools, one round Stool, a Walnut-wood Cheſt of Drawers, a Dreſſing-Glaſs, a Chimney-Glaſs, and two Sconces, a Braſs Hearth, Iron Back, Shovel, Tongs, and Bruſh, a Pair of Iron Dogs, and one Piece of Tapeſtry Hangings, a Wainſcot ſquare Table with Drawers.

Numb. XI.

John Fellowes.

The South Sea Company Inventories provide a wealth of information on the houses and belongings of rich City merchants.

These inventories were published in 1721 by Jacob Tonson, Bernard Lintot and William Taylor, a year after the disastrous crisis of the South Sea Bubble. This dark episode in the annals of the City led thousands across the land to lose money and prominent figures in the City mercantile community to go bankrupt.

The South Sea Company was set up in 1711 to trade with the South Seas (the Pacific). It was initially so successful that it offered to manage the National Debt, and went on to provide people of influence with shares on unrealistic terms. Fraudulent mushroom companies gave another negative twist to the financial risks that had been taken.

The Bubble burst in 1720 when there were insufficient funds to pay for shares being sold, leading to a general panic and a massive rush to sell. The Inventories are the outcome of the investigation that followed, and which led to the confiscation of goods and property. There are twenty-six inventories in all and they have been used by several contributors to this book, including Adriana Turpin who has thus summarised their contents:

Of the 26 directors listed, 11 had inventories of their London houses; 3 had lodgings in London; the remainder had no inventories of the contents of their houses. The majority had houses on the outskirts of London and a few had houses further away, such as Thomas Reynolds, who had a house in Manchester, as well as a house in the Victualling Office in London and at Kicksend in Middlesex. James Edmundson had recently pulled down his house to rebuild and William Astell's house had recently burned. There are copies of the inventories at the London Guildhall Library, The Public Record Office at Kew, the British Library and the Bodleian Library, Oxford.

The sample reproduced here is the first page of the inventory of Sir John Fellowes in *The Particulars and Inventories of the Estates of the late Sub-Governor, Deputy Governor, and Directors of the South Sea Company*. The inventory was taken on 13 March 1720 and ran over sixteen pages. It dealt with Fellowes's Carshalton property. Another separate inventory dealt with his London house in Old Jewry which was auctioned in 1723. The total value of his London house was £604 0*s.* 0*d.* The total value of his Carshalton inventory, a detail of which is reproduced here, was £753 6*s.* 6*d.*

A 1713 inventory also exists for this property when it belonged to Edward Carleton, tobacco merchant. At times the two inventories correspond closely and follow roughly the same route. The Fellowes inventory starts at the top of the house where servants' accommodation was found (Rooms I to VII). 'Mr Reeve's Room' was that of Samuel Reeves, stewart, who was responsible for the day to day running of the whole estate (see Jones in Bibliography). By the time the inventory reaches the Gallery, which contained thirty-two pictures, we are on the first floor and the last room on the page is clearly a substantial bedroom. It is interesting to compare the furnishings in this room with those of the 'Maids Garret' above.

Appendix Two Sample from the London Orphans' Court Inventories

The London Orphans' Court Inventories are unique documents kept in the Corporation of London Records Office. The Court was set up to protect the interests of the children of London freemen who happened to die leaving children under age. The inventories of moveable goods, plus debtors and creditors, were deposited with the Orphans' Court who operated the City Custom. This ensured that in the event of a father's early death, under age children would be guaranteed ⅓ of the value of all goods listed, while a second third would go to the wife of the deceased and the remaining third, or 'dead man's portion', was the freeman's to dispose of as he wished.

In London over 3000 inventories and associated accounts have survived. Most of them date from the period 1660 to 1740. They are much more difficult to consult than the South Sea Inventories, firstly because they take the form of manuscripts, secondly because they are written in a variety of handwritings, some more legible than others, and thirdly because they are found on narrow parchment strips kept tightly rolled. These documents can only be comfortably read with the help of weights which keep in place both ends of the section to study.

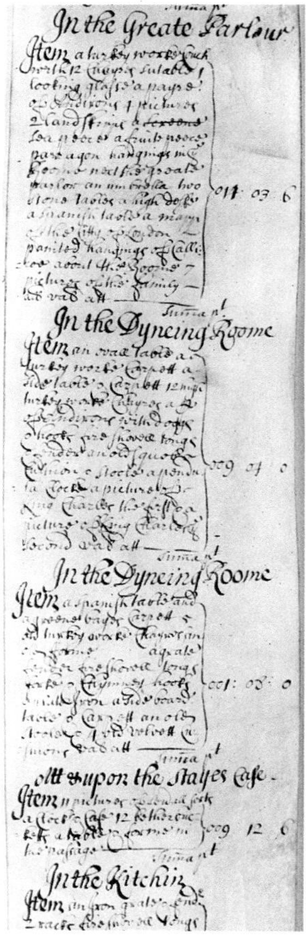
In the Greate Parlour

In the Dyneing Roome

In the Dyneing Roome

Att & upon the Stayes Case

In the Kitchin

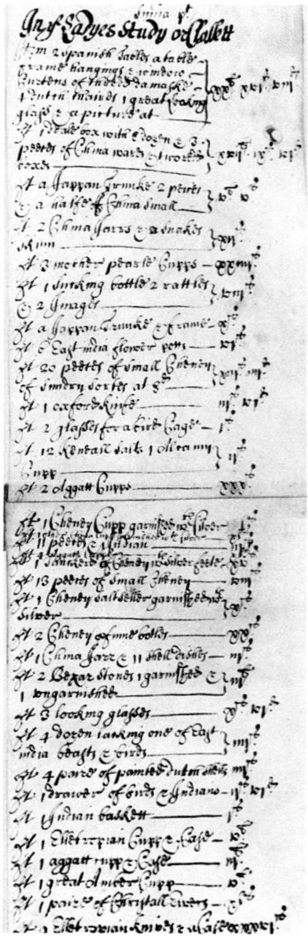
Ye Ladyes Study or Closett

We reproduce here two sections from two different rolls:

On the left is a section from the inventory of Sir Nathaniel Herne (Ref.1591), 31 March 1680, listing goods 'In the Great Parlour', 'In the Dyneing Roome', 'Att & upon the Stayes Case' and 'In the Kitchin'.

On the right is a section from the inventory of Sir Martin Noell (Ref.500), April 1666, listing goods in 'Ye Ladyes Study or Closett'.

Source: Carlton.

MERCHANTS' BIOGRAPHIES

ROBERT ABBOTT (*c.* 1610–58)

Born in Northamptonshire, Robert Abbott was apprenticed to the scrivener Francis Webb in London, completing his indentures in 1635. In 1637 he married Bertha, daughter of Jasper Chapman, a prosperous grocer. Abbott set up his own scriveners' shop, The Flying Horse, in Cornhill where his nephew Robert Clayton and John Morris later joined him as apprentices. Abbott prospered as a royalist money-scrivener in spite of his implication in the Waller Plot of 1643 and the adverse political climate thereafter. **LW**

Source: Melton 1986

PENNING ALSTON (d. 1668)

Penning Alston was born at Edwardston in Suffolk, the son of Edward Alston, gentleman, and Margaret Penning. He was the brother of Sir Edward Alston (1595–1669), President of the College of Physicians, who was knighted at the Restoration in 1660. Penning Alston was a member of the Grocers' Company and held property both at Greenlands in Buckinghamshire and in Suffolk. He was buried at St Botolph, Aldersgate, and according to Woodhead was possibly brother-in-law of Richard Chandler. **LW**

Sources: Beaven; DNB; Woodhead

JOHN BANCKES (dates unknown)

Described as a 'Hamburg merchant and Banker' in Vertue's *Note Books*, he was Sir Godfrey Kneller's first English patron. Kneller lodged with him in York Buildings for about a year, and painted him in 1676. It is tempting to assume that he is the John Bankes (*c.* 1627–99) described by John Evelyn as 'a merchant of small beginnings, but by usurie etc.: amass'd an Estate of 100000 pounds etc.' Unfortunately, Evelyn's John Bankes had a house in Lincoln's Inn Fields in 1676, and had been created a baronet in 1661; this distinction is unlikely to have been omitted from his portrait in which a letter is addressed to 'Mr John Banckes, Mrchant, London' or from Kneller's letters which describe his patron as 'Mr Bancks'. **VC**

Sources: Tate Gallery Collections Index; Vertue; Evelyn

SIR WILLIAM BOLTON (16??–??)

Apprenticed as a Merchant Taylor in 1623–24, he became Master in 1659 and was knighted in 1663. He served as Sheriff in 1660–61, and became Lord Mayor in 1666, immediately after the Fire. It was the Merchant Taylors' custom to present £100 to any brother who filled that office. Their income from property destroyed, they begged him to accept less, but he insisted on the full amount. He was accused of embezzling £1,800 of money collected for Fire victims, and was forced to resign. Becoming impoverished, Common Council allowed him a pension of £3 a week. He was brother-in-law to Patience Ward. **AS**

Source: Woodhead

RICHARD CHANDLER (1606–91)

The son of William Chandler of Stratford upon Avon, Richard Chandler served as Master of Haberdashers' in 1668–69 and 1682–83. He was apprenticed in 1628 to Thomas Stones and married twice, his second wife Winifred being the daughter of Sir Thomas Jervoise. He was one of the Alston Trustees and according to Woodhead possibly brother-in-law of Penning Alston. **LW**

Sources: Beaven; Woodhead

SIR ROBERT CLAYTON (1629–1707)

Born in Bulwick, Northamptonshire, the son of a carpenter, Robert Clayton was apprenticed to his maternal uncle, Robert Abbott, a money scrivener. In partnership with fellow apprentice John Morris he greatly expanded Abbott's banking business and became active in City affairs, stoutly defending its charter in the 1680s. He was Alderman of Cordwainer Ward (1670–76) and of Cheap (1676–83 and 1689–1707). He was elected sheriff and knighted in 1671 and elected Lord Mayor of London 1679–80 after translation to the Drapers' Company. A prominent Whig, he was active in national politics too, serving as MP for the City of London for many years between 1678 and his death. In 1659 he married Martha Trott (d. 1705), daughter of Perient Trott, a merchant trading to Bermuda, but he died childless. In addition to his business premises at Old Jewry, he owned Marden Park at Bletchingley in Surrey and extensive land holdings elsewhere in Britain. He was a Director of the recently-founded Bank of England (1702–07) and the many other offices he held are listed in the *DNB* and Woodhead. He also featured in contemporary literature, notably John Evelyn's *Diary*, Daniel Defoe's *Roxana* and Dryden and Tate's *The Second Part of Absalom and Achitophel.* **LW**

Sources: Beaven; DNB; Melton 1986; Woodhead

WILLIAM CLAYTON (1641–1716)

A younger brother of Robert Clayton, William trained as a carpenter and joiner with their father in Bulwick, Northamptonshire. By 1669 he was working in London for his brother and in 1671 directed the building of his brother's new house in Old Jewry. After the death of Robert Abbott in 1684 he lived at Hambleden Manor. It had been intended that William's eldest son, Robert, would be Sir Robert Clayton's heir, but he died abroad in 1698. Sir Robert Clayton's extensive properties therefore passed to William's second son, another William, who increased the family's holdings in Buckinghamshire, served as MP for Bletchingley and was created baronet in 1732. **LW**

Sources: Melton 1977; Melton 1986; VCH

SIR WILLIAM CRAVEN (1548?–1618)

Free of Merchant Taylors' Company in 1569 and Warden of the Company in 1593 he founded a grammar school in Burnsall, Yorkshire, which still flourishes as a junior school. He was knighted in 1603, at the accession of James I, was Lord Mayor of London in 1610 and President of Christ's Hospital in 1611–18. He gave £50 towards the building of the library at St John's College, Oxford. **AS**

Sources: DNB; Clode 1875

JONATHAN DAWES (1633–72)

Apprenticed to a member of the Fishmonger's company, William Lumbrey, Jonathan Dawes took on his master's trade in the Levant Company. He married Anne, daughter of Sir Thomas Bendish in 1663. He lent Charles II £6000 and was knighted in 1671. He held positions as Alderman for the Broad Street Ward (1669–72), and was also Sheriff (1671–72). **AT**

Source: Woodhead

JOHN FELLOWES (1670–1724)

A 1712 inscription in the City church of St Michael Paternoster Royal referred to 'Mr John Fellowes of London, merchant'. However, it seems that the only commodity in which he made a significant investment was 'cocheneal', the crushed beetle which produces such an effective red dye. This 'merchant', more a financier than a trader, was the fourth son of William Fellowes, another London merchant. John Fellowes was made a baronet in 1719, the year he was appointed Sub Governor of the South Sea Company. His involvement and responsibilities there meant that he was hit hard when the South Sea Company collapsed shortly afterwards. In London he resided in Old Jewry (See Appendix I) but he had also purchased Carshalton House in Surrey which is where he died and chose to be buried. His austere funerary monument at Carshalton Church may still be seen today. **MG**

Sources: South Sea Inventories, Jones

WILLIAM FREEMAN (*c.* 1645–1707)

William Freeman was the son of Colonel William Freeman of Bury St Edmunds who had arrived in St Kitts in 1629 and established an estate there. Colonel Freeman fought for Parliament in the Civil War but lost his St Kitts' lands when the French invaded in 1666. He became an agent for the Royal Africa Company in the Leeward Islands involved in the slave trade and sugar plantations. Between 1678 and 1684 the younger William Freeman acted as the agent in London for Sir William Stapleton, the Governor of the Leeward Islands. He inherited his father's remaining West Indian property after the Colonel's death in the early 1680s and according to Tyack he acquired a captain's commission under James II. In addition to the Fawley Court estate near Henley, William Freeman also owned Crosby Hall in Bishopsgate and a plantation on Montserrat. **LW**

Sources: Freeman's tomb at Fawley church; Hancock; Tyack

JERRARD GORE

There are two Merchant Taylors of that name, a father and a son. The elder served his Company as Master in 1567, contributed modestly but generously enough to various charities and was on the Court which established Merchant Taylors' School in 1561. The younger man served as Warden from 1601–04 and took part in the visitation of another of the Company's schools at Great Crosby in Lancashire. It was presumably to him that William Turner was apprenticed. **AS**

Sources: Clode 1875; Clode 1888

SIR NATHANIEL HERNE (1630–79)

Nathaniel Herne was apprenticed to John Frederick and married his daughter Judith in 1656, who brought with her a dowry of £5000; he later took over his father-in-law's business. His wealth was increased further on inheriting his half-brother Nicholas's estate, and he owned property in the City as well as in Stepney. He was a member of the East India Company and rose through its ranks, becoming Governor (1674–76 and 1678–79). He was also MP for Dartmouth and knighted in 1674. His brother was also apprenticed to John Frederick and married, for his second wife, Elizabeth, Judith's sister and co-heiress. He also became a Governor of the East India Company as well as becoming MP for Dartmouth in 1689. **AT**

Source: Woodhead

SIR THEODORE JANSSEN (*c.* 1658–1748)

Theodore Janssen was born in Angoulême where his father was a paper manufacturer. He came to London from Holland in 1683 as a Huguenot refugee. He seems to have had financial backing from the beginning and was naturalized in 1685. He traded in tin and lead with Genoa and Leghorn, as well as being a major importer of paper. In 1694 he was a founder member of the Bank of England. He also acted as a dealer in securities, negotiating with his brother and other contacts in Amsterdam. His biggest profits came from financing William III's war with France and in 1696 he was knighted by William. In 1711 he became one of the first directors of the South Sea Company. He was opposed to free trade and wrote a pamphlet in 1713 against the Treaty of Commerce between England and France. In 1717 he became MP for Yarmouth, Isle of Wight, to represent Whig interests. His wife Williamza Henley was the sister of Anthony Henley, a well-known classical scholar, wit and musician, with whom Theodore Janssen shared a strong love of the classics. One of his projects was the publication by the Cambridge University Press of a new edition of Suidas' Greek/Latin lexicon and new editions of Horace's works. After his ruin with the collapse of the South Sea Company and being barred from public office, he continued business with his sons, but moved out of Hanover Square to a smaller London house, as well as letting Wimbledon Manor. In 1731 at 73 he moved permanently to Wimbledon, where he died aged 90. **AT**

JOHN LANGHAM (1583–1671)

John Langham was the eldest son of a 'linendraper' and was brought up in Guilsborough, eight miles north of

Northampton. After the death of his father in 1607, he moved to London, served his apprenticeship for the Grocers' Company and was sent on two tours abroad as a factor. After his return to London, he married Mary Bunce, an alderman's daughter, in 1620. Langham built up his own fleet of ships and became a leading Turkey merchant. He traded in shipping cargoes and on one occasion he was reputed to have made a profit of £30,000 on a delivery of currants from the Mediterranean. He invested in the East India Company and was appointed director from 1626 to 1642. He served as treasurer of the Levant (Turkey) Company in 1632–34 and governor in 1654. He was elected alderman and sheriff of the corporation of London in 1642. As a stalwart royalist, his political career was fraught with difficulties during the Civil War and he was twice imprisoned in the Tower. A group of royalist aldermen, including Langham, refused to proclaim the abolition of the monarchy in 1649 and they were excluded from office by Parliament. As a result Langham did not serve as lord mayor, although he was reinstated as alderman and MP after the Restoration in 1660. Charles II granted him a knighthood and baronetcy, and he retired from his political offices shortly thereafter on account of his age. **AH**

Sources: Langham Ms (See Notes to Chapter 11 on p. 184); Beaven; Sharpe

JOHN MORRIS (d. 1682)

Born in Abingdon in Berkshire John Morris was the son of a John Hall or Hales, but took on the surname of his great uncle, a baker who had adopted his father. Morris was elected to a Bennett's scholarship at Abingdon School after his own father's early death. He was apprenticed to Robert Abbott and formed a close partnership in the banking business with his fellow apprentice Robert Clayton which lasted until his death. He was an Alderman in 1669 and served as MP for Bletchingley in Surrey in 1679–81. It seems he never married but lodged with the Claytons at the business premises. He bequeathed his property to Sir Robert Clayton. **LW**

Sources: Beaven, Melton, Woodhead

MARTIN NOELL (1614–1665)

Born in Stafford, Martin Noell was an active member of the Scriveners' Company all his life and may have been apprenticed to a London scrivener. He was a financier and revenue farmer who in the 1650s succeeded in obtaining quasi-monopoly rights on English salt. With Thomas Povey he promoted the creation of a West India Company and was also active in the Levant and East India Company. He is also remembered as the man who paid the considerable sum of £520 not to have to become an alderman. He was knighted in 1662 (much to Pepys' surprise) and died of the plague in 1665. His wife died of grief shortly afterwards. **MG**

Sources: Beaven; DNB

DUDLEY NORTH (1641–91)

The fourth son of Sir Dudley North (1602–77) and Anne Montagu of Boughton House, Northamptonshire, he was bound to Thomas Davis, a 'Turkey merchant' and was sent to Russia and then to Smyrna. He remained there until 1680, first as a factor for his master's firm and then becoming one of the leading figures of the Turkey Company. His influence in Constantinople was considerable, and it was suggested that he should be the British ambassador there. He left his business in his brother Montagu's hands, returning to England a very rich man. As a supporter of the crown, he was elected one of the sheriffs of London, and he continued to support both Charles II and then James II as MP for Banbury. From 1684 to 1685 he was Lord of the Treasury. He was very close to his younger brother, Roger, who was keeper of the Great Seal under James II. Both brothers lost their political influence after 1689. Dudley married a considerable heiress, Ann, widow of Sir Robert Gunning of Cold Ashton, Gloucestershire in 1683 and loving the country, bought an estate at Glemham in Suffolk. Considered 'one of the ablest men of his time', he wrote a tract advocating free trade, 'Currency', published shortly before his death. **AT**

Sources: DNB; Grassby 1994

THOMAS PAPILLON (1623–1702)

Thomas Papillon, born in Putney, was the third son of David Papillon, a merchant. He received his freedom of the Mercers' Company in 1646 and became a director of the East India Company (1675–82). He married Jane Broadnax of Godmersham Kent in 1651. He was member of parliament for Dover between 1672–81 and a staunch adherent of the country party, arguing for protection of merchants' interests, free trade within the United Kingdom and, in the case of the trial of Lord Shaftesbury in 1681, the right of grand juries to examine witnesses in secret. He became extremely unpopular with the court party, and, on being fined £10,000 in 1684 in an action of false indictment, fled to Utrecht to avoid payment. He returned to England in 1689 and was re-elected MP for Dover, which he represented until 1695, when he became MP for London. He had bought Acrise Place in Kent in 1666. **AT**

Sources: DNB; Scouloudi; Museum of London 1989

SIR JOSEPH SHELDON (1628–1681)

Joseph Sheldon was a rich and successful woollen merchant, a member of the Drapers' Company, alderman for the Bishopsgate ward from 1666 to his death and Lord Mayor of London. He was born in Staffordshire, the son of Ralph Sheldon of Wadley, Derbyshire and Stanton, Staffordshire, and was the nephew of Gilbert Sheldon, Archbishop of Canterbury. In 1655 he married Elizabeth Clifton, daughter of William Clifton of St Paul's Churchyard; there is no record for his second marriage to Margaret Rose. He lent extensively to the City of London and held a mortgage with Nicholas Charleton for £11,000 on the Duke of Buckingham's estate. **AT**

Sources: Woodhead; Alexander

DORMER SHEPPHERD (1644–?)

Dormer Sheppherd was born in 1644, son of William Sheppherd and Mary Dormer. He was born at Great Rollright, Chipping Norton in Oxfordshire. He was the youngest of six children, one of whom was Sir Fleetwood Sheppherd (who was appointed Steward of the household of Nell Gwynn and later was made usher of the Black Rod in 1694). As sole surviving sibling, letters of administration relating to Sir Fleetwood Sheppherd was granted to Dormer Sheppherd on 31 October 1699.

It is known that Dormer Sheppherd visited Maryland USA 3–18 August 1677.

He married twice, first to Katherine who died in 1680 and second to Sarah Hawes in 17 March 1681. He bought the land on Mile End Green and built the house around 1693. He had a black Servant called Lewis who ran away from the house in Mile End Green twice in 1707. He also had a son called Amos Sheppherd born at Great Rollright around 1683, who was admitted to Lincoln's Inn Field in 1703. **KG**

Sources: DNB, Public Records Office

JOHN SMITH (1628–73)

The son of James Smith, a member of the Salters' Company and alderman, John Smith followed his father in both professions. He married twice: first, Anne, daughter of William Wise of Windsor and secondly, Jane, daughter of Robert Deane of St Mary Aldermary. He owned city property, East India Company stock and brickworks in Redriffe and Isleworth, Middlesex, leaving an estate worth £19,895. As a sheriff from 1669–70, he was of the court party, considered in 1672 (Account of the Aldermen) to be 'an honest, good-natured person, desiring to serve his Majesty to his utmost and ready to oblige any of the king's friends.' His son married Mary, daughter of John Eyles, a director of the South Sea Company. **AT**

Sources: Woodhead

SIR WILLIAM TURNER (1615–93)

Born at Kirkleatham in North Yorkshire, the third son of John Turner, whose family had held land there since the 1620s. He came to London, was apprenticed to Jerrard Gore, Merchant Taylor, became free of the Company in 1640, and served as Master in 1661 and again in 1684. Knighted in 1662, he was Lord Mayor in 1668–69 and again in 1684, and MP for the City from

1690 till his death. He was President of Bethelem and Bridewell Hospitals, 1669–87 and 1690–93. A strict man but much respected, a eulogy, *Litterae Consolatoriae*, on his becoming Lord Mayor, declared that he would restore the devastated City, building 'the Groundwork of thy future fame'; an elegy on his death described him as 'the City's Darling and the Orphans Joy'. But his heart lay in his birthplace. He built there a hospital or almshouse which still thrives; originally a school was attached to it though now it is entirely a retreat for the elderly. According to the booklet published by the Trustees, work began on the building on 30 June 1674; the bricklayer Christopher King completed his task on 15 June 1676; and Charles II granted it a charter three years later. It may be coincidence but Robert Hooke's diary for 11 January 1672/73 reports '... at Sir W. Turner he desired modell for School Schoolhouses and 20 almshouses' and though that structure may not have been for Kirkleatham, yet the dates are close and a design can be used twice. Further research is needed here. Turner also left money to found a free school in the village and his heir and nephew, Charles, and great-nephew, Cholmley, honoured the bequest with a magnificent edifice which is now the excellent local museum. The school itself passed through two reincarnations and is now Sir William Turner's Sixth Form College in Redcar Lane, while Sir William's death mask sits benevolently in the Hospital Chapel, the interior of which was remodelled in the 1740s by Cholmley Turner, possibly with the advice of James Gibbs, Sir Christopher Wren's disciple. **AS**

Source: Local enquiries in Kirkleatham, North Yorkshire; Woodhead; History of Parliament, House of Commons, 1660–90.

SIR JOHN VERNEY (1640–1717)

John Verney was born the second son of Sir Ralph Verney of Claydon House, Buckinghamshire. At seven he joined his family in Blois, France, where they had fled during the Civil War. The family returned in 1653 and six years later John was apprenticed to Gabriel Roberts, a Levant Company merchant. He went to Aleppo as a factor, remaining there until 1672. He became free of the Levant Company and the Vintners Company in 1674 and was on the governing board of the Royal Africa Company between 1679–81, 1686–88, 1691–92 and 1696–97. He leased a house in Hatton Garden. His father died in 1696, and, he inherited his baronetcy that year, later created Viscount Fermanagh (1703). He married three times and there are portraits of Verney and his three wives at Claydon House, Buckinghamshire; wall tablets to his first two wives, Elizabeth Verney, died 1686, and Mary Verney, died 1694, are in the Church of All Saints, Middle Claydon. **AT & VC**

Sources: Whyman 1999; *A Guide to the People in the Pictures at Claydon House*, National Trust 2000

SIR ROBERT VYNER (1631–88)

Goldsmith-banker and partner, then successor to his uncle Sir Thomas Vyner. He remade much of the regalia for Charles II's coronation in 1661, and was a major government financier. He is believed to have had £400,000 on loan to the government when the Stop of the Exchequer was instigated in 1672. His creditors had him declared bankrupt in 1683/4. His business premises were in Lombard Street; after these were destroyed in the Great Fire of 1666 he was temporarily lodged at the African House in Warnford Court. He bought Swakeleys, Ickenham, Middlesex in 1665. Knighted 1665; created a baronet 1666; Sheriff of London 1666–67; Lord Mayor 1674–75. Married Mary Hyde (nee Whitchurch), widow of Sir Thomas Hyde in 1665, she died in 1675; one son Charles (1666–88). **VC**

Sources: Pepys (VI, VII, & X); Stevenson & Thomson

SIR THOMAS VYNER (1588–1665)

Goldsmith-banker who established the family firm at the Sign of the Vine, Lombard Street. He bought Eastbury House in Barking in 1650, now leased by the National Trust to the local authority as a community arts centre. His son George, 2nd baronet (*c.* 1639–73) was also a goldsmith-banker, but the family business was inherited by his nephew Sir Robert Vyner (q.v.).

Knighted by both Cromwell and Charles II; created a baronet 1661; Sheriff of London 1648/9; Lord Mayor 1653/4. **VC**

Sources: Pepys (X); Thorold

SIR JOHN WARD (1655–1726)

John Ward was born in Yorkshire, but had London connections through his uncle, Sir Patience Ward (1629–96), the seventh son of Thomas Ward of Tanshelf near Pontefract, who, after studying at Cambridge for the Ministry, had moved to London to seek his fortune as a merchant. As a dissenter he frequently opposed Charles II, but nonetheless became Lord Mayor in 1680–81. In 1683 he was exiled for perjury against the Duke of York, later James II, but was re-instated on the accession of William III, Thomas Papillon arguing in his defense. On his death, his nephew John Ward inherited his property and his business. John Ward was admitted to the Freedom of the Merchant Taylors' Company by patrimony (Patience Ward was also a member of the company) and became Master in 1709–10. He was an alderman (1709–26), Sheriff (1715–5) and Lord Mayor (1718–19). He was knighted in 1714. He was a member of the East India Company and Director from 1696–98 and 1709–12, as well as a director of the New East India Company and director of the Bank of England 1694–97, 1698–1711 and 1712–26.

His son, also John Ward, married Frances Bristow in 1719 and bought Squerryes in Kent from his friend the third Earl of Jersey in 1731. **AT**

Sources: DNB for Patience Ward; Beaven; information supplied by the Corporation of London Records Office.

SIR PATIENCE WARD (1629–96)

The eighth son of Thomas Ward of Pontefract in Yorkshire, he owed his unusual name to his father's yearning for a daughter; he swore that if his wife had another boy 'he would call him Patience'. He went to Cambridge, but, preferring to engage in trade, he unwillingly became a Merchant Taylor and went on to make a fortune as a cloth merchant. He became Master in 1671–72, Lord Mayor in 1680–81, and was knighted in 1675. During his year in office, the inscription was placed on the monument that the Great Fire was due to 'the treachery and malice of the Papists'. He was elected MP for Pontefract in 1679 and 1681. In 1683 he removed to Holland for religious reasons, and only returned when William III had obtained the throne; he then became MP for London. He died in 1696 and was buried at St Mary Abchurch. **AS**

Source: Woodhead; History of Parliament, House of Commons, 1690–1715.

ROWLAND WILSON (1613–50)

The son of a wealthy vintner of the same name who was involved with the Guinea Company in Africa, Rowland Wilson junior also became a vintner. His father came from Gresgarth, Kendal, in Westmorland but from 1624 the family owned Merton Abbey in Surrey. Rowland Wilson junior was an active Parliamentarian and served as a Lieutenant Colonel in the London Trained Bands during the Civil War. He was MP for Calne in Wiltshire in 1646 and although nominated to serve at the trial of Charles I he did not stand. He was Colonel of the Orange Regiment from 1645–50 and was elected to the Council of State in 1649–50. His marriage to Mary Carleton, daughter of Bigley Carleton, a grocer, was childless and he predeceased his father, dying while Sheriff of London on 19 February 1650. His widow became the third wife of Sir Bulstrode Whitelocke. **LW**

Source: Beaven; Spalding 1975

AH Anthony Hotson
AS Ann Saunders
AT Adriana Turpin
KG Katharine Goodison
MG Mireille Galinou
LW Laura Wortley
VC Valerie Cumming

Bibliography

A TO Z RESTORATION LONDON: *The A to Z of Restoration London* (Introductory Notes by Ralph Hyde), London Topographical Society, No. 145, 1992

ABBOTT: J. A. R. Abbott, 'City Money Scrivener and His Account Book 1646–1652' in *Guildhall Miscellany* No. 7

ACKLEY: Clifford S. Ackley, *Printmaking in the Age of Rembrandt*, Exhibition Catalogue, Boston Museum of Fine Arts, 1980

AILESBURY: Historical Manuscripts Commission, *The Manuscripts of the Marquis of Ailesbury*, 1898

ALCORN: Ellenor M. Alcorn, *English Silver in the Museum of Fine Arts, Boston*, Vol. I, 'Silver before 1697', Boston, 1993

ALLEN: Roy Allen, 'The Belsize Map of 1714', *Camden History Society Newsletter*, No. 134, November 1992

ARNOLD: Janet Arnold, *Perukes & Periwigs*, London, 1970

AUBREY: John Aubrey, *Brief Lives*, ed. Andrew Clark, Oxford, 1898

BAKER: T. M. M. Baker, *London. Rebuilding the City after the Great Fire*, Chichester, 2000

BARBON: Nicholas Barbon, *An Apology for the Builder, or a Discourse Shewing the Cause and Effects of the Increase of Building*, London, 1689

BEARD & GILBERT: Geoffrey Beard and Christopher Gilbert, *Dictionary of English Furniture Makers 1660–1840*, Furniture History Society, [London], 1986

BEAVEN, A. B. Beaven, *The Aldermen of London*, London, 1908

BECKETT: R. B. Beckett, *Lely*, London, 1951

BELL: Walter George Bell, *The Great Fire of London in 1666*, London, not dated

BIMBENET-PRIVAT & MITCHELL: Michèle Bimbenet-Privat & David Mitchell, 'Words or images: descriptions of plate in England and France 1660–1700', *Silver Society Journal*, 15, 2003

BOLD: John Bold, 'The design of a house for a merchant', *Architectural History*, 33, 1990

BOUGHTON Inventory: 'An Inventory of the Goods of His Grace the Duke of Montague (sic) at His Seat at Boughton in Northamptonshire taken Novr. the 27th 1717', Boughton House and Victoria & Albert Museum (Furniture, Textiles and Fashion Department)

BOWETT: A. Bowett, *English Furniture 1660–1714 From Charles II to Queen Anne*, Antique Collectors' Club, 2002

BRETT & IRWIN: Katherine B. Brett and John Irwin, *The Origins of Chintz*, 1970

BREWER: John Brewer, *The Pleasures of the Imagination, English culture in the Eighteenth Century*, London, 1997

BRIDGES: J. Bridges, *History and Antiquities of Northamptonshire*, 2 volumes, London [1662–91], 1791

BROWN & SCHWARTZ: Peter B. Brown & Marla H. Schwartz, *Come Drink the Bowl Dry: Alcoholic Liquors and Their Place in 18th Century Society*, York, 1996

BRYANT: Julius Bryant, 'Villa views and the uninvited audience, contemporary attitudes to the Georgian villa', *The Georgian Villa*, ed. Dana Arnold, 1998

BUCKERIDGE: Bainbrigg Buckeridge, 'Essay Towards an English-School, with the Lives and Characters of above 100 Painters', in Rogers de Piles *The Art of Painting and the Lives of the Painters ...*, London, 1706

CAMPBELL: Lorne Campbell, *Renaissance Portraits - European Portrait-Painting in the 14th, 15th and 16th Centuries*, New Haven & London, 1990

CARLTON: Charles Carlton, 'The Administration of London's Court of Orphans', *Guildhall Miscellany*, Vol. VI, No. 1, October 1971

CARSWELL: John Carswell, *The South Sea Bubble*, Stroud, 1993

CARTWRIGHT: *Mr Cartwright's Pictures*, Exhibition Catalogue, Dulwich Picture Gallery, London, 1987

CASSIDY: Brendan Cassidy, 'Largillièrre's portrait of Siberechts', *Burlington Magazine*, Vol. 128, June 1986

CHERRY 1993: Bridget Cherry, 'John Pollexfen's House in Walbrook', *English Architecture Public and Private* ed. John Bold and Edward Chaney, 1993

CHERRY 2001: Bridget Cherry, 'Edward Hatton's New View of London', *Architectural History*, Vol. 44, 2001

CLARENDON: S. W. Singer (ed), *The Correspondence of Henry Hyde, Earl of Clarendon with the Diary of Lord Clarendon 1687–1690*, London, 1828

CLIFFE: J. T. Cliffe, *The World of the Country House in Seventeenth-Century England*, New Haven & London, 1999

CLODE 1875: Charles M. Clode, *Memorials of the Guild of Merchant Taylors*, London, 1875

CLODE 1888: Charles M. Clode, *The Early History of the Guild of Merchant Taylors*, 2 volumes, London, 1888

CLUETT: Douglas Cluett, *Discovering Sutton's Heritage, the story of five parishes*, Sutton, 1995
COLEMAN: Donald C. Coleman, *Sir John Banks, Baronet and Businessman*, Oxford, 1955 (or 1963?)
COLLINS: Helen Collins, PhD thesis on Edward Jarman, London, 2001, published 2004
CONWAY DAVIES: J. Conway Davies, *Catalogue of Manuscripts in the Library of the Honourable Society of the Inner Temple*, London, 1972
COOPER: Michael Cooper, *'A More Beautiful City' Robert Hooke and the Rebuilding of London after the Great Fire*, 2003
CORNFORTH: John Cornforth, 'Kirkleatham, Cleveland, I & II', *Country Life*, 6 and 13 January 1977
COWAN: B. Cowan, 'Arenas of connoisseurship: auctioning art in later Stuart England', *Art Markets in Europe 1400–1800*, M. North and D. Ormord (eds), 1998
CRAWFORD: Anne Crawford, *A History of the Vintners Company*, London, 1977
CRAWFORD & GOWING: Patricia Crawford & Laura Gowing, *Women's Worlds in Seventeenth Century England*, London, 2000
CROFT-MURRAY 1955: Edward Croft-Murray, 'An English Painter of Chinoiseries', *Country Life Annual*, 1955
CROFT-MURRAY 1962: Edward Croft-Murray, *Decorative Painting in England 1537–1837*, London, 1962
CROOT: Patricia Croot, 'Before and after Drury House: development of a suburban town house, 1250–1800', *London Topographical Record*, 2001
CRUICKSHANK & WYLD: Dan Cruickshank and Peter Wyld, *London — The art of Georgian building*, London, 1977
CUMMING: Valerie Cumming, *A Visual History of Costume, The Seventeenth Century*, London, 1984

DNB: *Dictionary of National Biography*, London and Oxford, 1885–1990
DAVIES & SAUNDERS: M. Davies and Ann Saunders, *A History of the Merchant Taylors' Company*, London, 2004
DE PILES: Roger de Piles, *Abrégé de la vie des Peintres*, translated by John Savage as *The Art of Painting and the Lives of the Painters ...*, London, 1706
DONALD: Diana Donald, 'Mr Deputy Dumpling and Family – Satirical images of the City Merchant', *Burlington Magazine*, Vol. 131, 1989
DOOLITTLE: Ian Doolittle, *The Mercers' Company, 1579–1959*, London, 1994
DRAPER: Frederick W. M. Draper, *Four Centuries of Merchant Taylors' School, 1561–1961*, London, 1962
DUNKERLEY: S. Dunkerley, *Robert Bakewell, Artist, Blacksmith*, Cromford, 1988

EARLE: Peter Earle, *The Making of the English Middle Class: Business, Society and Family Life in London 1660–1730*, London, 1989

EDWARDS: Peter Edwards, *Dealing in Death: the arms trade and the British Civil Wars, 1638–52*, London, 2000
EVELYN: E. S. De Beer (ed), *The Diary of John Evelyn*, Oxford, 1955
EVELYN 1652: John Evelyn, *The State of France*, London, 1652
FOKKER: Timon H. Fokker, *Jan Siberechts, Peintre de la Paysanne Flamande*, Bruxelles and Paris, 1931
FORBES: J. S. Forbes, *Hallmark: A History of the London Assay Office*, London, 1999
FOSTER: Joseph Foster, *London Marriage Licences 1521–1869*, London, 1887
FOX: Celina Fox, *Londoners*, London, 1987
FRIEDMAN: T. Friedman, *James Gibbs Architect 'a man of great fame'*, Orleans House Gallery, London, 1982

GALINOU: Mireille Galinou, *The Painted Room, Sir John Cass's Foundation Primary School*, Corporation of London, 2002
GANZ 1998: James A. Ganz, 'Still Life Mezzotints by Robert Robinson', *Burlington Magazine*, Vol. 140, no. 1139, February 1998
GANZ 2000: James A. Ganz, *Robert Robinson (1651–1706): Painter-Stainer and Peintre-Graveur*, Ph.D. dissertation, New Haven: Yale University, 2000 (facsimiles distributed by UMI Dissertation Services, Ann Arbor, Michigan)
GIBSON K: Katharine Gibson, 'The Cult of Charles II', *The Royal Stuart Society*, Paper XLVII, London, undated
GIBSON R: Robin Gibson, *The Clarendon Collection, Catalogue of portraits in the collection of the Earl of Clarendon*, [London, 1977]
GIBSON-WOOD 2002: Carol Gibson-Wood, 'Picture Consumption in London at the End of the Seventeenth Century', *Art Bulletin*, Vol. 84. 3, Sept 2002
GIBSON-WOOD 2003: Carol Gibson-Wood, 'Laroon, Gaspars and portraits of Charles II', *Burlington Magazine*, 145, July 2003
GLANVILLE: Philippa Glanville, *Silver in Tudor and Early Stuart England*, London, 1990
GRANGER: J. Granger, *A Biographical History of England and Catalogue of Engraved British Heads*, Leicester, first edition 1769
GRASSBY 1994: Richard Grassby, *The English Gentleman in Trade: The Life and Works of Sir Dudley North 1641–1691*, Oxford, 1994
GRASSBY 1995: Richard Grassby, *The Business Community of Seventeenth-Century England*, Cambridge, 1995
GRIFFITHS 1989: Antony Griffiths, 'Early Mezzotint Publishing in England — I: John Smith 1652–1743', *Print Quarterly*, VI, No3, September 1989
GRIFFITHS: Antony Griffiths, *The Print in Stuart Britain 1603–1689*, British Museum exhibition catalogue, London, 1998
GUNNIS: Rupert Forbes Gunnis, *Dictionary of British Sculptors 1660–1851*, London, 1953

HANCOCK 1995: David Hancock, *Citizens of the World*, Harvard University, 1995
HANCOCK 2002: David Hancock (ed), 'The Letters of William Freeman, London Merchant, 1678–1685', *London Record Society*, 2002
HARE: Susan M. Hare, *Goldsmiths' Hall in the City of London*, London, 1996
HARRIS 1979: John Harris, *The Artist and the Country House*, London, 1979
HARRIS 1996: *The Artist and the Country House — From the fifteenth century to the present day*, exhibition catalogue, Sothebys, 1996
HATTON: Edward Hatton, *New View of London*, 2 volumes, 1708
HEAL: Ambrose Heal, *The London Goldsmiths 1200–1800*, Cambridge, 1935
HEARN: Karen Hearn, 'A Seventeenth Century Enigma: Jan Siberechts's View of a House and its Estate in Belsize, Middlesex', *Patrons' Papers 3*, Tate Gallery, London, 2000
HILTON PRICE: Frederick G. Hilton Price, *A Handbook of London Bankers*, London, 1890–91
HOLBORROW: J. Holborrow, *Fingest: Stony Ground*, London, 1999
HOLDER: Nick Holder, *7a Laurence Pountney Hill, London EC2*, Museum of London Archaeology Service report, 2003
HOLMES: G. Holmes, *The Making of a Great power — Late Stuart and early Georgian Britain, 1660–1722*
HONOUR: Hugh Honour, *Chinoiserie*, 1961
HOOKE: H. W. Robinson and W. Adam (eds), *The Diary of Robert Hooke 1672–80*, 1968
HOPE: Valerie Hope, *My Lord Mayor*, London, 1989
HORWITZ: H. Horwitz, "The mess of the middle class' revisited: the case of the 'big bourgeoisie' of Augustan London', *Continuity and change*, (2), 1987
HOWGEGO: James L. Howgego, 'The Guildhall Fire Judges' in *The Guildhall Miscellany*, London, February 1953
HUNT: Margaret Hunt, *The Middling Sort: Commerce, Gender and the Family in England 1680–1780*, Berkeley, 1996
HUNTING: Penelope Hunting, 'The Survey of Hatton Garden in 1694 by Abraham Arlidge', *London Topographical Report*, Vol. xxv, 1985
HURLEY PARISH: Hurley Parish Council, *The Five Villages of Hurley Parish — A Pictorial Record*, 1999
HYDE: Ralph Hyde, *London in Paintings, Guildhall Art Gallery*, London, 1999

INGAMELLS & FORD: J. Ingamells and B. Ford, *British and Irish Travellers in Italy 1701 to 1800*, New Haven & London, 1997
ISRAEL: Jonathan I. Israel, *Radical Enlightenment. Philosophy and the Making of Modernity 1650–1750*, Oxford, 2001

JEFFERY: Paul Jeffery, *The City Churches of Sir Christopher Wren*, London & Rio Grande, 1996
JENSEN: H. James Jensen (ed), *The Sensational Restoration*, Bloomington & Indianapolis, 1996
JESSOP: A. Jessop (ed), *The Lives of the Norths*, London, 1890
JONES: A. E. Jones, *The Story of Carshalton House, now St Philomena's*, London, 1980
JONES R: Rica Jones, 'Jan Siberechts: View of a House and its Estate in Belsize, Middlesex 1696', *Paint and Purpose*, S. Hackney, R. Jones, J. Townsend (eds), London, 1999

KNIGHT: Caroline Knight, 'The Irish in London: post-Restoration suburban houses', in *Irish Architectural and Decorative Studies*, Vol. 1, Oysterhaven, 1998
KNOOP & JONES: Douglas Knoop and Gwilyn P. Jones, *The London Mason in the 17th century*, London, 1935

LAMBERT: U. Lambert, *Bletchingley: A Parish History*, privately printed, 1929.
LAUDERDALE: Peter Barber, Oliver Cox, Michael Curwen, *Lauderdale Revealed*, Lauderdale House Society, London, 1993
LINDEY: Laurie A. Lindey, 'Edward Traherne: a study of the furniture trade in Restoration London', unpublished dissertation, V&A/RCA MA Course in the History of Design, London, 2003
LONDON DIRECTORY: *The London Directory of 1677*, facsimile, 1878
LUGT: F. Lugt, *Répertoire des catalogues de ventes publiques intéressant l'art ou la curiosité*, 1938

MANNING & BRAY: O. Manning and W. Bray, *History of Surrey*, 3 volumes, London, 1804–14
MACLEOD & MARCIARI: Catharine MacLeod and Julia Marciari Alexander (eds), *Painted Ladies. Women at the Court of Charles II*, London & New Haven, 2001
MAGALOTTI: Count Lorenzo Magalotti, *Travels of Cosmo the Third, Grand Duke of Tuscany through England, During the Reign of King Charles the Second* (1669), London, 1821
MEADOWS: A. Meadows, 'Collecting Seventeenth-Century Dutch Painting in England 1689–1760', unpublished PhD thesis, University of London, 1988
MELTON 1977: Frank T. Melton, 'Sir Robert Clayton's building projects in London, 1666–72', *Guildhall Studies in London History*, Vol. III, No. 1, 1977
MELTON 1986: Frank T. Melton, *Sir Robert Clayton and the Origins of English Deposit Banking 1658–1685*, Cambridge, 1986
MÉROT: Alain Mérot, *Retraites mondaines. Aspects de la décoration intérieure à Paris au XVIIe siècle*, Paris, 1990
METCALF: Priscilla Metcalf 'Living over the Shop', *Architectural History* (27), 1984
MILLAR 1978, Oliver Millar, *Sir Peter Lely*, National Portrait Gallery exhibition catalogue, London, 1978

MILLAR 1997: Oliver Millar, 'Artists and craftsmen in the service of Sir Stephen Fox and his family', *Burlington Magazine*, June 1997

MILLS & OLIVER: Peter Mills & John Oliver, *The Survey of Building Sites in the City of London*, London Topographical Society (98), 1967

MINGAY: Gordon E. Mingay, *English Landed Society in the Eighteenth Century*, London & Toronto, 1963

MISSON: Henri Misson de Valbourg [ed. by Francois Maximilien Misson], *Mémoires d'Angleterre*, La Haye [The Haghe], 1698

MITCHELL 1993: David Mitchell, 'Dressing plate by the "unknown" London silversmith "WF"', *The Burlington Magazine*, June 1993

MITCHELL 1995: David Mitchell (ed), *Goldsmiths, Silversmiths and Bankers Innovation and the transfer of skill*, 1995

MITCHELL 2004: David Mitchell, 'The influence of Tartary and the Indies on social attitudes and material culture in England and France, 1650–1730', *Riggisberger Berichte*, 2004

MONTGOMERY: Florence M. Montgomery, *Textiles in America 1650–1870*, New York, 1984

MONTIAS: John Michael Montias, 'Auctions of works of art in seventeenth-century Amsterdam (1597–1638)', *Nederlands Kunsthistorisch Jaarboek* (50), 1999

MOORE: Andrew Moore, *Dutch and Flemish Painting in Norfolk*, Norfolk Museum Service, 1988

MORGAN: Victor Morgan, 'The Norwich Guildhall Portraits: Images in Context', *Family and Friends — A Regional Survey of British Portraiture*, Andrew Moore with Charlotte Crawley, London, 1992

MUNDUS MULIEBRIS: *Mundus Muliebris or the Ladies Dressing Room unlock'd, And her Toilette spread*, London, 1690

MURDOCH: Tessa Murdoch, 'The Lord Mayor's Procession of 1686: The Chariot of the Virgin Queen', *Transactions of the London & Middlesex Archaeological Society*, Vol. 34, 1983

MUSEUM OF LONDON, 1985: *The Quiet Conquest The Huguenots 1685 to 1985*, Museum of London exhibition catalogue, 1985

NICHOLS: John Gough Nichols 'Thomas Godfrey's Diary', *Topographer and Genealogist* (II), 1852

O'DONAGHUE: Freeman M. O'Donaghue, *Catalogue of Engraved Portraits in the British Museum*, 5 volumes, London, 1908

OGDEN: Henry V. S. and Margaret S. Ogden, *English Taste in Landscape in the Seventeenth Century*, 1955

OGILVY: James Ogilvy, *Relics and Memorials of London City*, London, 1910

OMAN: Charles C. Oman, *Caroline Silver 1625–1688*, London, 1970

ORMROD: David Ormrod, 'The Origins of the London Art Market,1660–1730', *Art Markets in Europe, 1400–1800*, M. North and D. Ormrod (eds), 1998

PAPILLON: Alexander Frederick W. Papillon, *Memoirs of Thomas Papillon of London, Merchant*, Reading, 1887

PARES & TAYLOR: Richard Pares & Alan J. P. Taylor 'A London West-India Merchant House' in *Essays presented to Sir Lewis Namier*, London, 1956

PARRY: G. Parry, 'John Talman A Life in Art', *Walpole Society* (59),1997

PEARS: Ian Pears, *The Discovery of Painting — the Growth of Interest in the Arts in England, 1680–1767*, New Haven & London, 1988

PEBERDY: R. B. Peberdy, 'The Economy, Society and Government of a Small Town in Late Medieval England: a study of Henley-on-Thames from *c.* 1300 to *c.* 1540', unpublished PhD thesis, Leicester University, 1994

PEPYS: Robert Latham & William Matthews (eds), *The Diary of Samuel Pepys*, London, 1995

PETRIE: A. F. Petrie, *A Short History of Yewden Manor & Greenlands*, Henley Archaeological and Historical Group, 1979

PIPER: David Piper, *Catalogue of 17th century portraits in the National Portrait Gallery*, Cambridge, 1963

PLATT: Colin Platt, *The Great Rebuilding of Tudor and Stuart England*, London, 1994

PRICE: Jacob M Price, 'The Tobacco Adventure to Russia', *Transactions of the American Philosophical Society*, 1961

RAVENHILL: William Ravenhill, 'Joel Gascoyne's Stepney: his last years in pastures old yet new, 1638–1664', *Guildhall Studies in London History*, Vol. II, No. 4, April 1977

RIBEIRO: Aileen Ribeiro, *The Gallery of Fashion*, London, 2000

RIDDELL: Charlotte Eliza Lawson Riddell, *Mitre Court. A Tale of the Great City*, London, 1885

RUBINSTEIN 1994: Gregory M. G. Rubinstein, 'Artists from the Netherlands in seventeenth-century Britain: an overview of their landscape work', *The exchange of ideas, religion, scholarship and art in Anglo-Dutch relations in the 17th century*, ed. Simon Groenveld and Michael Wintle, Zutphen, 1994.

RUBINSTEIN 2004: Gregory M. G. Rubinstein, 'The Drawings of Jan Siberechts', *Master Drawings*, [forthcoming]

SAUNDERS: Ann Saunders (ed), *History of Royal Exchange*, London, 1997

SAUMAREZ-SMITH: Charles Saumarez-Smith, *Eighteenth-Century Decoration, Design and Domestic Interior in England*, London, 1993

SCHARF: George Scharf, 'Portraits of Judges in the Guildhall', *Archaeological Journal*, Vol 50, pp. 264–73

SCHOFIELD 1995: John Schofield, *Medieval London Houses*, New Haven & London, 1995

SCOULOUDI: Irene Scouloudi, 'Thomas Papillon, merchant and Whig 1623–1702' *Proceedings of the Huguenot Society*, Vol XVIII, No. 1, 1947

SEDGEWICK: Richard Romney Sedgewick, *The House of Commons 1715–1754*, London, 1970

SHAFTESBURY: Anthony Ashley Cooper, 3rd Earl of Shaftesbury (1671–1713) *Characteristics of Men, Manners, Opinions, Times*, ed. Philip Eyres, Oxford, 1999

SHARPE: Kevin Sharpe, 'Restoration and reconstitution: politics, society and culture in the England of Charles II', *Painted Ladies. Women at the Court of Charles II*, Catharine MacLeod & Julia Marciari Alexander (eds), New Haven & London, 2001

SHAW: Bridget Shaw, 'Pieter Roestraten and the English Vanitas', *Burlington Magazine*, June 1990

SCHRODER: T. Schroder, *The Art of the European Goldsmith Silver from the Schroder Collection*, 1983

SIMON: Jacob Simon, 'Gilded Frames', *Painted Ladies: Women at the Court of Charles II*, ed. Catharine MacLeod & Julia Marciari Alexander, National Portrait Gallery, New Haven & London, 2001

SLOAN: Kim Sloan, *A Noble Art, Amateur Artists and Drawing Masters c. 1600–1800*, British Museum, London, [2000]

SNODIN & STYLES: Michael Snodin & John Styles, *Design & the Decorative Arts. Britain 1500–1900*, London, 2001

SORBIÈRE: Mons. [Samuel] Sorbière, *A Voyage to England*, London, 1709 (The Epistle Dedicatory, Paris Dec. 12th, 1663)

SOUTH SEA INVENTORIES: *The Particulars and Inventories of the Estates of the late Sub-Governor, Deputy Governor, and Directors of the South Sea Company*, London, 1721 (Guildhall Library, Public Record Office and also as facsimile in House of Commons Sessional Papers of the Eighteenth Century 1721: Reports & Papers 1721: South Sea Inventories)

SPALDING 1975: Ruth Spalding, *The Improbable Puritan: A Life of Bulstrode Whitelocke 1605–1675*, London, 1975

SPALDING, Diary 1990: Ruth Spalding (ed), *The Diary of Bulstrode Whitelocke 1605–1675*, Oxford, 1990

SPALDING, 1990: Ruth Spalding, *Contemporaries of Bulstrode Whitelocke 1605–1675 — Biographies, Illustrated Letters and other Documents*, Oxford, 1990

SPENCE: Craig Spence, *London in the 1690s. A Social Atlas*, London, 2000

SQUIBB: G. D. Squibb, *The Register of the Temple Church*, London, 1979

STAINTON & WHITE: Lindsay Stainton and Christopher White, *Drawing in England from Hilliard to Hogarth*, British Museum exhibition catalogue, London, 1987

STALKER & PARKER: John Stalker and George Parker, *A Treatise of Japaning and Varnishing*, Oxford, 1688

STANTON: A. H. Stanton, *On Chiltern Slopes. The Story of Hambleden*, Oxford, 1927

STEELE: [Richard Steele], *Town Talk, in a letter to a Lady in the Country*, No. 1, London, Saturday December 17, 1715

STEVENSON & THOMSON: Sara Stevenson and Duncan Thomson, *John Michael Wright, The King's Painter*, Scottish National Portrait Gallery, 1982

STOW 1720: John Stow, *Survey of London*, ed. by John Strype, 1720

SWAIN: Margaret H. Swain, 'Nightgown into Dressing Gown', *Costume 6*, London, 1972

SURVEY OF LONDON: *The Survey of London*, 45 volumes, 1900–2000

TATE GALLERY: *Manners & Morals — Hogarth and British Painting 1700–1760*, Tate Gallery exhibition catalogue, London, 1987

TAWNEY: R. H. Tawney, 'The Rise of the Gentry, 1558–1640', *Economic History Review*, II, No1, 1941

TILLEMANS: Robert Raines, 'Peter Tillemans — Life and Work', *Walpole Society*, 47, 1978–1980

THORNTON: Peter Thornton, *Seventeenth-Century Interior Decoration in England, France & Holland*, New Haven & London, 1978

THORNTON & TOMLIN: Peter Thornton and Maurice Tomlin, *The Furnishing and Decoration of Ham House*, London, 1980

THOROLD: Peter Thorold, *The London Rich, The Creation of a Great City from 1666 to the Present*, London, 1999

TRISTRAM: E. W. Tristram, 'A Painted Room of the Seventeenth Century', *Walpole Society*, Vol. 3, 1914

TURPIN: Adriana Turpin, 'Thomas Pistor, father and son, and Levens Hall', *Furniture History*, Leeds, 2000

TYACK: G. Tyack, 'The Freemans of Fawley and their Buildings', *Records of Buckinghamshire*, XXIV, 1982

VCH (Victoria County History): The Victoria History of the Counties of England
A History of Buckinghamshire, Vol III. London, 1969
T. F. T. Baker (ed), *Middlesex*, Vol. IX, Oxford, 1989
Surrey, Vol. IV, London, 1967

VEALE: Elspeth Veale, 'Sir Theodore Janssen, Huguenot and merchant of London c1658–1748', *Proceedings of the Huguenot Society*, Essays in Memory of Irene Scouloudi, Vol XXVI, No. 2, 1995

VERTUE: M. Bignamini, 'George Vertue Art Historian and Art Institutions in London 1689–1768', *Walpole Society*, Vol. 54, 1991

VERTUE: George Vertue, *Note Books*, Walpole Society, 1930–55

WALPOLE: Horace Walpole, *Anecdotes of Painting in England*, London, 1888

WATERHOUSE: Ellis Waterhouse, *Dictionary of 16th and 17th century Painters*, 1988

WATSON: Isobel Watson, 'From West Heath to Stepney Green, Building Development in Mile End Old Town, 1660–1820', *London Topographical Record*, Vol XXVIII, 1995

WHITE: A White, 'A Biographical Dictionary of London Tomb Sculptures c.1560–c.1660', *Walpole Society*, LXI, 1999

WHYMAN 1997: Susan Whyman, 'Land and Trade Revisited: The Case of John Verney, London Merchant and Baronet 1660–1720', *London Journal*, 22(I), 1997
WHYMAN 1999: Susan E. Whyman, *Sociability and Power in Late Stuart England, The Cultural Worlds of the Verneys 1660–1720*, Oxford, 1999
WILD: Antony Wild, *The East India Company*, London, 1999
WILSON & MACKLEY: Richard Wilson and Alan Mackley, *Creating Paradise: the Building of the English Country House 1660–1880*, Hambledon & London, 2000
WOLLEY: Hannah Wolley, *The Queen-Like Closet or Rich Cabinet*, London, 1670
WOODHEAD: John R. Woodhead, *The Rulers of London 1660–1689. A Biographical Record of the Aldermen and Common Councilmen in the City of London*, London, 1965
WYCHERLEY 1675: William Wycherley, *The Country Wife*, London, 1675
WYCHERLEY 1677: William Wycherley, *The Plain Dealer*, London, 1677

Picture Credits

1 The Sally from Mincing Lane, etching published by W. Humphreys in February 1777.
Library of Congress, Washington D.C.

2 Map of London, engraving by Johannes de Ram, *c.* 1690.
Guildhall Library Print Room, Corporation of London

3 View of the City of London on a linen damask napkin, *c.* 1665.
By courtesy of the Stedelijk Museum, Kortrijk, Belgium

4 Bird's-eye view of Covent Garden, etching by Wenceslaus Hollar, *c.* 1658.
© *Copyright The Trustees of the British Museum*

5 Prospect of London, engraving by Johannes Kip, 1720.
© *Copyright The Trustees of the British Museum and The London Topographical Society, who published a facsimile of this prospect, with notes by Ralph Hyde, in 2003*

6 Detail from William Morgan Survey of London, 1682, engraving.
Guildhall Library Print Room, Corporation of London

7 Late 15th-century silver gilt Cup owned by goldsmith-banker Robert Clayton.
By courtesy of the Schroder Collection

8 Embroidered bed cover, *c.* 1700, drawing by John Stilwell.
Photograph © 2003 Museum of Fine Arts, Boston

9 'Madness' and 'Melancholy' by Caius Gabriel Cibber on the pediment of the gate of the Old Bethlehem (Bedlam) Hospital, 1783, engraving by William Sharp after Thomas Stothard.
Guildhall Library Print Room, Corporation of London

10 Invitation to St Luke's Feast at Painter-Stainers Company, 24 November 1687, etching by an anonymous artist.
Guildhall Library Print Room, Corporation of London

11 A sheet of London trade cards, Samuel Pepys' collection.
By courtesy of the Pepys Library, Magdalene College, Cambridge

12 Still life, oil painting on canvas by Pieter Gerritsz van Roestraten (1630–1700).
Private Collection

13 Interior of Goldsmiths' Hall, 1692, watercolour by John Ward.
By courtesy of the Worshipful Company of Goldsmiths

14 A London Coffee House, *c.* 1705, anonymous gouache drawing.
© *Copyright The Trustees of the British Museum*

15 The artist in his studio, *c.* 1716, oil painting on canvas by Peter Tillemans.
Norwich Castle Museum and Art Gallery

16 View of a merchant's house at 32 Botolph Lane in the Ward of Billingsgate, 1886, watercolour by John Crowther.
Guildhall Library Print Room, Corporation of London

17 'Houses on the South Side of Leadenhall Street', drawn (1796) and published (1814) by J. T. Smith.
Guildhall Library Print Room, Corporation of London

18 Entrance to the Fleet River, *c.* 1750, oil painting on canvas, School of Samuel Scott.
Guildhall Art Gallery, Corporation of London

19–20 Cheapside row of shops on the corner of Wood Street, 2003: front façades (*top*) and back façades (*bottom*).
© *Mireille Galinou*

21 Ye Old Watling Pub at the junction of Bow Lane and Watling Street, 2003.
© *Mireille Galinou*

22 Wardrobe Place, off Carter Lane, 2003.
© *Mireille Galinou*

23 The House of Sir John Houblon in Threadneedle Street in the early 19th century, watercolour by T. C. Dibdin.
By courtesy of The Governor and Company of the Bank of England

24 No 7a Laurence Pountney Hill in the City of London, 2003, photograph.
Maggie Cox, Museum of London Archaeology Service
© *Museum of London*

25 No 23 Great Winchester Street, 1880, watercolour by John Crowther.
Guildhall Library Print Room, Corporation of London

26 Entrance to the house of Sir Robert Clayton in Old Jewry, etching published by A. Beugo in 1812.
Guildhall Library Print Room, Corporation of London

27 Detail from William Morgan's Survey of London, 1682.
Guildhall Library Print Room, Corporation of London

28 The Painted Room at 32 Botolph Lane, watercolour by E. W. Tristram. From 'A painted room of the seventeenth century' by

E. W. Tristram in the Third Annual Volume of the *Walpole Society*, 1913–14.
Guildhall Library, Corporation of London

29 Dean's Court, south of St Paul's Cathedral, *c.* 1986, photograph.
Guildhall Library Print Room, Corporation of London

30 Plan from Mills & Oliver's *Survey* (see bibliography).
Corporation of London Records Office. Photo: By courtesy of the London Topographical Society

31 The main staircase at 32 Botolph Lane, *c.* 1900, pencil drawing by Robert Randoll.
Guildhall Library Print Room, Corporation of London

32 Plan of the ground floor at 32 Botolph Lane. From C. J. Paget 'Wren's Reputed House in Botolph Lane' in *The Architectural Review*, April 1906.
Corporation of London Records Office: Archives of the Sir John Cass's Foundation

33 The Painted Room at Carshalton House, photograph.
© *Burt Crawshaw, By courtesy of Sutton Local Studies Library*

34 Panel from the Painted Room at Norton Court in Kent.
© *Mireille Galinou, by courtesy of the owners of Norton Court*

35 Norton Church, from the grounds of Norton Court.
© *Mireille Galinou, by courtesy of the owners of Norton Court*

36 Front elevation of Stepney Green House in Mile End Old Town, photograph.
By courtesy of Katharine Goodison

37 Anonymous mid-18th-century oil painting depicting property (wrongly) labelled 'Kenfield Hall'.
Collection Marylebone Cricket Club. Photo: Bridgeman Art Library

38 Detail from Joel Gascoyne's 'A map of the hamlet of Mile-End Old Town, in the parish of Stepney', 1703.
Guildhall Library Print Room, Corporation of London

39 Detail of shell hood over the front door of Stepney Green house, photograph.
© *Katharine Goodison*

40 Detail of front façades of Nos 1 & 2 Laurence Pountney Hill, *c.* 1900, woodcut by an anonymous artist.
Guildhall Library Print Room, Corporation of London

41 Shell hood in Sherborne Lane, City of London, *c.* 1840 drawing.
By courtesy of London Metropolitan Archives

42 Detail of stucco head of putti over the door of Stepney Green House, photograph.
© *Katharine Goodison*

43 Detail of stucco heads on a house in Queen Anne's Gate London, photograph.
© *Katharine Goodison*

44 Detail of ironwork railings by Robert Bakewell, Stepney Green House, photograph.
© *Katharine Goodison*

45 'The Anatomy of Carriage Gates', drawing by Sam Dunkerley, 1988, from his book *Robert Bakewell artist.*
By courtesy of Mrs Dunkerley and of the publishers Scarthin Books, Cromford

46 The main staircase, Stepney Green house, photograph.
© *Katharine Goodison*

47 Staircase and mural at 75 Dean Street, photograph.
By courtesy of London Metropolitan Archives

48 Interior view of the staircase, Stepney Green House, wood engraving from *The Pictorial World*, 23 November 1878.
Guildhall Library Print Room, Corporation of London

49 Panelling in a ground floor room, Stepney Green House, photograph.
© *Katharine Goodison*

50 Ground floor fireplace, Stepney Green house, photograph.
© *Katharine Goodison*

51 John Lofting, Detail from A New draught and description of the fire engine . . ., photogravure of *c.* 1720 engraving.
Guildhall Library Print Room, Corporation of London

52 Bed from Glemham Hall, embroidered silk, *c.* 1700.
Country Life Picture Library

53 Carved and gilt side table, *c.* 1715–20.
By courtesy of Squerryes Court, Kent

54 Turkey work chair, *c.* 1680.
Temple Newsam, Leeds Museums & Galleries. Photo: Bridgeman Art Library

55 The Tea Table, engraving, *c.* 1710.
© *The Trustees of the British Museum*

56 The Blue-Paper Warehouse in Aldermanbury, *c.* 1720, engraving.
Bodleian Library, University of Oxford

57 Long-case mahogany clock by Quare and Horseman.
By courtesy of Squerryes Court, Kent

58 Lady of quality at her Toilette, late 1680s, anonymous engraving, published by Jean van der Bruggen, Paris.
Bibliothèque nationale de France

86 Fantastic Palace, 1696, oil on panel by Robert Robinson, from The Painted Room, formerly No. 32 Botolph Lane, London.
Sir John Cass's Foundation Primary School, Aldgate. Photo: Corporation of London

87 Tobacco Cultivation, 1696, oil on panel by Robert Robinson, from The Painted Room, formerly No. 32 Botolph Lane, London.
Sir John Cass's Foundation Primary School, Aldgate. Photo: Corporation of London

88 El Dorado, 1696, oil on panel by Robert Robinson, from the Painted Room (overmantel), formerly No. 32 Botolph Lane, London.
Sir John Cass's Foundation Primary School, Aldgate. Photo: Corporation of London

89 Enthroned Prince, oil on panel by Robert Robinson.
Present whereabouts unknown. Photo: The Paul Mellon Centre for Studies in British Art

90 The Family of Sir Robert Vyner, 1673, oil on canvas by John Michael Wright.
By courtesy of the National Portrait Gallery, London

91 Wife of the Lord Mayor of London, 1649, etching by Wenceslaus Hollar.
Private Collection. Photo: by courtesy of Valerie Cumming

92 Portrait of John Banckes, 1676, oil on canvas by Sir Godfrey Kneller.
© *Tate, London, 2004*

93 Detail from the interior of a Cloth Merchant's, with a buyer inspecting bales of cloth, 1690, oil on canvas by Egbert van Heemskerk the Younger.
© *Museum of London*

94 Eleanor James, *c.* 1695, oil on canvas by an anonymous artist.
By courtesy of the National Portrait Gallery, London

95 Detail from Illus. 90

96 Detail from Illus. 90

97 The Chariot of the Virgin Queen of the Mercers' Company, Lord Mayor's Procession, 1686, pen and wash drawing by an anonymous artist.
© *Museum of London*

98 Alternative proposal for Clayton monument, pencil, black & brown wash drawing attributed to the elder William Woodman (*c.* 1654 – *c.* 1731).
Henry Moore Institute, Leeds (Acc.LEEAG, PA, 1999.0008). *Photo: Conway Library, Courtauld Institute of Art*

99 Langham family monument, Cottesbrooke, Northamptonshire, 2002, photograph.
© *Anthony Hotson*

100 Details from the Langham family monument, 2002, photograph.
© *Anthony Hotson*

101 Half length portrait of John Langham, *c.* 1650, oil on canvas, by Gerard Soest (according to 1769 inventory).
Dunham Massey, The Stamford Collection (The National Trust). Photo: by courtesy of the Photographic Survey, Courtauld Institute of Art

102 Three quarter length seated portrait of Mary Bunce, Lady Langham, 1650, oil on canvas by Gerard Soest (according to 1769 inventory).
Dunham Massey, The Stamford Collection (The National Trust). Photo: NTPL/John Hammond

103 The Clayton family monument, engraving by E. Kirkall after J. Wrigglesworth.
Guildhall Library Print Room, Corporation of London

104 Detail from the Clayton Monument: Dame Martha's effigy.
© *Anthony Hotson*

105 Portrait of Dame Martha Clayton, 1680, oil on canvas by Lorenzo da Castro. Sold at Christie's, 23 June 1950.
Present whereabouts unknown

106 Detail: portrait of Sir Robert Clayton, *c.* 1680, oil on canvas by Lorenzo da Castro.
Courtesy of The Governor and Company of the Bank of England. Photo (2002): © *Anthony Hotson*

107 Still life of City insignia, *c.* 1676, oil on canvas attributed to Pieter Gerritsz van Roestraten.
Guildhall Art Gallery, Corporation of London. Photo (2002): © *Anthony Hotson*

108 Mayoral Portrait of Robert Clayton, mezzotint by John Smith (1654–1720) after the *c.* 1680 painting by John Riley in the Guidhall Art Gallery, published by John Smith *c.* 1707.
Guildhall Library Print Room, Corporation of London.

109 Portrait of Sir Matthew Hale, Chief Justice of the King's Bench, *c.* 1670/1, oil on canvas by John Michael Wright.
Guildhall Art Gallery, Corporation of London

110 Portrait of Sir Hugh Wyndham, Judge of the Common Pleas, *c.* 1670/1, oil on canvas by John Michael Wright.
Guildhall Art Gallery, Corporation of London

111 Interior of the Guildhall looking East, 1724, engraving by an anonymous artist.
Guildhall Library Print Room, Corporation of London

112 The Ceremony of Swearing In Alderman Nathaniel Newnham, 8 November 1782, oil on canvas by William Miller.
Guildhall Art Gallery, Corporation of London

113 Portrait of Gilbert Sheldon, Archbishop of Canterbury, *c.* 1665, oil on canvas, Studio of Sir Peter Lely.
By courtesy of the National Portrait Gallery, London

114 Portrait of Sir John Robinson, *c.* 1672, oil on canvas by John Michael Wright.
Guildhall Art Gallery, Corporation of London

115 Portrait of George Monck, 1st Duke of Albemarle , *c.*1665–1666, oil on canvas, Studio of Sir Peter Lely.
By courtesy of the National Portrait Gallery, London

116 Portrait of Sir Joseph Sheldon, 1678, oil on canvas by Gerard Soest (1600–1681).
By courtesy of the Worshipful Company of Drapers, London

117 Unveiling The Coronation Luncheon at Guildhall, 1937, oil on canvas by Frank O. Salisbury.
Guildhall Art Gallery, Corporation of London

118 Full-length portrait of William Turner, 1675, oil on canvas by Mary Beale.
By courtesy of the King Edward's School, Witley, Surrey

119 House of William Turner at 73 Cheapside in 1883, photograph by Henry Dixon.
Guildhall Library Print Room, Corporation of London

120 Interior of a merchant taylor's workshop , 1749, etching and engraving by Louis Philippe Boitard, published by George Bickham.
© *The Trustees of the British Museum*

121 Detail from William Morgan's Survey of London, 1682.
Guildhall Library Print Room, Corporation of London

122 Detail from a prospect of London from Southwark taken after the Great Fire of London, *c.* 1666, etching by Wenceslaus Hollar.
Guildhall Library Print Room, Corporation of London

123 Cheapside: detail from 'The Curds and Whey Seller', *c.* 1730, oil painting on canvas by an anonymous artist.
© *Museum of London*

124 Marriage suit worn by James Duke of York (1633–1701) in 1673.
The V&A Picture Library

125 View of the Parish of St Martin Outwich in 1599, showing the Merchant Taylors' Hall as it appeared before the Great Fire; 1824 lithograph by Whishaw based on the lost original attributed to William Goodman.
Guildhall Library Print Room, Corporation of London

126 South West Prospect of the Royal Exchange, as rebuilt after the Great Fire. Engraving by William Sherwin, 1674.
© *Copyright The Trustees of the British Museum*

127 View of the Merchant Taylors' Hall in Threadneedle Street as rebuilt after the Great Fire, *c.* 1810, watercolour by George Shepherd.
Guildhall Library Print Room, Corporation of London

128 View of Merchant Taylors' School in Suffolk Lane, 1864, coloured lithograph by James Fahey.
Guildhall Library Print Room, Corporation of London

129 View of the Old East India House in Leadenhall Street, etching.
Guildhall Library Print Room, Corporation of London

130 See Illus. 51

The Contributors

VALERIE CUMMING

Valerie Cumming was a costume curator at Chertsey Museum, the Museum of London and the Court Dress Collection, Kensington Palace in the 1970s. Then she became Assistant Director and later deputy Director at the Museum of London. Research interests include seventeenthth-century dress and society, royal and ceremonial dress and nineteenth-century theatre costume. Her numerous publications include *A Visual History of Costume: the 17th Century; Royal Dress*; (with Aileen Ribeiro) *The Visual History of Costume*; *The Visual History of Costume Accessories.*

MIREILLE GALINOU

Mireille Galinou is a freelance arts and museums consultant. She worked for over 20 years with the collection of Paintings, Prints and Drawings at the Museum of London. In 1996 she founded the London Arts Café, a charitable arts organisation which campaigns for the better understanding of cities through art. She has curated numerous exhibitions for both institutions. She was the editor of *London's Pride – A History of the Capital's Gardens* (1990) and the co-author of *London in Paint – Oil Paintings in the collection of the Museum of London* (1996).

JAMES A. GANZ

Dr James A. Ganz is Curator of Prints, Drawings and Photographs at the Sterling and Francine Clark Art Institute in Williamstown, Massachusetts where he has organised numerous exhibitions. Dr Gant is also Part-Time Lecturer in the Williams College Graduate Program in the History of Art. His extensive doctoral research on the life and oeuvre of City-based artist Robert Robinson remains mostly unpublished.

GORDON GLANVILLE

Dr Gordon Glanville, former Head of History at Kingston University, has a long-standing research interest in Tudor and Stuart economic and social history.

PHILIPPA GLANVILLE

Philippa Glanville has recently retired as Academic Director at Waddesdon Manor, Buckinghamshire. She was previously Chief Curator in the Metalwork Department at the V&A Museum and Keeper of the Tudor and Stuart Department at the Museum of London. Both posts led to landmark redisplays of the permanent collections. She has published widely on English social history, London topography and goldsmiths' work including *London in Maps* (1972), *Silver in England* (1987), *Silver* (1996); and *Silver in Tudor and Stuart England* (1990).

KATHARINE GOODISON

Katharine Goodison read History of Art at Edinburgh University before qualifying as a lawyer in the City. She nows runs a successful millinery business. She is also a Trustee of the Dulwich Picture Gallery and The Clerkenwell Green Association. Katharine Goodison continues to research her house and is slowly restoring it back to its former glory.

KAREN HEARN

Karen Hearn is Curator of sixteenth- and seventeenth-century British art at Tate. She was the curator of the Tate Gallery exhibition *DYNASTIES: Painting in Tudor and Jacobean England 1530–1630* (1995–96), for which she received a European Women of Achievement award. She subsequently co-curated *In Celebration: The Art of the Country House* (Tate, 1998-99), *Marcus Gheeraerts II: Elizabethan Artist* (Tate, 2002) and is currently preparing a catalogue of the sixteenth- and seventeenth-century works in the Tate collection.

ANTHONY HOTSON

Anthony Hotson is completing a PhD at the Courtauld Institute of Art on late Stuart moneyed men and their patronage of sculpture and architecture, *circa* 1660 to 1720. He studied Philosophy, Politics and Economics at Balliol College, Oxford, and he subsequently took a master's degree in Economics at Nuffield College, Oxford. He has worked at the Bank of England, McKinsey & Company, and as a director of S. G. Warburg. Before embarking on his PhD he completed a master's degree at the Courtauld Institute.

VIVIEN KNIGHT

Vivien Knight has been Curator of Guildhall Art Gallery and the Corporation of London's Permanent Collection since 1982. During this period she was closely involved with the development of the design of the new Art Gallery and in the building process. She has written short themed books on the history of the Gallery and aspects of its collections, a research article in *Apollo* on Luke Clennell, and most recently an essay on seventeenth- to nineteenth-century paintings of women, in the catalogue accompanying the Japanese touring exhibition *Muses, Madonnas and Maidens*.

DAVID MITCHELL

Dr David Mitchell is a Visiting Research Fellow at the Centre for Metropolitan History, Institute of Historical Research, University of London. He has written widely on the design, production and use of linen damask napery in Europe and on the textile, goldsmith's and other trades in Restoration London. Apart from an ongoing research project for the Goldsmiths' Company, his current work includes two papers entitled, 'Social change and the design of plate 1660–1700: the debt to

France', and 'The influence of Tartary and the Indies on social attitudes and material culture in England and France, 1650–1700'.

ANN SAUNDERS

Dr Ann Saunders worked at Lambeth Palace Library, helping to restore it after the bombing of the last war, then the British Museum and Marylebone Library before going freelance in 1965. She is a Fellow of University College London and was awarded an MBE in 2002. She is the Honorary Editor of the London Topographical Society and the Costume Society. Her numerous publications include *The Art and Architecture of London: an illustrated guide* (1989), *The Royal Exchange* (1997), *St Paul's The Story of the Cathedral* (2001). She is presently working on a history of the Merchant Taylors' Company.

ADRIANA TURPIN

Adriana Turpin is an independent scholar, specialising in the history of the decorative arts. She was Senior Lecturer and Deputy Director of Sotheby's Institute between 1978 and 2002. Her research has focused on the late seventeenth century and she has written several articles on furniture of that period, among them 'A Table for Queen Mary', in *Apollo*, January 1999. She wrote an essay for the William Beckford exhibition catalogue (Bard Graduate School, New York & Dulwich Picture Gallery): 'Filling the Void: William Beckford's collecting of furniture'. She is currently working on an article on Cornelius Gole, a late-seventeenth-century cabinet-maker working in England.

LAURA WORTLEY

Laura Wortley's study of Jan Siberechts' Henley paintings developed out of her long term research at the River and Rowing Museum in Henley-on-Thames into *Artists Working on the Non Tidal Thames*. She works as a freelance art historian and, in addition to compiling catalogues on British paintings 1750–1950, she is the author of several books, including *British Impressionism: A Garden of Bright Images*, *Wilfrid de Glehn: A Painter's Journey*, and *Lucy Kemp Welch: The Spirit of the Horse.*

Index of People and Places